LINCOLN'S CRITICS

The Copperheads of the North

". . . in essence, a Copperhead Bible"

by
Frank L. Klement

Edited and Introduced by
Steven K. Rogstad

 WHITE MANE BOOKS

This White Mane Books publication
was printed by
Beidel Printing House, Inc.
63 West Burd Street
Shippensburg, PA 17257-0152 USA

In respect for the scholarship contained herein, the acid-free paper used in this book meets the guidelines for permanence and durability of the Committee on Production Guidelines for Book Longevity of the Council on Library Resources.

For a complete list of available publications
please write
White Mane Books
Division of White Mane Publishing Company, Inc.
P.O. Box 152
Shippensburg, PA 17257-0152 USA

Library of Congress Cataloging-in-Publication Data

Klement, Frank L.
    Lincoln's Critics : the Copperheads of the North / by Frank L.
Klement ; edited and introduced by Steven K. Rogstad.
        p.   cm.
    Includes bibliographical references (p.   ) and index.
    ISBN 1-57249-128-0 (alk. paper)
    1. Copperhead movement. 2. Lincoln, Abraham, 1809-1865--Public
opinion. 3. Northwest, Old--History--Civil War, 1861-1865--Protest
movements. 4. United States--History--Civil War, 1861-1865--Protest
movements. 5. United States--Politics and government--1861-1865.
6. Public opinion--United States--History--19th century.
I. Rogstad, Steven K. II. Title.
E458.8.K68   1999
973.7--dc21   98-46687
                                                                                    CIP

PRINTED IN THE UNITED STATES OF AMERICA

CONTENTS

Part Four: Rewriting Copperhead History

A Personal Note as a Preface

Occasionally someone asks me how I became entangled in the web of Copperhead historiography. My answer is short and simple: "Chance and circumstance."

With a master's degree in history already in hand, I was one of twelve members of Professor William B. Hesseltine's seminar during a six-week summer session at the University of Wisconsin. All twelve of us were sitting around a T-shaped table in a seminar room when "our master" entered, greeted us gruffly, smiled snidely after making a humorous remark, and said with authority, "Here is a sheet with twelve topics; put your name after the topic that you choose for this summer's work." He handed the paper to the person at his left. Since I sat at his right, all the topics except one had been chosen when I received the sheet. "Hobson's choice," I said to myself as I wrote my name after the last remaining topic: "The Democratic Opposition during the Civil War." Chance and circumstance had scored again.

We researched our topics as best we could, using both secondary and primary sources, gave reports on progress and aspects, and wrote papers that were read and judged critically. The class discussions and debates were spirited, contentious, and constant. Our mentor, evidently, thought that the members of the seminar should be a pack of wolves.

Early in the course I accepted the traditional interpretations about the so-called "Copperheads": they were pro-Southern, belonged to subversive secret societies, became involved in conspiracies, plumbed for peace, constituted a collection of ingrates, and criticized a president whose policies were proper and who deserved sainthood. By the end of the summer term

I had some doubts and suppositions, but not enough to change the equation. Lincoln, however, no longer walked on water.

The next summer, Professor Hesseltine was visiting at an English university and T. Harry Williams, a recent Ph.D. of Hesseltine's, directed the Civil War seminar. He and I agreed upon the topic "The Democratic Party in Wisconsin during the Civil War"—it was a good choice. At the end of the term I handed in a ninety-two-page paper and felt that I was becoming better acquainted with an evasive and complex subject.

At the start of my third summer term, I met with Professor Hesseltine to discuss a dissertation topic. "How about 'The Copperheads in the Upper Midwest'?" I asked somewhat apprehensively. His smile seemed to indicate assent. His remark was, "I've been waiting for someone to take hold of that topic and chew on it."

During more summer terms, a year "in residence," and every vacation, I plunged into the Copperhead wilderness, sometimes losing my way. Eventually I completed a dissertation entitled "Middle Western Copperheadism: Jeffersonian Democracy in Revolt." There were some challenges to the traditional interpretation but not enough. There were also gaps and other areas that needed exploration. I decided, therefore, to set aside the dissertation and my large stack of notes and start anew, this time with the resources of the Library of Congress and the National Archives as the starting point. Democratic newspapers were balanced by Republican ones and Republican collections of letters outnumbered the Democratic two to one. A research grant and fellowship enabled me to spend a full year in Washington, tapping the rich resources of the Library of Congress and the National Archives. Then there were visits to scores of midwestern libraries and research centers. Occasionally, I took time from my book project to write articles like "Economic Aspects of Middle Western Copperheadism," "Middle Western Copperheadism and the Genesis of the Granger Movement," "Copperheads and Copperheadism in Wisconsin," and "Carrington and the Golden Circle Legend in Indiana During the Civil War."

Meanwhile, in 1952, Wood Gray's *The Hidden Civil War: The Story of the Copperheads* and George Fort Milton's *Abraham Lincoln and the Fifth Column* gained headlines. The traditional interpretation of Copperheads was woven into Civil War fabric in brighter colors.

My concepts and contentions concerning Copperheadism, developed over about fifteen years of research, were in stark contradiction to those in the oft-praised books of Gray and Milton, and they were presented in my first book, *The Copperheads in the Middle West*, published in 1960 by the University of Chicago Press. A few reviews were favorable, most were otherwise. The most cutting, and published in a Sunday *Chicago Tribune*, was written by Avery Craven; he had directed Wood Gray's doctoral dissertation out of which *The Hidden Civil War* had evolved. He evidently believed Wood Gray's contentions rather than mine, evidently feeling compelled to defend assumptions that he had endorsed earlier. In a letter, the editor of the University of Chicago Press characterized Craven's review as "unkind" and "unfair" but never sent me a copy of it.

Research trips followed research trips, and two tangents of *The Copperheads in the Middle West* became books: the University Press of Kentucky published *The Limits of Dissent: Clement L. Vallandigham and the Civil War* in 1970, and the Louisiana State University Press published *Dark Lanterns: Secret Political Societies, Conspiracies, and Treason Trials in the Civil War* in 1984. Then there were articles and more articles, about fifty in all, dealing with one aspect or other of middle western Copperheadism.

I have never thought of myself as a "revisionist" although that tag has been tossed my way. I have considered myself an orthodox historian, drawing conclusions and concepts from the evidence provided by digging deeper than most. I have, in some ways, concentrated upon the "whys" of Copperheadism and contend that midwestern Copperheads must be judged by what they said and did *in their historical setting*. They should not be judged by what Republicans said that Democrats said and did.

Graduate and undergraduate students of Civil War history ought to welcome this book for, within its covers, articles and essays deal with most aspects of Copperheadism. There is still so much to be explored as regards this ephemeral and fascinating subject. If this book engenders controversy and further research and more assumptions, it will have served a purpose.

❊ ❊ ❊

Acknowledgements

No man is an island, and this author is indebted to many. First of all, there are "Thank yous" to editors of historical quarterlies—these editors wrote letters giving me permission to republish articles. The editor of White Mane, Dr. Martin K. Gordon, gave his endorsement to the project. Kristin Hoffman, a work-study student at Marquette University typed six chapters. Mrs. Jane Gray, Assistant to the Chair, History Department, Marquette University supervised the typing and did much of it herself. Special thanks also goes to Steven K. Rogstad, secretary and editor for the Lincoln Fellowship of Wisconsin, for taking time out of a busy, busy schedule to write the "Introduction." Clio, the Muse of history, was a constant companion who repeatedly said that retirement is a myth.

Frank L. Klement
Emeritus Professor of History
Marquette University
March 15, 1994

INTRODUCTION

"Without Frank Klement wild Copperheads would continue to run rampant through the Civil War Midwest," John Y. Simon noted soon after learning of the professor's death. "He forced all historians to re-think their assumptions about wartime disloyalty."[1] It was hardly an exaggeration, for the Marquette University professor did more to erase myths about Copperheads than has any other scholar. His meticulously researched and lucidly argued studies about Civil War dissenters and secret political societies have been so influential for a better understanding of the conflict that Mark E. Neely, Jr. wrote: "The shrewd and painstaking work of historian Frank L. Klement over the last thirty years has proved, beyond any reasonable doubt, that no systematic, organized disloyal opposition to the war existed in the North."[2] Even James McPherson, the most prominent of contemporary Civil War writers, who has not always agreed with Klement's interpretations of the Copperheads, confessed that he still "found them unfailingly stimulating. His books and articles are invaluable for anyone working in the Civil War field."[3]

Nearly sixty-two percent of the 221 items listed in Klement's bibliography (minus book reviews)—which is included as an appendix in this volume—discuss Copperheadism and subversive organizations which were active during the Civil War. Including this work, five of his seven books address anti-Lincoln themes. The professor's unpublished 1946 Ph.D. dissertation, "Middle Western Copperheadism: Jeffersonian Democracy in Revolt," and another unpublished book-length manuscript about the Knights of the Golden Circle bring the total to seven independent studies of Lincoln's Northern adversaries. The thirty essays he wrote about a variety of Copperhead activities comprise over half of the total number of articles he composed in fifty years of scholarship. In Eugene C. Murdock's 1987 work, *The Civil War in the North: A Selective Annotated Bibliography*, the number of entries for Klement's name is surpassed only by Bruce Catton and Edwin C. Bearss.[4] Klement's last article, "Catholics as Copperheads During the Civil War," appeared in print just months before his death on July 29, 1994. It was a fitting conclusion to a career which had sought to enlighten the historical community about President Lincoln's Democratic critics in the Upper Midwest, a group of people which Klement firmly believed had been wrongfully stereotyped by Northern propagandists during the war and by nationalist historians who wrote about the conflict afterward.[5]

Frank Ludwig Klement was born on a dairy farm near Leopolis in Shawano County, Wisconsin on August 19, 1908, the third oldest of eight children born to Jacob and Barbara (Kutil) Klement. Frank's paternal grandparents, Jakob (Jacob) and Maria (Mary) Klement, immigrated to America in 1883 with their three sons from Taus, Czechoslovakia, then under Austrian rule. Frank's father was about seven years old when the family arrived in Leopolis. It is not known why the family settled in Wisconsin and became dairy farmers, but Frank's younger brother John remembers hearing that there was a small settlement of Bohemians who came to the area around the same time, and Frank once told an interviewer that they lived in an area of second generation Americans, "many of them also from Bohemia and Czechoslovakia, many from Germany....The land they farmed was cut-over timber area that had to be cleared, then worked up for farming."[6]

Upon successfully passing a small rural school's eighth grade in Leopolis most of the county's boys and girls usually returned to assist with the hard labor needed to operate the family farm, while those students with higher aspirations entered a two-year high school program offered by public schools in either Clintonville or Shawano, larger farming communities about thirteen miles in either direction from the Klement farm. Frank decided to make the journey east to the state-graded Shawano High School, where students took courses for general knowledge, college preparation, business, or education. Hoping to follow in his older brother George's footsteps by becoming a school teacher, he enrolled in classes on August 31, 1925.[7]

Frank attended classes regularly and was soon recognized by faculty and classmates alike as one of the most ambitious students at the school. A philosophy he tried to personify—the one he chose to have placed next to his senior photograph—prophesied his subsequent accomplishments: "Eagerness seems to be the note of the whole man."[8] He easily excelled in the courses he took in English, history-social science, and mathematics. It is not known where Frank fit into the academic ranking of his class, but the 87 percent he received in spelling and writing was his lowest grade during his years at Shawano.[9]

As a continuous recipient of school honors, he earned the admiration and respect of other students. "I wish I had your knowledge for all my work in school," a schoolmate told him. "Where did you ever get all the information you've got in your head? I guess you must have a few more wisdom teeth than I have," another schoolmate said. One friend lamented, "Don't take all the honors next year—leave some for me." Evelyn Winther kiddingly chided him for the same thing: "Be sure and cap all the honors next year—in averages I mean. No chance for the rest of us when you're around." His friend Bernice Krueger enjoyed having Frank near her because he was "so brilliant," and Marcella Umland thought he was the "most capable student in everything." A fellow senior said he would remember Frank as the "possessor of all knowledge."[10]

To his male school chums, Frank was dubbed simply "Leopolis," but to the girls who admired his athletic build and wavy brown hair, he was affectionately referred to as "Curly" or "Frankie." More than one person thought he was a "shark" in geometry, the "star" of English class, and a chemistry expert. At the conclusion of his junior year, a friend could not pass up the opportunity to lump a few more adjectives before Frank's name when he wrote good-humoredly:

> Hello Smart Bright One! There is so much <u>bunk</u> in here about you being so <u>darn smart</u> that I'll change it for once. I think you're the dumbest animal I've seen in a long time and they just hand you this line because they don't know you like I do. You must enjoy studying because you fall asleep over your books 5 nights out of every four— Dream about it I suppose. A good idea, I must try it.[11]

It soon became apparent to many people that Frank had a special fondness for studying history. "I was very much interested in history," he recalled years later, "maybe because I had a good history teacher, but then I was interested in every subject. I was enamored with Algebra and English and all of the High School studies, and I read voraciously in those days."[12] The books which intrigued him the most were biographies of world leaders like Napoleon, Bismarck, George Washington, and Abraham Lincoln.[13] The curriculum included courses in Ancient History, Modern History, United States History, American Problems, Citizenship, and Civics—taught by Robert J. Icks and Loretta Iwen. Icks was voted the most popular teacher of the school in 1927 because of his frankness and friendliness with the students, and Frank probably admired Miss Iwen as much as the student who poetically penned:

> Many and oft there must needs be done,
> Things not listed in curriculum,
> Through just this type of work we claim
> Miss Iwen wins much of her fame.[14]

Frank gained a reputation for his uncanny ability to recall names, places, and events. "You sure were capable of 'earing' history," one admirer noted. "I often envyed [*sic*] you." "Won't you give me your recipe for remembering history?" asked Irene Bowman. Margaret McCarter echoed many when she said, "You sure are a bright one in history class. And I guess in all classes from what I hear." A senior classmate recorded in Frank's year-book at the end of 1926: "Will remember you as being so smart in history. You sure have the ability to remember." Oscar Swanson, who taught senior English and some history, complimented him on being "quite an asset to our history class." While some of his peers poked harmless fun at the serious scholar, most of his Shawano peers simply stood in awe of his ability to master so much information about so many different subjects. "To be great is to be misunderstood," one girl told him near graduation. "You are great, Frank, because you're so wise and you are also misunderstood. Wish I had half the brains that you have."[15]

Frank enjoyed other pursuits during his high school years. He was one of thirty students who participated enthusiastically in the projects of the Philakean Society, a literary group that promoted forensic activities and stressed a systematic practice in parliamentary usages. During his senior year the club entertained the school with a skit that had been "ingeniously worked out," in which two fictitious companies battled in a mock court over patent rights. Already a stickler for accuracy and detail, Frank impressed a fellow society member as the person "always calling for Robert's Rules of Order."[16] In his senior year he served as secretary for the Science Club, which studied the principles of electricity as applied to radio, discussed various topics of nature, and had its members attend a lecture on the facts about radium. He joined the school's Athletic Association, landed a position on Shawano's football team, and played for the Leopolis Cagers basketball team.

After graduating on June 4, 1927, with excellent marks, he enrolled in a one-year rural teacher training program at the high school. He completed its curriculum in June 1928 and taught for three years at the Pella District Number 2 School just south of Leopolis before accepting another offer to become the principal and upper grade instructor at a two-teacher state-graded school near Angelica at the far eastern part of Shawano County. He was teaching in Pella when a friend arrived at the Klement farmhouse one day in 1931 and simply said to him, "Let's go to college!" The suggestion instantly appealed to Frank, and the two ambitious young men started taking classes at Central State Teachers College (today the University of Wisconsin-Stevens Point) in the fall of that year.[17]

At Stevens Point, Klement soon declared himself a history major and studied in earnest under the direction of Professor Herbert R. Steiner, a native Wisconsinite and Harvard University graduate student who also served as dean of men. Steiner called his students to moral reflection and inspired them to labor for lofty ideals—not simply to work to accumulate money. "The college period is a probationary time when intellect and character are tested and refined," he advised them. "To come under the influence of a college environment where individuals are made ready for the highest type of human service is a privilege worth seeking for those who analyze and develop their potentialities."[18] He encouraged young people to aspire to only the highest traits of human character: loyalty, duty, hard work, and personal responsibility. "The world is delegating its duties more and more to you young people in whose character and intellectual ability it has confidence," he told students in 1933. "The amount of confidence reposed in you is never accidental. It is based upon what you have been and what you are. Your attitudes, your habits, and your conduct build this reliance which others have in you. May you build consciously and well."[19]

To the pious and serious-minded Klement, Dr. Steiner embodied all that was good and honorable; a superb model after which he would fashion his own academic dreams. In 1988, Frank would recollect the professor's courses as "a most pleasant experience." Steiner brought history alive in a way that Frank hoped to emulate in his own classroom someday. "He was a marvelous lecturer, and I became his favorite student. I took every course he offered. After his death, his son brought over boxes of books, and said: 'My father, I know, would like you to have these because he thought so highly of you.'" Beneath one of the history tests he had pasted into a scrapbook Klement had written the words, "Mr. Steiner was my History teacher. What a teacher!"[20]

Besides diligently pursuing the study of history, young Klement continued to pursue his interest in sports. He was one of almost two dozen members of the "S" Club, an organization he helped to establish his freshman year, which was designed to spark an interest in athletics in other students. During each of his four years at Stevens Point he was a star player of the school's basketball, football, baseball, and track teams.[21]

His interest in social organizations did not wane, either. He added his name to the list of members for the Forum, a professional group of aspiring high school teachers who provided personal direction to each other in the advancement of scholarship, and who gave students a chance to work as a group in solving problems which faced new instructors. He was elected vice president and president of the Chi Delta Rho Fraternity, and represented the group on the Greek Council. His high averages in all studies permitted him to become a member of the Zeta Chapter of Sigma Zeta, a scholarly fraternity that promoted science. He assisted in conducting a class in Parliamentary procedure as a leader of the Margaret Ashmun Club, an English honorary society, while promoting its short story competition. A devout Catholic, he worked hard as president of the Loyola Club, which sought to unite Catholic students together in a social setting to encourage the study of religion, "promote unswerving loyalty to faith, and to foster good will among all students on the campus."[22] His popularity enabled him to be elected vice president of his sophomore class, and in 1935 he became editor in chief of the school's weekly newsletter, *The Pointer*. His efforts to enhance the publication were recognized when the yearbook announced that the newsletter's "staff has given the students more pages than ever before in the school's history...."[23]

The United States was experiencing one of the worst economic depressions in its history as Frank approached graduation in 1935. Yet he was confident that his bachelor's degree in secondary education and strong athletic background would soon land him numerous interviews with schools which would beg for his services, not only for his talents in the classroom, but for his skills as a coach or assistant coach. He had grown tired of farm life in Leopolis and longed for a teaching position. While he waited at his parents' home during the 1934 Christmas holiday for job opportunities to present themselves, a local banker who also served as a director for the community's school board notified him that a principalship was available in Shawano. "I wouldn't teach in my hometown," young Klement told the man. Three months later, after he once again returned to the farm to celebrate Easter with his family, the school official repeated the offer. Frank had been interviewed several times, but no job offers followed. Still, he had a little more than a month remaining in school and remained confident that a better opportunity was imminent. "I wouldn't teach in my hometown," he repeated. The next few weeks brought no new results. When the banker showed up for a third time shortly after school had ended, he found Frank still tending to the cows on his father's farm. "He said, 'We've kept the principalship open for you,'" Klement recalled with a smile years later, "and I said, 'I'll take it.'"[24]

He soon found himself working hard as an instructor and principal of a four-teacher, state-graded country school. Keeping in mind advice he had received from Dr. Steiner ("The time to leave is when you're appreciated most"), Frank resigned after two years to obtain a master's degree at the University of Wisconsin-Madison. For him, Madison was the only "sensible place to matriculate...for additional upper education."[25] Little did he realize that he was approaching a turning point in his career; a period of time when another instructor—whose demeanor and classroom presence was the opposite of the gentlemanly and polite Steiner, and who seemed to be conducting a circus rather than a graduate seminar—would alter the direction of his historical studies forever.

In the autumn of 1937 Klement reported to Dr. Paul Knaplund's office at Madison. He was the third student in line for an interview, and when it was his turn the professor asked him what field of history he wanted to specialize in. The pointed question surprised and confused him, for he had no idea what "field of history" meant. Knaplund explained that he had a choice between Medieval, Latin-American, American, Modern European, Far Eastern, and others. "I had to make up my mind right on the spot,"

Frank recalled. "I had taken an extension course in Ancient History and was in love with it while I was teaching at Leopolis, but on the spot I said, 'American History.'" Knaplund then instructed him to choose whether he wanted to major in the early, middle, or recent era. "I had to decide upon the three and being a compromiser I said, 'The middle period'....I became, thus, a Civil War historian, which you see is largely chance and circumstance and spur-of-the-moment decisions." Frank was told to see assistant professor William Best Hesseltine, who would act as his academic mentor.[26]

To students who took his history courses at Madison, William B. Hesseltine loomed large as an ogre; a gruff and seemingly unpleasant individual who seemed to relish in insulting students' work. His critical and distrustful nature, when coupled with his sharp tongue and sometimes shocking behavior, struck fear in many who attended his classes. Hesseltine had come to Wisconsin in 1932 as an assistant professor after brief teaching stints at the University of Arkansas and University of Chattanooga. He was only thirty-five years old when Frank began taking his courses, but had skyrocketed to fame as an unpredictable and provocative lecturer, grueling taskmaster, and successful author. When he died in 1963 he was considered one of the leading revisionists in Civil War historiography.[27]

Richard N. Current, one of Hesseltine's thirty-two Ph.D. students, recalled that a first encounter with the renowned instructor could be a "terrifying experience," especially for young students who met with him in his Bascom Hall office.

> The professor was so short that his head did not extend much above the back of the swivel chair in which, his stubby legs crossed, he sat tilted rearward at a precarious angle....Before responding to the excuses of his visitor, he fixed upon him for a while an unrelenting stare. He took from his mouth a curved-stem pipe, which had gone out again, and held it in his right hand. He passed the other hand lightly across his bald dome, and his heavy mustache twitched once or twice, almost imperceptibly. When he finally spoke, his words came rumbling up as if from a cavernous depth; his voice must have been a full octave lower than that of any other member of the Wisconsin faculty. What he proceeded to say, as well as the way he said it, was memorable. Gruffly, he got to the point, with few of the circumlocutions that professors customarily use in reproving their students.[28]

With Knaplund's referral in hand, Frank entered Hesseltine's first floor office in Bascom Hall and found him "sitting in a lean back chair with smoke rings coming out of his bent pipe. He greeted me with a huff—gruffly—as if I were intruding upon him, and said, 'What are you here for?'" After some discussion, the professor enrolled him in his seminar dealing with the Civil War and Reconstruction, and in courses about historical methods, American constitutional history, and history of the West.[29]

Hesseltine's students knew him as a "lively if eccentric performer in the lecture hall." One student paid tribute to his ability to present a lecture which was "alternately lucid, mystifying, challenging, and outrageous, but always exciting." Current admitted that "his lectures seldom were models of organization, and even bright students might occasionally find him confusing. But only dullards ever found him dull." He had the gift of making history highly palatable by orating with a mixture of "mock pomposity," and chatting "as if reminiscing of men and events he personally had known...." All the while, however, "he was showing the relevance of the past to the present."[30]

Although students enjoyed his classroom antics, Hesseltine was at his best when conducting what he called his "seminary"; the graduate seminar he taught weekday afternoons in rooms at the Wisconsin State Historical Society. Frank L. Byrne, who earned his Ph.D. under him in 1957, wrote that the professor conceived of his seminar as "a continuing body, somewhat like the Mafia or the Irish Republican Army. His rule was, 'Once in, never out.'" He instructed his students to regard those individuals who had preceded them in his seminar as colleagues.[31]

All new arrivals to the seminar were made to attend special orientation lectures before they joined the existing group around an ancient T-shaped table, which Hesseltine stated had been used by the students of Frederick Jackson Turner. "The assertion achieved its purpose of challenging us with the tradition of the university," Byrne recalled. "He continued by assuring us that we were there because we knew that historical research was more important, in fact more fun, than anything else....He then told us that we were not in an educational institution but in a trade school."[32]

Most of the students who attended these meetings were stunned by the lack of order and respect afforded to the young seminarians. Current has described them as "dramatic happenings," where students were encouraged to vigorously dispute with one another, as well as with the professor himself! Hesseltine thoroughly enjoyed the sessions, "and the sharper the verbal combat, the better he liked it." T. Harry Williams, who was one of Hesseltine's first students and remained his favorite, quoted the professor as saying that the best seminar was like a dog fight. The specific content of each session was unpredictable, "but the usual atmosphere was more reminiscent of the Roman arena," another student remarked. Each student showed up with an assignment, and was expected to find fault with each other's construction, interpretations, and conclusions.

> Inspired by Hesseltine's injunctions to negative, not positive criticism, the students would harry the victim whose paper they had read in advance. Meanwhile, Hesseltine would sit quietly, puffing his curved pipe. Often he would seem to pay little attention—turning his back, walking to the window to weave the shade cord, writing Delphic inscriptions on

the blackboard. At the psychologically appropriate instant, he would leap in for the kill. One seminarian recalled his "incredible seminar method" whereby "he would knock down your paper, find the fatal flaw, and then find the key to the subject and proceed to reconstruct the material on the basis of his view of what the story really was." It was a searing experience, mitigated by a sense of shared and successive suffering. Far more traumatic were those few occasions on which Hesseltine avoided discussing the paper at all—his strongest rebuke.[33]

A major thrust of Hesseltine's message to aspiring scholars was to be skeptical historical writers; to "distrust each witness; to view every document as designed to deceive." He thought the best historians were those who approached their subjects with a marked degree of hostility which he believed aided an author's objectivity. Taking for granted that every paper submitted to him had been meticulously researched, Hesseltine always asked for more information from primary sources, questioned the author's logic and interpretations, and painstakingly dissected their imperfect prose. Gossip spread across campus about an occasion when he expressed displeasure with a seminarian's thesis by quickly throwing its several chapters off his desk onto the floor, where it skidded into the hallway outside his office. Although Hesseltine often heard such stories and denied that he had ever thrown a paper *on the floor*, he clearly had no patience for sloppy scholarship and often scrawled contemptuous remarks in the margins of offending paragraphs.[34]

Compiling an impressive collection of facts was worthless, Hesseltine asserted, unless writers could communicate them in clear, exciting prose. Write "books," not "dissertations," was his advice. One of his Ph.D. students has said that "writing sentences and assembling them into a narrative was for Hesseltine the culmination of the historian's task," and he urged students to tell their story so that the reader is "convinced, converted, and pleased."[35] More than once "whb" (as he often signed himself) was compelled to deliver his "Twenty-Minute Lecture On How To Write" and to distribute his list of "Commandments" on historical writing, which consisted of fifteen exacting admonitions which declared war on the misuse of senseless rhetoric, quotations, footnotes, judgements, chronology, and methodology. When being interviewed at Marquette in 1964, Klement expressed his opinion as to why amateur historians such as Bruce Catton were so successful at their trade compared to professionally trained historians: "Catton has mastered an art in which we do not get adequate development in graduate school: Catton can write. The fact that he does it so well certainly attracts public interest to history." Hesseltine prided himself on being a gifted writer, and insisted that his students learn to "organize clearly, write with vigor, choose words of strength, and imprison the acts of men upon the written page."[36]

The acts of men, however, were not to receive an author's judgement. Unlike many of his colleagues, Hesseltine rejected the idea that history should be used to teach political or moral lessons. "Thou shalt not pass judgements on mankind in general, yet thou shalt not pardon anyone for anything," he growled often. "Morality is not immutable." A variation of this commandment ended with the words: "If a man is in error thou shalt seek the reasons for his error, but not the excuses."[37] Frank learned the rule well. When he spoke to the Civil War Round Table of Chicago in 1966 on Clement L. Vallandigham, the most popular of Civil War dissenters, he prefaced his remarks by saying to listeners: "I hope you will allow me to paraphrase Shakespeare and say: 'I come to talk about Vallandigham, not to praise him. The evil that men do lives after them; the good is often interred in their bones. So let it be with Vallandigham.'" Hesseltine's "Commandments" were taken to heart by many of his students who went on to become college professors, and have been reproduced in various forms. When Klement joined the history department at Marquette University two years after he obtained his Ph.D., one of the first handouts he issued to undergraduates was his rules for good writing, which included four reworded Hesseltinian commands.[38]

As budding historians, Hesseltine's students were not only expected to fastidiously ferret out facts and present them coherently as a story, they were expected to do it continually without interruption only on subjects which were worthy of publication. Even after his Ph.D. students found positions in academe, he frequently sent small postcards to those laggards who did not publish according to his schedule, admonishing them to "GET BUSY." Ceaseless research and writing was a practice which he used as a benchmark to gauge academic success. It was not a goal which Hesseltine found unreachable, for his own bibliography shows a total literary output of nineteen books, 164 articles, and over 400 book reviews over a thirty-three year period. In 1948 alone, he announced to his department chairman the publication of two books, thirty-two articles, forty-four reviews, and forty-seven public lectures, which included twenty-five in Latin America for the U.S. State Department. He noted as an afterthought that 206 essays for encyclopedias still awaited publication. His colleagues viewed him as an unexhaustible fountain from which poured forth effortlessly a steady stream of books, essays, and reviews which few historians have been able to match in number. Whenever Klement had an opportunity to sit down and chat with his former professor years afterward at historical conventions, he usually went home with the feeling that he had not done enough writing and needed to do more.[39]

Compared to Stevens Point, the amount of work required at Madison was grueling. In "History of the West: 1783–1837," taught by Dr. John D. Hicks, taken during his first semester, Klement was required to read large sections in forty-two books. In Hesseltine's course, "Sectionalism and the

Civil War," students read three entire volumes (totaling over 1,200 pages) in addition to parts in forty-one others.[40] To some of his classmates, who came to Madison after already completing a few years of study at other notable universities and were acclimated to the heavy workload, Frank appeared less equipped to handle what was expected of him. Current has observed that "the Frank Klement that I knew was a little different from most of William B. Hesseltine's students at the University of Wisconsin in the 1930s. Though somewhat older, he was less well prepared for graduate work in history, as he confided many years later. Whatever he lacked in preparation, however, he more than made up in intelligence, determination, and hard work." Three decades later, when one of his own students expressed self-doubts as an undergraduate, Frank shared with him the problems he had faced at Madison, "where it was difficult to succeed and be a staunch Roman Catholic at the same time." In fact, Hesseltine warned Frank more than once that he would have difficulty getting ahead in the academic world because of his Catholicism, which many considered at that time to be the "mark of the Beast."[41]

Frank finished his master's thesis, "John Buchanan ('Scapegoat') Floyd: A Study of Virginia Politics Through a Biography," by the spring of 1938. Klement said in retrospect many years later, "It was, I guess, an acceptable Master's thesis, but nothing to write home about." That summer he accepted a teaching position at Beloit High School, some fifty miles south of Madison, where he taught Government, History, and English. Frank always maintained that he had been offered the position because of his athletic credentials, and he quickly became a successful B-Team coach in football and basketball, as well as co-coach in track. He emulated Hesseltine by making his classroom lectures memorable events and kept in mind the lessons he learned from Dr. Steiner and Robert Icks by taking a sincere interest in his students. One student said that he was "a mighty fine man. Fair and trusting," while another said that he was "the grandest teacher I ever had." An aspiring educator told Frank in 1941: "I really enjoyed being in your English class. Someday when I'm a teacher (Ahem!) I'm going to try to be like you. Perhaps I won't be quite as frank though, and I won't say impossible as much as you have, but if I make half as good a teacher as you—that will be something." The school's yearbook for that year described him as "serene and undisturbed. His face is tranquil and still, but yet there is a certain fixed position of his mouth and chin which suggests a steady and firm personality."[42]

Soon after taking the job in Beloit he married twenty-five-year-old Laurel M. Fosnot on August 27, 1938. School photographs show her as a pretty and petite dark-haired young woman. As a student at the University of Wisconsin-Madison, she was enamored with the arts and wrote her 1938 master's thesis on "Gestalt Psychology Applied to the Graphic and Plastic

Arts." Like Frank, she was active in university clubs, such as the Delta Phi Delta national art fraternity and Sigma Lambda, a professional sorority for students in the school of art education. The Klements were married for fifty-three years, and raised a family of three sons.[43]

When high school ended for the summer, Frank would journey to Madison to take additional graduate courses. When he returned to Hesseltine's graduate seminar in the summer of 1940, he was one of twelve students in the classroom. They were seated at the T-shaped table at the first meeting when the professor passed around a sheet of paper with twelve topics on it. "Each of us were supposed to sign up for one of those topics as a seminar topic for the year," said Frank, who had positioned himself immediately to Hesseltine's left. "He started it at the other end of the table, so by the time that list got to me, I got the last topic, and the last topic was, 'The Democratic Party in the Civil War.' So, thus I became, by chance, a student of the Democratic party during the Civil War."

The course outline for the summer 1940 session shows that his assigned topic was initially called "Seymour and Lincoln," which called for him to interpret Governor Horatio Seymour of New York as the representative of Northern Democracy and analyze the position of the Democratic party and Lincoln's relations with Democratic-ruled states. Frank retitled the topic "Lincoln and the Border-States" in his preliminary report to the seminar on July 16, and later changed it again to "The Democratic Party vs. the Administration in the Civil War." Unfortunately, the paper has not survived, for it represents Frank's earliest work on Copperheadism. Those first readings on the subject from books Hesseltine used in his seminar did nothing to dissuade him from accepting the traditional interpretations that Copperheads were a motley group of pro-Southern ingrates who affiliated with subversive secret societies, organized conspiracies, and "criticized a president whose policies were proper and who deserved sainthood." "By the end of the summer term," as Klement writes in the pages that follow, "I had some doubts and suppositions, but not enough to change the equation. Lincoln, however, no longer walked on water."

The following summer he focused his attention on his native state under the direction of T. Harry Williams, who was substituting for Hesseltine, and wrote a succinct study of the "Democratic Party in Wisconsin During the Civil War."[44] At the beginning of his third summer term in 1942 he approached Hesseltine somewhat cautiously with the proposal of writing a thesis entitled, "The Copperheads in the Upper Midwest." Hesseltine greeted the idea with a smile and the comment, "I've been waiting for someone to take hold of that topic and chew on it."

Hesseltine's harsh training regimen did not succeed with every student. Many were unable to accept or unwilling to submit to his harsh rules. Others Hesseltine simply rejected as prospects. "Most who remained comforted one another," one seminarian recollected. "Those who endured their professor's brusque demeanor, rigorous work standards, and exacting directions came to learn that they had earned a loyal comrade to sustain them upon completing his course work. "One reason why we did not collapse under his scathing, sometimes tyrannical, criticism was that we knew outside of seminar he was our friend," a former student wrote. Although he rarely paid even his favorite students any compliments, Hesseltine took great pride in their subsequent literary accomplishments and took armloads of his former students' books to class to demonstrate what his young scholars were capable of. Current has said that "all looked for him for aid in getting a job, and then for further help in securing a better one, and seldom did they look in vain." It is little wonder, therefore, that his undergraduate students greeted their professor daily in class with the "skyrocket"—a "siss boom bah" sort of cheer which lasted several minutes, once even accented with lit fire crackers. Many of his students agreed that "his kindness and gentleness—reflected in the twinkling eyes which belied the gruff manner he liked to put on—made him an irreplaceable friend."[45]

Hesseltine's benevolence extended to Frank on several occasions in the form of friendly advice and favors. Anxious to return to Madison to complete his year of residency in the Ph.D. program, Frank resigned from his teaching position at Beloit High School in 1942 and was able to offset expenses due to Hesseltine's influence in obtaining for him a Charles Kendall Adams Fellowship.[46] He was making fine progress on his doctoral thesis while taking courses and studying hard for his foreign language requirement when Hesseltine, to Frank's dismay, recommended him to the history department chairman at Madison as a candidate for a teaching assistant to Dr. Chester P. Higby, whose assistant had suddenly left the university to join the navy. He immediately implored Hesseltine to find somebody else for the job, explaining he was reluctant to take on added school responsibility because he did not want to be diverted from his doctoral work, but Hesseltine was unmoved. "They need your help now," he told Frank, referring to the department. "You may need their help later."[47]

As America deepened its involvement in World War II the following spring, Frank also felt the surge of patriotism when he received a letter offering him a navy commission. "Well, if it comes down to you the war is as good as lost," Hesseltine told him with characteristic curtness, "You can do more good teaching soldier-students somewhere, and they'll need you there." The United States had begun forming Army Specialized Training Programs during World War II in colleges for those who were serving in the war, and the professor's prophesy proved correct. In 1943, Frank accepted a job at Lake Forest College in Lake Forest, Illinois, supervising twelve quiz sections and teaching European and American history, plus courses on education to 325 soldiers who had to take classes there before continuing on to officers' school.[48]

In the late spring of 1962 Klement was serving as a member of the Wisconsin Civil War Centennial Commission. Leslie J. Fishel, Jr., director for the State Historical Society of Wisconsin, proposed to the commission the idea of having a history of Wisconsin's contribution to the Civil War effort published in the state's legislative volume, *Blue Book*, as part of the nationwide commemoration of the conflict. Fishel persuaded the members to adopt the project and select an author. Hesseltine was also serving on the commission and sitting at the table that day. As Klement recalled later, Hesseltine said with his "characteristic brasso profundo" that he knew just the right person. "Gesturing in my direction with his pipe, he said, 'You've been chosen.'" Although Klement greatly respected his mentor and believed he "owed him a large professional and intellectual debt," he was averse to accepting the assignment because he was teaching four courses at Marquette at the time and swamped with classwork. Before he could object, however, Hesseltine growled, "The due date is around Thanksgiving." "With that I meekly submitted," Klement wrote. "Wisconsin and the Civil War," appeared in 1962 and was published by the State Historical Society of Wisconsin the following year as a 112-page paperback book, also courtesy of Hesseltine's influence. In introducing the essay, Hesseltine proudly told readers that Klement mixed a "superb sense of balance" with "judicious selection." "Professor Klement has given each phase of Wisconsin's many-sided development careful attention; and from his brief, succinct narrative, there emerges a balanced, scholarly account of the total development of an American state involved in a great national crisis...[and] a story which deserves to be read, and deeply pondered by every citizen of Wisconsin." Wisconsin Governor Gaylord A. Nelson honored them, along with Alan T. Nolan, as distinguished state historians who added much to the understanding of the Civil War.[49]

Klement always remained devoted to his former professor and even dedicated his 1970 biography of Clement L. Vallandigham to his memory. Although he admitted that Hesseltine intentionally tried to be gruff and rough, and had a reputation for maltreating his students, he maintained that he "was a man with a big heart. When he finally had heart trouble, they diagnosed that he had an extra large heart. He was very, very, very proud of those who survived the ordeal of his seminar and got their doctorates." Hesseltine boasted that his students published more books and articles than those of any other professor in the country, and his personal magnetism also showed itself in the fact that practically all of his Ph.D. students went on to become eminent historians who made their mark in the study of the Civil War or its aftermath.[50]

On May 26, 1945, Frank was selected to deliver the Senior Chapel Address to students graduating from Lake Forest College. Standing before them in a reflective and somber mood, he reminded those young people what they should have learned from their four years of study in college.

First, "you should have acquired some understanding of things as they were, a well-rounded knowledge of things as they are, and a vision of things as they might be," he began. Also, he hoped they had acquired a better understanding of themselves. "You should have become better acquainted with your prejudices and possessed of a desire to eradicate them." Last but certainly not least, Frank was hopeful that they had been inspired to embrace "a desirable set of intellectual, aesthetic, moral, and spiritual values." After all, he told those assembled, "the main function of a liberal arts college is the clarification and the inculcation of the humanistic view of life. One's training may make materialistic values loom large on the horizon, *but one's education should be concerned with human values*." Possibly recalling to mind the moralistic advice Dr. Steiner often tendered to Stevens Point students, he left them with this charge:

> Do not float with the current which is over-emphasizing material values at the expense of human values. Keep facing the river's source; fight your way against the current. Only a dead fish floats downstream. Only a dead fish floats with the current. As long as you have any pride in yourself and life in your body, keep yourself headed upstream. War upon the intolerance which surrounds you on every side. Make democracy more than a hollow symbol....My generation has been critical of your generation—that is the perpetual story; each generation satisfies its ego by criticizing the one which follows....But, I am not proud of my generation's record. Between two devastating world wars we sandwiched two decades of hypocrisy and misery—during the 1920's we worshipped the golden calf, so that millions were ill-clothed, and ill-fed during the 'terrible thirties.' Human wreckage, as a consequence, litters the scene on every side. Now, my generation is passing the baton to yours. I have faith that your generation will carry it well. Certainly, you can do no worse than we have done. With God's help, you will do better.[51]

The military discontinued its specialized training programs and Klement moved to northern Wisconsin to begin a three-year teaching stint at Eau Claire State College, only because he wanted to teach strictly American History and actively write about Civil War-related topics. His first published article, "The Soldier Vote in Wisconsin During the Civil War," had appeared the previous fall and two more were near completion. This new opportunity, however, proved disappointing because the university did not encourage or reward its instructors for such activity. In September 1948 he joined the faculty of Marquette University in Milwaukee, where he would remain for the rest of his life.[52]

At Marquette, Klement was able to recreate historical events in such a vivid fashion during lectures that students were enthralled with the subjects he taught and sought to emulate him by becoming history professors themselves after graduation. John E. Walsh, current legislative historian for the Indiana State Archives, first met Frank as a freshman in September 1951. "The exposure to European history that Fall proved a life-altering experience. By semester's end I decided to make history my life's work." While he was working on his master's degree years later, he encountered the incomparable "Genesis of the Civil War, 1830–1860," a course that "epitomized the genius of Frank Klement as a teacher." Walsh has said that the course's examinations were unforgettable. "For instance, who but Frank Klement would pair the Maysville Road Bill with John C. Dickinson in a multiple choice question because Andrew Jackson killed them both? As explained by Klement, Old Hickory vetoed the former in 1830 and shot the latter in a duel in 1806." One student recalled a quiz where Frank asked the name of Robert E. Lee's horse and the author of the course textbook. Former student and author Mercedes Maloney said that she was "awed at the amount of knowledge this man possessed and how he was able to transmit that knowledge to his students. For me he made the Civil War come alive and I enjoyed every moment in his classes."[53]

Frank Klement also never forgot the favors which came his way as a result of colleagues who took action for his benefit, and frequently went out of his way to assist fledgling scholars who studied under him. He worked behind the scenes to get Walsh a teaching position at the University of Wisconsin-Oshkosh in the mid-1960s, and offered constant counsel while the young historian expanded his dissertation on Chicago Copperhead Wilbur F. Storey into a book-length biography.[54] Herman Viola was a senior at Marquette in 1960 when he decided to enlist in the navy rather than attend graduate school. Shortly before his two-year enlistment expired, he returned to Wisconsin on leave with the intention of returning to Reserve Officer Training School and becoming a naval officer. Probably recalling his own ambition to enter the navy and Hesseltine's reluctance to let him go, Klement did his best to discourage the former student from finishing out his enlistment. "Why not get a master's in history at Marquette instead?" he asked. Viola explained that his undergraduate record, coupled with the expense of graduate school, precluded such an idea. "Nonsense," Frank retorted, and explained that he certainly would qualify for a fellowship. Frank made him fill out an application, which required him to obtain three faculty references. Frank wrote out one on the spot, and two other professors promised to forward theirs soon. Viola returned to duty and received a letter from Frank a few weeks later, saying that his application had been too late and that all available fellowships had been awarded. When he arrived in Scotland, he received an urgent message from Marquette which said that one of the assistantships had been rejected by the recipient and that he could have it and gain admittance to the history department graduate program if he could report to the campus within two weeks. With still three months to go on his enlistment, Viola doubted that he could accept the offer, but his commander cut orders immediately for him to begin academic life. "What I subsequently discovered is that the other two professors never did write the letters of recommendation," Viola wrote later, who went on to become Curator Emeritus for the Smithsonian Institution. "Klement, however, pressured the graduate school and the department chairman to take a chance on me when the assistantship became available....I owe much of my success as a historian and scholar to his tutelage, friendship, and encouragement....He took a genuine interest not only in me, but also in my life's work." Walsh expressed similar sentiments in 1994 when he said that Frank was a "valued colleague and friend who maintained a prideful interest in our careers right to the end."[55]

For more than three decades at Marquette, Klement actively pursued his dream of combining teaching and writing. From 1958 until 1960 he served as chairman for the history department, and in 1965 won Marquette's prestigious "Award for Teaching Excellence." In the summer of 1956 he taught at Michigan State University, and in 1967 became a visiting Huntington Library Fellow at Sacramento State University. In 1972 he was named an "Outstanding Educator in America." After he officially retired for the first time in 1975 at age sixty-eight, Klement taught abroad as a Leverhulme Fellow and Visiting Professor of American History at the University of Sussex in England for one year. Marquette bestowed on him the title of Emeritus Professor of History in 1980 for his thirty-five years of dedication to the university and exemplary talents in the classroom. He continued to offer at least one course each semester until he finally quit teaching altogether in 1988. The university again honored Klement four years later by creating a lecture series in his name, only the third such series since Marquette's founding in 1881. The beloved professor became linked with Father Jacques Marquette (1637–1675) and Thomas Aquinas (1225–1274), when the "Frank L. Klement Lectures: Alternative Views of the Sectional Conflict" was inaugurated on October 19, 1992.[56]

Other awards also came his way. In 1973 he was named an honorary member of the Marquette chapter of Alpha Sigma Nu, the National Jesuit Honor Society. Ten years later he became an honorary member of Phi Beta Kappa, and six years after that he received the Meritorious Service Award from the Phi Alpha Theta Society.

Just after he departed for England in 1976, Klement caused a national furor when an enthusiastic Madison newspaper editor published sensationalized excerpts of his essay, "History and the Humanities," which dealt with his suspicion of nationalist historians.[57] Capitalizing on a few statements Klement made about underhanded tactics Lincoln used as a young politician in Springfield, the newspaperman sent them out over the Associated Press and United Press International wires a week before Lincoln's birthday under a "dirty tricks" designation. The headlines which screamed the news—"Abe Lincoln myth shred by historian," "Abe's halo is slipping," "Lincoln no saint, professor says," "Prof says Abe used dirty tricks," "A Different View of Lincoln," "Professor attacks Lincoln's legend," "Historian Says Myths Immortalized Lincoln," "Researcher says Lincoln not above a few dirty tricks," "Say it ain't so, Abe," "Lincoln's image tarnished?"— caused many a Lincoln loyalist to write him critical, often vehement letters.[58] The fact that Klement was already in London at the time the story broke prompted "nagging rumors" that he wrote the "dispatch on 'St. Abe,' then, under the cover of night, fled the U.S. to avoid the storm of controversy," one person told him. Within a week, one writer rebutted the protests by editorializing that "Klement makes a good point, and his revelations about one of our country's heroes should not detract from our admiration of the man or our appreciation of what he accomplished."[59]

Klement's early investigations into the lives of prominent midwestern "malcontents"—a word he frequently liked to use to describe Lincoln's Democratic critics—soon convinced him that those individuals who menaced supporters of the Union cause had been labeled traitors chiefly by religious leaders who backed the administration and Republican propagandists, whose writings would influence over a hundred years of scholarship about the Civil War. His conclusions from available evidence were at odds with previous historians who had delved deeply into the subject, especially two scholars who had books published in 1942, during the time when Klement was still on his own fact-finding mission.

The label of traitor was easily hung upon the Copperheads as America entered World War II because of books like *The Hidden Civil War: The Story of the Copperheads* by Wood Gray, and George Fort Milton's *Abraham Lincoln and the Fifth Column*, which described disloyal acts in the North during the Civil War at the time when the United States faced similar activities performed by "fifth column" saboteurs and other undercover internal groups. Although both writers took great pains not to make any comparisons between the problems faced by the Lincoln administration and those encountered by President Franklin D. Roosevelt, it was obvious that both books were hurriedly prepared to address disloyalty during wartime as an effort to comment upon contemporary domestic threats, and it did not escape notice that Milton even used a popular modern term in the title of his work which reflected its obvious slant.[60]

Because both books were published almost simultaneously, scholars had the opportunity to compare one against the other, and many found both wanting. Gray's research was not complete and certainly not definitive, one reviewer noted, but the book's strength was that it ably surveyed the repeated ebb and flow of public confidence in the North and defeatist movements in the Old Northwest by drawing from period newspapers and manuscript collections. Unfortunately, critics pointed out, very little new information was introduced, although Gray drew a composite picture of public and newspaper opinion, local politics in the Midwest, and the acts of opposition which took place outside secret societies. The text, however, was riddled with minor errors, and documentation was incomplete and often unsatisfactory, calling many of the author's judgements into question.

Most who reviewed *Abraham Lincoln and the Fifth Column* agreed that Milton's book surpassed Gray's in readability and provided a clearer picture of the national scene. But one disappointed reader said that its chapters lacked unity and attacked its bibliography and references by saying both were "worthless to scholars." Another review concluded: "The gentle reader may prefer this volume, but the serious student will do better to read both [books]."[61] Elbert J. Benton's *The Movement For Peace Without Victory During the Civil War* (1918) and *Peacemakers of 1864* by Edward Chase Kirkland (1927) were virtually the only secondary works which dealt with Copperheadism up until 1942, so it was not too surprising that both books, even considering their shortcomings, were heralded as the "first full-length studies ever to appear" on the subject.[62]

Klement had closely examined the research of Kirkland, Gray, and Milton, and scoured many of the same manuscript collections, but arrived at drastically different determinations about Lincoln's Northern carpers. The seeds of Klement's beliefs about Copperheadism had firmly taken root by the time he had finished his Ph.D. dissertation, "Middle Western Copperheadism: Jeffersonian Democracy in Revolt," in 1946.[63] Its title accurately reflected what he now earnestly believed about the Copperhead movement: that it was an offshoot of Jeffersonian and Jacksonian democracy which influenced the subsequent formation of Greenbackism, Populism, and the Granger and Progressive movements. Rather than a pro-Southern or pro-Confederate campaign, Klement reasoned that Copperheadism advocated the economic interests of the *west*, whose farmers resurrected the argument of states rights to protect them from the growing economic-political power of New England and the fear that a foreign power might take control of the Mississippi River, if the country became divided by a domestic war and other nations intervened. Its slogan, "The Union as it was," told of the abhorrence these westerners had for the radical Republican economic, social, and political changes which were taking place in the Federal and state governments.[64]

Klement argued that the Lincoln administration, backed by patronage, power, and money, was capable of taking strong counter-measures which labeled every Copperhead or Butternut a traitor to his country. The stigmatization of Copperheadism was further stamped on the American psyche by the defeat of the Democratic Party in the 1864 election, the rising power of Radical Republicans in Congress, an engendered spirit of nationalism, Robert E. Lee's surrender, and the apotheosis of Lincoln after his death at the hands of a pro-Southern assassin.

Klement believed that scholars who endorsed consensus history were doing an injustice to Abraham Lincoln by castigating his opponents "as chumps or clodhoppers" because it deprived the martyred Civil War president of credit and honor which was rightfully his.

The sea captain who reaches a distant port when aided by favorable winds and friendly seas accomplishes a routine chore. But the capable and courageous skipper, who exhibits qualities of leadership and greatness as he guides a frail craft o'er stormy seas and treacherous shoals, deserves the plaudits of posterity. A president who achieves his objectives when fools and cowards comprise the opposition merits no medals, but the president who overcomes and outwits an able and energetic opposition deserves both credit and honor....Lincoln achieved his goal in spite of an enterprising opposition—he guided the ship of state over a hazardous and uncharted course, and the mighty waves blown up by the winds of opposition but proved the captain an exceptional sailor. The waves of criticism and the winds of adversity tested the man, proved his greatness, and added another jewel to his crown of achievement.[65]

When Frank addressed a joint session of the Mississippi Valley Historical Association and the Economic History Association in 1950, he told those assembled that it was time Lincoln's critics had their day in court:

Nationalism as a force and apotheosis as a process have tempted writers to laud Abraham Lincoln and to denounce his enemies. Lincoln cultists and nationalist historians have wielded a weighty whip when chastising Copperheads....Investigators of the Copperhead theme have busied themselves in unearthing Copperhead quotations from newspapers, letters, and speeches and hanging them upon the line of treason. They have denounced these administration critics as traitors pure and simple—in effect, as men whose hearts were black, whose blood was yellow, and whose minds were warped.[66]

Within a year Klement was once more pointing out how "the barometer of popular opinion gauges Civil War Copperheadism as cloudy, foul, and pro-Southern. Historians have encouraged such a rating by reciting and exploiting the views of the fanatical fringe, by apotheosizing the Civil War heroes, and by ignoring the forces which underwrote discontent."[67] Examining the activities of prominent anti-Lincoln men such as Clement L. Vallandigham, Sam Medary, and S.S. Cox of Ohio, O.B. Ficklin and Samuel Buckmaster from Illinois, Daniel Voorhees and Thomas J. Hendricks of Indiana, William E. Morrison and Abner Pratt of Michigan, and Marcus M. "Brick" Pomeroy, Edward G. Ryan, George B. Smith, and Frederick W. Horn of Wisconsin, persuaded him that the fire-tongue language of the Copperheads were hardly "bolts out of the blue." Rather, they were the natural expressions of men who promoted western sectionalism by protesting against the deteriorating influence of agriculture, the increasing nationalization of business, centralization of the federal government, and the escalating efficaciousness of Puritan culture, character, and industrialism.[68]

Klement became the leading authority on Northern dissenters in 1960 with the publication of *The Copperheads in the Middle West*—an expansion of his graduate work—which drove a wedge into what had been for almost a hundred years a predominantly nationalistic interpretation of Lincoln's ardent Northern chastisers. Reviewers for the most part criticized his assessment that Copperheadism was not a seditious, pro-Southern movement, but was an organized effort on the part of ardent conservative Northern Democrats who opposed the draft, feared black equality, and hated Lincoln's deliberate infringement on civil liberties. Although its sectional, economic, social, religious, and political roots were deeply planted and its aspects often difficult to refine, Klement acknowledged that ardent Copperheads were out of step with the social and political realities of the day, but gave them credit for their dauntlessness, saying that "midwestern Copperheads, like supporters of the Lincoln administration, were human beings—motivated by the same wants and emotions that have been possessed by people throughout the ages...."[69]

Wayne C. Temple, however, was quick to judge that Klement had written "the definitive treatment of the Copperhead story. For the first time, a picture of the actual operations of the Copperheads is presented." The book was highly recommended "for the reader who finds the truth more satisfying, even if less strange, than fiction," said former classmate Richard N. Current. United States Supreme Court historian Emma Lou Thornbrough was the first person to identify the real significance of Klement's research in a review for *The Historian*: his "more critical and intensive use of the sources has resulted in an interpretation which is distinctly 'revisionist.'" The appellation would accurately characterize all of his labors on the subject for the next thirty-four years.[70]

The notoriety which was now Klement's brought him into contact with many researchers who sought information about the king of Copperheads, Clement L. Vallandigham. He had often wondered why this famous dissenter's life had not been studied in greater detail, but felt constrained from handling the subject because Charles H. Coleman, Professor of History at Eastern Illinois Teachers College, had been writing and speaking on the subject since the 1930s and announced to fellow historians in 1955 that he would be putting together a full-scale life of the Ohio politician. Coleman's shallow diggings permitted him to accumulate a case full of primary source material at his house and locate a few obscure letters which Vallandigham had written. Once the well-known episodes of Vallandigham's life took center stage in Coleman's lectures, Klement always dutifully referred inquiries about the Copperhead to him because "in this profession we honor each other's pre-emptions." However, when he was informed that Coleman was in declining health and could never finish his investigations, he wrote to him and received his blessing to continue the work.[71]

Klement soon realized that piecing together Vallandigham's biography would be an exhausting and lengthy process. It certainly had not escaped his notice that the only other book which described Vallandigham's career had been written by a sympathetic and devoted brother, who pictured him as a heroic figure, a man of high intelligence and signal courage, devoted to principle, who had been wrongfully depicted by fanatics and bigots. Klement approached the topic characteristically with the conviction that "nationalist historians of the post Civil war era have judged him harshly."[72]

The historical road which Klement now traveled was rutty, for he soon discovered a paucity of readily available primary source material. A 1913 flood in Dayton, Ohio where Vallandigham lived during most of his career, destroyed many valuable documents and those that remained were withheld, neglected or dispersed by sensitive descendants, so that there was not a single large collection of Vallandigham material at any depository. Most of his correspondence, as Klement soon learned, lay in dusty files in museums and libraries throughout the United States and Canada, which required long absences from his family and teaching duties. "It has been a tiring, long, slow research project," he told the Chicago Civil War Round Table four years before he finished the study, "and I can understand why some would turn away from it when they once expressed an interest in it."[73]

Klement superbly wove the details of Vallandigham's life into a striking story which enthralled readers when *The Limits of Dissent: Clement L. Vallandigham and the Civil War* was published in 1970. What emerged was the portrait not of a radical plotting to overthrow the federal government or a traitor to the North who supported the South, but rather a man attempting to preserve the pre-war federal system with slavery intact. It was the first scholarly appraisal of the famous Union critic, and most reviewers lavished it with praise because, as one noted, his research was based on primary sources and he used every scrap of available material to tell the interesting story. Klement "displays the careful research and meticulous attention to detail that marks all of his work; it is unlikely that a more thorough study of Vallandigham's Civil War activities could be written, noted a reviewer in the *The American Historical Review*. Wayne C. Temple was so impressed with the way Klement was able to put together such a splendid biography from fragmentary documentary evidence and a thorough examination of period newspapers that he exclaimed, "This book should win an award."[74]

Although many scholars were slow to accept Klement's revisionist views, he was no historical slouch and was always prepared to put on the gloves and battle those critics who questioned his findings. Such was the case in 1983 when he disputed with Mark E. Neely, Jr. over statements Neely made about his research concerning an 1862 arbitrary arrest case in Illinois. In the March issue of *Lincoln Lore*, Neely criticized Klement's apparently superficial examination of a collection of papers which contained valuable information about the case, and concluded that Klement's views must have been based on opinions expressed in a secondary source rather than on the documents themselves.[75] Angered by such an accusation, Klement wrote Neely a letter, parts of which were reproduced in the newsletter seven issues later. "He promised to print my letter in a forthcoming issue of *Lincoln Lore*. He printed about a third—the parts where I needled him he omitted," Klement wrote later. He refuted Neely's assertions point by point so successfully that The Lincoln Museum director telephoned him to apologize and was forced to concede at the conclusion of Klement's argument that the Marquette professor had indeed been the one responsible for getting the collection in question opened to scholars in the first place, and was the very first researcher to use them. "His was the pioneering archival research on the question of arbitrary arrests, and his interest...continues," he confessed. "Even now, he is at work on another book on the subject of secret societies...."[76]

The following year, *Dark Lanterns: Secret Political Societies, Conspiracies, and Treason Trials in the Civil War* was published by Louisiana State University Press. The story about subversive groups and conspiracy trials needed to be told, said Klement, because revisionist historians, like himself, had gained for the Copperheads a certain measure of rehabilitation which now showed that they were conservatives or misguided partisans rather than traitorous scoundrels who had enormous power in the North. The only area that Klement still believed needed re-examination was the accounts dealing with secret political societies and the Indianapolis and Camp Douglas conspiracies which "remain as they were a hundred years ago. The dark lantern societies, like the Knights of the Golden Circle, Order of American Knights, and Sons of Liberty are still misrepresented by Civil War historians, for myths and legends make it difficult to separate fancy from fact." Eight years earlier he had said: "A mythical cat had nine lives. Some Civil War myths have had ten." Now he again warned his readers to beware of the opinions that flowed from the pens of writers who promoted consensus history, who he believed present "majority views as the true views" and color the roles of dissenters in black or gray "because nationalism shapes the minds of men and guides the hands of the historians." "Nationalism," he stressed, "it seems, blesses the marriage of myth and history." *Dark Lanterns* made an extremely strong and convincing case that most of the surreptitious Copperhead groups were in fact poorly organized, paper-based organizations with small memberships, exaggerated influence, rather vague goals, and little ability to carry them out.[77]

Now in his eighties, and entering his eighteenth year of retirement, Klement's literary output continued uninterrupted, although the failure in 1986 of publishing firms to take an interest in his 835-page manuscript, "The Most Critical Year: Events of 1863," seems to have discouraged him from devoting any more time to book-length projects. Instead, he turned his attention solely to writing articles, most of which discussed Ohio politics, Copperheadism, and the Gettysburg Address.[78]

In the 1960s, the story behind Lincoln's most famous public utterance had been a fascination for Klement, but grew into somewhat of a pre-occupation while he was combing Ohio Governor David Tod's papers at the Ohio State Historical Society during the preparation of the Vallandigham biography. That collection shed light on Ohio's role in the dedication ceremony for the Gettysburg cemetery, and Klement took time away from his Vallandigham research to write a lengthy monograph about the subject for *Ohio History*. It marked the beginning of an interest in the Gettysburg event which resulted in nine more articles over the next twenty-three years, but he was quick to tell people that the essays were always secondary to his work on Copperheadism.[79]

In recognition of the speech's 130th anniversary, Klement collected all but one of his Gettysburg articles and wrote several controversial new ones, all of which were published as *The Gettysburg Soldiers' Cemetery and Lincoln's Address: Aspects and Angles* in November 1993. Reviewers praised this book, too, which was a significant contribution to Gettysburg literature primarily due to Klement being the first historian to go on record as whole-heartedly accepting artist Lloyd Ostendorf's claim that he had discovered a fragment of a sixth copy of the immortal speech written in Lincoln's own hand. Although the book was "prodigiously researched and brilliantly presented," many readers were still skeptical of Klement's reasoning in the Ostendorf matter.[80] To one who questioned his judgement, he wrote:

> I regard it as legitimate (the real McCoy), and I think with good reasons....I know that I climbed out on a limb in stating...that "the document" in Ostendorf's hands "is indeed the second page of the third draft of Lincoln's Gettysburg Address." It is possible that the branch may be sawed off and I will have an embarrassing fall. Or, put another way, I may have egg on my face. When I wrote my endorsement I believed it to be the real thing....And I still believe that.[81]

Almost the entire first printing of 1,500 copies sold in pre-publication sales, and *The Gettysburg Soldiers' Cemetery and Lincoln's Address* became Klement's best-selling book. Encouraged by the book's popularity, he decided to employ the same style for a fourth book about Lincoln's critics which he intended to be, "in essence, the Copperhead Bible." The volume that follows is the result of that vision, and the essays herein reflect the standard ideas which Klement preached about underground Civil War insurgency. He finished the book, along with a complete revision and expansion of his history of Wisconsin in the Civil War, for the State Historical Society of Wisconsin by the following March, just three months before he was diagnosed with cancer. Both manuscripts were in the hands of editors

when he passed away on July 29, 1994. Four of the chapters in this book—
"Copperheads in the Upper Midwest during the Civil War: Traitors, Politicians, or Dissenters," "Controversy Regarding the Copperheads,"
"Nationalism and the Writing of Civil War History: An Essay in Historiography," and "In Retrospect and More"—contain fresh insights and represent
Klement's final thoughts on a subject which fascinated him for over four
decades. The twelve articles are divided into four themes, which Klement
introduces in penetrating prefaces at the beginning of each section.

On April 18, 1989, Klement wrote to a friend: "Historians do not believe that success is due to chance and circumstance, but to good planning, hard work, and perseverance."[82] Although his thought-provoking
deliberations about Lincoln's Northern critics, which resulted in a landslide
of further revisionist work on the subject of Copperheadism, seem to validate his point, he was also the first to admit humbly in conversations and in
letters that the direction his life took was anything but the result of expert
foresight, and often spoke of his graduate days at Madison when so many
chance events and the kindness of so many individuals helped to shape
the course of his career.

While Frank Klement remains the undisputed champion of the Copperheads, he had not always received accolades from his academic peers,
even from fellow historians who admired his tenacity and indefatigable research. Thirty-six years after the appearance of *Copperheads in the Middle
West*, scholars continue to grapple with his conclusions about civil liberty
and wartime dissension in the North. Students of the conflict praise Klement
for supplying indisputable evidence that the Republicans misled the Northern people by convincing them that the Copperhead movement was not
shrewdly organized and centrally directed. However, many historians today question whether he took his revisionist deliberations to an opposite
and often inaccurate extreme; that he somehow overlooked or purpose-
fully ignored overt acts which anti-Lincoln men took to undermine the federal government during the war. In an essay published only seven years
after the appearance of *The Copperheads in the Middle West*, Richard O.
Curry identified Klement as one of seven prominent Civil War historians
who analyzed midwestern Democratic opposition to Lincoln's war policies
"in Unionist, if not entirely sympathetic terms."[83] Lincoln assassination authority William Hanchett has argued that, although calls for Lincoln's murder by many Copperheads did not meet the Constitutional criteria for treason,
"many other Copperhead activities, about which Klement had little to say,
did." Pointing to the fact that Copperhead organizations often disrupted the
draft, incited desertion in the army, established spying and smuggling con-
tacts with Confederate agents, and had a hand in sabotage, Hanchett believes Klement's inexorable position that many Civil War dissenters were
relatively harmless is far too mild and misleading. "Such treasonable actions took place all over the North....If they were the spontaneous acts of

outraged citizens rather than the planned operations of secret societies, the danger they represented to the nation was all the greater."[84] James McPherson agrees with Hanchett, having said in 1988 that Klement "sometimes protests too much in his attempt to exonerate the Copperheads from all such calumnies."[85] David E. Long, who has studied the election of 1864, worries that "many contemporary historians seem willing to accept the work of Klement implicitly" and may be misguided by his view that clandestine secret societies and conspiracies were merely fairy tales and figments of Republican imagination. Long asserts that there was "a sizeable and dangerous opposition to the war," a point which other scholars readily accept as well.[86] "There was a 'fire in the rear' of the Union war effort," Hanchett also insists, "and it was no myth."[87]

How would Klement answer such charges if he were alive today? Never one to shy away from a good historical debate, he was always prepared to defend his belief that the Copperhead threat was little more than a large Republican smear campaign, a smoke screen behind which in reality only a few weak and disorganized groups of dissenters actually maneuvered. Klement's inflexible stance should not surprise Civil War historians, for he performed his earliest Copperhead research in the 1940s and 1950s—just after World War II and at the beginning of the Cold War. Threats to the nation were still a fresh memory and politicians like Wisconsin Senator Joe McCarthy were finding Communists under every rock during televised investigations for all Americans to see. The chilling, almost paranoid, national political climate, when coupled with Hesseltine's charge that historians doubt the credibility of each witness and document, unquestionably fostered skepticism in Klement as he scoured Republican propaganda, period newspapers, Civil War reminiscences, and popular Civil War histories. He told an interviewer in 1964: "You can't separate a historian's philosophy of life or the era in which he lives from his scholarship. That is why each generation reinterprets for itself."[88] Twenty years later he alluded to himself in the third person when he wrote that "revisionists have challenged the contentions of earlier historians who believed the Civil War to be ordained, inevitable, and irrepressible. They have been challenged in turn by those who would revise the revisionists."[89]

When Dr. James Marten first met Klement at Marquette, the aging professor grimaced slightly when he learned that Robert H. Abzug, who criticized Klement's Copperhead beliefs in his very first published essay, was Marten's dissertation advisor. "His reaction to Abzug's article was very representative of his character: professional, scholarly, and confident—but also generous, kind, and forgiving," Marten said later.[90]

To the end, Klement maintained that his field of scholarship was not one which received much glory because the academic world clung too tightly to the work of scholars who chose to amplify the Lincoln Legend. "Nationalist historians really praise that which has happened and glorify that which has happened," he said in a reflective mood in 1988. "When you deal with Lincoln's critics and the Copperheads and the Democratic politicians, you're going down a road that is not appreciated by nationalist historians."[91]

Many historians, however, have not been reticent in saluting his success at brushing aside the myriad of false information and impressions which have influenced generations of scholars as they endeavored to understand some of America's earliest malcontents. Mark E. Neely, Jr. summarized Klement's legacy best when he wrote that the "works of Frank L. Klement in the 1950s, 1960s, and 1970s would demolish the myth of a large, secret, well-organized disloyal Northern opposition to the Lincoln administration."[92] It is a remarkable legacy indeed.

Steven K. Rogstad
Racine, Wisconsin
February 12, 1998

PART ONE

A Case for Lincoln's Critics

Civil War dissent is an intriguing subject with many angles and aspects. Court decisions have been somewhat ambivalent, so the topic rests in a kind of no-man's land, making it subject to varying interpretations. Nationalist historians have taken one approach, usually defending the party in power—this is especially true regarding President Abraham Lincoln and his policies, for they gloss over the many violations of civil rights. On the other hand, the so-called "revisionists" find Judge David Davis's indictment of the Lincoln administration in *Ex Parte Milligan* (1866) a justification for their views.

The first chapter, "Copperheads in the Upper Midwest: Traitors, Politicians, or Dissenters?" summarizes my many contentions regarding the so-called "Copperheads." It attempts to answer six questions: 1. What were the traditional views regarding the so-called "Copperheads" as expressed in Wood Gray's *The Hidden Civil War: The Story of the Copperheads* and George Fort Milton's *Abraham Lincoln and the Fifth Column* (both books published in 1942)? 2. Exactly who were the dissenters in Civil War days; that is, what socioeconomic elements of the Midwestern populace cast Democratic ballots and subscribed to Democratic newspapers? 3. Why was there widespread dissatisfaction with the Lincoln administration and was criticism valid and legitimate? 4. Why did Democratic dissent, so vibrant and widespread at times, become a losing cause? 5. What are the six basic contentions of those who challenge the suppositions of Gray, Milton, and others? 6. Should Lincoln's Democratic critics be labeled "traitors," "Copperheads," "politicians," or "dissenters"?

The second chapter surveys the violations of civil rights that took place during Lincoln's presidency. In his Pulitzer Prize-winning book, *The Fate of Liberty: Abraham Lincoln and Civil Liberties* (1991), Mark E. Neely did an excellent job with the subjects of habeas corpus and arrests of civilians. Book-length studies of related subjects like "The Military Trial of Civilians in the Civil War" and "Restrictions of Freedom of the Press during the Civil War" are needed. This last topic should include the many mobbings of Democratic newspapers and their exclusion from military districts and departments.

The two chapters comprising "Part One" set the base for a variety of questions. How legitimate was Civil War dissent? What is the responsibility of the opposition party—even in a war—when civil rights are widely violated? Should both the Republicans and Democrats have shelved partyism during the Civil War? Did Clement L. Vallandigham err when he criticized Gen. Ambrose E. Burnside's "General Orders, No. 38" and Gen. Milo Hascall's "Order No. 9"? If Burnside was wrong, was Vallandigham right? Soldiers broke down the door to Vallandigham's house in order to arrest him. Did the English axiom "a man's house is his castle" apply to Vallandigham? Ironically, Vallandigham could recite a selection from William Pitt's speech in the House of Commons:

> The poorest man may, in his cottage, bid defiance to all the forces of the Crown. It may be frail—its roof may shake—the wind may blow through it—the storm may enter—the rain may enter—but the King of England cannot enter. All His force dares not cross the threshold.

And finally, should all historians view Lincoln's Democratic critics as "the loyal opposition"?

Copperheads in the Upper Midwest during the Civil War: Traitors, Politicians, or Dissenters?

Those who like wine or books about the so-called "Copperheads" could say that 1942 was "a very good year." Two books that helped to fasten the traditional interpretation of Copperheads and Copperheadism upon Civil War historiography were published in 1942—the second year of U.S. involvement in World War II. Both books were praised by Allan Nevins in his presidential address to members of the American Historical Association; wittingly, he put his seal of approval upon the traditional interpretation of Civil War dissent.[1]

The traditional interpretation espoused by those two notable books—highly praised by most reviewers—included four major suppositions: (1) that the so-called "Copperheads" were Northerners "who sympathized with the South during the Civil War"—the definition given in the latest *American Heritage Dictionary*,[2] (2) that the so-called "Copperheads," in great numbers, joined such subversive secret societies as the Knights of the Golden Circle, the Order of American Knights, and the Sons of Liberty, (3) that the so-called "Copperheads" were involved in two gigantic conspiracies in the Upper Midwest, and (4) that the so-called "Copperheads" had no reason to criticize the Lincoln administration and the honorable war—this means that the traditional interpretation ignored most of the socioeconomic, constitutional, and political aspects associated with Civil War dissent in the Upper Midwest.

One of the two books published in 1942 bore the title *The Hidden Civil War: The Story of the Copperheads*. Its author was Wood Gray, then

3

a member of the History faculty of George Washington University. It evolved out of his doctoral dissertation, directed by Avery Craven, at the University of Chicago. This dissertation gathered dust for ten years, until World War II rekindled an interest in dissent, subversion, and treason—Gray's dissertation dealt with all three. Professor Gray, a meticulous historian, had collected hundreds and hundreds of quotations of the Copperheads and their Republican critics and hung them all on the line of treason. The phrase "it was reported that" preceded many of the contentions culled from Radical Republican newspapers and election time tracts and pamphlets. Gray endorsed each of the four suppositions that were ingrained in the traditional interpretation of the so-called "Copperheads." He endorsed the supposition that the so-called "Copperheads" sympathized with the South. He accepted Gen. Ambrose E. Burnside's contention that Clement L. Vallandigham, President Lincoln's foremost Democratic critic in the Upper Midwest, was "a traitor."[3] And he characterized the so-called "Copperheads" as persons who "must be guarded against in time of crisis among a free people."[4]

Gray also saw members of secret subversive societies behind every tree, writing "membership in the secret societies was numerous, widespread, and ready for concerted action if the opportunity should arise,"[5] and he recited the canard that the Sons of Liberty had 80,000 members in 1864 in Ohio. Gray also swallowed whole Republican-sponsored propaganda about conspiracies centered in Indianapolis and Chicago. One tall tale, recited by Gray, contended that Copperhead "generals" had promised to have "50,000 followers present" to instigate a Chicago-based uprising with Clement L. Vallandigham giving the signal to revolt.[6] Gray seemed to believe that Democratic dissenters had no reason to criticize the Lincoln administration and the honorable war as there was no analysis of them, for, from start to finish, the so-called "Copperheads" were "the bad guys"—"a type that is dangerous in a democracy."[7]

The second book published in 1942 bore the intriguing title *Abraham Lincoln and the Fifth Column*. Its author was George Fort Milton, a newspaperman turned historian. His three previous books dealing with the Civil War era had won high praise, so he had the credentials to write another Civil War book. But *Abraham Lincoln and the Fifth Column* was a poorly researched and hurriedly written potboiler, intended to take advantage of the war psychosis of the day. Milton accepted much Republican party Civil War-time political propaganda as historical fact. He blamed the Knights of the Golden Circle and the Order of American Knights for draft disturbances, widespread discontent, and wartime conspiracies.[8] He made much of both the Order of American Knights and the Sons of Liberty, involving both in conspiracies. His chapters dealing with the Indianapolis and Chicago conspiracies read like detective thrillers. He repeated the old myth that one of these societies had the password "Nu-Oh-Lac"—Calhoun spelled backwards.[9]

Milton praised Lincoln profusely with terms like "master politician," "states-man," "Commander in Chief extraordinary," "poet and prophet," and "ge-nius"—one who was true to the duties.[10] On the other hand, Milton viewed Lincoln's Democratic critics as "the disloyal opposition," "Southern sympa-thizers," and men who possessed black hearts and wore black hats. Vallandigham, Lincoln's best known Democratic critic in the Upper Mid-west, drew only Milton's scorn; he was called "almost a fanatic," an active conspirator "who preferred [Union] defeat to victory," "guilty of treason," and "the actual leader of a conspiracy to revolt."[11] In the end, Milton con-cluded, truth won out over treason, Lincoln was re-elected for another four years, and scored "a complete victory over the secessionists' fifth column in the Loyal States."[12]

Henry Steele Commager, one of the country's most respected histo-rians, heartily endorsed Milton's *Abraham Lincoln and the Fifth Column*, calling it "a stirring, and on the whole, a heartening story" of how the Civil War president "outmaneuvered and confounded the appeasers, the de-featists, and the fifth columnists of the Civil War era."[13] Even President Franklin D. Roosevelt, who had given Milton a desk job in Washington, gave the book a plug by calling his own critics "Copperheads" and equat-ing them with Lincoln's Democratic critics; Roosevelt also arranged to be photographed holding Milton's book before boarding a plane for one of his conferences with Joseph Stalin and Winston Churchill.

The supposition that Civil War Copperheads were pro-Southern, that they joined subversive societies, and that they engaged in gigantic con-spiracies, appeared in other books, in scores of articles, in college and high school textbooks, in encyclopedias and dictionaries, and in historical novels during the 1940s, 1950s, and 1960s.[14]

Revisionism, gaining a foothold here and there, began to challenge Gray's and Milton's four suppositions during the 1950s. Revisionists asked a variety of questions. Just who were the Copperheads? Who voted for Clem-ent L. Vallandigham in Ohio, Daniel W. Voorhees in Indiana, and James J. Allen in Illinois? Who subscribed to the so-called "Copperhead newspapers" like the *Cincinnati Enquirer*, the *Chicago Times*, or the *Dubuque Herald*? What kind of persons belonged to local Democratic clubs? Why did Demo-cratic leaders criticize Lincoln's policies and were any criticisms valid? Was there a socioeconomic basis to Democratic dissent in the Upper Midwest?

Through grass-roots research, and the discrediting of Radical Re-publican political propaganda, nonentities became real people with real concerns. These Democratic voters and Democratic subscribers of the so-called "Copperhead newspapers" generally belonged to one of four socio-economic groups: (1) Irish-Americans, (2) German-American Catholics, (3) "Butternuts," a term applied to upland Southerners who had crossed the Ohio River and preempted the poorer lands in the Upper Midwest, and (4) middle-class Americans who identified themselves with Jacksonian Democracy.

Irish-American newspaper editors included such self-proclaimed "Copperheads" as James J. Faran of the *Cincinnati Enquirer*, Daniel Flanagan of the *Mason (Ohio) Democrat*, Thomas Coughlin of the *Bucyrus Forum*, and Dennis A. Mahony of the *Dubuque Herald*. Then there were fellows like David Sheean of Galena (Illinois), Andrew D. Duff of Benton (Illinois), David McCarty of Madison County, Iowa, and Lambdin P. Milligan—all were among those arrested and accused of belonging to subversive societies.

Why were these Irish-Americans Democrats rather than Republicans in 1860? There are a number of reasons. In the first place, Irish-Americans were attracted by the "all men are created equal" concept associated with Jeffersonian Democracy and the "common man" phrase linked to Jacksonian Democracy. John O'Sullivan, editor of the *Democratic Review* in an earlier era, helped to steer fellow Hibernians into the party of James K. Polk and Stephen A. Douglas, and events of the 1840s and 1850s cemented the relationship. Furthermore, the new Republican party seemed to be tainted with three *isms*: prohibitionism, abolitionism, and Know-Nothingism. Most Irish-Americans detested all three. They liked whiskey, an integral part of their culture, feared that emancipation would release a flood of cheap labor to the Upper Midwest, and cursed Know-Nothingism, "the American neurosis" of the 1840–1860 era which seemed to threaten their Catholicism.[15] The election of William Pennington, a Know-Nothinger from New Jersey, as Speaker of the House of Representatives in early 1860, fused the Know-Nothing movement with the Republican party. Nor did Irish-Americans forget earlier events: Maria Monk's *Awful Disclosures* (a pack of lies that went through twenty printings), the burning of the Ursuline Convent near Boston, and the posters "No Irish Need Apply." Perhaps ninety-eight percent of the Irish-Americans voted the Democratic ticket in 1860 and distrusted President Lincoln.

Snotty Republicans viewed the Irish-Americans with contempt and disdain. The Freeport *Journal*, edited in Illinois by a rabid Republican, spoke scornfully of the "Irish 'cattle' who disgrace our soil."[16] The editor of the *Chicago Tribune* characterized the Irish as "blear-eyed sots" and "the voting tool of corrupt Democratic leaders."[17] The editor of the *Cincinnati Commercial* called the Irish "stuffed apes."[18] An editorial in the *Detroit Advertiser and Tribune* called Irish-Americans "locusts."[19] And the editor of the Chicago-based *Western Railroad Gazette*, after Democrats swept the spring elections of 1863, described the sons of Erin as "knaves," "voting cattle," and "filthy, stinking, God-forsaken wretches" in a lengthy tirade.[20]

German-American Catholics shared the same scorn that some Republican editors heaped upon Irish-Americans. The three New England *isms* were anathema to German-American Catholics as they were to Irish-Americans. German-Americans wanted their schnapps and lager beer, not prohibitionism. Know-Nothingism, fused with the Republican party, seemed to threaten their Catholic religion. And emancipation, the stepchild of abolitionism, seemed to threaten their livelihood if newly freed blacks came northward to seek jobs. "The jealousy of the low Germans and Irish against the free negro," an English journalist who was visiting the Upper Midwest wrote, "was sufficient to set them against the war which would have brought four million black rivals in competition for the hard and dirty work which American freedom bestowed on them."[21]

"Butternuts," a term applied to upland Southerners who had migrated northward to settle in the Upper Midwest, formed the third socioeconomic group that found a home within the Democratic party. "Butternuts" gained that name because they colored their jeans and linseys with a dye made by boiling the bark of butternut trees in water—the result was a color best described as "dirty dark yellow." These folks were the heirs of the "Barefoot Democracy" of Andrew Jackson's day. Scions of New England who became the leaders in the Upper Midwest scorned the so-called "Butternuts who lived in areas where the farms were smaller, the soil poorer, and where illiteracy was more widespread."[22] That contempt was evident in the entry which an observer, living in Cincinnati, made in his journal after watching a Democratic parade in "Butternut country":

> I went out and saw the Copperhead demonstration today. It was large. There were a number of women in the procession on horseback. Many of their riding skirts were so old, ragged & dirty, they might have belonged to their grandmothers. It was the unterrified, unwashed democracy.[23]

These Democrats carried hickory branches, honoring Andy Jackson, in parades, wore butternut emblems, and returned New Englanders' scorn with their own.

These ex-Southerners brought their stills with them when they crossed the Ohio River, settled on land they transformed into farms, and manufactured "corn liker" for themselves and their friends—prohibitionists, whom they associated with New England, received naught but curses and contempt. They also brought their anti-black prejudices with them and helped to give a base to the latent racism existent in the Upper Midwest. Their spokesmen included such fellows as John W. Kees of the *Circleville (Ohio) Watchman* and Dr. Edson B. Olds of the *(Lancaster) Ohio Eagle*. Neither had any sympathy for prohibitionists and abolitionists. Kees called abolitionists "damned disunionists"; he wanted them hung "till the flesh would rot off their bones and the winds of Heaven whistle Yanky doodle through their loathsum skelitonz."[24] Dr. Olds may have had the same anti-abolition feeling but he expressed his sentiments more moderately as he wore a butternut as a badge with considerable pride.[25]

These ex-Southerners occupied the lowest tier of counties in Iowa, the lower halves of Illinois and Indiana, and scattered counties in Ohio.[26] Local residents in Michigan and Wisconsin referred to these ex-Southerners in their states as "Kentuks." Most of them were rural residents and most of them were Baptists who attended revivals and camp meetings.

The fourth element within the Democracy of the Upper Midwest consisted of middle class Americans who considered themselves disciples of Jacksonian Democracy and apostles of Jeffersonian Democracy. Most espoused states' rights principles, many considered themselves to be Western sectionalists, and all thought that Northern abolitionists and Southern "fire-eaters" were "disunionists"—a threat to national unity and the balance of power enjoyed by the Upper Midwest in the antebellum years. Most considered themselves conservatives—patrons of Edmund Burke. Clement L. Vallandigham fit that mold, and so did congressmen like Samuel S. Cox of Ohio, Thomas A. Hendricks of Indiana, and James W. Singleton of Illinois as well as newspapermen like Samuel Medary of *The (Columbus) Crisis*, Henry N. Walker of the *Detroit Free Press*, and Wilbur F. Storey of the *Chicago Times*. Then add the names of such curmudgeons as Henry Clay Dean of Iowa and Marcus Mills Pomeroy of Wisconsin—the latter editor of the *LaCrosse Democrat*. This fourth class provided most of the spokesmen for the Democracy of the Upper Midwest but they knew full well who their constituents were.

Why did members of these four socioeconomic groups become dissenters, i.e., critics of the Lincoln administration and the war? There seem to be seven partial answers to that question. In the first place, Democratic partyism, tainted with emotion and partiality—especially during election campaigns—brought forth criticism of the Lincoln administration. In a two-party system, the "outs" invariably criticize the "ins" and seek votes wherever they can be found. Democrats believed that, as members of the opposition, they had the responsibility of keeping the Lincoln administration in tune with the wishes and wants of the people—as they understood them. The opposition party also had the responsibility of being the guardian of civil liberties and protesting vigorously when constitutional guarantees were ignored or violated—and there were many violations. Democratic partisanship, whether right or wrong, played a major role in subsidizing dissent and setting a solid base for it.

In the second place, there were economic aspects to Democratic dissent in the Upper Midwest, especially in the first half of the war. The patriotic surge that swept the North after the firing on Fort Sumter ebbed as time tempered the emotions and as an economic depression visited the Upper Midwest. The closing of the Mississippi River and the loss of Southern markets created economic havoc: the river trade collapsed, factory owners suffered, farm prices plummeted, and many banks whose paper money was based upon Southern bonds closed their doors—examples are that half of Wisconsin's banks failed and only seventeen out of 112 Illinois banks survived the bank panic of 1861.[27] Many midwesterners transformed their economic complaints into political dissent. Even some Republicans damned the Lincoln administration. In December of 1861, a Democratic observer in Cincinnati wrote:

Matters look blue enough here; business men have long faces and short money receipts. One Jim Brown & Co. say they have lost $40,000 since the election by depreciation in stock. There are three of them and they each voted for Lincoln, "God & Liberty," and say now they "wish Lincoln and all political parties were in hell."[28]

In midyear, 1862, Gen. John A. McClernand toured the Upper Midwest as President Lincoln's special envoy to assay the widespread disaffection and dissent. In his report to Lincoln, McClernand attributed the disaffection to economic factors and recommended a military campaign that would reopen the Mississippi River as a trade route and regain New Orleans as an export base for Midwestern farm produce.[29] Economic discontent, in part, explains why the Upper Midwest "repudiated" the Lincoln administration in the fall elections of 1862.[30]

A third cause of dissent in the Upper Midwest centered around "western sectionalism" and was expressed in complaints against New England and the Northeast. Economics underwrote some of the resentment. The closing of the Mississippi put the farmers of the Upper Midwest at the mercy of the eastern owners of the east-west railroads and Great Lakes' cargo vessels—both tripled their freight rates in 1861–1862, literally "skinning the West alive."[31] The postwar Granger movement, an expression of western sectionalism, had its roots in the Democratic-controlled Illinois state constitutional convention of 1862 and the state's Copperhead-controlled legislatures of 1863.[32] Furthermore, high tariff duties enacted by Congress in 1861 and 1862 seemed an insult to some midwesterners. Speaking for western farmers, congressman Vallandigham said he could not see the justice in exchanging four bushels of corn for one pound of coffee.[33] An Indiana merchant, railing against the Morrill Tariff Bill, said that if it became a law it would make him "disloyal."[34] Frederic W. Horn, a respected Democratic leader in Wisconsin, resigned his captaincy in the state militia rather than fight in a war that might "subjugate" his section of the country to "Pennsylvania's Iron mongers and New England manufacturers."[35] Lambdin P. Milligan, an Indiana Democrat who gained notoriety as a critic of the Lincoln administration, was an out-and-out free trader and western sectionalist, and so were Samuel S. Cox and Clement L. Vallandigham. Cox repeatedly expressed his contempt for Puritan culture, the Puritan character, and New England industrialism; Vallandigham, who once called himself an avowed western sectionalist, stated bluntly that he was "inexorably hostile to Puritan domination in religion or morals or literature or politics."[36] Democratic congressman James A. Craven of Indiana thought that more than words were necessary to prevent the Upper Midwest from becoming "slave and servant" of New England and—teaching those selfish states a lesson—"cut loose from the New England states."[37] Obviously, western sectionalism played a role in promoting dissent in the Upper Midwest during the Civil War.

A fourth aspect of midwestern dissent and discontent revolves around the word "emancipation." No other issue so aroused Democratic wrath, and it energized the latent racism existent in "Butternut," Irish-American, and German-American Catholic communities. From the beginning some Democrats called their political opponents "Black Republicans" and feared that President Lincoln would bow to abolition pressure.[38] They were prophets when the 37th Congress, in its second session (December 2, 1861, to July 17, 1862), passed half a dozen "abolition measures"—like freeing the slaves in the District of Columbia and the territories, recognizing Haiti, allowing blacks to serve as stage coach drivers, and permitting blacks to testify in the courts of the District of Columbia. "If this is a war...of Abolition," the Democratic editor of the *Oshkosh (Wis.) Courier* stated in an editorial, "then the sooner the Union goes to the devil the better."[39] No one put his racial prejudices on the line more strongly and viciously than Nelson Abbott, the "Butternut" editor of the *Macomb (Ill.) Eagle*. Complaining about the actions of the 37th Congress, editor Abbott wrote:

> Congress has the negro-phobia. It is nigger in the Senate and nigger in the House. It is nigger in the forenoon and nigger in the afternoon. It is nigger in motions and nigger in speeches. It was nigger the first day and it has been nigger everyday. Nigger is in every man's eye, and nigger in every man's mouth. It's nigger in the lobby and the proceedings are black with nigger...The nigger vapor is a moral pestilence that blunts the sense of duty to the constitution and destroys the instinct of obedience to the law.[40]

Democrats who feared that emancipation might threaten the jobs of white workers found evidence to support these fears here and there. In May and June of 1862, the Republican proprietor of the Burnet House, a Cincinnati hotel considered the finest in the West, dismissed fifty Irish workers (chambermaids, porters, cooks, and others) and replaced them with "contrabands," a term applied to ex-slaves—*at lower wages*. Boat owners and dock owners, especially in Cincinnati and Toledo, replaced their Irish boathands and dock workers with "contrabands"—*also at lower wages*. The departure of a Cincinnati-based steamboat with an all-black crew sparked a race riot in Cincinnati in July of 1862.[41] Race riots, with the same cause, also took place in Toledo, Chicago, and other midwestern cities. "Contrabands," hired as farm workers, were at times chased out of farming communities by white racists, usually Democrats.

As far as Democrats were concerned, Lincoln's Emancipation Proclamation of January 1, 1863, was the last straw. Dennis A. Mahony's *Dubuque Herald* trespassed on treasonable ground when he stated that the president's proclamation excused Democrats from further support of the war. "Abolition," the editorial said, "created the Administration, has shaped its policy,...and must be left to furnish the material requisites of men and money." For good measure, the editorial added that "Lincoln, his Cabinet, Congress, and all, should be hurled into the Potomac."[42]

Spokesmen for German-American Catholics and the "Butternuts" also criticized the Emancipation Proclamation viciously. So did many of the middle class Democrats, perhaps best illustrated by young Thomas O. Lowe whose father and brother were Union soldiers. Lowe, a disciple of Vallandigham, wrote to his soldier-brother: "In my heart I believe our policy [opposing emancipation] is the best for the white race, the black race, the country, and humanity, and I can die on the scaffold if need be, but I cannot change my faith."[43]

The fifth aspect of Democratic dissent in the Upper Midwest concerned civil rights and developed because the Lincoln administration violated the time-honored rights again and again. Freedom of the press, assured to citizens in the first amendment, suffered when editors were arrested, when newspapers were suppressed or denied mailing privileges, when generals excluded newspapers from their districts or departments, or when soldiers or self-styled "patriots" mobbed Democratic newspapers. More than a dozen Democratic editors were seized by federal marshals in 1862; the list included such diverse Democrats as John W. Kees of the *Circleville (Ohio) Watchman*, Archibald McGregor of the *Canton (Ohio) Stark County Democrat*, Dr. Edson B. Olds of the *Lancaster (Ohio) Eagle*, Daniel Sheward of the *Fairfield (Iowa) Constitution and Union*, and the ubiquitous Dennis A. Mahony of the *Dubuque Herald*. In 1863, when an Indiana editor called Gen. Milo S. Hascall "a donkey" for issuing an order restricting freedom of the press, the general promptly arrested the editor[44]—proving that the editor was right. On March 5, 1863, and during a blinding snowstorm, about a hundred soldiers armed with sabers and revolvers, did a thorough job of wrecking the offices of *The (Columbus) Crisis* before returning to nearby Camp Chases.[45] Freedom of the press suffered during the Civil War.

Freedom of speech, too, felt the hand of suppression; Gen. Ambrose E. Burnside's "General Orders, No. 38" and Gen. Milo S. Hascall's "Order No. 9" attest to that. So does the arrest of such fellows as Clement L. Vallandigham, Dr. Israel Blanchard, Henry Clay Dean, and others. In his Pulitzer Prize-winning book, *The Fate of Liberty*, historian Mark E. Neely called the arrest of Dr. Blanchard "a most sensationally wrongheaded arrest" and added that there were "many useless arrests."[46] Partisan U.S. marshals like David L. Phillips in Illinois and Harold M. Hoxie of Iowa abused their authority disgracefully, making arrests that never should have been made. Small wonder, then, that Democrats viewed themselves as defenders of civil liberties, and some mistakenly feared that the republic might evolve into a despotism. Democratic critics challenged President Lincoln's suspension of the writ of habeas corpus, claiming that he was usurping a congressional right. They also criticized Secretary of War Edwin M. Stanton's suspension orders of August 8, 1862, intended to enforce the "limping draft" proposed in the Militia Act of July 17, 1862. Suspension of the writ of habeas corpus enabled generals and U.S. marshals to make arrests and keep arrestees imprisoned without recourse to justice. The word "bastille," borrowed from the French, became a part of the Civil War vocabulary.

The sixth amendment promised "a speedy and public trial by an impartial jury in the district where the [supposed] crime had been committed." Instead, and in order to obtain convictions, generals tried civilians via military commissions. Vallandigham, after his arrest on the orders of General Burnside, faced a military commission because no jury in his district would have found him guilty of more than intemperate language.[47] The same holds true in the case of Lambdin P. Milligan and others in the second Indianapolis "treason trial" and Charles Walsh and others of the so-called "Chicago conspirators" in their Cincinnati-based trial before a military commission.[48]

The sixth aspect of dissent revolved around the policy and practice of federal conscription. Irish-Americans and "Butternuts," as one would expect, preferred the volunteer system with its generous bounties to enforced conscription. The commutation clause that allowed a draftee to buy his way out of service for $300 discriminated against the poorer elements of society. This clause gave Democrats a chance to say that it was "a rich man's war and a poor man's fight." Editor John McElwee of the *Hamilton (Ohio) True Telegraph*, speaking for the Irish-Americans, German-American Catholics, and the "Butternuts" of his area, wrote: "As a general thing, the Abolitionists are in office or in a condition to buy themselves free. Democrats, on the other hand, are the yeomen of the country. They live by labor and are the tillers of the earth; and [are not] in a condition to buy their freedom of the Administration."[49] Peter V. Deuster, editor of the Catholic-oriented German-language *(Milwaukee) See-Bote* denounced conscription as "despicable." The Irish and German-Americans, he stated in an editorial, "must be annihilated to make room for the Negro." The Conscription Act of March 3, 1863, he added, allowed "rich Republicans" and "aristocratic New England Yankees" to buy their way out—it was "the Polish forcing act (drafting Poles into the Russian army) taking place on American soil."[50]

The issue of peace-through-compromise occupied a central place, throughout the war, in the story of Democratic dissent in the Upper Midwest. There were some Democratic spokesmen who opposed military coercion of the South as the means to reunion from the very beginning; Vallandigham, Medary of *The Crisis*, Mahony of the *Dubuque Herald*, Lambdin P. Milligan of Indiana, and Frederic W. Horn, spokesman for Wisconsin's Luxembourgers, fell into that category. Others turned to compromise because they were concerned with the slaughter of soldiers as one bloody battle followed another. The economic depression of 1861–1862, growing sectionalist sentiment, and Union military defeats played into the hands of the peace mongers. The Democratic-controlled state legislature of 1863 in Illinois and Indiana proposed resolutions for the calling of a national peace-through-compromise convention—such resolutions were adopted by a score of county and local conventions. "Peace is on a million lips," editor McElwee of the Hamilton *True Telegraph* wrote in February of 1863, "and it will thunder, ere long, in the ears of our leaders like an Alpine storm."[51] Lincoln's Emancipation Proclamation of January 1, 1863, however, changed the equation, removing peace-through-compromise from the realm of possibility and making its advocates mere dreamers. Furthermore, the issue of peace-through-compromise proved to be a two-edged sword; it was a divisive issue that tore the Democratic party apart, exemplified by the Democratic National Convention of August 29–30, 1864. That convention spoke with a forked tongue, for it nominated a war man (Gen. George B. McClellan) as the party's presidential nominee while adopting a peace plank in its platform.

The seven aspects of Civil War dissent in the Upper Midwest melded together to make it, at times, a threat to the well-being of the Lincoln administration. In the first year of the war the voices of dissent were moderated and muffled by the surge of patriotism that swept over the entire North. Then, in late 1862, dissent gained force and respectability due to the economic depression of 1861–62 in the Upper Midwest, growing sectional sentiment, reaction to a spate of arbitrary arrests, the animosity to President Lincoln's preliminary proclamation of emancipation of September 22, Democratic victories in the fall elections, and General Burnside's devastating defeat in the battle of Fredericksburg. Dissent, portrayed by Republican newspapers as Copperheadism, reached high tide during the first six months of 1863, fueled by the widespread opposition to Lincoln's Emancipation Proclamation of January 1, 1863, a growing sentiment for peace, the defeat of Gen. Joseph Hooker's Union army at Chancellorsville, and the indignation associated with the arrest of Vallandigham and his illegal trial by a military commission. The peace crusades, an appendage of Democratic dissent, flourished during the first six months of 1863.[52]

Union victories at Gettysburg and Vicksburg, early in July of 1863, checkmated the high tide of Civil War dissent in the Upper Midwest, heartening morale and regaining respectability to the Lincoln administration. Dissent, as a viable movement, suffered another set-back when two Democratic gubernatorial candidates, both proponents of peace-through-compromise, lost to Republican opponents in October 1863 elections—Vallandigham, self-styled "apostle of peace" lost to "Honest John" Brough in Ohio, and George W. Woodward lost to incumbent Andrew G. Curtin in Pennsylvania. Gen. U.S. Grant's victory at Chattanooga on November 24–25 countered the contentions of some peace-mongers who said that the South could not be defeated. Republican party political propaganda and Union League activities, meanwhile, relit the fires of patriotism and kept the dissent movement in check during 1864. Although the peace movement experienced a revival in that year, due largely to the heavy, heavy losses in the Union armies, led by General Grant, before Richmond, the Democratic dissenters were rebuked by Lincoln's re-election in November of 1864.

Why did Democratic dissenters, so hopeful at times that their cause would triumph, end up as losers? The reasons are manifold. In the first place, the Democratic party in the Upper Midwest was without a strong leader after the death of Stephen A. Douglas in July 1861—no one stepped forward to fill his shoes. And the diverse elements that made up the Democracy made it difficult for the party to speak with one voice—kept it from being a unified opposition party. Then, too, the Democratic party was divided over the issue of peace-through-compromise. Disunity, in effect, was a Democratic disease.

In the second place, *nationalism* and *patriotism*, during the war, served to counter Democratic *dissent*, making it less effective. War rallies in cities large and small, with emotional oratory, martial music, and songs like "The Battle Hymn of the Republic," kept the fires of nationalism and patriotism burning brightly. Nationalism, which tends to tie the nation to God's apron strings, helped to make the war a holy war that carried out the Almighty's will. Patriotism received an assist from the Union League, which became a network for preaching patriotism and support of the Lincoln administration and the war. The call of patriotism, in some cases, overcame loyalty to the party, among some civilians and among many Democratic soldiers. James P. Sullivan of the famous Iron Brigade of the Union army illustrates the point. This Irish-American farm lad, known as "Mickey" to his fellow soldiers, possessed anti-black prejudices and was an avowed Democrat; he enlisted three times and served throughout the war, loyal to his country and eventually supporting emancipation.[53] In fact, army life abolitionized many soldiers, so the Democratic party of the Upper Midwest lost some who were once adherents. Patriotism, surely, was an ephemeral yet pervasive force and it played an intangible role in affecting dissent.

In the third place, President Abraham Lincoln was a political genius, adept in statescraft and with an uncanny ability to maintain the confidence of the populace. He kept the faith of the majority of his countrymen by saying the right things in the right way at the right times—negating dissent. His query regarding Vallandigham's arrest is a case in point: "Must I shoot a simple-minded soldier boy who deserts, while I must not touch a hair of the head of the wiley [sic] agitator who induces him to desert?"[54] The emotional cloak that Lincoln threw over the question suffocated the central issue of civil rights and covered the unfair implications. Another example rests in Lincoln's reply to Horace Greeley's "Prayer of Twenty Millions." With his preliminary proclamation of emancipation *already drafted and in a desk drawer*, Lincoln crafted a clever response that stated that any action taken regarding slavery must be related to saving the Union.[55] Thus, when he issued it exactly a month later, it impressed a "save-the-union" aspect into the public mind. President Lincoln's pragmatism flexed with ingenuity, his political intuition and leadership qualities, and his premeditated strategies enabled him to out-fox his political enemies, be they Radical Republicans or dissenting Democrats.

In the fourth place, the economic depression that plagued the Upper Midwest during the first year and a half of the war, gave way to war prosperity during 1863 and 1864. Economic prosperity is always a silent partner of the party in power. War prosperity, a Cincinnati observer wrote, served as "the lance of Achilles, healing by its touch the wounds of war."[56] Russell, the touring English reporter of the *Times* (London), said the same thing in a different fashion: war prosperity covered a multitude of sins.[57]

In the fifth place, the activities of the Union League affected the political climate, especially in the Upper Midwest, and helped to undermine Democratic dissent. Founded by Republicans in Pekin, Illinois, as a secret patriotic society on June 25, 1862, it soon grew into a state-wide organization. Midwestern Republican governors like Richard Yates of Illinois and Samuel Kirkwood of Iowa endorsed the Union League, envisioning it as an agency to help win elections and undermine Democratic dissent. A regional meeting in Chicago on March 25, 1863, took steps to promote a national convention, and it met in Cleveland on May 20. In the days that followed, council members worked in the political vineyard and established publishing houses that printed Republican political propaganda as tracts and pamphlets by the score, distributing many in the Upper Midwest. "All young men," one state council directive stated, "should be brought within the influence of the organization, before their opinions become fixed in the wrong direction." There was further advice: "All returned soldiers should be immediately sought out and cordially invited within your councils."[58] The League did yeomen work in countering Democratic critics and in helping to re-elect Lincoln in November of 1864, enabling the Grand President to chortle: "The Union League was a very powerful engine in the canvass, and, in the opinion of members, was the organization of all others that brought about this glorious result."[59] Truly, the Union League had a hand in rebuilding public morale in the North, winning elections, and negating Democratic dissent.

In the sixth place, Republicans adopted two political stratagems that paid dividends ten-fold: (1) one was to smear their Democratic critics as "Copperheads," brethren of South Carolina's "Rattlesnakes," and (2) the other was to devise bogeymen like the Knights of the Golden Circle to scare voters and win elections. Two Cincinnati newspapers, both Republican-oriented, launched the crusade to stigmatize Democrats as "Copperheads," and, before the war was over, that partisan propaganda became the most vicious, most extensive, and most successful smear campaign in American history. Wartime propaganda, charging Democratic critics with being pro-Southern in sympathy and proclivity, polluted the stream of history for more than a hundred years. It was so effective that the 1992 edition of the (Harper's) *American Heritage Dictionary* still defines a "Copperhead" as "a Northerner who sympathized with the South during the Civil War."[60]

Although not a single castle or council of the Knights of the Golden Circle existed north of the Ohio River and the Mason-Dixon line, Republican-sponsored exposés as pamphlets and newspaper accounts connected Democrats to the supposedly subversive organization. Hoaxes were also Republican-sponsored. Joseph K.C. Forrest in Illinois and Brig. Gen. Henry B. Carrington (the governor's man Friday) in Indiana were the chief fabricators of tall tales about the Golden Circle—they charged that hundreds of thousands of Democrats belonged to the order. In the last half of the war Republican propagandists added the Order of American Knights and the Sons of Liberty to the list—both of these two could be categorized as paper tigers. The propaganda campaign was so extensive and so effective that it was accepted as history, even into the middle of the 20th century. It played a part in discrediting Democratic dissenters of Civil War days, serving as a masterful if dishonest political stratagem.[61]

Still another means that Republicans used to checkmate the Democratic dissenters was to defeat them via the polling booths, for ballots are always better than bullets. After Democrats won the fall elections in the Upper Midwest in 1862, Republicans, using a variety of strategies, made a determined and deliberate effort to reverse the political trend. They had many advantages. In the first place, a Republican sat in the White House, and he could influence the election returns in a number of ways. Republicans controlled both houses of Congress and had a most effective congressional campaign committee. Then too, every governor of the seven states making up the Upper Midwest was a Republican (this included David Tod and John Brough of Ohio, although both posed as Unionists). Lincoln's party controlled all but two of the state legislatures in the Upper Midwest. Indiana and Illinois states legislatures were Democratic-controlled, but the two Republican governors used ingenuity and technicalities to prorogue them and nullify their programs—after all, the Democratic leaders in the two legislatures were more interested in playing political games than taking care of the business at hand.

The Republican-controlled state legislatures devised still another political stratagem to keep their party in power—giving the vote to soldiers in the field. Soldier-voting-in-the-field was a wonderful political ploy and that vote, in time, became a "controlled vote."[62] Ballots, in those days, were printed and distributed by the political parties, so Democrats were at a disadvantage because most of the colonels of regiments were Republicans and so were the "state agents," appointed by governors to oversee the welfare of soldiers in the field or in hospitals—Democrats claimed that the "state agents" were political "commissars" when it came to elections.

Some Republican colonels sought to gain political favor by having their regiments give a unanimous party vote; some gave "patriotic" speeches to their regiments the evening before the election,[63] and others destroyed the bundles of Democratic ballots shipped to regiments in the field.[64] A Wisconsin experience substantiated Democratic complaints that the soldier vote was a controlled vote: in the election of 1862 the total vote for Wisconsin's congressional candidates gave a four-to-one edge to the Republican candidates; in the election of 1864 the ratio was fifteen-to-one.[65] "The whole thing of this army voting is a most consummate humbug," one Democratic editor wrote; he added, "The scheme is like a jug handle—on one side."[66] In states that had no soldiers-in-the-field voting laws, Secretary of War Stanton heeded the pleas of Republican governors who requested that soldiers from Republican districts be furloughed so they could go home to cast "patriotic votes." Soldier votes, garnered in battlefield areas, decided a number of local elections, some state elections, and several congressional elections.

Using a variety of stratagems, Republicans made gains in some areas in the April 1863 elections. Then, in October of 1863, Lincoln's party scored two notable election victories, defeating two pro-peace gubernatorial candidates: "Honest John" Brough trounced Vallandigham (then in exile in Canada) in Ohio, and incumbent Republican governor Andrew G. Curtin narrowly won out over George W. Woodward in Pennsylvania—with the help of the soldier vote.[67] The final test took place in November of 1864 when Lincoln defeated McClellan. Without question, winning elections was a most important way to keep dissent and dissenters in check.

Revisionists, after investigating the causes of midwestern dissent and the reasons for its decline and defeat as a viable political force, face the responsibility of stating their contentions. Those who challenge the four contentions of Wood Gray and George Fort Milton should place their own on the line. There seem to be six. In the first place, the meaning of the word "Copperhead" as expressed in the *American Heritage Dictionary* ("a Northerner who sympathized with the South during the Civil War") and interpreted by Gray and Milton is in error—a lie. That definition was borrowed from Republican political propaganda of Civil War days. A corrected definition would read "a Democratic critic of the Lincoln administration."[68]

In the second place, the Democratic critics of Lincoln and the war should be characterized as CONSERVATIVES, persons who opposed the revolutionary changes that the Civil War brought to the country.[69] The opening paragraph in *The Copperheads in the Middle West* (1960)—characterized in Eugene C. Murdock's *The Civil War in the North: A Selective Annotated Bibliography* (1987) as "the first revisionist book on the Copperheads which directly challenges the conclusions of Gray, Milton, and others"—states the theme that the so-called "Copperheads" were really conservatives:

Those crucial years [1861–1864] helped to give a new meaning to the term "democracy" and the doctrine of equality crossed new frontiers in American thought. The war years also witnessed the transformation of a federal union into an American nation....On the economic scene, industry made gains over agriculture—the high tariff policy and the philosophy of industrialism became integral parts of postwar America.

All Northerners did not favor the changes which the War was bringing to America. Most of the midwestern Democrats put themselves on record as critics of change. In a sense, those Democrats were conservatives; they thought that the wheel of revolution turned too fast and too far. Their wartime slogan, "The Constitution as it is, the Union as it was," proved that they looked toward the past and feared the changes that the war foisted upon the country.[70]

Clement L. Vallandigham, the best-known midwestern critic of the Lincoln administration, considered himself a conservative and a disciple of Edmund Burke. Vallandigham had seven books by Burke in his 1200-volume library,[71] and, like Burke, he believed that changes should be evolutionary and not revolutionary and that tradition and the past should be considered when changes are made. Other Democratic critics of the Lincoln administration, like Lambdin P. Milligan and Daniel W. Voorhees of Indiana, Samuel S. Cox of Ohio, and Wilbur F. Storey of the Chicago Times, also considered themselves conservatives—opposing the ascendancy of industrialism, the centralization of the national government, and emancipation of the slaves.

In the third place, revisionists repudiate the contentions of Gray and Milton regarding the so-called "Copperhead secret societies": the Knights of the Golden Circle, Order of American Knights, and the Sons of Liberty. Actually, not a single chapter of the Knights of the Golden Circle existed in any of the seven states making up the Upper Midwest during the war. The Golden Circle was a figment of Republican imagination, based, in part on lies composed by Col. Henry B. Carrington in Indiana and Joseph K.C. Forrest in Illinois. Exposés, devised as political propaganda, were commonplace. The Golden Circle, in reality, was a bogeyman devised for political gain.[72]

The Order of American Knights and the Sons of Liberty, the first based in St. Louis and the second in Indianapolis, were paper-based organizations designed to appeal to conservative Democrats who favored peace-through-compromise and subscribed to the tenets in the Virginia and Kentucky Resolutions, adopted as protests against the Alien and Sedition Acts of 1798. Neither had a paid membership list and neither actually got off the ground. Harrison H. Dodd printed four small booklets as the basis for the Sons of Liberty,[73] yet not a single chapter existed in Indiana. Republican political propaganda, however, transformed the two paper-based organizations into many-membered subversive societies. Both Wood Gray and George Fort Milton built big mountains out of little hills of fluff and bluff.

In the fourth place, revisionist historians discredit Wood's and Milton's contentions regarding the two "gigantic conspiracies," one supposedly based in Indianapolis and the other in Chicago, both in 1864 and on the eve of the fall elections. Dodd, founder of the Sons of Liberty, actually did suggest "a revolution" to a handful of friends, who rebuked "the silly idea"; he also received a shipment of two dozen revolvers from New York City—purchased by a friend and shipped to Dodd in Indianapolis. Federal authorities seized the shipment. Governor Morton and his agents built a few facts into a grand and extensive conspiracy leading to the establishment of a northwestern Confederacy—propaganda intended to help reelect Governor Morton and discredit the Democrats. Dodd was guilty of indiscretions, but Morton's net entrapped innocent men like Lambdin P. Milligan. The first of the two military trials held in Indianapolis found Dodd guilty; the second, in which four Democrats were found guilty, was a farce.[74]

The Chicago or Camp Douglas conspiracy was built on even flimsier evidence. A local Democratic leader named Charles Walsh, convinced that Republicans might try to purge the polls, collected two dozen muskets and revolvers that he would "loan" to Democratic poll watchers if force was necessary to keep the elections "free and open."[75] Walsh thought that there were reasons to be concerned—Union Leaguers reportedly had organized "militarized auxiliaries" and Governor Richard Yates, in July of 1864, had asked Secretary of War Stanton to declare martial law in Illinois. Federal authorities seized Walsh's small store of arms and Col. Benjamin J. Sweet, commandant at Camp Douglas, devised an election eve exposé, expanding a few facts into another "gigantic conspiracy." According to Colonel Sweet, Copperheads would raid Camp Douglas, free the 9,000 Confederate prisoners held there, plunder and burn Chicago, spread rebellion over the entire Upper West, and establish a Northwestern Confederacy. All in all, the so-called "Camp Douglas Conspiracy" was a fantasy passed off as fact, a ploy to help reelect Governor Yates and President Lincoln, a travesty of justice, and a tall tale believed by historians Gray and Milton.[76]

In the fifth place, revisionists assign socioeconomic aspects to middle Western Democratic dissent. The so-called "Copperheads" belonged to four socioeconomic groups: Irish-Americans, German-American Catholics, "Butternuts," and middle class disciples of Jacksonian and Jeffersonian Democracy. There also was a sectionalist aspect, with an economic basis, to Democratic dissent in the Upper Midwest. There were real reasons for criticism of the Lincoln administration: the economic depression of 1861–1862, the furtherance of emancipation, numerous violations of civil rights, military failures, repulsions to the high, high battlefield casualties, unabashed Democratic partyism, and the fear that the Upper Midwest was losing its role in balance of power politics.[77]

In the sixth place, revisionist historians challenge an underlying theme in Gray's *The Hidden Civil War* and Milton's *Abraham Lincoln and the Fifth Column* that Copperheads were "the bad guys" and had no reason to criticize the Lincoln administration and the honorable war. But President Lincoln deserved censure on several counts, according to midwestern Democratic critics: in suspending the writ of habeas corpus, the president usurped a congressional prerogative; there were too many arbitrary arrests and the Bill of Rights was ignored when civilians were tried too often by military commissions; Lincoln's Emancipation Proclamations were clearly unconstitutional; military failures were commonplace. As members of the out-of-power party, Democrats had the responsibility to condemn the many violations of civil rights that took place during the war—many unnecessary. Steeped in history, they knew that civil wars in Europe had ended in dictatorships; the Great Civil War in England had evolved into an army dictatorship under Oliver Cromwell while the French Revolution had ended with Napoleon Bonaparte holding a scepter.

Amidst the widespread violations of civil liberties, Democratic leaders in the Upper Midwest acted with considerable restraint. After all, they were constitutionalists and conservatives. "Let whatever may come," Wisconsin's foremost Democrat (Edward G. Ryan) wrote in 1862, "the Democracy will abide by their time-honored principles, by the Constitution and the Union... We are for the Constitution as it is, and the Union as it was."[78] Time and again, Democrats said that their loyalty was to the Constitution and the Union, not the Republican administration. Clement L. Vallandigham, Samuel S. Cox, and Daniel W. Voorhees toured the back country where opposition to conscription could become violent and plead for restraint; they asked their constituents to obey the laws and to turn to the courts and the polls for justice—truly a conservative approach. Historian Mark E. Neely, generally a defender of Lincoln, said that Democratic protests, opportunistic at times, "played a role crucial to a democratic country involved in war" and added, "The Democratic party was a loyal opposition...it also played a legitimate role in preserving civil liberties in wartime America."[79] Yet Clio, the Muse of history often at the mercy of nationalism, invariably judges those who swim against the current rather harshly. Gray and Milton go further, one judging Lincoln's Democratic critics as traitors and "a type that is dangerous in a democracy" and the other characterizing them as traitors and "the secessionists' fifth column."[80]

Were Lincoln's Democratic critics in the Upper Midwest traitors, "Copperheads," or dissenters? If historians accept the definitions of treason as stated by Gen. Ambrose E. Burnside or the illegal military commission that tried Clement L. Vallandigham, then many of the so-called "Copperheads" were traitors. If historians accept Benjamin F. Wade's assertion, "Anyone who quotes the Constitution in this crisis is a traitor," or Thaddeus Stevens' supposition that Lincoln's war powers were unlimited, then many Democratic critics of the Lincoln administration could be accused of treason. The implication of treason could also be read into an utterance of John W. Forney (owner of the *Philadelphia Press* and the *Washington Chronicle* as well as secretary to the U.S. Senate and confidant of Lincoln) when he said, "Let us unite the North by any means...Silence every tongue that does not speak with respect of the cause and the flag."[81] If historians accept the assertion of one Republican who, after Vallandigham's arrest, asked that Vallandigham be "hung first and tried afterward," or Col. Alexander McCook's outrageous statement, "Yes, by God, I say, damn any man who is not for the Union, and damn Vallandigham, too. He is worse than a Judas; he is a damned traitor!"[82] then the controversial Democrat was a purveyor of treason. Editors of Radical Republican newspapers, time and again, accused Democratic critics of Lincoln of treason—"traitor" was a favorite smear term—especially during heated political campaigns—but it was little more than political propaganda. If historians follow in the footsteps of Wood Gray and George Fort Milton and accept campaign rhetoric and Republican political propaganda as historical fact, they will view the so-called "Copperheads" as *traitors*.

Revisionists take the constitutional approach to Democratic dissent—they sift through Republican political propaganda of Civil War days to get the facts. If historians accept the definition of treason in the U.S. Constitution[83] or accept the opinion of Chief Justice John Marshall in *United States v. Burr* (1807),[84] they will not view Vallandigham and other Democratic critics as traitors. More to the point are the words of Associate Justice David Davis (a Lincoln appointee) when he wrote the majority decision in *Ex Parte Milligan* (1866): "The Constitution of the United States is a law for rulers and people, equally in war and peace, and covers with its shield of protection all classes of men, at all times and under all circumstances. No doctrine involving more pernicious consequences was ever invented by the wit of man that any of its great provisions can be suspended during any exigencies of Government."[85] Democrats who had been critics of the Lincoln administration during the war shouted "Amen!"

If the word "Copperhead" is defined as "a Northerner who sympathized with the South during the Civil War"—as given in the *American Heritage Dictionary*—and that meaning is applied to Democratic critics of the Lincoln administration, then the definition is in error and needs revision. That, however, was the meaning devised by Radical Republicans and it became an integral part of their political propaganda.

Most of Lincoln's Democratic critics in the Upper Midwest were western sectionalists; they were pro-western rather than pro-Southern. As stated previously, Vallandigham, Cox, Milligan and scores of other so-called "Copperheads" fall in the pro-western category. Of course there were a few who rightly deserved to be labeled "pro-Southern." Some "Butternuts" had brothers or other relatives in the Confederacy and they had not yet fully sloughed their Southern heritage. A few—very few—left southern Indiana or Illinois or Iowa to join the rebel army. George Wallace Jones, a one-time governor of Iowa and a one-time slaveholder, had been a personal friend of Jefferson Davis and two of Jones' sons joined the Confederate army. Republicans had the right to assume that he was pro-Southern.[86] William A. Bowles of French Lick, Indiana, fit the same category. He had claimed that he had more respect for Jefferson Davis than for Abraham Lincoln, defended slavery as an institution, and gave an acquaintance who wanted to fight for the South a letter of introduction to a Confederate general.[87] Midwesterners had no one to match two Pennsylvanians; one (a woman) who put arsenic into pies that she baked for soldiers at a nearby army camp, another asked their minister to baptize a baby boy "Beauregard." The few midwesterners who were pro-Southern had no influence within the Democratic party, characterized by some revisionist historians as "the loyal opposition."[88]

The *American Heritage Dictionary* defines the word "dissent" as "to feel or think differently; disagree; differ."[89] This definition certainly fits Democratic critics of the Lincoln administration, especially those who lived in the Upper Midwest. They disagreed with administration policy on many counts: emancipation, conscription, high tariffs, arbitrary arrests, suspension of the writ of habeas corpus, as well as other issues. Such critics of the Lincoln administration as Vallandigham, Faran of the *Cincinnati Enquirer*, Voorhees, Storey of the *Chicago Times*, Milligan, and many others certainly were dissenters—this without argument.

But not all midwestern Democrats who opposed the policies of the Lincoln administration were without sin; some were guilty of outrageous statement. Mahony's *Dubuque Herald* was off base when the editorial writer, upset with Lincoln's Emancipation Proclamation of January 1, 1863, said that the people, "by revolution," ought to hurl Lincoln, his Cabinet, and Congress "into the Potomac."[90] "Brick" Pomeroy's *LaCrosse Democrat* was guilty of more outlandish utterances during the emotion-packed presidential election of 1864, putting a picture of Lincoln's on the front page with the caption "The Widow-Maker of the 19th Century." Worse than that, an editorial asked for the assassination of the president:

> The man who votes for Lincoln now is a traitor and murderer. He who pretending to war for, wars against the Constitution of our country is a traitor and Lincoln is one of these men...And if he is re-elected to misgovern for another four years, we trust some bold hand will pierce his heart with dagger point for the public good.

The editor even suggested an appropriate epitaph:

> Beneath this turf the Widow-Maker lies
> Little in everything, except in size.[91]

Heated political campaigns usually witness bigotry and fanaticism mixed with fact. Ridiculous assertions are commonplace, and, in reality, tend to discredit movements or parties. The opposition throws the cloak of the fanatical fringe over the entire movement or party in an effort to discredit. This certainly was true as far as Civil War dissent is concerned.

Midwestern Democratic critics of the Lincoln administration, generally, and when placed in their historical setting, were moderate in words and actions. After all, they were conservatives and constitutionalists, destined to oppose the Lincoln administration with words and votes and court cases, not revolution. Their protests restrained Lincoln and his partisans. It was the responsibility, of Democrats—in the country's two-party system—to criticize the transgressions of the party in power, and there were many. It was natural for Democratic critics to view themselves as the defenders of civil liberties. After Republican political propaganda of Civil War days is sifted and separated from historical fact, Democratic critics of the Lincoln administration will be recognized as *the loyal opposition.*[92] Revisionist historians have reached that conclusion. Ironically, that is exactly the way wartime Democratic critics in Civil War days viewed themselves.

CHAPTER II

President Lincoln, the Civil War, and the Bill of Rights*

The Civil War was a unique event in American history, brother fought against brother. The principle and practice of secession was settled by military might. King Cotton was toppled from his throne. Emancipation became a central issue. Congress and the president followed uncharted courses. It was the first war in which the president suspended the writ of habeas corpus. It was the first war with federal conscription. In the crucible of war the federal union of antebellum days evolved into a new nation, with more power centered in Washington. And civil liberties fared badly, worse than in any other American war.

The White House was occupied by a son of the western prairies. Abraham Lincoln, at the time that he took the oath of office, lacked administrative experience—unless operating a country store that went bankrupt falls into that category. But he was bright, perceptive, pragmatic, possessed of political savvy, adept at dealing with friends and foes, and skilled in statecraft. He had been mesmerized by the inspiring words of the second paragraph of the Declaration of Independence, especially the sentence: "All men are created equal and endowed by their creator with certain inalienable rights—among which are life, liberty, and the pursuit of happiness." Although Lincoln occasionally expressed respect for the Constitution, he had a rather "cavalier" attitude toward it—it seemed secondary to the Declaration of Independence.[1] Historian Mark E. Neely, a top Lincoln scholar, wrote "... he [Lincoln] played fast and loose with the Constitution after the firing on Fort Sumter;

---

*Reprinted (with permission) from the *Lincoln Herald*, 94 (Spring 1992): 10–23.

it was never the most important document in his thought."[2] And later: "For him [Lincoln] it was not the crucial document. He said repeatedly that he got all of his political ideas from the Declaration of Independence and from Thomas Jefferson."[3]

Time and again, President Lincoln said that his chief concern was to save the Union. In that famous letter to Horace Greeley—in response to the "prayer of twenty millions"—Lincoln said that he was willing to destroy slavery it if would save the Union, even though slavery was vaguely guaranteed in the Constitution.[4] Later Lincoln wrote a justification of his emancipation proclamations in rather shocking words: "...measures, otherwise unconstitutional, might become lawful, by becoming indispensable to the preservation of the constitution, through the preservation of the Union."[5] In simple words, this is the doctrine of necessity.

President Lincoln employed the same doctrine of necessity in suspending the writ of habeas corpus and in justifying the arrest of Clement L. Vallandigham, the best known Democratic critic of the war and the Lincoln administration. In a long letter really prepared as a state paper, Lincoln said that the arrest of the outspoken Dayton Democrat was based on the doctrine of necessity: "...he [Vallandigham] was damaging the army, upon the existence and vigor, of which, the life of the nation depends."[6] The Civil War president, thus, gave his Democratic critics a chance to resurrect the old axiom "Necessity has ever been the excuse of tyrants."

President Lincoln's doctrine of necessity offered a threat to the rights and privileges listed in the first ten amendments—the so-called "Bill of Rights." This was supplemented by the workings of the provost marshal system (provided for in the Conscription Act of March 3, 1863) and many of the U.S. marshals, usually Republicans. Small wonder, therefore, that the record of the Lincoln administration in regards to civil rights is a rather dismal one, although nationalist historians try to defend it while discrediting the Democratic dissenters.

Historian Mark E. Neely, in his study of civil rights in the Civil War, says, "For it is well known that President Lincoln suspended the writ of habeas corpus and thereafter managed the home front, in part, by means of military arrests of civilians—thousands and thousands of them." Again: "Critics of the Lincoln Administration have seen in the internal security system a potential for partisan abuse and political exploitation."[7]

The first amendment promises freedom of speech and freedom of the press to citizens, yet both were frequently violated during the Civil War. Some Democratic speakers, as critics of the Lincoln administration, were arrested soon after they finished their political speeches. Others were arrested for comments made on street corners. Philip Huber, a Philadelphian, called the war "a nigger conflict," adding, "God had put a curse on negroes and Abe Lincoln had put himself above God by trying to remove the curse"; he was arrested a few days later.[8] In August of 1862, a Pennsylvania citizen said that he would rather serve in the Confederate army for five cents a day than accept a generous bounty to join the Union army; he was arrested the next day.[9] Charles Ingersoll, a prominent Philadelphia dissenter, was arrested on August 23, 1863, after speaking in Independence Square and saying that "the despotism of the Old World" could furnish no parallel to "the corruption of the [Lincoln] administration."[10] Judge Andrew D. Duff and Dr. Israel Blanchard, respected Illinois Democrats, were arrested in August of 1862 because they "had spoken disrespectfully of President Lincoln."[11]

Dr. Edson B. Olds' arrest deserves mention because of repercussions and its importance. He was arrested after a speech in which he blamed Republicans rather than Southerners for the war and asked for compromise to stop the shedding of blood. Dr. Olds' friends regarded him as "a martyr for freedom of speech," and while still in prison, elected him to fill a vacancy in the Ohio state senate. After his release, and without any charges filed against him, he returned home to Lancaster to a "tumultuous reception." The crowd, estimated at 10,000 by a Democratic editor, gave him "a hero's welcome."[12]

The most notable of the arrests was that of Clement L. Vallandigham on May 5, 1863. The Dayton Democrat was a controversial fellow and a popular public speaker. After practicing law and serving a term in the state legislature while a resident of New Lisbon, he moved to Dayton to edit the *Dayton Empire*, and revive the Democracy of Montgomery County. He won election to Congress on his third try and, after the start of the war, become both "Lincoln's gadfly" and "the apostle of peace." He failed in a bid for a fourth congressional term, but only because the Republican-controlled state legislature changed the boundary of the Third District by substituting a fifty-fifty county for a predominantly Democratic one.[13] Vallandigham, then, decided to seek the Democratic gubernatorial nomination although members of the party hierarchy had already decided upon someone else. Knowing that Dr. Olds had been rewarded with state office after becoming "a martyr for freedom of speech," Vallandigham decided to try the same tack.[14]

Maj. Gen. Ambrose E. Burnside, commanding the Department of the Ohio and headquartered in Cincinnati, inadvertently provided Vallandigham with the opportunity to seek "martyrdom" by issuing "General Orders, No. 38" on April 27, 1863. Burnside's military edict stated that "the habit of declaring sympathies for the enemy [would] be no longer tolerated."[15] Since the rather rash general regarded any vocal or written criticism of Lincoln or the war as "aiding the enemy," freedom of speech and the press was definitely threatened within Burnside's jurisdiction.

Friends of Vallandigham organized a Democratic rally in Columbus, Ohio, on April 30, 1863, in order to give the ex-congressman a chance to bait General Burnside. Vallandigham took advantage of that platform appearance to ridicule and criticize President Lincoln as well. Burnside's ears burned, and when he learned that Vallandigham would speak at Mount

Vernon (Ohio) on May 1, he sent two members of his staff, dressed as civilians, to the Democratic rally to "observe" and "take notes."[16]

Knowing that General Burnside had two agents in attendance, Vallandigham rose to the occasion. After some remarks about the historic role of the Democratic party in the country's history, he turned to the discussion of his rights as "a freeman." Holding a copy of Burnside's "General Orders, No. 38" aloft, Vallandigham denounced it as "a bare usurpation of power"—it was no more than "a detestable document" deserving to be burned. He could spit upon it, he said, and trample it underfoot; he stood on "General Orders, No. 1—the Constitution of the United States." There was more.[17]

Several days later, after receiving the reports of his "agents" and ascertaining that Vallandigham was back home, Burnside sent a "midnight special" to Dayton; it contained the general's aide-de-camp as head officer and sixty-seven soldiers with their muskets. The soldiers broke down the back door of Vallandigham's home, seized him in his upstairs bedroom, marched him to the awaiting train, and took him back to Cincinnati. The precept that a man's house is his castle did not hold in Vallandigham's case.[18]

Another of the more notable arrests was that of Lambdin P. Milligan of Huntington, Indiana. He was an outspoken critic of Lincoln and the war— he had called it "unjust, unnecessary, infamous."[19] His hatred of Lincoln was genuine, but he detested his governor even more. Earlier he had characterized Governor Oliver P. Morton's war proclamations as "silly twaddle." For good measure, Milligan called his governor "a common liar" who was "as false as his own black heart, as villainous as his own nature is cowardly and infamous."[20] Morton returned Milligan's hatred in full measure, for the governor imagined that he was Sir Galahad and that Milligan was Sir Modred. Governor Morton wanted Milligan taken prisoner but had to wait until he found a subservient general (Brig. Gen. Alvin P. Hovey) to arrest the Huntington curmudgeon. On October 6, 1864, a detail of soldiers appeared at Milligan's home and a special train took prisoner Milligan back to Indianapolis.[21]

Sometimes free speech was violated in other ways than by arrests. During a party rally, held at the Central Democratic Club in Philadelphia, armed soldiers invaded the hall and routed the speaker and the audience.[22] Once army units commanded by rash officers broke up a large Democratic rally in Indianapolis. Featured speakers held forth on the central stand while lesser lights spoke on satellite platforms. Samuel R. Hamill, one of the lesser lights, was criticizing Lincoln, Morton, General Burnside, and the arrest of Vallandigham when armed soldiers from nearby Camp Morton rushed the platform and stopped the speech-making. Later, when U.S. Senator Thomas A. Hendricks was speaking at the central stand, soldiers with fixed bayonets advanced toward the speaker and threatened "to make a summary disposal of him." Hendricks promptly ended his speech and the Democratic crowd dispersed in a rather ugly mood.[23] That evening squads of soldiers stopped the excursion trains taking Democrats back home, boarded the cars, and confiscated all the pistols and revolvers that they could find[24]—violating the second amendment that stated that "the right of the people to keep and bear Arms, shall not be infringed." Neither the commanding officer at Camp Morton nor General Burnside nor Governor Morton issued a reprimand to the soldiers or an apology to the Democrats. The Indianapolis Republican newspaper, more concerned with patriotism than the principle of freedom of speech, endorsed the soldiers' actions.[25]

Free speech also suffered when Republican rowdies shouted down Democratic speakers at local political rallies or harassed them—results were the same when Democratic rowdies disrupted Republican party rallies. Intimidation was a common practice, illustrated by the experiences of Harrison H. Dodd of Indianapolis. Dodd took the train to Danville to be the featured speaker at a Democratic party rally. When he arrived there, he found that local Republican officials had denied local Democrats use of the room in the county courthouse that they had reserved earlier. So they held their rally outdoors. During the speech-making, Republican rowdies rushed the platform and cursed and insulted Dodd. On the way home, and at one railway station, a group of citizens gathered around Dodd; members of the mob called him a traitor and the more savage suggested a tar-and-feathers party or hanging him to the nearest tree.[26] Small wonder that Dodd thought it necessary for Democrats to organize a secret mutual protection society to save civil rights of members of his party.[27]

Freedom of the press, like freedom of speech, was also violated frequently during the Civil War. Federal authorities arrested James A. McMaster, editor of the *(New York) Freeman's Journal* for defending secession as a viable doctrine and for opposing the war. Albert D. Boileau, editor of the *Philadelphia Evening Journal*, was arrested on January 23, 1863, after the newspaper printed an article that compared Abraham Lincoln's "intellectual capacities" with those of Jefferson Davis; rumors said that Lincoln ordered the arrest because he came out second-best in the comparison.[28] Dennis A. Mahony of the *Dubuque Herald* was arrested in 1862 for being too critical of Lincoln and the war.[29] Daniel Flanagan, an Irishman and editor of the *Mason (Ohio) Democrat* was arrested the day after his newspaper reprinted an anti-draft article from another newspaper.[30] The Flanders brothers, co-editors of the *Franklin County Gazette* (published in Malone, N.Y.) were arrested on October 22, 1861, and carted off to Fort Lafayette.[31] John W. Kees of the *Circleville Watchman*, an Ohio weekly, was most intemperate in calling Lincoln a fool, a fanatic, and a figurehead of the abolitionists—he was arrested in 1862, supposedly for discouraging enlistments and flirting with treason. The editor of the *Plymouth Democrat,* published in Indiana, called a general "a donkey" for issuing an edict limiting freedom of the press—the general promptly arrested the editor,[32] proving that the editor was right. There were many, many others.[33]

Sometimes newspapers were suspended and their editors not arrested. A Philadelphia newspaper, *The Christian Observer*, was "closed down" in August of 1861; its Presbyterian editor left for Richmond.[34] Another Philadelphia newspaper, *The Jeffersonian*, was suppressed "upon the authority of the President" on August 23, 1861; when a court handed the paper back to the editor (John Hogdson), Postmaster General Montgomery Blair barred the paper from the mails.[35] Half a dozen Democratic newspapers were suppressed in Indiana after General Milo S. Hascall was named commander of the Military District of Indiana, a subdivision of General Burnside's Department of the Ohio. Hascall issued "Order No. 9" as a supplement to Burnside's "General Orders, No. 38." Hascall's edict said that all newspapers (and speeches) that advised resistance to measures intending "to bring the war policy of the Government into disrepute" would be violating "General Orders, No. 38." Hascall's edict added, "...the country will have to be saved or lost during the time this Administration remains in power, and therefore he who is factiously and actively opposed to the war policy of the Administration is as much opposed to his Government."[36] When the editor of the *South Bend Forum* said that he intended to defy Hascall's edict, his paper was closed down.

Other newspapers like the *Louisville Courier, Boone County Standard* (a Missouri newspaper), *New York Day Book, Baltimore South, New Orleans Crescent*, and others were also suppressed. In the final edition of the *Day Book*, editor N.R. Stimson wrote: "An attempt is now being made to suppress all the organs of opinion in the North that differ with the will of the party temporarily in possession of the Federal Government."[37] The editor exaggerated, but too many Democratic newspapers were suppressed.

The best-known of the suspensions took place in June of 1863 when General Burnside closed down the *Chicago Times* and accused editor Wilbur F. Storey of making "disloyal and incendiary statements" in his newspaper.[38] The incident gave President Lincoln a chance to redeem himself, for he was still being strongly criticized for the arrest of Vallandigham. Through his secretary of war, the president revoked Burnside's suspension of the *Chicago Times*.[39]

Freedom of the press also suffered when mobs destroyed Democratic printing plants—this happened scores of times. *The Palmetto Flag*, a Philadelphia newspaper, was the first in the North to feel the effect of mob action—its editor had published an editorial defending the firing on Fort Sumter; the newspaper ceased publication and its editor headed south.[40] A few days later, on June 18, 1861, the *Booneville Observer*, a Democratic newspaper in Missouri, was wrecked by a mob.[41] On August 12, 1861, an angry mob invaded the quarters of the *Bangor (Maine) Democrat*, carried the office furniture and type cases into the street and celebrated around a town bonfire.[42] Indiana's governor, Oliver P. Morton, seemed to favor the suppression of Democratic newspapers, and quite a few felt the hand of mob action; the list included the *Terre Haute Journal and Democrat, Lafayette Argus, Rockport Democrat, Richmond Jeffersonian, LaPorte Democrat, Franklin Democrat, Vincennes Western Sun, Princeton Union Democrat*, and the *Columbia News*. Indiana, Ohio, Illinois, and Pennsylvania were the political battlegrounds in 1863 and witnessed the destruction of more Democratic newspapers than the other Northern states. Ohio's most celebrated case involved a Columbus newspaper called *The Crisis*, edited by Samuel Medary, a friend of Vallandigham. On March 5, 1863, and during a blinding snowstorm, about a hundred soldiers armed with sabres and revolvers, did a thorough job of wrecking the editorial offices of *The Crisis* before returning to nearby Camp Chase[43]—neither the governor of Ohio nor the camp commander apologized for the incident.

Freedom of the press was not served when Democratic newspapers were barred from the mails. This happened time and again. Even faraway California Democrats felt the long arm of Washington's restricting mailing privileges for the party's newspapers; in February of 1862 eight newspapers lost their postal rights; they were the *Placerville Mountain Democrat*, the *Los Angeles Star*, the *Stockton Argus*, the *Stockton Democrat*, the *Visalia Equal Rights Expositor*, the *Visalia Post*, the *Tulane Post*, and the *San Jose Tribune*.[44]

There were times when generals prohibited the circulation of Democratic newspapers within their jurisdiction. The list is long, and two examples must suffice. On the same day that General Burnside suspended the publication of the *Chicago Times*, he prohibited the circulation of the *New York World* within the Department of the Ohio.[45] In the spring of 1863, Major General Samuel Prentiss, headquartered in Helena, Arkansas, and commanding the Department of the Southwest, prohibited the circulation of the *Chicago Times, Milwaukee News*, and the *LaCrosse Democrat* within his jurisdiction. Marcus Mills "Brick" Pomeroy, editor of the *LaCrosse Democrat* and correspondent for the other two, had a rather unpleasant experience. General Prentiss called the *LaCrosse Democrat* editor into his office, read him the riot act, and banished him from the area—warning him that, if he returned, he would be arrested and hung as a spy.[46]

Lincoln's attitude toward the arrest of Democratic editors or orators was "somewhat ambivalent." In the case of Vallandigham, the president wrote to General Burnside that "all [of] the Cabinet regretted the necessity of arresting...Vallandigham."[47] Perhaps Lincoln did too, but was it because General Burnside had violated the first amendment or because the widespread reactions lessened public respect for the Lincoln administration? Not only were moderate Republicans concerned, but so were the Radical Republicans. Governor Morton, who had little concern for the rights of the

Democrats, wrote a four-page letter to the president, emphasizing that Vallandigham's arrest has multiplied "the extent and intensity of opposition to both Lincoln and the war."[48]

When Brig. Gen. John M. Schofield arrested William McKee, editor of the *(St. Louis) Missouri Democrat,* President Lincoln wrote, "I regret to learn of the arrest of the Democratic editor. I fear this loses you the middle position I desire you to occupy."[49] Later, Lincoln wrote to General Schofield again:

> You will only arrest individuals and suppress assemblies or newspapers when they may be working palpable injury to the military in your charge, and in no other case will you interfere with the expression of opinion in any other form or allow it to be interfered with violently by others. In this you have a discretion to exercise with great caution, calmness, and forbearance.[50]

The key phrase seems to be "palpable injury to the military." Lincoln has justified Vallandigham's arrest on just that ground and it could be used again and again against Democratic dissenters, be they editors or orators. In other words, the president was authorizing a general to invoke the doctrine of necessity. "Yet though critical of individual cases in private and fully aware of their potential to harm the administration," historian Mark E. Neely wrote in his famous book on civil rights in the Civil War, "he publicly defended a policy that permitted suppressing disloyal papers."[51]

But who defined "disloyal"? Should the definition be left only to Lincoln and the Radical Republicans? Democrats thought otherwise. Could the Civil War president have been influenced by John W. Forney, a confidant of Lincoln as well as editor of the *Philadelphia Press* and secretary of the U.S. Senate, who wrote: "Let us unite the North by any means...Silence every tongue that does not speak with respect of the cause and the flag."[52]

In addition to freedom of speech and the press, the first amendment also states that Congress should make no law prohibiting the free exercise of religion. One wartime congressional enactment did discriminate against Jews. The federal law that allowed the appointment of chaplains to army regiments specified that they must be of Christian denominations—rabbis, thus, were excluded. As a congressman in 1862, Vallandigham took the lead to change the law so that rabbis could also be army chaplains.[53] On September 18, 1862, President Lincoln appointed Rabbi Jacob Frankel as a military chaplain—the first in U.S history.[54]

Sometimes discrimination against Jews took place in military districts or departments. On December 17, 1862, for example, Maj. Gen. U.S. Grant, commanding the Department of the Tennessee, issued "General Orders, No. 1"; it expelled "Jews as a class...from the department." Some sutlers and merchants had violated trade regulations—the excuse used by General Grant to issue his order. Several Illinois congressmen called on President

Lincoln to protest Grant's discriminatory edict and so did Caesar J. Kaskel, a Jewish merchant from Paducah, Kentucky. Lincoln then expressed his opposition to Grant's "General Orders, No. 11" to Maj. Gen. Henry W. Halleck, the president's general-in-chief. In turn, General Halleck revoked the discriminatory edict and, on January 3, 1863, wrote to Grant: "The President has no objection to your expelling traders and Jewish peddlers [*sic*], which I suppose was the object of your order, but as it in terms prescribed [*sic*] an entire religious class, some of whom are fighting in our ranks, the President deemed it necessary to revoke it."[55] In the area of religious toleration, Lincoln had an impeccable record.

There were some restrictions upon freedom of religion here and there, but they were usually against individuals by church authorities. Henry Clay Dean, an Iowa populist and preacher, alienated members of the hierarchy of the Methodist Church because he blended too much Democratic politics with scripture in his sermons. Dean opposed the war and "Washington-based tyranny." He had his license canceled by his church superiors.[56]

Two Illinois preachers who spoke at a Democratic party rally were reprimanded by the Methodist Episcopal Conference in Springfield on October 13, 1863.[57] A Presbyterian clergyman who preached a sermon on the theme "Blessed Are the Peacemakers"—one of the beatitudes from the Sermon on the Mount—was arrested soon after in Newark, Delaware.[58] After the war, a prominent Methodist Episcopal cleric wrote, "Our ministers were true to the National cause; no one would have been tolerated if he had shown any sympathy for the enemy."[59]

The suspension of the writ of habeas corpus, intertwined with civil rights, was a most controversial issue during the Civil War. After a mob attack upon Massachusetts' troops passing through Baltimore on their way to Washington, President Lincoln authorized Maj. Gen. Winfield Scott, general-in-chief at the start of the war, to suspend the writ of habeas corpus along the line of the Philadelphia-to-Washington railroads. About a month later, a Union general arrested a Maryland citizen named John Merryman and hustled him off to Fort McHenry. Chief Justice Roger B. Taney, sitting on circuit court duty in Maryland, issued a writ of habeas corpus in behalf of Merryman. After some refusals and maneuvering, Chief Justice Taney wrote a statement (*Ex Parte Merryman*) that reprimanded Lincoln for suspending the writ of habeas corpus, arguing that the president had assumed a congressional function. The president, Taney said, was responsible for maintaining constitutional guarantees and anyone suspected of treason or wrongdoing should be reported to a district attorney and have his day in court.[60] Lincoln, on the other hand, believe that, as commander in chief of the army, he had the right to take action and suspend the writ of habeas corpus in this case. He would be faithless to his oath of office, he believed, "if the government should be overthrown when it was believed that disobeying the single law would tend to preserve it." This was Lincoln's first use of the doctrine of necessity.

President Lincoln continued to authorize the suspension of the writ of habeas corpus in specific cases and areas, here and there, and his

Democratic critics continued to insist that he was usurping authority and desecrating the rights of citizens. Then, on March 3, 1863, Congress suspended the writ, and the question of presidential prerogative on this question ceased to be a point of contention. But time and again, citizens were arbitrarily arrested and held in prison without charges being filed against them and having the right to appear before a judge to have their case heard.

The fourth amendment, seemingly promising citizens "to be secure in their persons...against unreasonable searches or seizures," was violated more frequently than any other. Most of the arrests, especially those concerned with the enrollment and draft, were right and proper. Many were of spies, violators of trade regulations, smugglers, blockade runners, Southern citizens entering the Union lines, or outright criminals. A Harrisburg woman, pro-Southern in her sympathies, sold poisoned pies to Union soldiers in a nearby army camp; seven of her customers died and she was arrested.[61] In Chicago, a woman armed with a knife and aided by a vicious dog, prevented the enrollment of her husband—both were later arrested.[62] A back country Pennsylvanian named Samuel Reinert chased away an enrolling officer with a shotgun after his wife had dumped a bucket of hot water upon him; ironically, Reinert was over forty-five and blind in one eye, so his name would not have appeared on the draft list.[63] Hundreds of such incidents and sometimes violence that resulted in deaths occurred too often. Thirty-eight of those involved in the enrollment process were killed and more than sixty wounded.[64] Arrests ran into the thousands.

On the other hand, too many of the arrests were political, some vindictive. Since most of the provost marshals, involved in the enrollment and the draft, and U.S. marshals, enforcers of federal laws, were Republicans, they had a partisan interpretation of the word "disloyalty." David Sheean, a lawyer and onetime mayor of Galena, Illinois, was arrested in August of 1862 after he sought a writ of habeas corpus for a Democrat accused of discouraging enlistments—Republicans called the lawyer's action in seeking a writ "disloyalty."[65] Secretary of War Simon Cameron ordered the arrest of a New Jersey Democrat named James W. Wall after a Republican postmaster reported that the fellow was "a dangerous person."[66] Dr. John M. Christian, a Democratic spokesman of Marion, Ohio, and Thomas H. Hodder, editor of the county's Democratic newspaper, were arrested after dishonest Republicans fabricated a subversive society plot and bogus documents to substantiate it.[67] Brig. Gen. Henry B. Carrington, headquartered in Indianapolis as commander of the Military District of Indiana, took a force of 250 soldiers into Illinois to arrest Judge Charles H. Constable because he disagreed with the Democratic judge's judicial reasoning[68]—Falstaff could have done better. The list goes on and on as Republican-sponsored intolerance gave a slanted meaning to the word "disloyalty"—the justification for most of the political arrests.

Then there were those imprisoned after mass arrests here and there. In September of 1861, Federal authorities arrested more than fifty Marylanders, including nineteen members of the state legislature—supposedly to prevent the state's secession. After the Cincinnati race riot of July 1862 was suppressed (black freemen were chased off boats and docks and their section of town put to the torch) close to fifty arrests were made—almost all were Irish-Americans and Democrats. In Wisconsin, after the Port Washington anti-draft riot in November 1862 ended, 150 area residents were arrested—most were German-Americans and Democrats.[69] Authorities arrested several hundred after the four-day New York City anti-draft riot had run its course—most were Irish-Americans or German-Americans and Democrats.[70] The so-called "Fishingcreek Valley Conspiracy," in Columbia County, Pennsylvania, was a rather bizarre affair; the soldiers sent on the mission to seize the four cannons (supposedly smuggled from Canada), an arsenal of arms, and a hundred armed "resisters," soon recognized they were engaged in a wild goose chase. Nevertheless the troop's officers "seized" a hundred of the valley's residents to prove that the so-called conspiracy was more than a fantasy. Most of those arrested in the August 1864 farce were German-Americans and Democrats.[71] Then, in November of 1864, the commandant at Camp Douglas claimed that he arrested 150 "suspects" on Chicago streets to nip an uprising in the bud—Col. Benjamin J. Sweet's fantasy evolved into the "Camp Douglas Conspiracy."[72]

The number of civilian arrests in the North (including the border states of Missouri, Kentucky, and Maryland) can never be precisely determined. Sometimes provost marshals or U.S. marshals or army commanders "detained" an individual for an hour or a day and never reported the event to Washington. In the past, estimates of civilian arrests during the Civil War ranged from 10,000 to 38,000[73]—a guess of 15,000 would be better than most.

A considerable number of civilians who were arrested were tried by military commissions rather than in the civil courts—a clear violation of the sixth amendment that promised "a speedy and public trial by an impartial jury in the district where the [supposed] crime had been committed." Edmund J. Ellis, Democratic editor of the *(Columbia) Boone County Standard* in Missouri, was one of the first civilians to face a military commission; he was found guilty, exiled to the Confederacy, and had his printing press confiscated.[74]

The military trial of Clement V. Vallandigham received more publicity than all of those that preceded it. After arresting Vallandigham, General Burnside promptly organized a military commission and put the trial in motion—this procedure was promised in "General Orders, No. 38." The military commission, presided over by Judge Advocate Henry L. Burnett, consisted of eight of Burnside's subordinates, insuring a conviction even before the trial began. Vallandigham refused to enter a plea, insisting that he was a civilian and subject to the civil courts of Ohio. Judge Advocate Burnett ignored Vallandigham's repeated assertion that, since he was neither a soldier nor sailor, he could not be tried by a military commission. In the end, the commission found Vallandigham guilty of violating "General Orders, No. 38"—Burnside announced that the prisoner was guilty of treason—and the Democratic dissenter was sentenced to prison.[75] President Lincoln, after discussing the affair with his cabinet, changed Vallandigham's sentence to exile—presumably to be shipped south so he would be with his "friends."[76]

Another oft-discussed military trial took place in Indianapolis where Lambdin P. Milligan and several others were charged with belonging to a subversive secret society and involved in a conspiracy. As far as Milligan was concerned, the so-called conspiracy was mostly fantasy, concocted for political gain and to discredit the Democracy. The commission, in its verdict, found each of the prisoners guilty as charged—three (including Milligan) were sentenced to be "hanged by the neck until...dead" and the fourth was to be "confined at hard labor for the duration of the war."[77]

Another of the more interesting military trials took place in Cincinnati, beginning on January 11, 1865. Nine of the many arrested for involvement in the Camp Douglas conspiracy faced a military commission with Major Burnett again as Judge Advocate. Several were found guilty, but only one (an Englishman at that) was sentenced to death by the commission.[78]

The most notable of the military trials took place in Washington, D.C. early in May of 1865 and involved those charged with the assassination of President Lincoln. Here too, according to the sixth amendment, the defendants should have been tried in the civil courts. Professor Ludwell H. Johnson, a nationally known Civil War historian, once wrote a stinging indictment of that trial:

> The trial of the conspirators was an utter disgrace. Some witnesses were bullied into perjury by threats of hanging; other sold their false testimony for cash. Stanton [Secretary of War] and Holt [Judge Advocate General] first tried to hold the trial in secrecy, but word of their plan reached the press and Stanton backed down. Some members of the military commission conducted themselves so as to dishonor the uniform they wore. The commission itself, of course, lacked any jurisdiction known to either civil or military law. The blatant partisanship of Assistant Judge Advocate John Bingham, Stanton's old friend from Ohio, was shameful in a man whose official position required him to present evidence of innocence as well as guilt to protect the rights of the defendants. Witnesses were heard and testimony admitted that would have made Sir George Jeffrey blush. As for the prisoners they were (except for Mary Surratt) not only heavily ironed in court and out, but at Stanton's direction, were tormented to the point of madness by having to spend weeks in their cells blinded and deafened by heavy padded canvas bags that were tied over their heads.[79]

Friends of the prisoners could have argued that use of the heavy padded canvas bags was a barbaric practice and a violation of the eighth amendment that opposed "cruel and unusual punishments."

Not all Civil War dissenters were without sin. Some residents of southern Indiana, Illinois, and Pennsylvania left for Dixie to fight for the Confederacy—their political views may have had little to do with their decisions. Two sons of George Wallace Jones, earlier a governor of Iowa and one-time slave owner, left for Dixie to become Confederate soldiers. There were pockets of sympathy for the Confederacy in some parts of Ohio, Indiana and Illinois.

Outrageous statements were commonplace. A New Jersey resident named Daniel Cory said that he would "like to put a bullet through President Lincoln."[80] Moses Stannard, a Connecticut resident, raised "a secession flag" and expressed the wish that the Confederates would kill the president and capture Washington.[81] In York County, Pennsylvania, a couple asked a minister to baptize their baby boy "Beauregard"—after the Confederate general who won the first major battle of the Civil War.[82] John Laird, editor of a week newspaper (*Greensburg Argus)* in Pennsylvania, asked his readers to "suspend Old Abe—by the neck if necessary—to stop the accursed slaughter of our citizens."[83] John W. Kees of Circleville, Ohio, referred to abolitionists as "damned disunionists" and wanted them hung "till the flesh would rot off their bones and the winds of Heaven whistle yanky doodle through their loathsum skelitonz."[84] The editor of the *Dubuque Democratic Herald* trespassed on treasonable grounds when he wrote that Lincoln's emancipation proclamations were unconstitutional and therefore "excused" Democrats from further support of the war and that the people, "by revolution," should "hurl him [Lincoln] into the Potomac...Cabinet, Congress, and all."[85]

No one abused President Lincoln more than "Brick" Pomeroy of the *LaCrosse Democrat*—his criticisms fall into the outrageous category. Spewing invective, Pomeroy called Lincoln "a fool," "blockhead," "moron," "flatboat tyrant," "despised despot," "imbecile," "fanatic," "widow-maker," and "orphan-maker." He characterized the war as "insane action" and "a murderous crusade for cotton and niggers." During the presidential campaign of 1864, Pomeroy composed new words for the old song "When Johnny Comes Marching Home"; one stanza read:

> The widow-maker soon must cave!
> Hurrah! Hurrah!
> We'll plant him in some nigger's grave!
> Hurrah! Hurrah!
> Torn from your farm, your shop, your raft;
> Conscript! How do you like the draft?
> And we'll stop that too,
> When Little Mac takes the Helm.[86]

Worse than that, another editorial that overstepped the bounds of decency contained the following words:

He who pretending to war for, wars against the constitution of our country is a traitor and Lincoln is one of these men...And if he is elected to misgovern for another four years, we trust some bold hand will pierce his heart with dagger point for the public good.[87]

Spewing more invectives, editor Pomeroy even recommended an epitaph:

Beneath this turf the widow-maker lies,
Little in everything except in size.[88]

Pomeroy did not retreat a single inch when word of Lincoln's assassination reached LaCrosse, a small city in the Wisconsin backwoods. Dipping his pen in gall, Pomeroy wrote, "God generously permitted an agent to make a martyr of the president." And again, "...we feel to thank God for calling Lincoln home, wherever that may be."[89] Pomeroy's irreverence and invective did not bring about his arrest. In theory, freedom of the press existed in LaCrosse during the Civil War.[90]

Many Democratic dissenters believed that it was more essential for the president to abide strictly by the guarantees included in the Bill of Rights during a war than in times of peace. Therefore, they were concerned when it was reported that, early in the war and in conversation with the British ambassador (Lord Lyon), Secretary of State William H. Seward had said, "My lord, I can touch a bell on my right hand, and order the arrest of a citizen of Ohio; I can touch a bell again and order the imprisonment of a citizen of New York; and no power on earth except the President, can release them. Can the queen of England do so much?"[91] Democratic dissenters were also shocked by a statement attributed to U.S. Senator Benjamin F. Wade (Ohio) who chaired the powerful Joint Committee on the Conduct of the War: "He who quotes the Constitution in this crisis is a traitor." And, of course, they were concerned when President Lincoln, time and again, invoked the doctrine of necessity.

In their editorials, such confirmed Democrats as Mahoney of the *Dubuque Herald*, Samuel Medary of *The Crisis,* and James J. Faran of the *Cincinnati Enquirer* pointed out that civil wars in Europe had ended in dictatorships—Oliver Cromwell became an army-supported dictator after the Great Civil War in England while Napoleon Bonaparte was the end product of the French Revolution. Therefore, civil rights must be defended more vigilantly and valiantly in times of war than in times of peace—lest a despotism might evolve out of the American Civil War. "We are embarking upon a course," editor Faran wrote early in 1863, "that will certainly produce some Cromwell or Napoleon who will crush beneath his iron heel the democratic legacy we have so long enjoyed."[92]

But Lincoln had no desire to be a Cromwell or a Napoleon. He was more concerned with his responsibility than with power and glory. His job, as he saw it was to save the Union—"the last best hope on earth." The country's welfare, with reunion as his chief guideline, took precedence over his personal ambition and wishes. Elections took place as scheduled, and Lincoln was willing to step aside gracefully if the electorate chose another in the presidential election of November 1864.[93] He spoke of "government of the people, by the people, for the people" at Gettysburg—it must continue even if he felt it necessary to overstep constitutional boundaries occasionally.

What Lincoln did was important. What he did not do also had a bearing on the issues of the hour. He did not reprimand soldiers, whether in uniform or home on furlough, who destroyed Democratic printing presses—as commander in chief he should have been concerned. He did not reprimand federal marshals who made unnecessary and partisan political arrests. He let military commissions try civilians in areas where the civil courts were open and functioning. He seemed to treat the Bill of Rights in a rather "cavalier" fashion.

In a postwar U.S. Supreme Court case, *Ex Parte Milligan* (1866), the Lincoln administration received a reprimand for its transgressions. Justice David Davis, a Lincoln appointee, wrote the decision for the court. Two pertinent sentences said: "The constitution of the United States is a law for rulers and people, equally in war and peace, and covers with its shield of protection all classes of men, at all times and under all circumstances. No doctrine involving more pernicious consequences was ever invented by the wit of men that any of its great provisions can be suspended during any of the great exigencies of Government."[94]

Democrats who had been dissenters during the war years shouted "Amen!" Vallandigham believed that he and other Democratic critics of the Lincoln administration had helped to save the democratic system—prevented more abuses and kept a spotlight upon the Bill of Rights. Historian Mark E. Neely seems to see the Democratic dissenters in the same way: "The opportunistic protests played a role crucial to a democratic country involved in war....The Democratic party was a loyal opposition. If their rhetoric was calculated to goad Republicans, it also played a legitimate role in preserving civil rights."[95]

Background of Dissent

The three chapters comprising "Part Two" emphasize the socioeconomic base of middle western Copperheadism. Pocketbook issues were one aspect of dissent in the Upper Midwest and provide an interesting angle of it. Economic causation underwrote dissent during the first two years of the war and then lost its importance as war prosperity became a force and a factor during the last two years of the war.

Chapter IV, in an abbreviated form, was first presented as a paper at the joint session of the Mississippi Valley Historical Association and the Economic History Association at Oklahoma City on April 21,1950. It evidently sparked some interest because members of the audience asked one question after another. Sometime, later, Professor William B. Hesseltine (my graduate work mentor at the University of Wisconsin) told me that the paper was "the most discussed" in the halls and lobbies during the rest of the convention. Enlarged and reworked, it was published in the March 1952 issue of the *Mississippi Valley Historical Review*.

Using the same sources, and adding some new ones, a second paper centered around Western sectionalism as an aspect of Civil War dissent. It trespassed over some of the same ground as the Copperhead-Granger article but added some new angles. The paper, submitted to the editor of *The Historian: A Journal of History*, was published in the Autumn 1991 issue. It was later republished as one of the articles/topics in James A. Rawley's *Lincoln and Civil War Politics* (1969)—a popular book of readings.

Belatedly, my attention was called to an article co-authored by William G. Shade and Ronald P. Formisano, entitled "The Concept of Agrarian Radicalism," and published in the January 1970 issue of *Mid-America: A Historical Review*. Believing that I had been misrepresented, I wrote an article entitled "Copperheadism, Grangerism, and Quarrelsome Historians: A Rebuttal" and sent it to the editor of *Mid-America* with the following cover letter:

February 12, 1971

Managing Editor, *Mid-America*
Loyola University
6525 Sheridan Road
Chicago, IL 60626

Dear Editor:

The January, 1970 issue of *Mid-America*—this in Father Jacobsen's day—carried an article (by Messrs. Formisano and Shade), "The Concept of Agrarian Radicalism," which criticized my scholarship, misrepresented some of my contentions, and challenged my thesis that there was a connection between Mid-western Copperheadism and postwar Grangerism. It is a tradition that those who are attacked be given a chance to reply. Enclosed find a manuscript/article entitled "Copperheadism, Grangerism and Quarrelsome Historians: A Rebuttal."

Messrs. Formisano and Shade did not send me a reprint of their article (which it seems to me would have been the gentlemanly thing to do), and it was not until last July that I came across their handiwork while spending a day reading articles and book reviews in various historical quarterlies in the periodical section of our University library. I could not write a rebuttal then because I was busy with the index of my recent book *(The Limits of Dissent)* and with commitments to two editors. Recently and belatedly, I have prepared the enclosed rebuttal.

Since I believe that Messrs. Formisano and Shade misrepresented some of my contentions and were guilty of distortion as well as sins of commission and omission, you will admit, I hope, that I am entitled to a hearing. I also hope that I have kept our historiographical debate on a scholarly, gentlemanly, and non-personal plane.

The very fact that I have written a rebuttal to an argumentative article makes me a "quarrelsome" historian. The tone of their argumentation puts them in the same category—witness this sarcastic sentence on page 23 (of their article): "Thirty-three depressed Copperhead farmers would do wonders, no doubt, for the idea of agrarian radicalism." But I have no intention of letting our historiographical dispute degenerate to the level of the infamous Shannon-Craven debate. If historical disputation is good for the soul, I also hope it helps your journal.

Sincerely yours,

Frank L. Klement
Professor of History

Two months later I received a card, dated 4\13\71 and signed "Mgr Editor, MID-AMERICA" which read: "This is to inform you that we have your article, but no decision has been reached." Then, nine months later, acting editor John V. Mentag, S.J. wrote a letter as follows:

January 4, 1972

Dr. Frank L. Klement
Department of History
Marquette University

Dear Professor Klement:

Would that you had acted on your rebuttal before Father Jacobsen's death in August 1970, and would that definite decisions had been reached promptly as to the editorship of *Mid-America*. The latter situation is still unresolved and it look likes it will be some time before there is a resolution.

As a mere *locum tenens* acting editor I am unwilling to depart from a middle position in all things relative to the magazine. Consequently, after tardy consideration, I am returning your article.

Sincerely,

John V. Mentag, S.J.

Holding the belief that simple justice called for a chance to defend myself and state my case, I sent the manuscript back to the editor of *Mid-America* along with the following letter:

February 23, 1972

Rev. John V. Mentag, S. J., Acting Editor
Mid-America
Loyola University
6525 Sheridan Road
Chicago, IL 60626

Dear Father Mentag:

May I ask you to review my rebuttal/article and reconsider publication in *Mid-America*?

In the first place, a tradition exists in historical circles that one whose contentions have been attacked and/or criticized in a historical journal be given the privilege and/or courtesy of replying in print—and in the same journal. The same audience which read the Shade-Formisano article should have the opportunity to read the rebuttal. You will admit, I hope, that my rebuttal is neither personal nor vindictive and is in the scholarly tradition. And might I suggest a slight change in the title to make it less objectionable? How about "Copperheadism, Grangerism and Conflicting Contentions: A Rebuttal"?

In the second place, I base my request for reconsideration upon the principle of justice and fair play. At times the Shade-Formisano article misrepresented what I had earlier written in historical articles as well as in my Copperhead book. They not only criticized some contentions but also impugned my scholarship. How in the name of justice and fair play can you deny me the chance to reply? To use the excuse that the Shade-Formisano article was accepted by Father Jacobsen and that my blood is upon his hands seems like a technical evasion. You, as acting editor of *Mid-America* now have the responsibility to redress the balance. After all, I have asked for nothing more than justice and fair play—a chance to defend myself and my scholarship. I am sure that Father Jacobsen, were he alive today, would have given my the chance to reply and I hope you, too, want to see justice served.

Please review the enclosed rebuttal and reconsider the opinion you expressed in your letter of January 4.

Sincerely and respectfully,

Frank L. Klement
Professor of History

The acting editor of *Mid-America* did not respond to my letter. Nor did he return my manuscript. Evidently, he considered the case closed and, I suppose, that he practiced an editor's prerogatives.

Chapter V of this book gives me a chance to publish my rebuttal— somewhat belatedly. But readers should also know the contentions of Messrs. Shade and Formisano, so their article is included as the first half of the chapter. Now readers will have a chance to read and evaluate both of the controversial articles. They will also have an opportunity to see whether or not I answered their suppositions effectively—without sarcasm or arrogance. Readers of my letters will also have a chance to judge whether my requests were reasonable or whether I overstepped the bounds of propriety.

I really would like to have had a chance to revise and rewrite my rebuttal, for I see more chinks in Messrs. Shade and Formisano's armor now than I saw twenty-five years ago. But that would not be cricket. Today I would chide them for ignoring my Copperhead-Granger link in the Democratic-dominated Illinois State Legislature of 1863. A vote on a bill to set up a state railroad commission was derailed by Governor Richard Yates when he prorogued the legislature *on a technicality*. But there were Grangerlike arguments aplenty in that controversial legislature! Anyone who writes a history of Grangerism has to give midwestern Copperheadism, as expressed in the constitutional convention of 1862 and the Copperhead-controlled Illinois state legislature of 1863, its day in court.

Chapter III

Economic Aspects of Middle Western Copperheadism*

The barometer of popular opinion gauges Civil War Copperheadism as cloudy, foul, and pro-Southern. Historians have encouraged such a rating by reciting and exploiting the views of the fanatical fringe, by apotheosizing the Civil War heroes, and by ignoring the forces which underwrote discontent. By disregarding the environment which produces a corps of critics and by slighting causation, writers have tended to look upon Copperheadism from a legalistic and nationalistic point of view. But these midwestern malcontents did not operate in a vacuum! They represented widespread western views and championed western needs. Economic factors, in part, prompted their prolonged protests. The severing of west-south ties of trade, the excessive freight rates levied upon western produce shipped eastward, the economic program of the Northeast, the nationalization of business, and the centralization of government induced them to resurrect Jeffersonian principles to protect their section and its economy. They became western sectionalists because they opposed the increasing power of northeastern industrialism, which in seeking its goals threatened the balance of power the West had held politically and the sectional prosperity they had enjoyed economically.[1]

Sectional loyalty characterized most of the midwestern Copperheads. Clement L. Vallandigham's speech in the House of Representatives entitled "There Is a West" and his contention that he was "as good a Western fire-eater as the hottest salamander in this House" expressed his loyalty to

---

*Reprinted (with permission) from *The Historian*, 14 (Autumn 1951): 27–44.

his section.[2] That same western sectionalism was evident in the fears of those who claimed that the Northeast desired "to subordinate the agriculture of the West to her manufacturing interests."[3] The language of Samuel S. Cox and Sam Medary of Ohio, Orlando B. Ficklin and Samuel Buckmaster of Illinois, Daniel Voorhees and Thomas J. Hendricks of Indiana, Abner Pratt and William E. Morrison of Michigan, and Edward G. Ryan and Frederic W. Horn of Wisconsin was constantly sectional in tone—pro-western rather than pro-Southern.

Secession on the one hand and war on the other threatened the sectional balance, so those westerners subsequently stigmatized as Copperheads opposed both and advocated compromise in the dreary and disquieting days preceding the surrender of Sumter. The *Cincinnati Enquirer* recited statistics to show the economic interdependence of the Northwest and the South.[4] Medary's editorials in *The Crisis* goaded his readers to support compromise measures.[5] Cyrus H. McCormick regarded the Southern market, and his credits therein, important enough to warrant the purchase of the *Chicago Times* and to conduct a vigorous campaign in behalf of compromise.[6] Vallandigham even submitted a proposal which would allow a vote by sections in the Senate of the United States;[7] thus, the cotton South and the agricultural Northwest could protect their economic interests.

When compromise efforts failed, the same shots which brought about the surrender of Sumter and precipitated the nation into a civil war released an economic depression that ravaged the Northwest and undermined the patriotism evidenced by unfurled flags, marching feet, and emotional oratory. This business plague caused thousands to turn the keys in their office doors during the remaining months of 1861 and file petitions of bankruptcy.[8] That economic panic was a Hydra-headed monster, for the river trade collapsed, bank notes based upon Southern bonds depreciated in value, factory owners lost their Southern markets, and farm prices spiralled downward. The professional classes endured hard times, and the laboring men experienced unemployment.

The commercial interests dependent upon western-Southern trade suffered as civil conflict severed trade lines. Although the railroad trunk lines extending eastward and the Great Lakes' ports were turning the West from the South, the river trade of 1860 had set an all-time record both as to value and volume.[9] Hundreds of steamboats and thousands of merchants had participated in the river trade, sending large consignments of wheat, whiskey, corn, flour, bacon, poultry, hogs, horses, and merchandise down the river and receiving sugar, molasses, cotton, rice, and tobacco in exchange.[10]

Cincinnati, self-styled "Queen City" and the West's prize river port, entered upon a period of business retrenchment, for the coming of the war brought ruin to many wholesale merchants, shipbuilders, and steamboat owners as well as unemployment to a host of laborers. "Trade and business everywhere are almost at a standstill," reported an observer in May 1861. "Hundreds of merchants are weekly closing their business....and debts are scarcely thought of being paid."[11] The Cincinnati Chamber of Commerce blamed the city's economic plight upon the embargo which ended trade with the South.[12] The editorial columns of the *Enquirer* voiced dissatisfaction with the Lincoln administration and blamed the Republican party for the troubled times. One of the *Enquirer*'s owners, Washington McLean, owned several boiler-plate factories, giving him a special interest in the river trade.

Evansville occupied the position in Indiana that Cincinnati did in Ohio. It was the heart of "The Pocket," and the rivers were its arteries of trade. Lawrenceville, Aurora, Vevay, Madison, New Albany, and Cannelton experienced business distress and saw their mercantile interests prostrate. Cannelton's lucrative stone trade, financed by Louisville capital, prompted a New Year's eve resolution at the end of 1860, that Cannelton be included in the neighboring nation if an international boundary had to be drawn.[13]

Cairo traders, dreaming of making their city America's greatest river port, had seen twelve hundred tons of produce move southward daily late in 1860 and early in 1861.[14] War dealt a death blow to Cairo's roseate dreams and an economic nightmare replaced it. John A. Logan, blusterous and boisterous, spoke the mind of "Egypt" when he denounced Douglas for supporting the war: "You have sold out the Democrat party, but *by God,* you can't deliver it!"[15] The reduction in Cairo's commerce stunned the Illinois Central Railroad, which suffered a financial crisis.[16] Other Illinois rail lines also encountered hardship in the first half of 1861. The Burlington & Missouri Railroad, for example, had its receipts cut in half.[17] Even the Chicago commercial houses felt the effects of the opening of the war. The editor of the *Chicago Tribune* had earlier written: "In the Union we have our commercial wings stretched North and South, and sail with both...."[18]

The Ohio-Mississippi network funnelled southward many products of various manufactories of the Northwest, and the closing of the trade routes brought hardships and encouraged complaints. Cincinnati, for example, possessed at least nineteen different industries, each of which produced well over a million dollars' worth of goods annually; a considerable portion of the products depended upon a Southern market—eighty-five percent of the furniture, seventy-seven percent of the ale and beer, and sixty-three percent of the whiskey went down the river.[19] McLean, Democratic boss of Hamilton county and political patron of Vallandigham, shipped forty percent of his boiler plate to Southern purchasers. He resented the competition provided by Pennsylvania ironworks and bemoaned the collapse of his boiler-plate business. Early in the war McLean joined the antiadministration forces and helped to transform the *Enquirer* into one of the most critical and carping Copperhead sheets. The *Enquirer* repeatedly spoke in terms of western interests and advantage as it tied its own prosperity to that of Cincinnati and Cincinnati's to that of the West.[20]

The McCormicks had a lucrative market for their reapers in Virginia and other Southern states. War measures induced the eldest brother to write: "...our losses South will probably be heavy."[21] Quincy-packed pork usually moved down the Mississippi, and even the Chicago packers sent large quantities of meat southward.[22] Illinois distillers, who owned forty-two plants which produced 15,165,760 gallons of distilled spirits in 1860, were hard hit when the down-river trade dwindled. Dissatisfied distillers provided much of the opposition to the Lincoln administration in Belleview, Quincy, Chicago, Pekin, and Peoria.[23]

The collapse of the state banking systems of the Northwest aggravated the economic situation and added fuel to the fires of discontent. Bonds of Southern states constituted three-fourths (viz., $9,527,500) of the securities upon which Illinois paper money was based. Secession and war caused the Southern bonds to slide downward and, subsequently, to invalidate the state bank note issues. By November 1861 only seventeen solvent banks remained in the "Sucker State," whereas 112 had been functioning a year earlier. The currency circulation registered an even sharper decline, from $12,000,000 to $400,000.[24]

Wisconsin banks had relied heavily upon "Missouri Sixes," "North Carolina Sixes," and the state bonds of Louisiana, Virginia, and Tennessee to validate the $4,580,632 worth of state bank notes in circulation in 1860. By July 1, 1861, thirty-eight Wisconsin banks had declared bankruptcy, and a score more tottered on the rim of ruin as Southern bonds depreciated. Financial hocus-pocus, which substituted Wisconsin state bonds for the worthless Southern securities, saved the banks further embarrassment, although this action later received the condemnation of a legislative committee.[25] The banking institutions of other midwestern states also experienced a crisis.

These bank failures placed a heavy burden upon the struggling economy of the Northwest. There was a shortage of currency to handle the fall harvests. In addition, much of the direct loss was borne by farmers who held the stock of the defunct banks or who had the depreciating currency passed on to them.[26] A July 1861 entry in one Illinois farmer's diary told the story: "July 20, 1861—Sold some broken bank money at 35 cents to the $."[27] Workingmen, too, were victims of questionable practices, on occasion being paid in notes of which banks had cleaned their vaults.[28] A bank riot in Milwaukee and public protests in Watertown and Janesville weakened popular support of the Republican state and national administrations.[29]

These readjustments in financial, industrial, and commercial circles drove farm prices downward. In most agricultural sectors corn commanded only ten cents per bushel, and it reportedly sold for as low as seven cents a bushel in western Ohio and six cents in one section of Illinois.[30] Wheat brought less than twenty cents a bushel in many markets. Flour could be bought throughout the West for two or three dollars a barrel. No demand existed for butter or potatoes, while the Chicago quotations on hogs were cut in half in 1861. Some farmers burned their wheat for fuel rather than dispose of it at ruinous prices.[31] The wave of discontent which swept the Northwest in 1862 was rooted in the farmers' economic problems—arrival of interest-paying days, mortgage installments, unwanted agricultural surpluses, and empty pocketbooks.

The European demand for American foodstuffs failed to benefit the midwestern farmer. The closing of the southward trade routes made the Midwest solely dependent upon the east-west lines of transportation. The Great Lakes-Erie Canal waterways and the railroads leading eastward, many westerners felt, "skinned the West alive."[32] Railroad freight rates were more than doubled during 1861, and the tonnage rates assessed by the carriers on the Great Lakes rose in like manner. Corn commanded a price nearly sixty percent higher in New York than in Cincinnati. Not only had Illinois farmers lost fifty million dollars in 1861 because of reduced wheat prices, but they paid an additional thirty million in increased freight rates for the year.[33] Farmers' views were aptly expressed by the editor of the *Wisconsin Farmer:*

> The farmers work like heroes to produce their great crops of wheat, and then practically give to shipowners and transportation companies...all the profits of their toil.[34]

High freight rates helped to spread dissatisfaction throughout the West, gave strength and force to the Copperhead movement, and sowed the seeds of Grangerism, which blossomed into full flower in the 1870s. Gen. John A. McClernand, who toured the West in late 1862 as Lincoln's emissary and election analyst, blamed the political revolt of 1862 upon high freight rates.[35] William H. Osborn, the inquisitive and energetic president of the Illinois Central, who submerged his political views to business activity, recognized that Copperheadism combined sectionalism and economic exigency. He pointed out that in the "two years of war and distress" farmers paid "thirty-five to fifty cents per bushel to get their grain to market," so they had just cause to be malcontents. He added:

> The West won't stand the Albany and Buffalo monopoly much longer. A score of canal boat-men combine to get a higher price per bushel for ten days transportation than a farmer gets for toiling and sweating all through the summer months. He plows—they reap. He sows—they gather the harvest. The pressure is getting strong....A word to the wicked is sufficient.[36]

Prominent critics of the Lincoln administration—termed "Copperheads," by the Republican party press—continued their Grangerlike protests. Vallandigham, whose extremism was ultimately to cause his destruction, claimed that his section paid tribute to the Northeast:

Cut off as we are from all other means of outle...and with our railroads leading to the East, for the most part in the hands of Eastern directors or bondholders, the tariff of freights has at the same time been doubled, thus increasing the burden upon our trade both ways, so largely as to amount in a little while longer to absolute prohibition.[37]

Other complaints against the railroads were added to the list. Westerners charged that the elevators at the Great Lakes' ports were railroad-owned and railroad-operated and that a gigantic monopoly threatened the farmers' life. They claimed that rail rates were discriminatory in that they varied from section to section, favoring some and penalizing others. They resented the promotional practices which unloaded large blocks of railroad stocks and bonds upon local governmental units. They protested against railroad lobbying tactics, which were both sundry and devious. They censured pooling and stock-watering, for both tended to bring about higher rates. Prominent Copperheads, especially in Illinois, occupied the leading role in attacking questionable railroad practices.[38]

Republican-sponsored tariff acts were still another source of grievance to the midwestern farmer. Household needs as well as durable consumer goods climbed in price, while farm prices plunged downward. To farmers, it did not seem fair to exchange four bushels of corn for a pound of coffee. Vallandigham argued earnestly that the masses, the consumers and farmers, were penalized by protective tariffs; he contended that protection, as a tax, fell heaviest upon those least able to bear it.[39] The *Cincinnati Enquirer* labelled the Northeast's tariff policy as "extremely selfish and injurious to the interests of the North-West."[40] Stephen D. Carpenter, Wisconsin Copperhead, claimed that the high tariff was "as much a curse to the Great West as the South" and called it "a monster tax" levied "on the Mississippi Valley for the benefit of a few Eastern lords."[41] Frederic W. Horn, Carpenter's colleague in party and politics and three-time speaker of the state senate, resigned his captaincy in the militia rather than fight in a war which, he felt, would assure the sectional domination of New England; so he announced his opposition to a continuation of a Union in which the Middle West was "plundered" for the benefit of "Pennsylvania Iron mongers and New England manufacturers."[42] Other prominent opponents of the Lincoln administration spoke the same language. The editor of the *Milwaukee See-Bote* headlined a long editorial "The Irrepressible Conflict between East and West" and interpreted Copperheadism as a clash of the industrial Northeast and the agricultural Northwest.[43] Medary added his rasping voice to the antitariff chorus.[44] S.S. Cox of Ohio anathematized the tariff as "a great fiscal tyranny" by which the West paid a subsidy to "the iron-masters of Pennsylvania and the cotton millionaires of New England." Another congressman, speaking for Illinois farmers and emphasizing the sectional aspect of tariff legislation, noted,

> Every time we have a nail driven into a horse-shoe, we are taxed; every time we use a wire to ring the snout of a swine, we are taxed; and every time we use a cup of tea we are taxed....[45]

One dejected farmer referred to the tariff as "that ass' jawbone by which the Yankee manufacturers have slain their millions of Western agriculturists."[46] In fact, criticism of the tariff and claims of sectional loyalty were characteristic of Copperhead spokesmen and the antiadministration press. western realism was exemplified by the prominent Indianapolis merchant who studied one of the wartime tariff proposals and added, "If that tax is levied, it will make me disloyal."[47]

The institution of heavy excise duties upon distilled spirits[48] and malt liquors brought protests from distillers and farmers alike. Vallandigham and his cohorts viewed the excise tax as a blow against the West and as a war upon democratic doctrines. Many small distillers realized that, in practice, the internal revenue program discriminated against then, and they consequently closed their plants. Farmers who had disposed of their surplus grain at the distilleries complained bitterly as they were forced to find other markets for their grain.

The National Bank Act of 1863 aroused some anxiety in the West, but patriotic preachments, wartime confusion, and an antipathy to wildcat banking paved the way for governmental sanction of the principles of Whiggery. Sam Medary, fired by loyalty to section and to Jacksonian concepts, levied a heavy editorial barrage against the "monstrous Bank Bill" and spoke the language of the Southern fire-eaters: "The West will not bleed at every pore because well-preserved and fanatical New England declares that such is her patriotic duty."[49] The *Enquirer*'s editor raised the specter of monopoly:

> The enormity of this bill is sufficient to make General Jackson, who killed the old Bank of the United States, turn over in his coffin....The design is to destroy the fixed institutions of the States, and build up a central moneyed despotism.[50]

In the House of Representatives, Vallandigham and Voorhees restated the arguments against monopoly and centralization of power in the best Jacksonian and Jeffersonian tradition.[51] Two other midwestern Copperheads, James C. Allen and William A. Richardson, both of Illinois, led the forces that secured postponement of the taxing of the state bank notes and the granting of the "money monopoly" to the nationally chartered banks.[52]

Those who railed at the "railroad monopoly" usually raised their voices against the "money monopoly." Frederic W. Horn, ofttimes unfairly blamed for the Wisconsin draft riots of 1862, feared "the power and influence of New England capital."[53] Marcus M. Pomeroy, a *La Crosse Democrat* editor who developed criticism of Lincoln into an art and whose dictionary of diatribe was unabridged, believed that the war and its monetary measures made the trans-Allegheny West both "slave and servant of New England."[54] The *See-Bote*'s editor, too, contended that "the money monopoly of New England is absolutely controlling and the labor of...the Western states is tributary to it."[55] Another malcontent stated his unequivocal opposition to all banks, and criticized Hamiltonian doctrine by contending that "the doctrine of vested rights is a great humbug...."[56]

Labor, too, wore its crown of thorns. The business depression which plagued the West early in the war brought mass unemployment and labor unrest. The unemployed paraded the streets of Milwaukee, and other Midwestern cities witnessed similar scenes. A touring *Times* (London) correspondent observed that labor paid a heavy price in the war—that it was "ground down to the utmost extent of its power of endurance."[57] Although opportunities for employment increased after the first year of the war, because of the withdrawal of workers into army uniforms and the demands for war supplies, the influx of freed Negroes and border-state white refugees tended to give employers tighter control of the labor market.[58]

The greatest resentment against emancipation came from the ranks of unskilled labor. The *Times'* (London) correspondent observed,

> The jealousy of the low Germans and Irish against the free negro was sufficient to set them against the war which would have brought four million of their black rivals into competition for that hard and dirty work which American freedom bestowed on them.[59]

The *See-Bote* warned Milwaukee Germans against abolition. It headlined an editorial "Abolition the Worst Enemy of the Free White Laborer," warning its readers that employers desired abolition in order to secure "cheap labor" as it issued a call to action: "Workmen! Be Careful! Organize yourselves against this element which threatens your impoverishment and annihilation."[60] *The Crisis*, the *Chicago Times*, and the *Cincinnati Enquirer*, as leading Copperhead papers in the Midwest, repeated the same theme.[61] Efforts of some Chicago meat-packers to employ "contraband labor" forced Irish and German workers to protest. At a public meeting they adopted the resolution that

> ...the packing-house men of the town of South Chicago, pledge ourselves not to work for any packer, under any consideration, who will, in any manner, bring negro labor into competition with our labor.[62]

A score of midwestern cities suffered riots. The departure of a Cincinnati steamer, manned by an all-Negro crew, lit the fires of revolt; Cincinnati Irish attacked the Negro quarters with torches and guns.[63] Chicago's Bridgeport Irish, the city's "unwashed Dimmycrats," staged the "Omnibus Riot" and the "Lumberdock Riot"—a tragedy in two acts. Toledo, Milwaukee, Rock Island, and Quincy workmen, among others, strongly protested the influx of cheap and competitive labor.

Laborers had other complaints, too. The $300 exemption clause in the Conscription Act of 1863 appeared to be class legislation.[64] Wages, until late in the war, lagged far behind prices, which moved upward as the government sponsored inflation through the issuance of greenbacks.[65] In spite of Republican party propaganda, the tariff policy of the administration levied a heavy burden upon the millions of workers employed in the non-protected industries. The Contract Labor law, which permitted employers to bring in foreign workers by the boatload, encouraged laborers to strike and to organize. These dissatisfied workmen readily justified their opposition to the Lincoln administration and their presence in Copperhead ranks.

The protest of lamenting laborers and disgruntled agrarians underwrote midwestern Copperheadism. The malcontents, naturally, blamed the administration for many of their ills. They expressed their dissent in a variety of ways, sometimes engaging in negative measures and at times proposing positive programs. Some agitated for compromise and peace conventions, "for union without victory"; they believed that a patched-up peace would restore their western political balance of power, regain their economic ties with the South, and dissipate the domination of the Northeast. The West wanted the Mississippi opened and its markets restored.[66] Others bid for an outlet to the sea via Canada and for direct trade with Liverpool and London. The Illinois "Copperhead Legislature of 1863" supported such a measure to free westerners from the choking grasp in which east-west trade operators held them.[67] Most of them hid behind the facade of state rights to protect their democratic faith, their individual rights, their sectional wants, and their economic life; so they held the conscription act with its provost marshal system to be unconstitutional, the suspension of the writ of habeas corpus as a move toward tyranny, the muzzling of the press as dangerous to life and liberty, and revitalized Whiggery as heresy from Jeffersonian doctrine. Many resorted to verbal and written protests and petitions. All turned toward the polls as the medium to redress their grievances. The political revolt of 1862 subsequently rocked the Republican administration. In the legislatures of 1863 in Illinois and Indiana, the malcontents tried to restore politics with mudsill machinations. Their political blunders were a boomerang, and Governors Yates and Morton capitalized upon Copperhead errors of judgment and action. In the Illinois State Constitutional Convention of 1862 the Copperheads spoke a Grangerlike language and formulated antirailroad provisions, but the tail of treason dragged their constitutional kite into the ditch of defeat.

War prosperity, encouraged by administration measures, entered the western scene midway in the war, and rising prices pleased the agrarians as falling prices had earlier displeased them. The judicious distribution of war contracts changed some dissenters into defenders. Draft bounties tempted some of the poor laborers and drew them from their unhappy surroundings. Vallandigham, abstaining from tact and illogical in tactics, gained notoriety and stigmatized Copperheadism. Administration counter-measures and Republican party stratagems, combined with victory at Vicksburg, also helped mold men's minds. But it was war prosperity which contributed most to undermining this Jeffersonian protest against the progress of the Industrial

Revolution and its envelopment of the government. A Cincinnati editor viewed war prosperity as "the lance of Achilles, heading by its touch the wounds" of death and devastation,[68] and the touring correspondent of the *Times* (London) added that prosperity covered a multitude of sins.[69] Consequently, Copperheadism collapsed and died a slow death.

Southern sectionalism had resulted in secession and had threatened the Northwest with "geographic isolation." The political and economic advance of the Northeast, on the other hand, had threatened the power of the western sectionalists, who hid behind the tenets set forth by John Taylor of Caroline. The defeat of the South dealt a deathblow to the doctrine of secession and quashed the Jeffersonian protests of the West. Sherman's capture of Atlanta gave the lie to Copperhead charges that the war was a failure. Grant's victory at Appomattox successfully silenced those who had chanted the old refrain "The Constitution as it is and the Union as it was." So, in the end, both the South and the West failed to stem the tide of the Industrial Revolution in America. And the new nation, maintained as one by war, prepared to enter a new era.

CHAPTER IV

Middle Western Copperheadism and the Genesis of the Granger Movement*

Nationalism as a force and apotheosis as a process have tempted writers to laud Abraham Lincoln and to denounce his enemies.[1] Lincoln cultists and nationalist historians have wielded a weighty whip when chastising Copperheads, who were midwestern malcontents and opponents of the Lincoln administration. Investigators of the Copperhead theme have busied themselves in unearthing Copperhead quotations from newspapers, letters, and speeches and hanging them upon the line of treason. They have denounced these administration critics as traitors pure and simple—in effect, as men whose hearts were black, whose blood was yellow, and whose minds were warped.

Cause and effect as a principle of history has seldom been applied to the Copperhead theme. Northern critics of administration policy have been removed from their setting to be pilloried publicly. But Clement L. Vallandigham's views were not bolts out of the blue. He truly represented the majority views of his district. Nor was it an accident that Edward G. Ryan of Wisconsin headed the Copperhead clan of his state during the Civil War—the same Ryan who wrote the Jacksonian antibank clause into the proposed state constitution of 1846 and who, as chief justice of the Wisconsin Supreme Court, rendered in 1874 the greatest of the state decisions against the railroads.[2] Samuel Medary believed that his editorials in *The (Columbus) Crisis* preached the same Jeffersonian and Jacksonian

*Reprinted (with permission) from the *Mississippi Valley Historical Review*, 38 (March 1952): 679–94.

doctrines as his paper's earlier motto: "Unawed by the influence of the rich, the great, or the noble, the people must be heard and their rights protected." In fact, a good case could be prepared to prove that consistency created Copperheads and that midwestern Copperheadism linked Jacksonian Democracy and Grangerism. Times changed, but the views of the Copperheads did not. They were malcontents because they protested against the dwindling influence of agriculture, the nationalization of business, and the centralization of the federal government.

Midwestern Copperheadism was compounded out of a half dozen complex ingredients. At times Democratic partisans flavored it with political opportunism and sordid party tactics. At times religious hopes and fears served as a condiment, for a tinge of Know-Nothingism colored the Republican party and drove Irish and German Catholics into the ranks of the opposition.[3] The Wisconsin draft riots of 1862 were caused, in part, by the anti-Catholic policy followed in the naming of chaplains.[4] Frederic W. Horn's predictions that New England Puritanism would "war upon certain religious denominations" and that the region would try to establish its "sectional church" as a "national one" were based upon religious fears.[5]

Copperheadism in the Middle West also possessed social aspects. The designation "Butternut," used interchangeably with the term "Copperhead," suggested its rural and democratic basis. It was, in the main, a small farmer movement—for the Copperhead country was characterized by small homesteads, poor soils, and widespread illiteracy.[6] David Ross Locke, through his fictitious character Petroleum V. Nasby, ridiculed a social class and his economic inferiors as well as an opposition political party.

The ingredient usually referred to as "humanitarian sentiment" left occasional evidence of its presence. Mothers whose love of sons exceeded devotion to country, and those who feared the effects of conscription, endorsed the antiadministration arguments. Medary's Quaker heritage encouraged his propeace pleading. Marcus M. Pomeroy, a small-city editor who had given the war qualified support, visited the Arkansas sector in 1863 and returned to LaCrosse to become an ardent peace advocate and a vociferous Lincoln critic because rotting coffins, ravenous buzzards, and "cotton crusades" were an integral part of the war.[7]

Western sectionalism—so much a part and parcel of Grangerism[8]—was another ingredient out of which midwestern Copperheadism was compounded. Westerners, generally, sought to promote their own and their section's well-being. They were as section conscious as were the Southern planters or the New England Yankees. They were desirous of promoting their section's economic welfare, political aspirations, and cultural development. Vallandigham openly averred, "I became and am a Western sectionalist,"[9] and he restated that contention more expressively upon the floor of the House of Representatives: "I am as good a western fire-eater as the hottest salamander in this House."[10] The same sectional sentiments were repeated in all parts of the Midwest. A prewar *Chicago Times* editorial warned easterners: "The great Northwest will not submit to be a vassal to New England."[11] Samuel S. Cox repeatedly expressed his distrust of Puritan culture, the Puritan character, and New England industrialism.[12] His tactless colleague Vallandigham also resented the fact that New York and New England regarded "the western man...to be a sort of outside barbarian," and he stated that he was "inexorably hostile to Puritan domination in religion or morals or literature or politics."[13] Horn, the prominent Wisconsin Democrat whose name was closely tied to the state draft riots, understood the economic conflict which existed between western farmers and eastern industrialists; he early decried the "plundering of the Midwest" for the benefit of "Pennsylvania's Iron Mongers and New England manufacturers."[14] The editorial columns of *The Crisis* constantly voiced these sectional views. The *Milwaukee See-Bote*'s editor condemned the industrial and "codfish aristocracy," and often threw sharp editorial darts at New England.[15] The *Cincinnati Enquirer*, one of the principal Copperhead sheets, repeatedly spoke in terms of western advantages and interests.[16] Daniel W. Voorhees, capable Indiana Copperhead, often exploited the same sectional theme. So did Orlando B. Ficklin, later a prominent Illinois Granger, but he expressed himself more vividly; he was thankful "that God made the world before He made the Yankees, for they would have interfered with His business and destroyed the beautiful world in which we live."[17] Illinois Copperheads, acting in concert in the legislature, accused the Republican governor of pandering to New England capitalists.[18]

More than one midwestern critic of New England and its influence in the nation's capital asked for separation from the Northeast and the protection of western interests.[19] Sectional sentiment gave substance to the anti-New England resolution adopted at a Democratic meeting in Brown County, Indiana: "our interests and inclinations will demand of us a withdrawal from political association in a common government with the New England States, who have contributed so much to every innovation upon the constitution, to our present calamity of civil war, and whose tariff legislation must ever prove oppressive to our agricultural and commercial pursuits."[20]

Repeatedly midwestern Copperheads contended that New England caused the war and benefited from it while the West paid in money and men as well as in services and subserviency. Many malcontents insisted that the war elevated New England's "galvanized Federalism" to the driver's seat while western agriculturalists pulled the heavy load.[21] Truly, middle western Copperheadism makes sense only when it is viewed as a pro-western rather than a pro-Southern movement.

The sectional loyalty of the Copperheads was accentuated by the long list of economic grievances which they recited. The collapse of the banking system in several states bore heavily upon the farmers. Bank notes, based upon Southern bonds, depreciated in value, and institutions closed their doors in rapid succession as a bank panic gripped the Northwest when secession and war became a reality. In Illinois only 17 of the state's 112 banks remained solvent by the end of 1861. Nearly half of Wisconsin's banks closed their doors and scores failed in other midwestern states. Bankers, merchants, and employers passed on to farmers and working-men most of the depreciating state bank notes. An official of the Illinois Central Railroad suspected that the bankers were interested in keeping "the present trash afloat until such time as they can clean their vaults of it."[22] Farmers who held the stock of defunct banks as well as worthless currency complained bitterly. Furthermore, there was a shortage of cur-rency to handle the fall harvest.

The closing of Mississippi River trade also affected the farmers of the Midwest adversely. Although the growing eastbound trade severed, in part, the economic ties of the West and the South, the river trade was still nec-essary to the western farmers' welfare in 1860. Agricultural statistics and trade reports proved the Southern states bordering the mighty Mississippi depended upon the upper Midwest, in large part, for foodstuffs.[23] An article entitled "Illinois Corn and Secession" in the December 1860 issue of the *Prairie Farmer* reported that the New Orleans market had contracts for a million bushels of grain in 1861.[24] In fact, the year 1860 witnessed the hey-day of the down-river traffic.[25] Cincinnati alone shipped 105,332 sacks of corn, 47,801 bushels of wheat, and 158,592 barrels of flour southward in 1860.[26] Many manufactured items such as Cincinnati beer and Belleville whisky, produced from farm surpluses, went down the river.

The closing of the river trade forced farm prices downward, and flour, packed pork, and distilled spirits went begging for buyers. Corn commanded less than ten cents a bushel; potatoes could be had by the hundred bush-els for the asking; butter was a drug on the market, and hog prices were more than halved in 1861.[27] It was not pro-Southern sympathy but eco-nomic reality which prompted an Illinois newspaperman to entitle an edito-rial "Western Farmers, What Are Your Interests?" to deplore administration measures which erased the Southern market, and to ask the question, "Will the fighting farmers of the Upper Mississippi ever find out that it is the Lincoln's blood-and-murder party who has killed their 'goose with the golden egg'?"[28]

As farm prices dived downward, household necessities skyrocketed in price. The Morrill Tariff of February 20, 1861, and the supplementary act of the following August levied duties on tea, coffee, sugar, spices, and other items. Anticipating the effect, wholesalers and retailers raised their prices: before the end of 1861 sugar doubled in price, and coffee, which had sold for eleven cents a pound before Lincoln's election, brought more than three times as much by the end of 1862. A Wisconsin editor suggested to his Republican opponents that the best way they could support a "mistaken President" was by "drinking lots of coffee at...thirty-five cents a pound."[29]

The same Illinois legislature which considered a national convention as a way of ending the war, whimpered because Lincoln had "given sanction to a measure known as the Morrill Tariff, under which the East is enriching itself at the expense of the West."[30] In his editorial columns Medary thundered, "The West has been sold to eastern manufacturers by the politicians; the tariff is not a war measure, but a New England protective measure by which she expects to lay the great agricultural West tributary at the feet of her cotton and woolen mills."[31]

Farmers could not see the justice in requiring "four bushels of corn to buy one pound of coffee."[32] Their depressed spirits and deflated pocketbooks encouraged them to turn their backs upon the Lincoln administration in the fall election of 1862 and the spring voting of 1863. When the economic shoe pinched, midwestern farmers transposed their economic grievances into political arguments, personal pessimism, and open opposition.

The malcontents also directed a barrage of criticism against the railroads. The closing of the Mississippi had put midwestern farmers at the mercy of the railroads which made the most of their opportunity. "The railroads have put up their tariff on freights to almost an embargo price," moaned Medary in the columns of *The Crisis*; "they are literally skinning the West alive by advantage of the Mississippi blockade."[33] Immense purchases of American foodstuffs for the European market affected the western farmer but slightly, for prohibitory transportation rates of the trunk line railroads and lake freighters deprived western agrarians of the benefits they should have received.[34] In July 1861 barley commanded more than two and a-half times as much in New York as in Chicago, and much more in Chicago than at the local railway depots.

Complaints against excessive rail rates echoed from all parts of the Middle West. Iowans pointed out "that it cost more than *five times* as much to transport a bushel of wheat from Iowa to New York as the farmer received for it."[35] It seemed unfair to southern Illinois farmers that railroads which charged $1.10 to $1.20 per barrel to ship produce to New York in July 1861 should raise their rates to $3.00 per barrel by January 15, 1862—and that while farm prices spiraled downward. A downstate Copperhead Democrat asserted that Randolph County farmers paid $36,000 in increased freight rates in the last six months of 1861 and that Illinois residents paid a total of $18,000,000 in increases during the same period.[36] Vallandigham, self-styled "Western fire-eater," gave a sectional interpretation to the freight problem: "Cut off as we are from all other means of outlet...and with our railroads leading to the East, for the most part in the hands of eastern directors or bondholders, the tariff on freights has at the same time been fully doubled, thus increasing the burden upon our trade both ways, so largely as to amount in a little while longer to absolute prohibition."[37] Medary stated his sectional views more bluntly, asserting that administration policy would make westerners victims of the "skinning, brutally skinning despotism of Eastern railroads, and make us Western people paupers and slaves forever."[38] Gen. John A. McClernand, in reporting reasons why the Northwest repudiated the administration in the elections of late 1862, ascribed the general discontent to high freight rates.[39] The Great Lakes carriers were also included when the farmers protested against excessive freight rates. Even rail lines which brought farm surpluses to lake ports recognized that water transportation rates were so high that they pained and provoked the farmer and "reduced the nett [sic] price of his products...to so low a point as to leave no margin of profit."[40]

Grangerlike arguments against monopoly, discriminatory rates, pooling, stock watering, lobbying, and fraudulent promotion reverberated from many parts of the Midwest. Charges of coalescence between lake-port railroads and elevators appeared in many newspapers. One Copperhead spokesman, in an "Address to the People of Illinois," stated that the "aggregate indebtedness of counties, cities and towns for railroad companies has been ascertained to exceed fifteen millions" in his state.[41] Most of the charges which Grangers made in the 1870s were a repetition of the antirailroad arguments of the early 1860s.

Prominent "Peace Democrats" lampooned the "vested interests," condemning eastern capital and western railroad promoters. Republicanism, to them, was "revitalized Whiggery" or "Hamiltonian doctrine" galvanized to new life. Vallandigham preached that gospel, contending that the moneyed powers "found the nucleus of such an organization [Republican party] ready-formed to suit their hands—an organization...founded upon the most powerful passions of the human heart."[42] The correspondent of the *Times* (London), in touring the West, found evidence of the economic ties of Lincoln's party when he observed, "Wherever wealth is prevalent, there you have the stronghold of the Republican party."[43] Copperheads, generally, hated the New England influence, opposed "vested interests," and asserted faith in Jeffersonian principles.

Republican bigwigs, on the other hand, often deplored western sectionalism. "Palsied be the hand," stated Governor Richard Yates of Illinois, "that would sever the ties which bind the East and West."[44] Indiana's aggressive wartime governor, Oliver P. Morton, shadowboxed with "traitors" in his state and used emotional pleas to quash Copperhead sentiment. The *Chicago Tribune*, unofficial spokesman for the Lincoln administration, injected emotion into its editorials while tarring as traitors all critics of the party in power. While these and other champions of Radical Republicanism attributed "disloyal sentiments" to black hearts and blank minds, a more competent observer gauged Copperhead causation more rationally. William H. Osborn, competent president of the Illinois Central Railroad Company during the year of civil conflict, spent much time in Chicago and Springfield and noted that farmer discontent was closely tied to the question of high freight rates. In a series of letters he contradicted the views of his Republican colleagues, attributing the farmers' dissatisfaction to economic rather than biological or emotional factors. He scored the excessive tolls charged by the Erie Canal and trunk line operators, saying that "The West cannot consent to be held by the throat any longer to enrich Albany and Buffalo."[45] "The people of this State," he wrote from Chicago, "are bound to have an outlet to the Sea; this leaning towards Canada is a natural consequence of the apathy and indifference manifested by the State of New York touching a fair division of the spoils of the products of the prairies—$7/8$ to forwarders and $1/8$ to the poor devil who raises the corn. It is grievous."[46] The disgusted westerners, wrote Osborn, have paid "thirty-five to fifty cents per bushel to get their grain to market; it makes them grit their teeth." Then he pithily added: *"It is not a question of loyalty, but...one of bread and butter."*[47]

The Illinois state constitutional convention of 1862 illustrated the tie of midwestern Copperheadism and Grangerism. The *Chicago Tribune*, Republican party whip in Illinois, criticized the downstate Democratic delegates as "Copperheads," "secession conspirators," and "Southern sympathizers." Other administration papers followed suit. The *Tribune* charged that Democrats "who were members of, or sympathizers with, the Knights of the Golden Circle," controlled the convention and that treason was in process.[48] State Treasurer William Butler, a Republican, predicted that the partisan delegates would "attempt to take the State out of the Union."[49]

Four prominent Copperheads, Orlando B. Ficklin, Samuel Buckmaster, William J. Allen, and James W. Singleton, dominated the so-called "Copperhead Convention." Antirailroad arguments and action occupied the major share of its time—even the "Granger idea" that public utilities were subject to state regulation was forcefully promoted. The attack upon the railroads came from every quarter. Delegate Daniel Reilly, the miller who spoke for the farmers of Randolph County, asserted that the closing of the Mississippi gave the railroads an opportunity to defraud the farmers by excessive freight rates.[50] Delegate R.B.M. Wilson of Tazewell County resented the practice which forced local governments to buy railroad bonds or stock in order to determine the course of the line; he pointed out that every county from Terre Haute to St. Louis went into debt between $80,000 and $100,000 by subscribing for railroad stock. Morgan County, he said, subscribed to stock in two railroads and issued bonds to cover the $200,000 indebtedness. Foreclosures wiped out the stock and left the farmers shouldering a heavy yet empty bag. Too many farmers and too many local governmental units, complained Wilson, "have been bitten by this monster of appropriations for railroads."[51]

Downstate delegates from the "Copperhead country" denounced the free pass system as a form of bribery. They desired an oath from incoming state officials that they have never "received or accepted any free ticket, gift, or gratuity from any railroad company." Copperheads candidly condemned railroad officials who authorized bribes in the form of free travel, champagne suppers, or outright gifts.[52] Some complained that outsiders, representing "foreign capital," dictated "when we may ride and how much we shall pay per mile."[53] Others, continuing the Grangerlike arguments, insisted that it was the right and "the duty of a State" to control all corporations created by it and to relate restrictions to public welfare.[54] They weighed a demand for uniform rates per mile for both passengers and freight, but failed in the effort to write such a requirement into the state's fundamental law.[55] They discussed the desirability of disqualifying all railway corporation officials from membership in the legislature.[56]

The newly drafted constitution was loaded with provisions aimed at the railroads. It contained a clause, Jeffersonian and Grangerlike, that all private property was "subservient to the public welfare." It guaranteed to railway mechanics a lien upon the product of their work. Another section declared that rolling stock of railroads was "personal property and liable to execution of such." It prohibited local governments which were willing to lend their credit to chartered companies from becoming, in any way, subscribers to the stock of such corporations. Another clause bound the Illinois Central to its charter obligations and forbade any future legislature to release the company from them—nullifying the vigorous lobbying activities of William H. Osborn and John M. Douglas, president and attorney, respectively, of the railroad.[57] The convention membership tried to reduce the influence of lobbyists by increasing legislators' salaries. It tried to check "private and special legislation" by providing that bills should be read at large on three separate days and by specifying that only general laws should be passed on certain subjects—for special legislation had become a "crying evil" under the old state constitution.[58] The agrarian spokesmen were bold in contending, "There are other interests in the State besides commerce and industry."[59]

The agrarian-controlled convention undid its own work by an exhibition of rank partisanship, base politics, slipshod leadership, and inopportune extension of its authority into outlying fields. It halved the terms of the incumbent Republican state officials, and it gerrymandered when reapportioning the legislative and congressional districts. It busied itself with diverse and sundry investigations and played politics in wartime.

Governor Yates's Republicans capitalized upon Copperhead errors of judgment. Editor Joseph Medill led the attack upon the newly drafted constitution with its many antirailroad provisions. It was, he contended, a "secession swindle" and an "infamous fraud," engineered and supported by the "traitorous Knights of the Golden Circle."[60] Illinois Central officials opposed the new constitution, but they refused to proclaim their opposition openly for fear of a popular reaction.[61] But William B. Ogden, on the way to becoming "Railway King of the Northwest," campaigned actively for the defeat of the proposed constitution. He pointed out that railroads had contributed much to Illinois' development and declared that the old constitution was adequate. "We do not require a change in the present Constitution," Ogden told a Chicago audience on the eve of the election, "and we should hesitate ere we make one, lest we might apply to ourselves the inscription on the tombstone: 'I was well; I took medicine, and here I am.'"[62]

The new constitution failed of ratification, at least in part, because the banks, the express companies, and the railroads threw their weight against the document.[63] Douglas, the Illinois Central's efficient lobbyist, was "jubilant over the results."[64] Medill's *Tribune*, ignoring the economic issues, headlined an editorial, "Illinois Saved from the Grasp of Traitors," and expressed delight that "the traitors of Illinois and their infamous schemes are buried out of sight."[65]

The Illinois legislature of 1863—accused of "secesh sympathies" by the Republican press—again revealed the tie between Copperheadism and Grangerism. In this unusual session, prorogued by Governor Yates for its peace proposals and stigmatized as "traitorous,"[66] the antirailroad element was again active. Senator William Berry, McDonough County Democrat, introduced a significant resolution on January 9:

> *Resolved*, That the committee on Judiciary be instructed to examine whether or not the present exorbitant and ruinous rates of charges for transportation on the railroads of this state, can be restrained by law, and if so, to report a bill effectually guarding the interests of the country and the people against the same.[67]

The Senate soon passed a bill which threatened to put this "Granger idea" of the postwar era into law. The proposal restricted railroad earnings to 10 percent, and it set up a three-member commission with rate-making powers.[68] Ogden, who was then planning the consolidation of a number of lines into the Chicago and Northwestern Railroad system, gave the ablest speech against it, although he had capable support from a Republican colleague, William H. Underwood.[69] Railroad companies increased their activity at Springfield.[70] Edward L. Baker, president of the Chicago, Burlington & Quincy, opposed the bill and presented the railroaders' views:

> The idea of establishing a uniform system of fares and freights on the railroads is as preposterous as it would be to compel all your legislators—big men and little men—to eat the same quantity of roast beef and plum pudding daily, winter and summer, & to wear pen jackets of the same size all the year around.[71]

The *Western Railroad Gazette*, circulating by its own admission "with the especial view to subserve the interests of Railroad men,"[72] waged a vicious war upon "the fire in the rear scoundrels"—those "miserable, sneaking, God-forsaken, pusillanimous Copperheads" of the 1863 legislature. Governor Yates weakly defended the railroad against the monopoly charges,[73] while the *Chicago Journal*, the *Chicago Tribune*, and the *State Journal* aided the cause of the railroads by slandering the legislators as "pro-Southern schemers," "treason mongers," and "secessionist-disunionists." "Our Springfield dispatches," warned the keeper of the Republican party conscience, "say that the leaders of the Copperheads intend revolution against the authority of the General Government."[74] It accused them of perfecting a "secession movement under the auspices of the Knights of the Golden Circle."[75]

Meanwhile, the railroad commission bill found the going heavier in the lower house as the opposition organized and strengthened its lines. But the bill finally passed the preliminary hurdles and was made the special order for June 10.[76]

The legislature, however, had been concerned with more than the railroad commission bills. The Copperheads had adulterated their antirailroad brew with impure ingredients—poisonous politics and peace proposals. Popular opinion, framed and fanned by the Radical Republican press, Governor Yates's supporters, and the railroad interests, deserted the Copperhead legislators. On the morning of June 10, minutes before the railroad bill was scheduled or "special order" discussion in the lower house, Yates prorogued the legislature. This tactical and parliamentary victory of the governor and his partisans quashed the Copperhead plan to endorse a national peace convention and it nullified the schemes of Democratic plotters—plans to take army patronage out of Yates's hands and a conspiracy to reapportion in favor of the antiadministration party. But it also killed the railroad commission bill and invalidated the work of the antirailroad interests. While the railroad men applauded, Republican chieftains congratulated Governor Yates for his "brilliant coup d'etat" in proroguing "the copperhead swell mob known as the Illinois Legislature."[77] The Democratic malcontents, meanwhile, were left stewing in their own juice, a bitter compound of Copperhead incompetency combined with venal politics.

Administration strategy, highlighted by the attempt to tie the tail of treason to the Democratic kite, placed the opposition party at a disadvantage. Rising farm prices in late 1863, the pressure of patriotism, soldier-voting laws and practices, military-political control of the border states, and Copperhead clumsiness combined to render the protest of the midwestern malcontents ineffective. Vallandigham's persecution complex and his distasteful deportment also nullified the protests of the western sectionalists. New England's industrialism held the whip hand in the later phases of the Civil War, and the objections of the dissenting Democrats of the Midwest were overruled. The Jeffersonian protests of the western sectionalists against "revitalized Whiggery" and "galvanized Federalism," ably expressed by Illinois Copperheads in the constitutional convention of 1862 and the "Copperhead Legislature" of 1863, were hushed until revived in the postwar years by the Greenbackers and Grangers.

Midwestern Copperheadism had much in common with Grangerism. Both were sectional protests. Both were grounded in economic grievances.

Both flaunted the banner of state rights, emphasized civil liberties and individual rights, and muttered Jeffersonian phrases. They spoke of human rights and of opposition to the vested interests. Grangerism, yet unnamed, was evident in the claims and language of that lesser known Copperhead who represented Schuyler County at the Illinois constitutional convention and who succinctly stated, "I believe this doctrine of vested rights is a great humbug—a cobweb—gotten up by the lawyer to confuse the common man."[78] It was evident in the words of the Democrat Daniel Reilly, Copperhead from lower Illinois, when he lustily proclaimed:

> We believe down in Egypt—in that part of Egypt I have the honor of representing—that all our railroad corporations are creatures of the State; that what rights and immunities they have were all derived from the State; that they have derived their existence from the State. And we believe also, that railroad corporations are a power in the State not to be despised, but rather to be treated with favor; but that these great establishments are not worthy of favor if they do not favor the interests of the people...."[79]

Truly, Grangerism existed in the Middle West before Oliver Hudson Kelly contributed the name, the organic structure, and the organizing zeal.

Not all Copperheads were antirailroad men, nor were all antirailroad men Copperheads. But it was no coincidence that Illinois Copperheads in session, whether in the constitutional convention of 1862 or the legislature of 1863, took measures to check the railroad abuses and to proclaim the Granger doctrine of state control and regulation.

Chapter V

CONTROVERSY REGARDING THE COPPERHEADS

Section One

"The Concept of Agrarian Radicalism"
by Ronald P. Formisano and William G. Shade*

American historians have used the concept of agrarian radicalism to explain phenomena ranging from Shay's Rebellion in the eighteenth century to Progressivism in the twentieth. The idea has held strong fascination for scholars who are sympathetic to the Jeffersonian tradition and tend to see American history as a struggle between "radical" and "conservative" forces. The common formula usually involves angry debtor farmers who depart from their naturally pacific cultivation of the land to seek redress for their economic grievances in radical political action. Their radicalism lies not in their political involvement, but rather their economic programs which generally include schemes for monetary inflation and the control of corporate enterprise. Agrarian radicalism has served to characterize both the social sources and the ideologies of disparate movements and programs for politico-economic reform throughout the Middle Period, connecting the pre-war Locofocos and other "radical" Democrats with post-war movements for monetary reform and railroad regulation.

Since World War II a series of attacks on various aspects of this interpretation have appeared. The Jacksonian movement can no longer be viewed simply as an outburst of agrarian radicalism, and the many social movements of that age have assumed a complexity that the concept is inadequate to convey or suggest.[1] The groups behind the Granger Laws and railroad regulations after the Civil War were neither exclusively farmers nor

---

*Reprinted (with permission) from *Mid-America*, 52 (January 1970): 3–29.

exclusively western.[2] Antebellum demands for inflation came more often from the entrepreneurial elements than the farmers;[3] and simple generalizations concerning exclusively rural support for paper money following the war simply do not hold.[4] Recently Thomas P. Govan has demonstrated how historians have used the word "agrarian" with such imprecision and indiscretion that it is void of any meaning outside the particular context in which it appears.[5] But the appealing simplicity of a classic idea dies hard.

We wish to show not only the imprecision of this concept, but also that it has outlived its usefulness as a theory of causation in understanding the American past. To do this we shall focus on a particularly sweeping assertion of the concept, namely, that midwestern Copperheadism was essentially a radical and agrarian social movement which provided a bridge between Jacksonian Democracy and post-war reform. The work of two scholars allows us, moreover, to concentrate in detail on one allegedly spectacular manifestation of the phenomenon, the Illinois Constitutional Convention of 1862.[6]

Frank L. Klement in his influential article, "Middle Western Copperheadism and the Genesis of the Granger Movement," proposed that Copperheadism "linked Jacksonian Democracy and Grangerism."[7] Klement also asserted, in a later book, a similar tie between Jacksonian Democracy and Greenbackism.[8] A substantial part of Klement's case rested on his interpretation of the activities of the Illinois Constitutional Convention of 1862. A Democratic majority ran the convention, and the state's Copperheads, dominating that majority, used the convention to attack banks and railroads. Similarly, Stanley L. Jones in "Agrarian Radicalism in Illinois' Constitutional Convention of 1862," asserted the convention "illustrated the vitality of the Jackson movement in the West while it was also a portent of the Granger and Populist movements."[9]

The idea of agrarian radicalism is the backbone of both interpretations. Klement's antirailroad Copperheads were farmers of southern Illinois who before the Civil War depended on trade with the South *via* the Mississippi. The closing of the river in 1861 put them at the mercy of the railroads running north and east, which proceeded to hike their rates. In the Convention representatives of Copperhead agrarians struck back: "antirailroad arguments and action occupied the major share of its time."[10] In typical Granger fashion they denounced excessive freight rates, railroad bribery of public officials, the practice of local governments of buying railroad stocks and bonds, and, in addition to expressing other Granger grievances, "weighed a demand for uniform rates per mile for both passengers and freight, but failed in the effort to write such a requirement into the state's fundamental law."[11] According to Jones, the farmers of Illinois "had always distrusted corporations," and the southern Illinois farmers were "particularly opposed to banks and corporations."[12] Delegates from agricultural areas led the assault on banks and railroads; the "rural" counties of southern and central Illinois supported the constitution.

The two authors disagree on several important points. Jones described the leaders of the Convention as a "bipartisan group who had grown up in the Jacksonian tradition."[13] Klement's Copperheads were intensely partisan. Klement pictured antirailroad activity as all of one kind: Grangerlike. Jones believed that the hostility against railroads was directly mainly at the Illinois Central because it had delayed payments owed the state under the terms of its charter. Both Klement and Jones recognized that although some delegates demanded regulation of railroad rates, the convention made no provision for such laws. It is reasonable to ask for an explanation. *The great shibboleth of the Grangers was rate regulation.* "The primary source of complaint against the railroads...the principal motive for the enactment of the Granger laws—was the prevalence of unequal treatment [in rates] on the part of the roads as between persons and localities."[14]

Finally, Jones clearly related postures on the money question to the hard money, antibank ideas of the Jacksonians, but while suggesting ties to Greenbackism he left this matter obscure. He indicated that the question of the Greenbacks came up and "many anti-bank Democrats tried to persuade the convention to authorize the payment of taxes in the new medium."[15] However, he is aware that on this as well as rate regulation the convention failed to act.

Why this inaction? What was the nature of the monetary provisions? Who supported and opposed them? How were they related to the later Greenback agitation? Who demanded and who opposed rate control? How "Grangerlike" were the activities of the convention? What was the relationship between Jacksonian Democracy, Copperheadism, Grangerism, and Greenbackism in Illinois? Systematic examination of these questions affords an opportunity to test the validity of the concept of agrarian radicalism.

Most accounts of the preconvention political situation contain conflicting evidence, but it seems clear that before 1860 both Republicans and Democrats wanted a new constitution. During 1860, the Republicans made the cause their own. In November 1861, however, the Democrats swept the election of delegates, electing 47 Democrats to 21 Republicans, 7 "fusion" and 2 doubtfuls.[16] Most of the fusionists later acted very much like Democrats. The Republicans claimed that the Democrats had won by posing as Unionists and fusionists while privately holding Copperhead sentiments.[17] Other causes for the Democratic victory have been suggested. Very few voters turned out and the war may have sapped the issue of its attraction while also diverting the energies of Republicans. One student suggested that Democratic success was due to the "most prominent lawyers" being Democrats.[18]

The disastrous economic effects of the war during 1861 and the uncertain course of the struggle contributed to the repudiation of the Republicans. Bank notes based on Southern bonds became worthless and depreciated paper money flooded the state. By the end of 1861 only 17 of the state's 112 banks remained solvent. The entire business community felt the effects of an increasing shortage of capital.[19]

Whatever the causes of Democratic success, the convention met in Springfield in January, 1862, and the Democratic majority quickly established itself in the areas of partisanship and Copperheadism. It boldly assumed legislative powers, issued ordinances, and sought to instruct state officers in their duties. It functioned, in short, as a General Assembly and constitutional convention. For example, while framing an article on banks it issued an instruction to the state auditor forbidding him to circulate paper to any but specie paying banks. It reapportioned state and Congressional election districts and unblushingly gerrymandered in favor of the Southern, traditionally Democratic section. (Almost all the Democratic delegates came from southern and central Illinois.) The Republicans had swept the 1860 state election, and, to remedy that situation the Democrats made constitutional provisions to halve the terms of Republican incumbents. This naked partisanship contributed to the constitution's ultimate rejection by the electorate.[20]

The convention was less Copperhead than Republicans charged, and the historical record suggests that at times influential Democratic leaders pressed for moderation. Nevertheless, the convention sought to embarrass the Republican administration by showing misconduct and excesses in war expenditures. Yet, an investigation of the treatment of Illinois troops in the field ended in ludicrous failure.[21]

Rumors that the pro-Southern Knights of the Golden Circle wielded influence over the convention proved to be unfounded. The *Chicago Tribune*'s special reporter, Joseph K.C. Forrest, an unscrupulous adventurer, had instigated the rumors. When the convention hauled him before an investigation committee, he admitted to a total lack of evidence. Suspicion had been raised, however, and the Republicans exploited it.[22]

The Democrats took an aggressive stand on states rights, but denied the right of secession in the bill of rights. They exhibited Negrophobia and presented a set of "Black Laws" to be voted on separately, barring free Negroes from voting and from immigrating to Illinois. While the constitution was rejected by 16,051 votes, the Black laws carried by majorities of 107,657 and 176,271.[23] After adjournment the Democrats fought for the constitution as an antimonopoly, antispecial privilege document embodying the interest of the people. They accused the Republicans of being influenced by monopolies like the Illinois Central. The Republicans denounced Democratic partisanship, and emphasized the unpatriotic nature of the "Secession Constitution."[24]

The obvious and primary motive behind most of the convention's activity, hitherto slighted, was the regaining of political power.[25] Before 1860 the Democratic Party had been the dominant party. Many of the delegates had held positions of state and local power and the party tried to use the convention to regain control of the state.

Forrest repeatedly charged in the *Tribune* that the Democracy and the Convention were dominated by the pro-Southern "Egyptians."[26] He characterized them as both radical and conservative. The "radical majority," he said, had "little in common with the northern part of the state. Egypt is their ideal of social life and civilization." Egypt was a land of almost exclusively agricultural people and held a "natural prejudice toward all modern forms of progress: particularly banks, corporations, and even railroads." In the convention "the commercial or manufacturing interests in the state were not represented at all." There were two or three good lawyers present, but professional politicians "who [held] office pandering to public follies and prejudices" dominated the convention.[27]

Klement's characterization of Copperheads was more sympathetic—and subtler. He described Copperheadism as a complex blend of ingredients: partisanship, religious, social, and economic antagonisms; humanitarian sentiment; and western sectionalism based, above all, on economic grievances. Yet Klement, like Forrest, depicted Copperheads as both radical and conservative. Copperheads were agrarian radicals on one hand, and on the other were conservatives in a sense that they resisted change and objected to the "emergence of a new America of mills, cities, a stronger central government" and "revived Whiggery and the ascendancy of industrialism over agriculture."[28]

Four prominent Copperheads according to Klement dominated the convention: Orlando B. Ficklin, William J. Allen, Samuel A. Buckmaster, and James W. Singleton. Yet, it is not clear from the convention *Journal*, newspaper coverage, and secondary accounts that these men were the four *most* influential Democrats. Buckmaster, for example, lost the presidency of the convention to William A. Hacker, another Copperhead from deep Egypt, who acted as more than a figurehead. Over thirty men have been listed as leaders in various accounts of the convention. After comparing these accounts with the *Journal*, the *Illinois State Register*, and the *Chicago Tribune*, fourteen men, including the four mentioned by Klement, have been selected as primary and secondary leaders and examined, to determine their resemblance to the agrarian radical stereotype and their part in the antibank and antirailroad proceedings.

All four men mentioned by Klement were prominent Democrats and Copperheads. Allen, Buckmaster, and Ficklin fit fairly well into Klement's mold. "Josh" Allen became nationally known as an outspoken critic of Republican conduct of the war and may have been involved in the move to sever Egypt from Illinois. Following the war he advocated the "Ohio Idea" in the Democratic convention of 1868 and stood for a moderate stance on deflation in Illinois in the 1870s. Because of his reputation as a lawyer, President Cleveland appointed Allen to a federal judgeship which he held until his death.[29] As Speaker of the Illinois House of Representatives in 1863, Buckmaster led a bitter denunciation of the war and earned a reputation as a strong Copperhead.[30] Ficklin, a friendly political enemy and sometime law partner of Lincoln's, had been a Democratic congressman before the Civil War and was later a prominent Granger.[31] Of these three lawyer-politicians from counties in Southern Illinois, only Buckmaster introduced resolutions dealing with railroads, leading the Democratic assault on the Illinois Central. All three supported the antibank stand of the convention; and Allen, while not a Greenbacker, attempted to steer a moderate course following the war.

The case of Singleton conforms less easily to Klement's thesis. Lawyer, brigadier general, state legislator and congressman, Singleton began as a Whig but split with his part over the Kansas-Nebraska Act. In 1862 he was an influential if characteristically unpredictable Democrat and Copperhead. He came from Quincy in Adams County on the western border of central Illinois. Although active in the promotion of Illinois Agricultural College and the Illinois State Agricultural Society, Singleton's major private enterprise, both before and after the war, was building and presiding over railroads. On monetary questions he was at odds with the Democrats in the convention. Earlier Singleton had advocated free banking; in 1862 he opposed the antibank article of the constitution. Following the war he attacked the "Ohio idea." Understandably, Singleton also showed little interest in railroad regulation.[32] None of the four discussed introduced resolutions dealing with general railroad regulation. Categorizing Singleton as an "agrarian radical" divests the term of any meaning. This difficulty persists with other Democratic leaders, and "Long" John Wentworth makes the point with emphasis.

Contemporaries recognized that John Wentworth was a complex figure.[33] He was born in New Hampshire, attended Dartmouth College, and moved to Chicago in 1836. He rose to dominance of the city's Democratic party and repeatedly represented the Chicago district in Congress. "Able but demagogical," Wentworth championed river and harbor improvement, land reform, and hard money.[34] In 1850 he helped Senator Stephen Douglas gain an Illinois Central land grant from Congress, but he broke with the Democrats over the slavery issue and became a Republican supporting Lincoln, the war, and later radical Reconstruction.[35]

From 1857–1861 Wentworth served as a Fusion mayor of Chicago. Known as a "friend of the laboring man," he proposed a constitutional amendment giving laborers a prior lien on wages. In 1862 Wentworth was nationally an orthodox Republican, but locally he acted like a Democrat. He generally voted with the Democratic majority and campaigned vigorously for the new constitution. His main interest seems to have been in the banking provisions. He had long opposed banks and paper money and complained that "Men who were sound on the Negro position were rotten on the bank question."[36] Following the war he supported Hugh McCulloch's resumption policy.

Wentworth's dexterity in politics was matched by his success in business and journalism. For a long time he edited and then owned the *Chicago Democrat*. "One of the financial pillars of the First National Bank for many years,"[37] he also owned stock in the Chicago and Galena Railroad and the Illinois Central Railroad. To all this can be added his "magnificent farm estate" of 2,500 acres at Summit, Cook County, which he amassed while attacking land speculators and monopolists in the pages of the *Democrat*. Summit Farm served as headquarters of the Illinois Breeding Association which Wentworth had promoted. He was rumored to be worth $750,000 in 1862. His biographer, Don Fehrenbacher, believes that this is an exaggeration although he was a millionaire by the late 1870s.

Forrest observed that most of the Democratic talking was done "by the old school, Dement, Thornton, Edwards, Ross, Singleton, and others."[38] The first named gentleman, Maj. John Dement, represented Lee and Whitside Counties in northern Illinois. Although both counties were formerly Whig and thereafter predominantly Republican, they sent an old Democratic party wheel horse to the convention. The diminutive Dement—he was nicknamed "tom tit"—was a friend and mentor of Stephen A. Douglas, rewarded for his services by being appointed Receiver of Public Monies by three Presidents. In 1836 he moved to Dixon, Lee County, and in the early fifties became "extensively engaged in manufacturing" iron plows and flour milling. Later he took over the Dixon flax bagging mills and "spent his last years as a manufacturer and owner of much city property."[39] Dement worked with the Democratic majority, but was a Union man who supported the war until the Emancipation Proclamation. He had opposed banks in the 1847 Constitutional Convention, but in the 1862 convention he resisted the antibank provision of the constitution and joined the Republicans in endorsing the Congress' pending issuance of Greenbacks.[40]

Anthony Thornton was hardly an "old school" Democrat as described by Forrest. He represented Shelby County which was strongly Democratic with a predominantly Southern population. Although a Whig until 1856, he became a Copperhead during the war. A lawyer, state Supreme Court Justice, Congressman, and "aristocratic in mien, deportment, and bearing," Thornton owned the Thornton Bank, Thornton's Store, and a warehouse in Shelbyville. In the 1847 convention he had favored free banking, and although he voted for the antibank proposal in the 1862 document under constituent pressure, he personally opposed the Democratic position on banks; ultimately he campaigned against the constitution.[41]

Benjamin S. Edwards, son of the famous governor Ninian Edwards, had a background of Yale, Whiggery, and "aristocratic tendencies," a large and prosperous farm, saw and grist mills, and an "extensive mercantile business" in Illinois and Missouri. His wife was a leader of Springfield society. A prominent Copperhead in 1862, he made one of the strongest speeches in the convention against the evils of paper money.[42]

Lewis Ross represented Fulton County, the seat of which, Lewistown, had been founded by his father. "He was the acknowledged leader of the Democratic party in central Illinois," and served in both the state legislature and Congress where he sat on the Committee on Agriculture. A successful lawyer with "large and important" business interests, Ross lived in a seventeen room "mansion house" in Lewistown. A Copperhead, he supported the antibank resolution in the constitution although he would have preferred a gradual rather than immediate prohibition of paper money.[43]

Ex-governor Augustus French and Judge Norman Purple were both on the Committee on Banks and Currency. Purple, a prominent Peoria lawyer, promoted the adoption of the antibank resolutions.[44] French, a law professor at McKendree College, had led the Democratic opposition to banks as governor. In the convention he generally supported the antibank proposals, but agreed with Ross on gradual rather than immediate elimination of paper money. French speculated in land and railroads in the early fifties, but the extent of his holdings in 1862 is not clear.[45]

Alexander Starne was at most a second rank Democratic leader. From Pike County in west central Illinois, Starne had been a protege of Judge Purple and earlier ran a general store. He served one term as secretary of state; and later he assumed the presidency of the Hannibal and Naples Railroad. He was also "extensively engaged in coal mining with his sons."[46]

Finally, young Melville Weston Fuller must be counted as at least a second rank leader in the convention. The protege of Chicago Democratic boss, "Billy" Goudy, Fuller rose quickly in the party after the war. Appointed Chief Justice of the Supreme Court by Cleveland in 1888, he "became a staunch defender of private interests against social legislation."[47] A leading "Bourbon" Democrat with "considerable property interests in Chicago," Fuller bitterly opposed banks and favored hard currency. A vigorous opponent of inflation, he voted against receiving "the greenbacks in payment of State taxes...and condemned the Pendleton plan."[48] In 1862 he supported the antibank resolutions and had a mild reputation as a Copperhead although he fought Vallandigham.

None of the major leaders described here offered resolutions dealing with general railroad regulation and three opposed the antibank stance of the convention. All were lawyers and most became judges. The group included one sometime Republican, and three Democrats who had been Whigs. Four had interests in railroads, and at least seven could be accurately described as "businessmen." Although one moderately backed Pendleton's "Ohio Idea," none became a Greenbacker and three were known advocates of hard money. Only one figured prominently in the Granger movement. (Of eleven lesser figures also examined, all were lawyers. At least two pursued mercantile and banking interests. Two were former Whigs. One had worked as an attorney for the Illinois Central.)[49]

Antirailroad arguments and action occupied only a minor share of the convention's time, including discussion of the Illinois Central problem. Not one of the fourteen major leaders considered here introduced resolutions dealing with general railroad regulation. The leaders from southern Illinois did dominate the convention, and were mostly intense Copperheads, but they showed no interest in general railroad regulation. On monetary questions they reflected the long standing Democratic distrust of banks and paper money which had always been one of the "cardinal principles" of "the Egyptian democracy."[50]

It is impossible to characterize the Democratic leadership of the convention as "agrarian radicals." Their diversity and incomplete information makes it difficult to characterize them at all. Some of them held "Copperhead" and "agrarian" attitudes, but as a group they defy these labels. Living in a state recently emerged from the frontier stage, which was undergoing tremendous physical expansion, and living in an age before specialization and surplus, they worked at many varied occupations: law, public office, business, agriculture, industry, and almost universally, land speculation. Law and entrepreneurship in politics and business seem to be the most typical qualities of the men described. If they must be categorized, the term "Bourbon" suits these politician-entrepreneurs far better than "agrarian."[51]

The discussion of money and banking in the convention actually involved two quite different questions. That which occupied most of the convention's time concerned the elimination of banks and the prohibition from the state of bank notes under $10. This was the culmination of the long Democratic struggle to rid the state of banks and return to hard money.[52] Since the early 1840s the Democrats had contested unsuccessfully with first the Whigs and then the Republicans to achieve these ends. In the Constitutional Convention of 1847 the hard money forces lost a close battle to the advocates of free banking. The Democrats, led by Governor French, were able to hold off the demands for expanded banking and credit facilities until 1851 when a group of Democrats from the northern part of the state joined with the Whigs to pass a free banking bill. Throughout the decade Democrats maintained hostility to banks while their opponents tried to reform the inadequacies of free banking. Following the Panic of 1857 the Democracy revived the bank issue in an attempt to draw defectors to the new Republican party back into the fold. Although unsuccessful at first, the general revulsion against the banking system which followed its collapse during the economic crisis precipitated by secession gave the Democrats the opportunity to "play on new frustrations with old formulas."[53] Throughout the summer of 1861 the *Illinois State Register* made it clear that a revival of "Democratic principles" meant a return to the "constitutional currency."[54]

In the convention the antibank forces were led by Judge Purple who introduced a motion on the first day to eliminate banks of issue.[55] He later presented the majority report of the Committee on Banks and Currency designed to carry out this end. The report suggested that the convention instruct the auditor to issue no further notes to any bank which could not prove that it had at all times held $5,000 cash capital in its vaults and had never refused to redeem its notes in specie. Copperheads Harvey K.S. Omelveny and Benjamin Edwards endorsed Purple's plan with strong antibank speeches which drew praise from the Democratic press. Generally Democrats favored the antibank article and Republicans opposed it.[56]

As Jones pointed out, there was some discussion of Greenbacks in the convention, but this hardly lends support to the Jacksonian-Copperhead-Greenback thesis. On January 29, Alexander Campbell, who had earlier advocated the issue of Treasury notes redeemable in government stocks, presented his report on Treasury Notes in which he attacked the eastern banker's plan for financing the war and put forth his "people's plan" to issue legal tender treasury notes redeemable in government stock. Only a "sound reliable, circulating medium" could restore confidence, revive industry, "and facilitate production and commerce to a degree unknown in our history."[57] Campbell had probably been influenced by the writings of the New York Whig businessman, Edward Kellogg. Neither showed the reverence for specie nor fear of inflation typical of the Jacksonians. In 1861 he urged his legal tender proposal on Secretary Chase and in 1862 tried to get the convention to instruct the Illinois congressmen to vote for the legal tender law then pending.[58] His resolution received solid Republican support, but the Democrats rallied to defeat it.[59] Campbell later became a Greenback leader in Illinois and wrote one of the movement's most widely read pamphlets, *The True American System of Finance*.[60] He was neither a Copperhead nor a farmer, but rather a former Whig mayor of LaSalle, and in 1862 a Republican businessman with extensive interests in land speculation and coal mining. Although he favored the elimination of state banks, Campbell did not sign the constitution.

Jones vaguely connected antibank Democrats and the Greenbackers, but neither he nor Klement mentioned Campbell. Rather they assume that opposition to banks made one a Greenbacker. Following the war these were two distinct although sometimes related positions, but in 1862 and 1863 both Greenbacks and a national banking system were Republican measures which received nearly unanimous support from western Republicans and equally unified opposition from Democrats led by the Copperhead triumvirate, Pendleton, Voorhees, and Vallandigham. The Copperheads in the Illinois convention displayed the traditional Democratic fear of banks and paper money of any kind which motivated their congressional representatives. The Republicans in the convention continued to pursue their party's thirty-year quest for a sound and adequate currency to undergird rapid expansion of business enterprise. Alexander Campbell, the only member of the convention to become a leading Greenbacker, came from a minority faction of the Whig-Republican tradition which had long looked to a national paper currency to spur enterprise and limit usury. Far from being a Copperhead, he did not even support the 1862 constitution.

The main issue involving railroads in the convention concerned the Illinois Central. The road's original charter of 1851 required it to pay 7 percent of its annual profits to the state. In 1861 the road fell behind in payment and sought relief. It maintained that loss of Southern trade due to the war, cut rate services to the federal government, the wear and tear of troop transportation, and Illinois's general currency problems contributed to its perilous financial condition. In October the road's president, William H. Osborne, met with Governor Richard Yates; Osborne said publicly that he simply sought "indulgence" for the reasons stated above; however, it was more likely that he was trying to balance off the claims of the road on the federal government against the state. The federal government owed the road mainly for troop transportation, and Osborne argued that the troops could be considered state troops.[61]

During the first weeks of the convention both Democrats and Republicans introduced resolutions calling for investigation of the Illinois Central matter, to "clarify" the road's relationship to the state and to insure compliance by the road with its charter.[62] The Democrats quickly seized the issue in their general attempt to make political capital against the Yates administration.[63] In the convention, Samuel Buckmaster charged that the Republicans regarded the interests of the railroad more tenderly than those of the public. He and other Democrats postured as defenders of the public from a rapacious monopoly and deceitful public officials. Buckmaster even charged that Yates, who had been cooperating with the convention, removed a conscientious auditing commissioner to replace him with one properly considerate of the Illinois Central. Yates denied he ever knew the attitudes of the auditors in question, and insisted that he had not tried to set off the account of the road "against the seven percent of the gross earnings due the state, and that it was properly charged against the United States." He added that he respectfully did "not acknowledge the right of your honorable body to instruct me in the performance of my duty."[64]

Not nascent Grangerism, but partisan politics lay behind the Illinois Central issue. Jones found that most of the hostility against railroads was directed against the Illinois Central, because of "popular distrust" of the railroad's intention to comply with its charter.[65] But evidence concerning the attitude of public opinion on the Illinois Central, or railroads in general, has not been produced. Further, any account of the Illinois Central's public image at the time would have to consider the activities of its intelligent president. Keenly sensitive to public relations, Osborne promoted both the welfare of his clients and good will and business for the road. In the summer of 1861 Osborne accepted corn at Chicago prices from moneyless farmers as payment for land debts. This practice rose to a vast business in a few months and the company reluctantly gave it up in 1862. Similar attempts to retain the good will of politicians, editors, and farmers were generally successful. "Until the 1870's the Illinois Central was," according to its foremost historian, "undoubtedly the most popular railroad in Illinois."[66]

Although given less notice than the Illinois Central question, rate regulation was discussed in the press and at the convention. Daniel Reilly, a Randolph County Copperhead, fits neatly into the agrarian radical thesis although he did oppose the banking article in the constitution. Randolph County was on the northwest fringe of Egypt, bordered by the Mississippi, and in position to be affected by the Mississippi closing.[67] Reilly was a miller, who Klement believes "spoke for the farmers" of southern Illinois; and he spoke very much like a Granger. On January 15, he asked the convention to submit inquiries to railroads requiring them to tell how much they had raised their freight rates between July 1 and November 1, 1861, on such articles as flour (which Reilly manufactured), wheat, corn, hogs, cattle, salt, sugar, cotton, etc. The convention decided against his resolution on a non-roll call vote and referred it to the committee on manufacturing and agriculture.[68]

On January 21, Reilly resumed his campaign, denouncing railroads at length, and he was joined by other members. He asked the committee on railroads to uncover any conflict between railroad charters and state laws and to investigate the relation between state officials and the railroads.[69] The resolution was referred to committee where it died. Persisting, Reilly submitted a minority report, whereupon by motion of Mr. Burr, a Democrat, the whole subject was tabled.[70]

Reilly seems to have been the most strenuous opponent of railroads in the convention. He deserves the attention he has received, but his weight alone does not establish the agrarian radical thesis. No other Democratic delegates from southern Illinois offered resolutions dealing with general railroad regulation, and no other delegate from southern Illinois offered a resolution dealing with rate control. The Democratic leadership effortlessly sidetracked Reilly's proposals; the leading Democratic paper, the *Illinois State Register*, ignored them.

Resolutions calling for legislation affecting rate control came from three other men; two represented counties in the northern half of the state, the third Adams County in the western-central bulge. None were prominent Copperheads and one was a "war Democrat" from a strong Republican county. All the counties represented by these men, except Adams, voted against the constitution.[71]

James Paddock first presented regulatory legislation to the convention on January 13. He submitted one resolution holding the Illinois Central to its obligations, and another seeking constitutional requirements for railroads to adopt uniform rates for passengers and freight, "in proportion to the distance traveled, or freight carried thereon."[72] Paddock represented

Will, DuPage, and Kankakee counties of the prairie region south and west of Chicago. Born in Onondaga, New York, he came to Illinois in 1836 to practice law. Originally a Whig, he became a Douglas Democrat in the fifties and supported the war. In the convention he usually voted with the Republican minority. He opposed the banking article in the constitution, and the counties he had represented voted heavily against adoption. His last campaign found him in Sherman's army, where he died in 1863.[73]

From the same prairie region as Paddock came Perry A. Armstrong, a Democrat representing Grundy County, whom Jones described as an opponent of railroads.[74] On January 23 he offered a resolution that embodied much of the essence of railroad control laws after 1870. He proposed that a board of railroad commissioners be created, who could supervise tariffs and fares, regulate timetables and connections, and perform other duties that might become necessary.[75] Armstrong was the youngest member of a "brood of brothers active in [Democratic] politics and business." Perry himself ran a general store and served in various public offices. His interests ranged from poetry to history to railroad charters: he drew up the original charters of the Chicago and Rock Island, the Illinois Central, and the Burlington and Quincy Railroads. He too opposed the antibank stance of the Democratic majority.[76]

Austin Brooks, with General James Singleton, represented Adams County. Brooks, a former Douglas backer, edited the Democratic Quincy *Herald* which had proposed the discussion of rate regulation in mid-1861.[77] On February 11, he submitted a long resolution on corporations, one section of which empowered the general assembly to regulate "public carrying...in such manner that the charge for carrying shall be uniform per distance and below a fixed price per mile."[78] Historians have connected neither Brooks nor the *Quincy Herald* with the Copperhead movement though he was a strong Democratic partisan bitterly hostile toward banks. After the convention he defended the constitution as "a poor man's constitution, protecting as it does, against the encroachment of monopolies the rights of labor against the aggressions of chartered corporations."[79]

In addition to Reilly, Paddock, Armstrong, and Brooks, sixty-one citizens of Brown County asked for rate regulation. They submitted a petition through Delegate Archibald A. Glenn, praying that "some provision be inserted in the organic law of this state, making the different railroad companies common carriers in the fullest acceptance of the term, and requiring them to carry all freights at reasonable rates and in reasonable time." It would be most interesting to know the occupations and political affiliations of the 61 citizens. Thirty-three depressed Copperhead farmers would do wonders, no doubt, for the idea of agrarian radicalism. Glenn, at any rate, was a Democratic lawyer, banker, and merchant. Brown County, like Adams, voted for adoption of the constitution.[80]

Two delegates introduced resolutions dealing generally with railroads but not involving rate control. Both were Republicans: James B. Underwood from St. Clair County in southern Illinois, and Jonathan Simpson of Henderson County in the northwest central region. Although he voted against the banking article, Simpson not only signed the constitution, but later defended it in a county history which he wrote. His resolution called for the taxation of railroad property, such as rolling stock, which had hitherto been exempt. Simpson also asked the convention to foster agricultural interests by establishing a bureau of agriculture.[81] Underwood, who later fought the constitution, proposed "...that railroads, with their running stock, machine shops, and the appurtenances thereto, be made subject to execution in all cases against said corporations for torts, and also in favor of employees for wages against said corporations, and also for machinery furnished such roads, in preference to prior mortgages and trustees."[82]

Demands for general railroad regulation were non-partisan and any connection that they had with Copperheadism or opposition to banks was incidental. Demands for rate control came mainly from the northern part of the state, especially from the land of rich prairie soil stretching west from Chicago. To understand fully the significance of the agitation for regulation in 1862, both earlier and later developments must be considered.

Underlying the booming growth of the state from 1850 to 1860 were railroads. Population, cultivation of increased acreage, commercial farming, manufacturing, commerce, towns, all followed the coming of the roads. Eastern capitalists and speculators dominated the process, but local men pitched in eagerly. They led campaigns to raise local capital, and often combined the latter with eastern capital as well as their own. In the forties and fifties towns and counties competed for the routes and termini. Some of the major political battles of the era revolved around the location of railroads. Local governments competed for the privilege of buying stocks and bonds of a potential railroad to insure the road's running their way. This practice was denounced in the 1862 convention and the constitution would have prohibited "local jurisdictions" from "mortgaging themselves" in any way for such a purpose. It was a common method of building railroads and one which some of the delegates personally had practiced.[83]

Unlike the banks, railroads in general and the Illinois Central in particular were not points of partisan controversy before the war. Many opponents of free banking, including Governor French, advocated a general incorporation law for railroads.[84] The Illinois Central was a creation of the leaders of the Illinois Democracy; and conflicts over the road in the legislature were not partisan. For example, while the company was still shaky in the late fifties, a legislative fight over valuation for taxation developed. Abraham Lincoln, the Illinois Central's shrewd lawyer, secured passage of a bill which made the state Supreme Court auditor of the company's assets. The Court and railroad enjoyed friendly relations because of the power of Democrat Judge Sidney Breese whose "life ambition was identified with the success of the Illinois Central Railroad."[85]

Demands for general railroad regulation originated in the fifties in the northern part of the state among farmers and businessmen who were more often than not Republicans. From 1858 throughout the 1860s, merchants, shippers, grain dealers and exporters exerted more or less continuous pressure for various forms of regulation. These moves were promoted by the *Chicago Tribune* and pushed in the legislature by Republicans like Stephen J. Hurlbut and Allen C. Fuller. A sizable portion of the Chicago business community lobbied for rate control warehouse regulation in the Constitutional Convention of 1869–70 and the legislature of the following year which established a "strong" commission for those purposes.[86]

A majority of the Illinois Constitutional Convention of 1862 was not prepared to consider regulation of railroad rates, and the Democratic leadership showed no interest in such proposals. But the convention did write into its constitution laws typical of the first phase of the reaction against railroads. Rolling stock and movable property of railroads were made liable to taxation, "execution and sale," and local governments were prohibited from subscribing to or extending credit for railway stock.[87] The binding of the Illinois Central, while primarily political, can also be considered part of the "withdrawal of favors" stage in Illinois's second thoughts about railroads.

Although the Copperheads who dominated the Illinois Constitutional Convention of 1862 did not engage then in Grangerlike or Greenback agitation and few of these men were involved in the later movements, the agrarian radical thesis could be maintained by showing that ex-Copperheads led or supported these movements in Illinois.[88]

During the Civil War Copperheadism and southern Illinois were almost synonymous. Nationally known peace agitators, resistance to the draft, violent incidents, and secret Southern societies were associated with the area around Egypt. "The region," said Professor Paul Gates, "was honeycombed with Copperheadism."[89] Southern Illinois was the earliest part of the state to be settled and dominated by settlers whose families came originally from Virginia and the Carolinas by way of Kentucky and Tennessee. The early farmers avoided the broad prairies to the north because they thought that the absence of timber there meant that the soil was inferior.[90]

After 1830 New Yorkers and New Englanders began to occupy the northern prairie lands. They tended to come "in parties or even in well organized colonies" and "naturally they sought their kind and kin in the northern counties." Eventually, a sectional divergence and antagonism developed between the northern and southern sections, by no means uniform and complete in either but nevertheless distinct. Upstate critics of Egypt thought the area infested with swamps and malaria and thought its inhabitants shiftless, ignorant, and backward in their farming methods. The southerner desired "only to be left alone by the later immigrants whom he despised."[91]

By 1860 this pattern of settlement emerged in voting trends. Northern counties generally gave majorities to the Republican Party and the Egyptian counties returned the largest Democratic majorities in the state. The vote on the 1862 constitution reflected the cleavage: of some 50 counties below Springfield only seven voted against adoption. The north and the environs of Chicago voted solidly against adoption. The vote in central Illinois, like the strength of the two parties there, was distributed more evenly.[92]

Klement described the "Butternut Democracy" of southern Illinois as ex-Southerners, usually Methodists or Baptists, living on smaller homesteads and poorer soils. He drew the lines of his Butternut-Copperhead even more sharply than the type just delineated above. He mentioned their relatively greater illiteracy, the Negrophobia, their dislike of Congregationalism (a "bourgeois church") and Yankee money men. The Butternuts were "the debtors, the less learned, the small farmers who squeezed out a meager living."[93] This is the type of farmer that the agrarian radicalism thesis would ask one to regard as a typical later Granger and advocate of Greenback inflation.

Information on secondary Greenback leaders is scarce, but none of the state's three major leaders fit the proposed mold.[94] Alexander Campbell was a Whig and then a Republican. Jesse Harper who spoke at most of the Greenback party conventions and received 98 votes for the Presidential nomination in 1880 was a friend of Lincoln and a Republican editor until he split with the party in 1876.[95] Alson J. Streeter who was involved in a number of reform causes ranging from Grangerism to Populism was the Union Labor candidate for president in 1888. He was a Democrat, but not a Copperhead.[96] An examination of twenty other Greenback leaders shows that thirteen were from the northern part of the state, five from the central counties and only two from Egypt. Although Illinois Southerners complained that they did not get their share of the places on the various tickets, it could be argued that they did not provide many votes.[97] Sixty-five of Illinois' one hundred and two counties gave the Greenback Party at least ten percent of their vote in one or more elections between 1876 and 1884. Of the thirty-eight counties which did not, twenty-six were in the southern half of the state. Shelby is the furthest south of the five strongest Greenback counties. Livingston, southwest of Chicago, was the strongest. Among the ten most important counties only Hamilton is in Egypt; and of the top twenty-five, two others near the bottom of the list, Jefferson and Johnson, are in the southern half of the state. Greenback strength centered in a belt of counties approximately one hundred miles wide running south of a line drawn due west from Chicago. Since it had long been known that Greenbackism and Grangerism were related in Illinois, it is not surprising that this is the same area associated with development of the Grange.

There were actually two Granger movements in Illinois. One involved the expansion of the Patrons of Husbandry, the Grange, a farm organization whose purposes were social as well as economic. This is often confused with the earlier movement led by mercantile and commercial elements which resulted in legislative regulation of railroad rates. While these two movements drew support from the same areas, their leadership, organization and objectives were distinct.

The farmers of southern Illinois when not actually in opposition, played a minimal role in the agitation for rate control. Harold D. Woodman has demonstrated the leadership of Chicago businessmen in the passage of the Granger laws;[98] and George Miller has shown that support for rate control in Illinois followed a sectional pattern throughout the sixties, determined by whether or not an area was serviced by railroads. The persistent pattern of legislative voting revealed the serviced areas of northern Illinois as leading exponents of control and "unserved communities in the Egypt area of the south as its bitterest opponents."[99] In the 1870 Constitutional Convention the southerners still remained the staunchest opponents of rate control. The vote on the 1870 rate control law showed that "the centers of opposition were the south and west where the demand for railroads was greatest."[100]

The Patrons of Husbandry in Illinois first appeared in the northwest, the land of ex-Yankees, avid Republicanism, commerce, large-scale farming,[101] and railroads. The first permanent Grange in the state was organized at Nuanda in Henry County in November, 1869. In 1872, when Granger organization gathered momentum, 60–75 Grangers proliferated in Whiteside, Lee and other northern counties in the Henry area.[102] The first Grand Master of the State Grange, Alonzo Golder, came from Whiteside County. The next four Grand Masters lived in counties in the northern (2) and central (2) regions.[103] It has long been recognized that the appeal of the Grange rested on much more than the possibility of economic gain. It relieved rural isolation and loneliness, and socially and culturally acted as a "liberalizing and uplifting influence." It increased the self-esteem of the farmer and his wife, and made them more conscious of their appearance in the eyes of others. On one level of behavior this expressed itself in a "marked improvement in the dress and manners of members."[104]

All that has been said regarding northern and southern Illinois suggests that motives of self-esteem, concern for appearances and for self-improvement tended to affect northern Illinoisans more than their southern neighbors in the 1860s and 70s. Whether one measures such cultural outlooks in terms of improved land, literacy, or the Puritan desire to record the achievements of their past, it was the northern counties that were, as the *Alton Telegraph* said in the 1850s, "imbued with the spirit of 'go-aheaditiviness.'"[105] The "Genesis" of Grangerism and Greenbackism is properly associated with northern Illinois, and probably with the dominant characteristics of that region and its people, among which Copperheadism is not included.

Klement and Jones have placed historians in their debt by the dimensions they have added to our understanding of the Copperheads and by the questions they have implicitly raised.[106] But the assumption underlying their work, that agrarian radicalism explains and connects nineteenth-century protest movements before, during, and after the Civil War, is untenable. At no point does the hypothesis wholly fit the historical record. Although the majority of Copperhead leaders had been Jacksonian Democrats, they were more often lawyer-politicians with business connections than poor farmers. The issues they supported differed substantially from those which Greenbackers and Grangers championed. Few leading Copperheads went into the post war movements; and the leadership and support for those movements came from generally non-Copperhead sources.

David Potter has warned that until historians submit their assumptions and generalizations to critical scrutiny, they may not even understand what it is intrinsically they are discussing.[107] By focusing on an influential thesis employing the concept of agrarian radicalism, we have attempted not merely to dispute that thesis, but also to examine the implicit assumptions making up the concept. The refusal of Klement and others to examine these assumptions has led them into generalization—based on rhetorical similarities and a few atypical and often inaccurate examples—which are clearly at odds with explicit data.

In order better to understand these nineteenth-century social movements historians must develop precise concepts derived from the systematic examination of the socio-political context. This work has hopefully clarified some of the points of controversy regarding the Copperheads, Grangers and Greenbackers, and will make possible the needed re-examination of these movements unrestrained by the outmoded and invalid concept of agrarian radicalism.

University of Rochester   RONALD P. FORMISANO

Lehigh University   WILLIAM G. SHADE

Section Two

"Copperheadism, Grangerism, and Conflicting Contentions: A Rebuttal"

Setting up strawmen and knocking them down with arguments, analogies, and footnotes is an old practice. It is, however, more an art form than an exercise in historical methodology.

Two young historians used the strawman technique—at least in part—in an historical essay entitled "The Concept of Agrarian Radicalism," an argumentative article which appeared in the June 1970 issue of *Mid-America*. They set the stage by writing:

> Frank L. Klement, in his influential article, "Middle Western Copperheadism and the Genesis of the Granger Movement," proposed that Copperheadism "linked Jacksonian Democracy and Grangerism." Klement also asserted, in a later book [*The Copperheads in the Middle West* (Chicago, 1960)], a similar tie between Jacksonian Democracy and Greenbackism. A substantial part of Klement's case rested on his interpretation of the activities of the Illinois Constitutional Convention of 1862. A Democratic majority ran the convention, and the state's Copperheads, dominating that majority, used the convention to attack banks and railroads. Similarly, Stanley L. Jones in "Agrarian Radicalism in Illinois' Constitutional Convention of 1862" asserted [that] the convention "illustrated the vitality of the Jackson movement in the West while it was also a portent of the Granger and Populist movements."[1]

Then comes the strawman: "The idea of agrarian radicalism is the backbone of both interpretations."[2]

This I deny! Nowhere in my article ("Middle Western Copperheadism and the Genesis of the Granger Movement") did I state that midwestern Copperheads were "agrarian radicals"—in fact, I never used the term. Nor was there any reference to Democratic dissenters as "agrarian radicals" in my Copperhead book (*The Copperheads in the Middle West*). In fact, my interpretation is quite the opposite, for I viewed midwestern Copperheads essentially as conservatives who opposed the changes which the Civil War foisted upon their country and their section.[3]

Perhaps it is best to discuss who the Copperheads were—in order to discredit the "agrarian radicalism" label—before linking them to prewar or postwar movements.

The word "Copperhead" or "Copperheads," as smear terms, were devised by Radical Republicans who wanted to discredit Democratic dissenters of Civil War days. Republican editors like Whitelaw Reid of the *Cincinnati Gazette* and Republican propagandists contended that Democratic critics of the Lincoln administration were traitors, symbolized by the poisonous snake with the copper-colored head. Republican propagandists also contended that these so-called "Copperheads" (Democratic dissenters) were partisan, unpatriotic, and pro-Southern. For good measure the Republican propagandists developed the myth that midwestern Democrats or "Copperheads" organized the Knights of the Golden Circle as a subversive society and sponsored treasonable projects like the "Camp Douglas Conspiracy" and the "Northwest Confederacy."[4]

During the postwar years Republicans wrote their interpretation of wartime Democratic dissenters into history. Whitelaw Reid, who used "Copperhead" as a smear term with reckless abandon, and Horace Greeley, whose *New York Tribune* shaped policy and damned the Copperheads, exemplified Republican writers who muddied the stream of history. Reid's *Ohio in the War* and Greeley's *The American Conflict* [5] mixed fact and Republican propaganda in a readable ratio—both accused Democrats of cooperating with the rebels, engaging in treasonable activities, joining secret serpentine societies, and hampering the war effort.

The intensification of nationalism in the 1885–1900 era and the apotheosis of Lincoln helped Americans of those years to accept Republican opinions and contentions as facts. The nationalistic surge helped biographers like William D. Foulke, novelists like Constance Robertson and William Blake, and historians like James Ford Rhodes and Edward Channing to fasten the Republican/nationalist interpretation upon Civil War historiography—developing the myth that Copperheads were men "whose hearts were black, whose blood was yellow, and whose minds were blank." Foulke's *Life of Oliver P. Morton*[6] depicted Indiana's Civil War governor as Sir Galahad, engaged in heroic combat with the forces of evil represented by perfidious Copperheads and conspirators. Robertson's *The Golden Circle* and Blake's *The Copperheads* passed Republican contentions into the realm of popular knowledge; both of these historical novels began with the assumption that Copperheads were traitors, linked to subversive plots.[7] Rhodes' and Channing's historical works, permeated with the nationalism which dominated American thought around the turn of the century, depicted Copperheads as misguided recreants who deserved to be stigmatized for their partisanship and for overstepping the limits of propriety. Rhodes, for example, characterized Copperheads as men who loved "their party better than their country" and described Clement L. Vallandigham (best-known of the Democratic dissenters) as a "cold, calculating, selfish, ambitious, vindictive" man.[8] Channing, who gloried in "the victory of the forces of union over those of particularism," saw rebels and "their Northern sympathizers" (the Copperheads) as wrong-minded men from his view atop Olympus.[9]

The 1920s witnessed forces which rejected the "nationalist tradition" in the writing of history. Intellectuals who thought they had been taken for a ride by President Woodrow Wilson's crusade "to save the world for democracy" turned against war as a means to an end, embraced pragmatism as a philosophy, applauded Henry Mencken's iconoclasm, and began to rewrite nationalistic history. Debunking as a biographical art and Charles A. Beard's concepts regarding economic causation fitted the mood of the 1920s and 1930s. Revisionist historians, reacting to the "nationalistic tradition" of an earlier era, had a field day in rewriting Civil War history. James G. Randall and Avery Craven led the scholars who contended that fanaticism underwrote the crises of the antebellum era and that "a blundering generation" had stumbled into war.[10]

Revisionists also re-examined the role of the Radical Republicans and of President Lincoln—bringing Lincoln scholarship "out of the sheltered eddy, where it had been circulating rather aimlessly, back into the full current of the historical stream."[11]

Even the Copperheads received more sympathetic treatment in historical studies written during the 1920s and 1930s. Mary Scrugham, who detested war "as a just and desirable method of settling disputes between civilized people," argued that the majority of Americans wanted peace in 1861 but were led into war by extremists and selfish politicians who beclouded the "real" issues and manipulated events—she entitled her book *The Peaceable Americans of 1860–61*.[12] Most of Scrugham's "peaceable Americans" of 1860–61 became wartime Copperheads and critics of Lincolnian policy. Edward Kirland's *The Peacemakers of 1864* was void of the scorn which nationalist historians heaped upon those preaching the doctrine of peace and compromise.[13] Stuart Mitchell's *Horatio Seymour of New York*[14] was downright sympathetic to the Democratic war governor. A number of articles which appeared in the learned journals began to debunk some of the Republican propaganda of Civil War days—propaganda which had found its way into history. Earle D. Ross, for example, recognized that western sectionalism underwrote some of the arguments used against measures of the Lincoln administration,[15] and Charles H. Coleman absolved Democrats who had participated in the Charleston (Illinois) riot of 1864 of traitorous designs.[16]

The coming of World War II made patriotism and nationalism popular again and revisionist historians suffered a setback.[17] Wood Gray's *The Hidden Civil War* hung Copperhead quotations and incidents upon the line of treason—arranging them chronologically by chapters, while George Fort Milton's potboiler, entitled *Lincoln and the Fifth Column*, treated Copperheads as traitors, resurrected Civil War legends, and accepted Republican wartime propaganda as fact. Gray portrayed Copperheads as "defeatists" ("men of little faith") who were guilty of partisanship, "hidden weaknesses," and a willingness "to connive" with Confederate agents. "...Vallandigham, ablest and most determined of these men but an epitome of arrogant political egotism," Gray wrote, "was a type that is dangerous in a democracy."[18] Milton's hurriedly concocted thriller combined fact, fancy, and fiction in a readable ratio, damning Copperheads in general and Vallandigham in particular.[19] With subtlety, Milton brought the reader to see parallels between the Copperheads of Civil War days and Nazi sympathizers of his own day. Henry Steele Commager, blindly endorsing Milton's handiwork, character- ized the book as "a stirring and, on the whole heartening, story of how Lincoln out-maneuvered and confounded the appeasers, the defeatists, the malcontents, and the fifth columnists of the Civil War era."[20] Franklin D. Roosevelt gave the book his endorsement, arranging to be photographed holding Milton's book as he was ready to depart for one of his conferences with Churchill and Stalin. FDR's attorney general (Homer S. Cummings) also warmly recommended Milton's potboiler about "the appeasers, the seditionists, and the faint-hearted [Copperheads] of another day when the nation was in peril."[21]

While Milton and Wood gloried in the popularity of their best-sellers, some historians arose to challenge portions of the twice-told tales. Ken- neth M. Stampp's *Indiana Politics during the Civil War* demonstrated that partisanship during the war was practiced by Governor Oliver P. Morton and Indiana Republicans as well as by Indiana Copperheads and that Demo- cratic opposition to the dictatorial practices and policies of the self-righ- teous governor was not sedition or the manifestation of pro-Southern sympathy.[22]

Eleven years later my first book, *The Copperheads in the Middle West*, appeared. According to a student of Civil War politics and dissent, this book "substantiated Stampp's conclusions, but with much wider coverage and more thorough exploration of the aspects of opposition to the administra- tion. Conclusive proof was offered that legitimate discontent with adminis- tration policies and not a combination of treason and partisanship was the basic cause of disaffection in the North."[23]

I would like to think that my Copperhead book (and a series of ar- ticles) did much more than enlarge upon Stampp's contentions and repudi- ate the central themes of Gray's *The Hidden Civil War* and Milton's *Abraham Lincoln and the Fifth Column*. In the first place, I presented midwestern Copperheads as conservatives—"midwestern Democrats who put them- selves on record as critics of change."[24] They opposed the transformation of the federal union into a "new nation" (a centralized state), the ascen- dancy of industrialism over agriculture, the extension of freedom and rights to the black man, the erasure of the Midwest's chances to play balance-of- power politics, and the use of force and bloodshed as a means to reunion. Their slogan "The Constitution as it is and the Union as it was" revealed that Copperheads were traditionalists, tenaciously hanging on to old val- ues and old beliefs—even the doctrine that the black man was an inferior being undeserving of the white man's rights. In the second place, I tried to debunk some of the Republican political propaganda (like the stories about subversive societies, e.g., Knights of the Golden Circle) which polluted the stream of history. In the third place, I attempted to prove that Democratic discontent in the upper Midwest had a socio-economic[25] as well as a political basis. And finally I tried to prove that most Copperheads responded to appeals to sectional prejudice, applauding those who denounced "Puritan domination in religion or morals or literature or politics."[26] Such prominent midwestern Copperheads as Clement L. Vallandigham and Lambdin P. Milligan bluntly called themselves western sectionalists.[27] Some midwestern Copperheads accused President Lincoln of selling his soul and selling out his section to New York capitalists, New England manufacturers, and Pennsylvania iron-mongers.[28] Midwestern Copperheadism, in other words, *possessed a sectional base.*

I have also treated this sectional and socio-economic basis of midwestern Copperheadism in three articles: (1) "Middle Western Copperheadism and the Genesis of the Granger Movement," *Mississippi Valley Historical Review*, 38 (March 1952), 679–94; (2) "Economic Aspects of Middle Western Copperheadism," *The Historian*, 14 (Autumn 1951), 27–44; and (3) "Midwestern Opposition to Lincoln's Emancipation Policy," *Journal of Negro History*, 49 (July 1964), 169–83. Later, in a book entitled *The Limits of Dissent: Clement L. Vallandigham and the Civil War* (Lexington: University Press of Kentucky, 1970), I presented the best-known Copperhead as spokesman for three socio-economic groups (Irish-Americans, German-American Catholics, and the "Butternuts"), as a western sectionalist, and *as a conservative*—due in part to his early exposure to Calvinism, his training in law, and his devotion to Edmund Burke.

Other historians incorporated the Copperheads-as-conservatives thesis into their scholarly studies. Richard O. Curry developed the conservatives vs. radicals theme into his excellent book entitled *A House Divided: A Study of Statehood Politics in West Virginia* (Pittsburgh, 1964).[29] V. Jacque Voegeli touched upon the theme in an incisive work entitled *Free but Not Equal: The Midwest and the Negro during the Civil War* (Chicago, 1967). And Leonard P. Curry, an excellent student of Civil War politics, put conservative tags upon most midwestern Copperheads who served in the Thirty-seventh Congress in his well-researched book, *Blueprint for Modern America: Nonmilitary Legislation of the First Civil War Congress* (Nashville, 1968). Professor Leonard Curry not only put most Democrats who served in the Thirty-seventh Congress into the "conservative category" but he even designated such Copperheads as William J. Allen of Illinois and Clement L. Vallandigham of Ohio as "ultra-conservatives."[30] In other words, both of the Currys discarded the Republican contention that Copperheads were traitors, put these Democratic critics of the Lincoln administration into a historical setting, and classified them as conservatives—*not as agrarian radicals.*

Were the Grangers agrarian radicals? Historians generally agree that the Grange developed as an organization to promote the social, economic, and political betterment of the farmers. Conditions during the early postwar years made farmers and their friends concerned about the declining prices of farm products, the growing indebtedness of farmers to merchants and bankers, the excessive and discriminatory freight rates charged by railroads, the ascendancy of industry over agriculture, the "grading" of wheat by elevator owners and operators, the rise of monopolies (which raised the price of goods farmers purchased), and the social isolation and restricted educational opportunities for residents of rural areas. Although the Grange was reputedly a nonpolitical organization, members employed concerted political action to solve their problems.[31] But were the Grangers agrarian radicals or were they conservatives?

My contention is that Grangers, like midwestern Copperheads, were essentially conservatives, opposing changes and practices which they did not approve. My *American College Dictionary* defines a "radical" as "one who advocates fundamental and drastic political reforms or changes by direct and uncompromising methods."[32] The Grangers, as I understand them, do not fit the definition. They were men of property (often mortgaged, it is true) taking legal and traditional measures to protect their property and advance their interests. When they argued that states had the power to establish railroad commissions they were trying to revive states' rights, a doctrine nearly buried at Appomattox. They were men of law-and-order, turning to state legislatures to protect themselves from being victimized by corporations and capital. Grangers of the postwar era, like Copperheads of Civil War days, wear the conservative tag well. The terms "agrarian discontent" and "agrarian radicalism" are not synonymous!

Was there a link between midwestern Copperheads and Grangers, especially in Illinois? Copperheads of this state had a chance to air their complaints and promote their views in two different assemblages—the Illinois State Constitutional Convention which met on January 7, 1862, and the Democratic-controlled State Legislature of 1863. Both Copperhead-controlled bodies were guilty of "rank partisanship, base politics, slip-shod leadership, and the inopportune extension of its activity into outlying fields."[33]

The '62 constitutional convention, for example, halved the terms of the incumbent Republican state officials, gerrymandered when redrawing the state legislative and the congressional district lines, and conducted investigations intended to discredit the Republican governor. But the Copperhead members also spent considerable time condemning railroad practices which they considered unreasonable, discriminatory, and unfair— *levying the same complaints and advocating the same remedies as the Grangers of the postwar era*. Not only did most Democratic delegates support resolutions calling for an investigation of "the Illinois Central [Railroad] matter," but they also recited a litany of grievances against other railroads and talked of establishing a state commission to control freight rates and regulate railroads—this is the so-called "Granger idea."[34] A host of Democrats (aided by a couple of Republican insurgents like "Long John" Wentworth and Alexander Campbell) levied some of their heaviest siege guns against a number of railroad practices. Daniel Reilly,[35] a miller from Randolph County and active in Granger circles in the postwar era, was one of the leading critics of the railroads at the constitutional convention. He claimed that the closing of the Mississippi river provided the railroads with an opportunity to raise their rates to excessive levels.[36] Delegate R.B.M. Wilson of Tazewell County complained that railroad companies had forced local governments to buy bonds or stocks and that every county from Terre Haute to St. Louis had gone into debt between $80,000 and $100,000 by subscribing for railroad stock—some of which became worthless.[37] Some Democratic delegates denounced the "free pass system" (complimentary passes to state officials, legislators, and politicians generally) as a form of bribery which ought to be outlawed.[38] Some, like Grangers of a later day, complained that absentee capital, whether provided by Wall Street or Fleet Street, dictated rates—"when we may ride and how much we shall pay."[39] Perry A. Armstrong, another Democrat, proposed the establishment of a state commission to supervise freight and passenger rates and service[40]— this is the so-called "Granger idea" of the postwar years. Democrat Daniel Reilly also endorsed this "Granger idea" and espoused states' rights doctrine to give it validity:

> We believe down in Egypt—in that part of Egypt [which] I have the honor of representing—that all corporations are creatures of the State; that what rights and immunities they have are all derived from the State; that they have derived their existence from the State. And we believe also, that railroad corporations are a power in the State not to be despised, but rather to be treated with favor; but that these great establishments are not worthy of favor if they do not favor the interests of the people...[41]

Although the newly drafted constitution failed to provide for the establishment of a railroad commission, the Copperhead-forged document was loaded with provisions aimed at railroad companies. It contained the Grangerlike clause that all private property of a quasi-public nature was "subservient to the public welfare." It declared rolling stock of railroads to be "personal property and liable to execution as such." It guaranteed to railroad mechanics a lien upon the product of their work. It prohibited local governments from subscribing for stock of railroad companies. It bound the Illinois Central Rail Road Company to its charter obligations forbidding any future legislature from cancelling these obligations. It tried to restrict special legislation (often a form of favoritism) by specifying that bills should be read at large on three separate days.[42]

The Democratic-controlled convention, however, had alienated more than the railroad and banking interests. It alienated most Republicans because of its rank partisanship, and the party's editors and leaders waged a vicious campaign against its ratification, even linking the so-called "Springfield abomination" to Confederate influence and the Knights of the Golden Circle.

The "Copperhead Constitution," therefore, failed in its ratification test, in part because the railroads, banks, and express companies threw their full weight against the document.[43] John M. Douglas, attorney for the Illinois Central Rail Road Company, was "jubilant over the results."[44]

The antirailroad element of the Democracy was also active in the so-called "Copperhead Legislature" of 1863—Grangerlike arguments were again repeated and recited. Early in the session William Berry, a Democrat from McDonough County (in west central Illinois), introduced a Grangerlike resolution which read: "*Resolved,* That the committee on Judiciary be instructed to examine whether or not the present exorbitant and ruinous rates of charges for transportation on the railroads of this state, can be restrained by law, and if so, to report a bill effectively guarding the interests of the country and the people against the same."[45] Later the upper house passed a measure to put the so-called "Granger idea" into law, providing for a three-member state commission with rate-making powers.[46]

The railroad commission bill made slower headway in the lower house, but it eventually passed most hurdles and was made the "special order" for June 10, 1863.[47] Republican Governor Richard Yates, however, invalidated the work of the antirailroad Copperheads by proroguing the state legislature upon a technicality—nullifying the antirailroad hopes of Copperheads who had recited their Grangerlike grievances as well as the partisan and peace convention proposals of discontented Democrats.[48] So Governor Yates and Republican partisans were able to sabotage the programs of Copperheads in the state legislature as they had earlier nullified the efforts of Democrats who had dominated the constitutional convention a year earlier.

When the co-authors of the article "The Concept of Agrarian Radicalism" argued that few Copperheads of Civil War days became prominent in the postwar Granger movement, they are on solid ground. But it was ground I had earlier cultivated. I too found that Daniel Reilly was one of the few Copperheads who provided a lineal link with Grangerism. Twenty years ago I researched the early leadership of the Grange in Illinois—perusing Jonathan Periam, *The Groundswell: A History of the Origin, Aims, and Progress of the Farmers' Movement* (Cincinnati, 1874) and a dozen other sources. I, too, found that nearly all the Illinois leaders of the Granger movement came of Republican antecedents. Grange leadership had little to do with party; activity was most intense in those areas where railroads existed and where complaints against management practices were most numerous—and there were many more miles of railroads in the Republican counties than in the counties which were in Copperhead hands during the war years.

The co-authors of the article "The Concept of Agrarian Radicalism" seem to have ignored the conjunction in the title of my article "Middle Western Copperheadism and the Genesis of the Granger Movement." The conjunction is "and," not "as." The conjunction "and" was chosen deliberately—partially because the relationship of midwestern Copper-headism and the Granger movement was not lineal. The conjunction "and" gave one a chance to recognize that the Granger movement had eastern antecedents even before the Civil War.[49] It also gave one a chance to contend that the link of midwestern Copperheadism and postwar Grang-erism was philosophical—one of ideas rather than men—and to point out that antirailroad grievances repeated in the 1870s had been recited in the 1860s.

The concluding paragraphs of the article "Middle Western Copper-headism and the Genesis of the Granger Movement" are as valid now as they were twenty years ago:

> Midwest Copperheadism had much in common with Grangerism. Both were sectional protests. Both were grounded in economic griev-ances. Both flaunted the banner of state rights, emphasized civil liber-ties and individual rights, and muttered Jeffersonian phrases. They spoke of human rights and of opposition to the vested interests. Grang-erism, yet unnamed, was evident in the claims and language of that lesser known Copperhead who represented Schuyler County at the Illinois constitutional convention and who succinctly stated, "I believe this doctrine of vested rights to be a great humbug—a cobweb—gotten up by the lawyer to confuse the common man."[50] ...Truly, Grangerism existed in the Middle West before Oliver Hudson Kelley contributed the name, the organic structure, and the organizing zeal.
>
> Not all Copperheads were antirailroad men, nor were all antirailroad men Copperheads. But it was no coincidence that Illinois Copperheads in session, whether in the constitutional convention of 1862 or the leg-islature of 1863, took measures to check railroad abuses and to pro-claim the Granger doctrine of state control and regulation.[51]

Marquette University   FRANK L. KLEMENT

Democrats as Copperheads and Critics

Time and again, in various articles, I have pointed out that the so-called "Copperheads" drew their membership from four socioeconomic groups: (1) Irish-Americans, (2) German-American Catholics, (3) the "Butternuts," and (4) middle-class Americans who viewed themselves as disciples of Jacksonian and Jeffersonian Democracy. The first two groups get special treatment in Chapter VI. The last two groups receive full play in the last three chapters of Part Three.

What about German-American Lutherans? In Wisconsin, Iowa, and Illinois perhaps half of the German-American Lutherans were Democrats, most of whom belonged to the Missouri Synod. Rev. C. F. W. Walther, the genius of the Missouri Synod, had written treatises in defense of slavery. Party membership of German-Americans might depend upon what newspapers they read or the views expressed by local leaders or pastors.

German-American Lutherans in Ohio usually voted the Republican ticket, supposedly influenced by opinions expressed in German-language newspapers or by church leaders. The so-called "Forty-eighters" had their own category; some were free thinkers. With few exceptions the "Forty-eighters" voted for Lincoln. Men like Carl Schurz and Franz Sigel were first-rate abolitionists and second-rate generals.

Chapter VII, "Midwestern Opposition to President Lincoln's Emancipation Policy" and Chapter VIII "Ohio Politics in 1863" drew heavily upon newspapers as sources. Clement L. Vallandigham was an important character in both—he was the central figure in the latter.

91

The supposition that Vallandigham courted arrest as a means to gain his party's gubernatorial nomination in 1863 was first presented in my Vallandigham book *(The Limits of Dissent: Clement L. Vallandigham and the Civil War)*. It was challenged by a reviewer. But I am more convinced of it now than when I first presented it.

Vallandigham and "Brick" Pomeroy, both of whom gained a reputation as critics of Lincoln and the war, were men of different molds. Vallandigham remained a confirmed Presbyterian although he dropped his membership in a church where the pastor preached abolition doctrine; Pomeroy disdained organized religion. Vallandigham was a family man; Pomeroy, in a day when divorce was a disgrace, was married three times and divorced three times. Vallandigham carefully considered options; Pomeroy seemed to act haphazardly—Vallandigham's gun was a sharpshooter's rifle, Pomeroy's a blunderbuss. Vallandigham excelled in oratory; Pomeroy wielded a facile pen, and two books, *Sense* and *Nonsense*, earned him a reputation as a writer. When traveling medicine shows visited Dayton, Vallandigham stayed at home; when such shows visited LaCrosse, Pomeroy finagled a role in them. Vallandigham hid his ambitions and self-righteousness with a cloak of modesty—that word was not in Pomeroy's vocabulary and he gloried in being outrageous so he could be in the spotlight. Vallandigham deserves consideration as a dissenter; Pomeroy who blended eccentricity with ability, has already received more attention than he deserves.

Vallandigham should not be removed from his historical setting when he is evaluated. General Burnside's "General Orders, No. 38" deserved censure then as it receives now. Nor should historians ignore General Hascall's "General Order, No. 9," issued in neighboring Indiana, when judging Vallandigham. Hascall, like Burnside, stated that "the habit of declaring sympathy [as they interpreted it] for the enemy" would not be tolerated. Hascall added, "...the country will have to be saved or lost during the time this Administration remains in power, and therefore he who is factiously and actively opposed to the war policy of the Administration is as much opposed to his Government." Hascall proceeded to "save" the country by suppressing Democratic newspapers, denying Democrats the right to buy arms, censoring the mail, and making arrests here and there. When Vallandigham made the two speeches that led to his arrest, his call for civil rights was as much a critique of Hascall as it was of Burnside.

CHAPTER VI

Catholics as Copperheads during the Civil War

American Catholics were prominent in the ranks of the "Copperheads," a term applied to the Democratic critics of the Lincoln administration during the American Civil War. Most of the Catholic critics, with the exception of individuals like Orestes Brownson and Count Adam Gurowski, came from two elements of the heterogeneous population of the country: Irish-Americans and German-American Catholics.

Earlier, the Irish-Americans had developed an affinity for Jeffersonian and Jacksonian Democracy, and events of the 1840–1860 era cemented their affiliation with the Democratic party. John O'Sullivan, editor of the *Democratic Review*, had coined the phrase "Manifest Destiny," and James K. Polk and Stephen A. Douglas made it meaningful.

The Republican party, founded during the 1850s as Whiggery disintegrated, became the home of three *isms*: prohibitionism, abolitionism, and Know-Nothingism. Irish-Americans and German-Americans detested each of the three, ofttimes reacting emotionally. The Irish regarded whisky and pubs as part of their culture and the Germans felt the same way about schnapps and lager beer. The Irish and German-Americans detested abolitionism, for they feared that emancipation would release a flood of cheap labor that would threaten their very livelihood. American Irish and German-American Catholics also detested Know-Nothingism, an anti-Catholic movement that was "the leading American neurosis" of the 1840–1860 era.[1] The election of William Pennington, a Know-Nothinger from New Jersey, as speaker of the House of Representatives in early 1860 fused the Know-Nothing movement with the Republican party. Nor did the Catholics forget earlier events: Maria Monk's *Awful Disclosures* (a pack of lies that went through twenty printings), the burning of the Ursuline convent near Boston, and the published posters "No Irish Need Apply." Small wonder, then, that about ninety-eight percent of the Irish-Americans voted the Democratic ticket and distrusted President Lincoln. The German-American Catholics were not far behind.

Yet, after Confederate forces fired upon Fort Sumter and the president called for 75,000 men, most American Catholics supported the war. Miles O'Reilly, a poet and a Democratic partisan, put his sentiments into words:

> To the tenets of Douglas we tenderly cling,
> Warm hearts to the cause of our country we bring;
> To the flag we are pledged—all its foes we abhor—
> And we ain't for the "nigger" but we are for the war.[2]

Although most Catholics seemed to support the war, there were dissenters. James A. McMaster, the Irish-American who edited the (New York) *Freeman's Journal*, not only rejected war as a means to an end, but roiled Republicans by defending secession as a political principle—he was arrested and incarcerated while the paper was suppressed. Frederic W. Horn, a German-Catholic living in Cedarburg, Wisconsin, resigned his captaincy in the state militia rather than partake in a war that might "subjugate" his section of the country to "Pennsylvania Ironmongers and New England manufacturers."[3] James J. Faran, an Irish-American who edited the influential *Cincinnati Enquirer*, had reservations about the war and he gradually evolved into a carping critic. Dennis A. Mahony of the *Dubuque Herald* wrote that President Lincoln's call for 75,000 volunteers "was in one aspect at least, also violative of the Constitution."[4] When Lincoln, by proclamation of May 3, 1861, called for an additional 23,000 three-year volunteers for the army and 18,000 for the navy, Mahony protested strongly. He called that proclamation "a manifest and unquestionable assumption of arbitrary power." "The step between this and the *coup d'tout* of a despot," a Mahony-written editorial stated, "is short and easily taken."[5] Lambdin P. Milligan, proud of his Celtic background and his religion—he was a regular communicant at St. Mary's Church in Huntington, Indiana—opposed the military coercion of the South from the very beginning; he regarded himself as a strict constructionist and a state's righter.[6] There were others.

As the months passed by, these Democratic dissenters grew more brazen in their criticism of President Lincoln and the war. The patriotic surge that followed Fort Sumter's surrender ebbed with the passage of time. Worse than that, an economic depression visited the upper Midwest for the Mississippi River blockade, and the loss of Southern markets depressed farm prices. There also was "a bank panic" because the paper money of many midwestern banks was based upon Southern bonds in the hands of state auditors. Many, many banks "went under"; only seventeen out of 112 in Illinois, for example, survived in 1861. The agriculture and bank problems were followed by "a commercial recession." The hard times caused some who had earlier supported the war to turn against the Lincoln administration. A Cincinnati Catholic, writing to his Democratic congressman, appraised the situation:

> Matters look blue enough here; business men have long faces and short money receipts. One Jim Brown & Co. say they have lost $40,000 since the election by depreciation in stock. There are three of them and each voted for Lincoln, "God and Liberty," and now say they "wish Lincoln and all political parties were in hell."[7]

Dennis A. Mahony, the ebullient Irish editor of the *Dubuque Herald*, bluntly blamed the Lincoln administration for his section's ills: "Grain has gone down till it won't pay hauling charges." An editorial stated, "So much for electing a man—the exponent of Personal Liberty Bills, Nigger Suffrage, and Equality, Beecherism, Stoweism, Niggerism, and a dozen isms and Tom fooleries upon which the entire North under the lead of Abolitionized Massachusetts has gone mad."[8]

Although General U.S. Grant's victory at Fort Donelson in February 1862 regained a little respect for the Lincoln administration, the defeat of the Army of the Potomac in the Peninsula Campaign tarnished it again. Congressional action in several instances caused uneasiness among many Democrats: one act abolished slavery in the District of Columbia; another did the same for the western territories; the Confiscation Act gave the president a chance to strike at slavery; and there were more. Furthermore, President Lincoln suggested compensated emancipation in the border states in messages to Congress in March and April of 1862.

These so-called "abolition measures" aroused Irish and German-Catholic Democrats who resented the influx of "contrabands"—a term applied to ex-slaves entering the Union lines, many moving into the states bordering the Ohio River. Cincinnati Irish had reasons to be concerned. In May and June of 1862 the proprietor of the Burnet House, considered the finest hotel in the West, dismissed fifty Irish lads and lassies and replaced them with "contrabands"—at lower wages. During June and July, employers replaced Irish and German dock workers and boathands with "contrabands" flooding the Cincinnati area—again at lower wages.[9] "The jealousy of the low Germans and Irish against the free negro," an English journalist touring the upper Midwest wrote, "was sufficient to set them against the war which would have brought four million black rivals in competition for the hard and dirty work which American freedom bestowed on them."[10]

The Catholic editor of the *Cincinnati Enquirer* fanned the flames of discontent, pointing out that, in Philadelphia, the use of "colored workers" had depressed the market for whites, especially Irish-Americans:

Like causes will produce like results here. How do our white laborers relish the prospect that the emancipation of the blacks spreads before them? What do they think of the inundation of two or three thousand free [Negroes] into Ohio, which inundation will come if we carry out the emancipation policy of President Lincoln. How many whites will be thrown out of employment? How much will it reduce the price of labor?[11]

Editor Faran's comments, giving an economic base to racism, was the match that started a fire. Several dozen Irish, leaving pubs and adding recruits along the way, headed for the riverfront. They drove newly hired blacks off the docks and boats. Then, becoming a mob, they invaded "Shantytown" or "Bucktown," terms applied to the sections of Cincinnati where most of the blacks lived, and put houses and shacks to the torch. The participants in the riot beat up every black that they could catch—thus expressing their antipathy to emancipation. That night some blacks retaliated with a raid upon "Dublin," an area inhabited by Cincinnati's poorer Irish. The mayor of Cincinnati issued a proclamation denouncing the violence and the chief of police recruited a posse of about a hundred to stop the rioting.[12]

In the days and months that followed, the Catholic hierarchy of Cincinnati and the Catholic editor of the *Enquirer* waged a war of words for the minds and hearts of the Irish and German-Catholics of the area. Archbishop John Purcell and his brother, who edited the *Catholic Telegraph*, led the attack against both slavery and Civil War dissent. They were ably assisted by Bishop Sylvester Rosecrans, Purcell's coadjutor and brother of Gen. William S. Rosecrans—both of the brothers were German-Americans and converts to Catholicism. The *Catholic Telegraph* called slavery "a monstrous crime," adding, "It corrupts heart and soul, and we have no respect for the Christianity of any person who, now that the evil is dying out, would wish to see it restored."[13] Editor Faran did not say that he wanted slavery restored or destroyed, but he stressed the fact that he did not want his readers to have their livelihood threatened by the inundation of "contrabands." He was interested in reality, he said, favoring practicality to theory. He gained more subscribers from the Democratic ranks and became even more critical of the Lincoln administration and the war in the months ahead. Archbishop Purcell and his able assistants did not win the war of words. Cincinnati, with its large Irish and German population, remained a Democratic stronghold, adverse to abolitionism and the war.[14]

A similar scenario occurred in Dubuque, where the Catholic editor of the *Herald*, the city's Democratic and antiwar newspaper, saw politics through different spectacles than his bishop, Mathias Loras. The respected bishop believed that slavery was morally wrong and that the war merited the support of all good citizens. On the other hand, editor Mahony opposed President Lincoln and emancipation from the very beginning. The slender and slightly stooped editor's physique belied the presence of a strong mind steeped in Jeffersonian principles. Erudite, versed in law, history, and logic, the irascible editor was more than a match for his nemesis, Jesse Clement of the Republican-oriented *Dubuque Times* as well as his saintly bishop.[15]

Mahony, who distrusted Lincoln, berated the various presidential proclamations. His lengthy editorials, always argumentative, cited tradition and sections of the Bill of Rights. Earlier, he had applauded Chief Justice Roger B. Taney's reprimand of Lincoln in *Ex Parte Merryman* (1861) and he had scolded the president for the arrest of nineteen members of the Maryland state legislature.[16] The Catholic editor was especially critical of Secretary of War Edwin M. Stanton's order of August 8, 1862, which authorized U.S. marshals and others "to arrest and imprison any person who may have engaged by act, speech, or writing, in discouraging volunteer enlistments, or in any way giving aid and comfort to the enemy...."[17] This order, suspending the writ of habeas corpus, served as the excuse for a score of arrests in the upper Midwest—including that of Dennis A. Mahony.

About 3:30 a.m., very early on August 14, 1862, a federal marshal and two aides called at Mahony's residence, arrested the protesting editor, and carted him off to a waiting steamboat to begin the first leg of a long journey that took him to Old Capitol Prison in Washington, where he was confined in Cell No. 13.[18] No formal charges were ever filed against him, but the Republican press accused him of disloyalty, sympathizing with the South, and opposing the war. After nearly four months of confinement, Mahony and several others were released after they promised that they "would not prosecute Federal or State officers who had been concerned in our arrest."[19]

Irish-Americans often paid a heavy price for their loyalty to the Democratic party. In Chester County, Pennsylvania, an Irishman who voted the Democratic ticket in October of 1862 lost his job. His employer, after discharging him, said, "We can never have the same feeling towards you again; it would be disagreeable for you to remain and even more so for us."[20]

Some of the Catholic editors who had earlier given the war qualified support, turned against the Lincoln administration after the president issued his emancipation proclamations—the first on September 23, 1862, and the second on January 1, 1863. John Mullaly, the Irish editor of the *(New York) Metropolitan Record*, falls in that category; Mullaly's paper called itself "A Catholic Family Newspaper," and the editor would become a true Copperhead in 1863. The same was quite true of the *See-Bote*, a German-language weekly that catered to German-Catholics in the Milwaukee area. The *See-Bote* was mildly critical of Lincoln early in the war and strongly critical after the president added emancipation as a war policy. The *See-Bote* dated back to January 1852, when Bishop John Martin Henni authorized the establishment of a newspaper that could counter the anti-Catholic tirades of such Milwaukee papers as the *Flugblaetter*, the *Volksfreund*, and the *Humanist*. During the Civil War years the *See-Bote* was ably edited by a most capable German-American, Peter V. Deuster. Always opposed to abolitionism, he called that movement's leaders "disunion devils" or "disunion demagogues" and referred to the other Milwaukee-based German-language newspapers as "the German Nigger press." Noting the spread of emancipation sentiment in 1862, the Catholic editor of the *See-Bote* asked his readers to check its "infiltration." "Let us," he wrote with feeling, "resist this evil from the very beginning! The North belongs to the free white men, not to the Negro. To him Nature has provided other regions." One edition of Deuster's newspaper bore the headline: "Abolition the Worst Enemy of the Free White Laborer" and the editor gave some advice: "Workmen! Be Careful! Organize yourself against this element that threatens your impoverishment and annihilation."[21]

Edward G. Ryan, a Catholic attorney of Milwaukee, destined to become the greatest Chief Justice in the history of the Supreme Court of Wisconsin in the postwar era, also was most critical of President Lincoln's proclamations. Ryan considered himself a constitutionalist. He wrote the Democratic platform preceding the '62 elections and it took Lincoln to task in a scholarly way—this stinging indictment came to be known as "the Ryan Address." Ryan's public speeches were centered around the same theme.[22]

The criticism offered by three Milwaukee-area Catholics (Edward G. Ryan, Peter V. Deuster, and Frederic W. Horn) helped to set the stage for the best-known antidraft riot of 1862. Since some Wisconsin counties (Ozaukee, Washington, and Milwaukee Counties were among them) failed to provide their quota of volunteers, state officials decided to resort to a draft. Recognizing that such action might affect the results of the fall elections adversely, the Republican governor shamelessly postponed the draft until after the November elections. This political ploy was exposed by Deuster of the *See-Bote* as "a political trick."[23]

Antidraft sentiment was especially strong among the German-Americans and Luxembourgers in the Port Washington area of Ozaukee County. Some of the residents subscribed to the *See-Bote* and agreed with its anti-abolitionist and antidraft sentiments. "European immigrants," editor Deuster once wrote, would become "fodder for cannons" at the wishes of the abolitionists. The Irish and Germans, he added, "must be annihilated to make room for the Negro...."[24] Secondly, William Pors, a prominent Mason and the draft commissioner, was thought to have secured exemptions for his Masonic friends. Furthermore, only one Catholic priest had been named a chaplain in the first twenty-three Wisconsin volunteer regiments—this was for the nearly all-Irish 17th. Every Catholic, a Port Washington priest said, desires "the consolation of his religion in the hour of danger and death." The priest added, "...this accounts for the German Catholic reluctance to enlist."[25] Finally, Secretary of War Stanton had ruled that German and Irish-

Americans who had voted but were not yet full-fledged citizens were eligible for the draft—Stanton had once been a Know-Nothinger and he knew that the Irish and German-Americans were usually Democrats and that few Republican votes would be lost.

Early in the morning of November 10, as Commissioner Pors readied the machinery of the draft atop the steps leading to the county courthouse, a crowd gathered. There were some calls: "No draft!" The crowd, made up mostly of Luxembourgers and German-Americans, became uneasy as time for the lottery drew near. Amid calls of "No draft!" a couple of burly fellows moved forward, grabbed the commissioner, threw him down, and with a kick or two started him on his way down the steps. Others hit him or kicked and cursed him as he rolled and bounced to the bottom. Bruised and battered when he reached the street, Pors managed to get up and run for his life, pursued by a motley group of men, women, and children. He escaped into the basement of the post office, locked himself in, and prayed for his safety. Other members of the mob destroyed the machinery of the draft, seized the box with the enrollment records, and started a bonfire in the street.

The mob broke into segments and vented its wrath upon eight homes (Masons and Republicans). Commissioner Pors' house suffered the most as the ruthless invaders tore clothes to ribbons, raided the fruit cellar, spread jam and jelly upon upholstered furniture and fine carpets, and broke some furniture for a fire in the street.[26]

The governor of Wisconsin sent troops to Port Washington to restore order and resume the draft. Officials arrested about 150 of the rioters. Under orders from the governor, the prisoners were turned over to Federal authorities, to be tried by courts-martial in accordance with President Lincoln's proclamation (suspending the writ of habeas corpus) of September 24, 1862.[27] Edward G. Ryan, anxious to rebuke the Lincoln administration, offered his legal services free to his fellow Catholics—the fifty who remained as prisoners. He took their cause to the Wisconsin State Supreme Court in a case called *In Re Kemp*. Ryan presented an emotional yet reasoned plea. He damned the Lincoln administration for "government by proclamation." He insisted that Congress alone had the right to suspend the writ of habeas corpus. A dictatorship or a despotism might develop, Ryan said, if the rights of citizens could be restricted by presidential proclamations. The impassioned Ryan ended with a flourish: "I want to see the Court have the courage to set the brute law of the sword at defiance!"[28]

In January 1863 the Wisconsin State Supreme Court issued its decision (*In Re Kemp*). The majority of the judges, Democrats before their appointment to the court, accepted Ryan's line of reasoning that Congress, not the president, had the right to suspend the writ of habeas corpus. So *In Re Kemp* was a rebuke to Lincoln, and, in the eyes of his Democratic critics, a victory for civil rights.[29] Secretary of War Stanton and the president wanted a speedy review by the U.S. Supreme Court but backed off when they realized that Chief Justice Roger B. Taney (a Catholic) might reprimand the administration again—the first time was in *Ex Parte Merryman* (1861). The fifty prisoners were freed—a bitter pill for Stanton.[30]

Despite the antiwar sentiments and statements of some leading Democrats, many Irish and German-American Catholics enlisted in great numbers throughout 1862. Some were motivated by patriotism. Others sought an occupation or adventure. Many were tempted by the seemingly generous bounties offered to volunteers—several hundred dollars seemed like a fortune. "No fewer than thirty-eight regiments," a historian noted, "had used the word 'Irish' in their names."[31] As soldiers, the Irish and German-American Catholics generally fought well and the praise of their superiors was commonplace. At times casualties were heavy, with the battle of Gettysburg as but one example. Then there were the nuns, whom some hospital residents portrayed as angels. Even Lincoln applauded the charitable work of the Sisters of Mercy.[32]

The typical Irish soldier entered the war as a Democrat, unsympathetic to emancipation and opposed to blacks as soldiers. There was a latent prejudice, and it was exemplified by an Irish corporal who wrote, "We don't want to fight side by side with the nigger. We think we are too superior a race for that."[33] There were cases where Irish and German-American soldiers deserted after Lincoln's Emancipation Proclamations made abolition another objective of the war. But army life, and hatred of the enemy, gradually undermined the antiemancipation sentiments of many Irish and German soldiers.

Dissenters who hoped that the Democratic election victories in the fall of 1862 might tempt Lincoln to sidetrack the promised Emancipation Proclamation of January 1, 1863 were disappointed with the president's message to Congress of December 1, 1862. "The tenacity with which Mr. Lincoln holds to his emancipation proclivities, notwithstanding the rebuke administered in the result of the election in the north last fall," a Catholic Democrat named Thomas Dudley wrote, "cannot fail, I think, to alarm the friends of the Union and Constitutional liberty throughout our broad land."[34] Quite a number of Democratic editors, Mahony among them, suggested that President Lincoln be impeached. Events of the year prompted Count Adam Gurowski; a Polish-American who lived in Washington and often criticized President Lincoln, to write in his diary: "Dec. 31, 1862—midnight—Disappear! Oh year of disgraces, year of slaughter and sacrifices."[35]

As far as many Catholic critics of Lincoln were concerned, the Emancipation Proclamation of January 1, 1863, was the last straw. "Abolition created the Administration, has shaped its policy, has dictated its appointments, and must be left to furnish the material requisites of men and money," Mahony of the *Dubuque Democratic Herald* wrote.[36] This "last desperate measure," Mahony added, absolved Democrats from further support of the war:

The people who submit to the insolent fanaticism which dictated this last act, *are and deserve to be enslaved* to the class which Abraham Lincoln self-sufficiently declares free. If they possess a tithe of the spirit which animated Rome when Cataline was expelled from its walls...they would hurl him into the Potomac...Cabinet, Congress, and all.[37]

Mullaly's *Metropolitan Record*, originally partially subsidized by Archbishop John Hughes of New York, expressed sentiments quite similar to Mahony's. He even predicted a black-versus-white war in the United States, quite like that which had occurred in San Domingo. Mullaly called Lincoln's January 1, 1863, proclamation "a vile and infamous document" that would "release a flood of cheap labor" that would "ruin" Irish-Americans.[38] Echoing Mahony's views, Mullaly also said that Lincoln's proclamation "excused" Irish-Americans from further support of the war.[39]

Other Catholic editors also criticized the second emancipation proclamation. Faran of the *Cincinnati Enquirer* wrote harshly and appealed to the Negrophobia so widespread in the area. Deuster of the *See-Bote* again criticized the president, and his opposition to emancipation became an obsession that he cultivated during the remaining months of 1863.[40]

The Conscription Act of March 3, 1863, was as "despicable" to Irish-Americans and German-American Catholics as emancipation. The act's $300 commutation clause, allowing a draftee to buy his way out or hire a substitute, gave Democratic critics plenty of ammunition. "The immigrant, still without voting rights," Deuster wrote in the *See-Bote*, "would be the first to be sacrificed for the New England Yankees." The act allowed "rich Republicans" and "aristocratic New Englanders" to buy their way out; it was "the Polish forcing act," reminiscent of the drafting of Poles by the Russian government.[41] Mullaly of the *Metropolitan Record* played a similar tune. An editorial in the May 14, 1863, issue bore the headline: "The United States Converted Into a Military Despotism—The Conscription Act the Last Deadly Blow Aimed at Popular Liberty."[42] Mullaly's censure of the Lincoln administration alienated Archbishop Hughes, and the Catholic churchman severed his link with the newspaper. The critical editorials, written by Mullaly, finally brought about his arrest on August 19, 1864. Nearly every Catholic editor in the country was critical of the Conscription Act for one reason or another but few went as far as the editor of the *Metropolitan Record* as to vicious criticism.

Mullaly's antidraft editorials were sometimes reprinted in other Democratic newspapers. That practice brought unwanted results to Daniel Flanagan, the Irish-Catholic editor of the *Mason (Ohio) Democrat*; he was arrested by army officials, tried before a military commission in Cincinnati, and sentenced to six months imprisonment in Fort Delaware.[43]

Mahony left Dubuque for New York City in mid-January of 1863 to put together a manuscript that would be published as a book entitled *The Prisoner of State*. He dedicated the book to Secretary of War Stanton:

Sir—Having considered for some time to whom it was most appropriate to dedicate a work describing the kidnapping of American freemen
by arbitrary power, and their incarceration without trial or the judgment
of any court in Military Prisons, no one has so well earned the unenvi-
able distinction as yourself of having your name connected so imper-
ishably with the infamy of the acts of outrage, tyranny, and despotism
which the book, I hereby, dedicate to you, will publish to the American
people.

The last sentence of the two-page dedication read: "I am, sir [Stanton], one
of the many hundred victims of the despotism of the arbitrary power of
which you have become the willing, servile, and pensioned tyrant."[44]

The contents of the strange book, constituting the testament of a
Catholic dissenter of Civil War days, included a long introduction (a reasoned essay), editorials from the *Dubuque Herald*, a journal kept by Mahony
while he was confined in Old Capitol Prison, descriptions of prison life,
vignettes of other prisoners, and a hodgepodge of reminiscences. Although
blatantly partisan, it is nevertheless an important historical document.

During the early months of 1863, while Mahony was preparing the
text for his strange book and while Catholic soldiers were dying on far-
flung battlefields, Republican strategists took steps to discredit Democratic
dissenters and retain control of public opinion. One stratagem was to discredit Democratic critics as Southern sympathizers and "Copperheads"—
partisans with a disloyal bent. The smear campaign, headed by the Radical
Republican editors of Cincinnati newspapers, equated Democratic critics
with the poisonous snake that had a brown-blotched body and a copper-
colored head—allies of South Carolina's rattlesnakes. The campaign was
so effective that even today's dictionaries define a "Copperhead" as "a
Northern who sympathized with the South during the Civil War."[45]

A second stratagem was to devise a bogeyman—the Knights of the
Golden Circle. Although not a single chapter or castle of the Knights of the
Golden Circle existed north of the Ohio River during the war, Republican-
sponsored propaganda portrayed the K.G.C. as a subversive society with
hundreds of thousands of members—an auxiliary of the Democratic party.
In 1863 the Order of American Knights replaced the Golden Circle as the
favorite Republican bogeyman and in 1864 the Sons of Liberty took the
headlines. Most Catholic critics of the Lincoln administration were not only
smeared as "Copperheads" but falsely accused of belonging to secret subversive societies.

A third stratagem was to organize a secret society, the Union League,
and present it to the public as a patriotic, nonpartisan organization—to
secure the non-committed voters. Actually, the Union League was the right
arm of the Republican party and the various chapters became agencies to
distribute political propaganda and win elections. These three political stratagems, aided by Union victories at Gettysburg and Vicksburg, undercut

Democratic dissent and served as a sedative to the movement for peace and compromise.[46]

The three Republican stratagems, as well as the Union victories at Gettysburg and Vicksburg, did little to quash the dissent so widespread in New York City, especially the areas inhabited by Irish-American and German-American Catholics. Perhaps forty percent of New York residents were Irish-Americans and the approach of conscription cast an aura of gloom over their households. In the minds of many, the war to save the Union had evolved into a war to free the slaves. After all, blacks or "contrabands" had been brought in as "scabs" to break a bitter dock strike staged mainly by Irish stevedores in April 1863—there was a residue of resentment in the days that followed.

Early in July, authorities decided to set the machinery of the draft in motion. When quotas were assigned to the various congressional districts, Irish blood boiled. "One district with a population of 131,000 had a draft quota of 5,881," one historian wrote, "while a neighboring and slightly larger district had a quota of only 2,697."[47] Was this blatant and unfair discrimination against the Irish-Americans?

The discriminatory aspects of the $300 exemption clause were also cussed and discussed in the grog shops and on street corners, giving critics a chance to say that "it was a rich man's war and a poor man's fight." A newspaper man visiting an Irish grog shop "to sample Celtic sentiment" got an earful. One unhappy Irishman asked the reporter, "Does he [Lincoln] think that the poor men are to give up their lives and let rich men pay three hundred dollars in order to stay home?" A second said that he would not shoulder a musket "in defense of an abolition administration." And a third, who opposed the draft, proved to be a prophet: "If Lincoln attempts the draft in New York, in violation of State authority, there will be black eyes and bloody noses."[48]

Col. Robert Nugent, an Irish-Catholic who served as the state's assistant provost marshal, set Saturday, July 11, 1863, as the day for drawing the names of draftees in the Ninth District, consisting of the nearly all-Irish 18th, 20th, and 21st wards.[49] The draft, held only in the 9th District on that day, proceeded without incident despite the presence of a large crowd; by four o'clock, p.m., 1,236 names had been drawn, announced, and recorded.[50] But it was a mistake to begin the draft on a Saturday and let unrest fester in the overflowing pubs the next day. Some members of an all-Irish fire-fighting company (Black Joke Engine Company No. 33) met secretly Sunday night to discuss ways to stop the drafting scheduled to be resumed next morning. Reports of "the plan" spread through the neighborhoods.

Next morning, crowds assembled in the streets. Men, in groups, walked into factories to recruit more members for the task ahead. Soon the mob approximated several thousand. Someone in some way directed the milling mob to the 9th District office where drafting had been resumed at 9:00 a.m.

Soon a huge crowd, rather unruly, had gathered there. After the fifty-sixth name had been drawn, announced, and recorded, someone shouted "No more!" and the crowd surged forward. Individuals threw stones, bricks, and paving blocks—the hose cart of Black Joke Engine Company No. 33 was soon emptied of its "missiles."

The rioters routed the draft officials and the police squad present, set fire to the building, and celebrated. Vandalism, arson, and violence spread over the city. The mob attacked and drove off a detail of policemen and even a company of marines. A portion of the milling mass trudged off to attack the Second Avenue Armory, a fortresslike building, routed the defenders (including forty policemen), wrecked the furniture, carted off thousands of muskets, and set fire to the building.[51]

The first day's rioting seemed to be directed at the draft and symbols of authority. The second day's violence featured attacks upon blacks and their businesses. Some buildings were burned and black men were assaulted and beaten or killed. A mob attacked and burned the Colored Orphan Asylum (all 237 children escaped)—there was no such institution for the orphans of Irish-Americans and German-Americans. Arson and plunder and killings continued for two more days.

Herman Melville, visiting New York City, stood appalled atop a roof and scanned the area where fires still burned and smoke rose skyward. He saw man "reverting aeons back in nature" and later wrote: "Balefully glares red Arson—there—and there."[52]

Some Catholic priests went into the streets to restrain the rioters, often their own parishioners. One talked some looters into returning their plunder. One prevented the burning of a block of houses inhabited by Protestants. Another prevented an attack upon buildings making up Columbia College (now Columbia University). Still another succeeded in dispersing a mob in his neighborhood. But generally, neither the pleas of the priests nor the proclamations of the authorities could stay the whirlwind of destruction and death.[53]

The mayor of the city, George Opdyke, and Governor Horatio Seymour begged for help in every direction. Governor Seymour even sought help from Archbishop Hughes. "I do not wish to ask you anything inconsistent with your duties," the governor wrote to the archbishop, "but if you can with propriety aid the civil authorities at this crisis, I hope you will do so."[54] Archbishop Hughes, in turn, wrote a letter and sent copies to the city's newspapers, hoping that the letters would be published and his advice heeded. He asked all "Catholic rioters" to "cease and desist" from mob action and "unchristian practices," and return to peaceful pursuits and bring "the disorders" to an end.[55] Then he circulated an announcement (via a flyer) stating that he would give "a talk" next morning (the sixteenth) from the steps of his residence.[56]

Next morning a crowd estimated at 5,000 assembled in front of Archbishop Hughes' residence. Suffering from rheumatism and a recent illness, and enfeebled with age, the revered churchman appeared, wearing the insignia of office. He addressed his flock as "my friends," saying that some had gone "astray." They were Catholics, he said, and so was he. They were Irish and so was he. The "disturbances" must stop for the sake of their religion and for the sake of Ireland. "Violence begets violence." There was more. In closing, he asked "all" to return peacefully to their homes and avoid mobs "where immortal souls are launched into eternity." After waving farewell, he limped back to his quarters. The crowd dispersed; its members returned peacefully and quietly to their houses and shacks.[57]

Archbishop Hughes, thus, had a hand in bringing the four-day antidraft riot to an end. There were other factors, of course. Troops had arrived in force and helped authorities to arrest many. Reasonable community leaders made their influence felt. Word that the draft had been suspended and postponed served as a sedative. The fires of resentment in the hearts of the rioters simply burned themselves out. The costs were high: 119 known dead, about 400 wounded or injured, and property damage approximating three million.[58]

With the streets of the city flooded with troops, federal authorities resumed the draft in August. Irony held sway at the 8th District headquarters when the lottery was held there on August 25; the first name drafted was that of Mayor Opdyke's son—his father paid $300 to exempt the son from service. The second name drafted was that of Timothy O'Hara, 267 First Avenue—since his Irish parents could not afford the $300 exemption, he marched off to war.[59]

A Catholic bishop in Pennsylvania did yeoman work in defusing a riot in Schuylkill County. Miners, mostly Irishmen, opposed the draft. Some ignored their draft notices, and rumors of a rebellion made the rounds in the back country. A crowd of about a thousand miners, bent on preventing the induction of friends, stopped a trainload of draftees in Tremont. It appeared that events might escalate into a major riot or open rebellion. Bishop James Wood, the spiritual leader of the area's Catholics, made his presence felt. He not only toured the area and asked all to obey the laws, but even sent directives to his priests to give sermons supporting law and order.[60]

The war dragged on. Republican political party stratagems paid dividends. Republicans won most of the important elections in the Northern states in the fall elections of 1863.[61] But the peace movement that had reached high tide early in 1863 and ebbed after Union victories at Gettysburg and Vicksburg, had a resurgence as the Army of the Potomac suffered heavy, heavy casualties in the Richmond area in 1864. Republicans, of course, wondered about the upcoming presidential election in November 1864; they sought Lincoln's reelection. Two midwestern governors, Oliver P. Morton of Indiana and Richard Yates of Illinois, also worried about reelection; each sought another four-year term. Each of these two governors had a hand in giving shape to "a Copperhead conspiracy" as a way to affect the election returns in his state.

Lambdin P. Milligan, an antiwar Democrat who had called his governor "a liar," "sleazy pretender," and "unprincipled villain" got tangled in a web of conspiracy woven largely by Governor Morton of Indiana. Milligan, at the time, was busy practicing law in Huntington, criticizing both Lincoln and Morton, and attending Masses regularly at St. Mary's Catholic Church. Governor Morton, on the other hand, contended that a conspiracy was brewing in Indiana and that the Indianapolis-based Sons of Liberty were involved. In early October, and shortly before the state's gubernatorial election, the governor pressured a subservient general (Alvin P. Hovey) to arrest Milligan and a dozen others and set the wheels of a military trial in motion. Republican newspapers published exposés that contained more fiction than fact and helped Governor Morton to win reelection.[62]

Following the arrests, two separate military trials took place in Indianapolis. In the first, a military commission found Harrison H. Dodd, founder of the Sons of Liberty, guilty as charged. But he escaped from the quarters where he was confined and headed for Canada, seemingly giving credence to the charges that he was guilty. The second trial, featuring Milligan and others, began on October 21, 1864. They were charged with "disloyal practices" and "conspiring against the United States," supposedly via the Sons of Liberty. As far as Milligan was concerned, the charges were false. The Huntington curmudgeon believed that Governor Morton was guilty of a personal vendetta against him and that the so-called "conspiracy" was concocted for political gain—he was right on both counts. Nevertheless, the military commission found four of the defendants "guilty as charged" and sentenced three (including Milligan) to be "hanged by the neck."[63] Sentencing was postponed periodically, and the end product was a U.S. Supreme Court case known as *Ex Parte Milligan* (1866). The Court, in a notable decision, ruled in Milligan's favor; it voided the military trial, ordered the defendant to be set free, and reprimanded President Lincoln and Secretary of War Stanton for employing military commissions to try civilians in areas where the civil courts were free and functioning.[64]

Governor Richard Yates wrote a sequel in Illinois. He, too, wanted reelection in 1864. Rather edgy and vindictively partisan (he also drank too much too often). Yates earlier had begged President Lincoln to institute martial law in Illinois.[65] Like Morton, Governor Yates had bested a Copperhead-controlled state legislature, more bent on political mischief rather than reasonable law-making, in early 1863. An editor of the *Chicago Tribune*, with considerable help from Yates, devised "a conspiracy" and secured the assistance of Col. Benjamin J. Sweet, the commandant at Camp Douglas, to flesh out the format. The Yates-Sweet fantasy included Copperhead help in freeing the 8,000 Confederate prisoners held in Camp Douglas (on the outskirts of Chicago), plundering and burning Chicago, carrying the rebellion to other Northern states, and establishing a separate Northwestern Confederacy.

Like in Indiana, one of the central characters in the supposed Chicago-based conspiracy was an Irish-Catholic and a Copperhead. Charles Walsh, the leading member of a local Democratic club in an Irish section of Chicago, owned a prosperous dray business. He was also the father of ten children ranging in age from three to nineteen. As a zealous Democrat, Walsh distrusted both Governor Yates and President Lincoln and, like others, believed that they might use military force to effect their reelection—purging the polls—especially if their reelection was in doubt. Rumors spread that Governor Yates was arming the Union Leagues—some Union League chapters were believed to have armed auxiliaries. This fear became an obsession with Walsh; so he collected some muskets and revolvers and recruited some fellow Democrats to serve as "armed poll watchers"—needed only if the Republicans tried to purge the polls. Walsh stipulated that "these arms," to be lent to "poll watchers," must "be returned after the elections."[66]

Three detectives hired by Colonel Sweet joined Walsh's local Democratic club and urged its members into treasonable activities—unsuccessfully. Then, on the eve of the November presidential election, Colonel Sweet arrested Walsh and many others, seized the arms in Walsh's basement, and devised a "conspiracy." The *Chicago Tribune* published an exposé entitled "Camp Douglas Conspiracy." The allegations of the three detectives, liars and rascals of the first order, startled the public.[67]

After most of those arrested were released, Charles Walsh and seven others were shipped in irons to Cincinnati to be tried for treason by another military commission. In the end, Walsh was found guilty as charged and sentenced to a five-year prison term, but seven of the nine commissioners signed a recommendation that he be pardoned. Only one of "the Chicago eight"—and an Englishman at that—was sentenced to death; he was an English adventurer named George St. Leger Grenfell. Walsh, then, returned to Chicago to resume his dray business, marry off two of his teenaged daughters, and continue to claim that a great injustice had been done to him.[68]

The role that Irish-American and German-American Catholics played in the American Civil War is filled with contradictions and steeped in irony. In the first place, there were the soldiers, generals as well as those serving in the ranks. Thomas Meagher, leading New York's Irish Brigade, and William S. Rosecrans, always carrying a rosary in his pocket as he took part in the western campaigns, represented the generals. More than two hundred thousand Irish Catholics and German-American Catholics served in the ranks as good soldiers who marched, camped, fought, and died. Then there was the noble work of the Catholic nuns who served as nurses. On the other hand, some of President Lincoln's better-known critics, the so-called

"Copperheads," had names like Mahony, Ryan, Faran, Mullaly, Milligan, and Deuster. Catholics were the chief participants in the antiblack riot of July 1862 in Cincinnati, the Port Washington draft riot of November 1862, and the devastating New York City antidraft riot of July 1863. Mahony's book, *The Prisoner of State,* and court cases like *In Re Kemp* (1863) and *Ex Part Milligan* (1866) remain as reminders that the story of Civil War Copperheadism is incomplete without giving a role to American Catholics.

CHAPTER VII

Midwestern Opposition to President Lincoln's Emancipation Policy*

Long before Charleston batteries fired upon Fort Sumter and broke the uneasy peace, many midwestern conservatives had learned to hate abolition and abolitionists. Douglas and other Democrats warned all who would listen that the "fell spirit of abolition" was destroying the comity of sections and endangering the life of the republic. "The irrepressible conflict is about to be realized," contended Congressman William Allen of Ohio, "not as the natural result of the institution of slavery, as recognized by the Constitution, but the result of the perversion of public sentiment by mad partisans..."[1] Democrats, generally, frowned upon the radical utterances of William Lloyd Garrison, and they criticized John Brown for stoking the fires of violence in Kansas. Brown's "act of folly" at Harper's Ferry caused their cup of bitterness to overflow. They designated him "a fiend incarnate" and "a mistaken madman," and they objected to the efforts of New England abolitionists to canonize him.[2] Clement L. Vallandigham, destined to become one of the controversial figures of the Civil War, wrote his contempt for John Brown into the record. Noting the respectability which abolition had gained in certain sectors and circles, Vallandigham wrote, "Thirty years ago, John Brown, hung like a felon, would have been buried like a dog."[3] Neither Vallandigham nor Douglas viewed slavery as morally right, even if they regarded Negroes as inferior people who could be denied social or political equality.[4] They regarded slavery as "a domestic institution"—subject to the laws of the states—and to which the federal Constitution gave its tacit approval.

*Reprinted (with permission) from The Journal of Negro History, 49 (July 1964): 169–83.

A few Democratic colleagues residing in the Northern states were outright defenders of slavery. Jesse Bright of Indiana and George Wallace Jones of Iowa had onetime owned slaves. John Reynolds of Illinois and the Reverend C.F.W. Walther, genius of the Missouri Synod of the Lutheran Church, had written treatises in defense of slavery.[5] Some of the conservative Democrats even argued that abolition was "the father of disunion," the secession movement but the son.[6]

Western sectionalists like Vallandigham and Samuel S. Cox of Ohio blended their antipathy for abolition with a hatred of New England. They saw the image of New England in the abolition crusade, and they condemned both in the same breath. They feared that New England wished to dominate the Midwest economically, revitalize Whig doctrines, and impose its religious and social views upon the rest of the country. Both Vallandigham and Cox announced that they were "inexorably hostile to Puritan domination in religion or morals or literature or politics."[7]

The antiabolition and anti-New England views of Vallandigham and Cox appealed to three elements of the diverse population of the Midwest. The Irish-Americans, concentrated in the cities, feared that abolition would release a flood of cheap labor that would engulf the industrial centers of the North. They could envision losing their jobs to free Negroes, whose living standards were even lower than those of the Irish workingmen. Small wonder that the Irish-Americans cursed the abolitionists and voted the straight Democratic ticket.[8]

Most German-Americans, whether yeoman farmers or city workmen, also opposed abolition and looked with distrust toward New England. Many New Englanders had taken part in the Know-Nothing movement, a nativist and anti-Catholic crusade of the 1850s. Furthermore, New England preached prohibition and abolition, two doctrines which most midwestern Germans opposed. Since the Republican party bore the scarlet mark of Know-Nothingism and was tainted with abolitionism and prohibitionism, the rank-and-file German workmen voted the Democratic ticket and applauded those speakers who condemned Republicans and abolitionists. The well-publicized Forty-eighters might speak out for "freedom" and emancipation, but the typical German-American joined the Irishman at the polls in support of the Democratic party and in casting an antiabolition ballot.[9]

Southern emigrants who had crossed the Ohio River to preempt the poorer soils of Ohio and southern Indiana and Illinois formed the third element of the midwestern population most easily affected by Negrophobia and most likely to vote the Democratic ticket. They brought their anti-Negro prejudices with them, their ego enchanted by the knowledge that there was a class below them on the social and economic scale. They became the "Butternut Democracy" of the back-woods regions—so-called because their linsey cloth and jeans were dipped in a yellowish-brown dye made by boiling the bark of the lowly butternut tree. They were usually illiterate and poor, leading a hand-to-mouth existence. They mistrusted the sons and scions of New England who wished to re-fashion the cultural practices of others in line with the Yankee image. They applauded when stump-speakers damned the abolitionists and they became "the unterrified, unwashed Democracy."[10]

During the first year of the war most Democratic spokesmen gave qualified support to the government and the Lincoln administration. Douglas set a heroic example, and the patriotic tide which surged over the North after Southern guns fired upon Fort Sumter seemed to sweep all before it. It seemed as if patriotism had triumphed over partyism. "Party lines burn, dissolved by the excitement," wrote Count Adam Gurowski from his observation post in Washington. "Now the people is fusion, as bronze."[11] A member of Lincoln's Cabinet also expressed pleasure at the support Democrats gave the war. "The Democrats generally as well as the Republicans," he wrote, "are offering themselves to the country."[12]

Only a handful of recalcitrant Democrats swam against the current. Dennis A. Mahony, outspoken editor of the *Dubuque Herald,* criticized every proclamation which President Lincoln issued, and he predicted that abolitionists would seek their objectives through war and the white man's blood. Samuel Medary, the "Old Wheelhorse" of Ohio politics and defiant editor of *The (Columbus) Crisis*, feared that a despotism would take over the country and abolition emerge triumphant. John W. Kees, erratic editor of the *Circleville Watchman*, ranted against the Lincoln administration and excoriated the abolitionists. Congressmen Clement L. Vallandigham and George E. Pugh of Ohio talked of peace and civil rights and denounced "Black Republicans" at every opportunity. Kentucky congressmen also feared that abolition fanatics wished to change the stated objectives of the war. Kentuckians, generally, were pleased that President Lincoln ignored the "effusion of the Fanatics" and drove a moderate course.[13] "If anything is to be abolished," wrote the Democratic editor of the *Detroit Free Press*, "we say by all means let it be abolitionism..."[14]

As the fall elections of 1861 approached, partisanship made its influence felt. Democrats realized that they were "on the outside looking in." An economic depression plagued the upper Mississippi Valley and it undermined popular support for the Lincoln administration. Reports of corruption and military defeats gave Democrats ammunition for the fall political campaigns. Democratic orators and editors brushed off the old arguments against abolition and against New England.

President Lincoln complicated the picture by revoking Gen. John C. Fremont's proclamation of August 30, 1861. General Fremont, in proclaiming martial law throughout the Department of the West, stated that the property of rebels within his jurisdiction would be confiscated and their slaves "declared free men."[15] Abolitionists applauded Fremont's action, while conservative Democrats moaned in protest. Kentucky Unionists also protested publicly against Fremont's proclamation. "I am now satisfied that we could stand several defeats like that at Bull Run," wrote a complaining Kentuckian, "better than we can this proclamation if endorsed by the administration."[16] Cognizant that Fremont's proclamation embarrassed Unionists in the border states and aware that public sentiment was not yet ready for such stern measures, Lincoln revoked Fremont's proclamation and soon after removed him from command.

Abolitionists denounced President Lincoln; they heaped curses and censure upon his head.[17] Democrats and conservatives hurried to the defense of Lincoln. For a period of several months the most vicious attacks upon Lincoln came from the right wing of his own party, whereas leaders of the opposition party "hailed with delight" the president's reproach of Fremont and the "discomforture of Abolitionists."[18] One Democratic editor, who labeled Fremont a "fool," Garrison "a maniac," and Ben Butler a "beast," put his stamp of approval upon Lincoln late in 1861. With considerable satisfaction he wrote, "Lincoln is sound on the nigger question."[19]

The antislavery activities of the abolition-minded members of the second session of the Thirty-seventh Congress, caused conservatives considerable concern. Abolition seemed to gain momentum, for the Radical Republicans wanted the war to destroy slavery as well as to save the Union. One measure proposed to end slavery in the District of Columbia—with compensation to the slaveholders. Another act emancipated slaves in the territories—without compensation. One bill authorized the use of "fugitives" as soldiers in the Union army. The Confiscation Bill, introduced by Lyman Trumbull of Illinois, stated that slaves of all persons supporting the rebellion should be "forever free of their servitude, and not again held as slaves." Furthermore, President Lincoln's efforts to get Congress and the border states to move in the direction of compensated emancipation, seemed to prove that the war's objectives were changing.

Conservatives spoke out against the "disease of abolition." John W. Kees, an Ohio editor who was later arrested for his anti-administration tirades, referred to abolitionists as "damned disunionists," and he wanted them hung "till the flesh would rot off their bones and the winds of Heaven whistle yanky doodle through their loathsum skelitonz."[20] Disconsolately, Kees added, "It is a pity that there is not a more tormenting hell than that kept by Beelzebub for such abolition fields."[21] One discouraged Democrat wrote in an even more hostile spirit. "If this is a war...of Abolition," stated the editor of the *Oshkosh Courier*, "then, the sooner the Union goes to the devil the better."[22]

Democratic politicians launched an attack upon "the fell spirit of abolition" on every front. The attack upon abolition or emancipation measures in Congress was led by a dozen midwestern Democrats. Clement L. Vallandigham spoke against the measures which would erase slavery in the District of Columbia and in the territories. Samuel S. Cox of Ohio and

Daniel W. Voorhees of Indiana saw the confiscation bill as a threat to civil rights as well as a wedge to wreck slavery. Lazarus Powell, a Kentucky senator, argued that Lincoln's advocacy of compensated emancipation contradicted the pledge that he had made in his inaugural address. Congressman Charles A. Wickliffe of the same state thought that the Administration moved toward establishment of a despotism. Democratic critics viewed Lincoln's policy of compensated emancipation as unconstitutional, impractical, and absurd.[23] Vallandigham tried to don the toga of Democratic leadership by calling a meeting of congressmen who objected to the course of events and by drafting an "Address of the Democratic Members of the Congress to the Democracy of the United States." That Address argued that States had jurisdiction over "domestic institutions," urged compromise as national policy, and bemoaned the drift toward despotism. It popularized the slogan "The Constitution as it is, the Union as it was." Vallandigham wanted the Union of pre-war days restored, with states rights and with slavery.[24]

The Democratic press also attacked the various emancipation or abolition measures. The *Cincinnati Enquirer*, the *Detroit Free Press*, and the *Chicago Times* invited workingmen to cast Democratic ballots and to check the trend toward abolition. The editor of the *(Milwaukee) See-Bote*, plagued by Negrophobia, entitled a long editorial "Abolition, the Worst Enemy of the Free White Laborer" and he issued a call to action: "Workmen! Be careful! Organize yourself against this element which threatens your impoverishment and annihilation."[25]

In their state and local conventions Democrats also denounced abolition. Six of the resolutions adopted by the Ohio Democracy, assembled in convention on July 4, 1862, in Columbus, condemned abolition.[26] Local Democratic rallies applauded resolutions that called upon Democrats to fight the rebels with bullets and the abolitionists with ballots.[27]

A couple of anti-Negro riots occurred in midwestern cities in July 1862. The Toledo riot occurred because employers hired free Negroes at "the old wages" after Irish dock hands had struck for higher wages. The fighting spread from the docks to the Negro quarter of Toledo—some houses were destroyed, workmen injured, and Negrophobia intensified. The Cincinnati riot, much more serious, had a like cause. When Irish deck hands struck for higher pay, the boat owners retaliated by hiring "contrabands" at lower prices. Enraged Irishmen drove the strike-breakers off the boats and the wharves. Then a mob invaded "Shantytown" and a section of the Negro ghetto was put to the torch. The two riots seemed to give some substance to contentions that emancipation threatened the economic security of white workers in Northern cities. Democratic politicians tried to use the riots to advantage—welding workmen into a solid Democratic bloc.[28]

While Democrats like Dennis A. Mahony of Dubuque and Samuel Medary of Columbus were convinced that the war to save the Union was being "perverted" into a war to free the slaves, some conservatives still had faith that President Lincoln would hold back the flood tide of abolition. When the president overruled Gen. David Hunter, it seemed as if the conservatives' faith in Lincoln was justified. Democrats again came to Lincoln's defense, while Radical Republicans turned a torrent of abuse against the President.[29]

In the months that followed, abolition pressure upon Lincoln increased. Prominent abolitionists argued that God would favor Union arms if emancipation became official policy.[30] Abolition-minded churchmen argued in behalf of antislavery measures. Radical congressmen demanded a more aggressive war policy which included emancipation measures. Horace Greeley penned the "Prayer of Twenty Millions," boldly demanding a presidential proclamation which would set the slaves free.[31]

Conservatives who depended upon Lincoln to hold abolitionism in check received a rude jolt when the president issued his preliminary proclamation of emancipation on September 22, 1862. In one voice, Democrats protested. The outraged editor of the *Louisville Journal* denounced the proclamation as "a gigantic usurpation"—"unauthorized" and "pernicious." The angry editor of the *Chatfield Democrat* called the measure "a piece of fanatical folly that will do more harm than good."[32] Joseph Bingham of the *Indianapolis State Sentinel* defined the proclamation as "a blunder...fraught with evil," and he wrote a two-column editorial arguing that the document was unconstitutional, unnecessary, and unwise. An editorial writer for the *Cincinnati Enquirer* pronounced the proclamation "ill-timed and unfortunate," an insult to patriotic men in the border states.[33] "But the crowning act of folly," wrote a Kentuckian, "is the *Emancipation Proclamation*...to make war on Union men of the country, as the Proclamation does, is calculated to create consequences."[34] The defiant editor of the *Canton (Ohio) Stark County Democrat* turned his back upon the administration: "This is another step in the nigger business, and another advance in the Robespierrian highway of tyranny and anarchy."[35]

The proclamation of September 22 stirred the Democrats to political activity. They stirred anew the coals of Negrophobia and launched attacks upon New England, "the hotbed of abolition." Democrats appealed to all conservative men to throw "the ins" out and put "the outs" in.

The October election returns in Ohio, Indiana, and Pennsylvania jolted the Lincoln administration. The editor of the *Dayton Empire* wrote, "Abolition lies prostrate..."and Joseph J. Bingham of the *Indianapolis State Sentinel* composed the headline "ABOLITION SLAUGHTERED."[36] "The people of the great States of Ohio, Indiana, and Pennsylvania," wrote the editor whom Clement L. Vallandigham had brought to Dayton to edit the *Empire*, "have spoken in thunderous tones through the ballot box against the fanatical Abolition legislation of the last Congress."[37]

The November elections added insult to injury—Lincoln and the Republicans were shocked at the antiadministration trend. "The Home of Lincoln Condemns the Proclamation," read the headline in the Democratic paper published in Springfield, Illinois.[38] Democrats claimed that the election returns repudiated President Lincoln's radical policies, his sanction of arbitrary arrests and his endorsement of abolition.[39] Democrats gloried in the election returns. "The Lord sent us *sunshine* in the late election," wrote the venerable John Reynolds of Illinois; "we must drive back the Abolitionists into the same holes they came out of."[40]

Democrats who interpreted the election returns of 1862 as a repudiation of Lincoln's emancipation policy hoped that the president would withdraw his proclamation of September 22, and "return to the original objectives of the war." They hoped in vain, for in his December 1, 1862, message to Congress the president expressed his determination to move forward. He made no concessions to the election returns. "The tenacity with which Mr. Lincoln holds on to his emancipation proclivities, notwithstanding the rebuke administered in the result of the election in the North last fall," wrote a disillusioned Democrat, "cannot fail, I think, to alarm the friends of the Union and of Constitutional liberty throughout our broad land."[41] The editor of the *Lexington (Ky.) Observer* read Lincoln's message with "the deepest mortification." He found Lincoln's defense of emancipation "weak and puerile," the conclusions "fallacious and discreditable."[42] Vallandigham's friend, the editor of the *Dayton Empire*, wrote in like vein:

> The message is chiefly, and almost exclusively, devoted to the negro question. The 'poor African' seems always uppermost in Abraham's mind. He argues at length in favor of his various emancipation schemes, but entirely fails to show that it is either possible, practical, or constitutional.[43]

A few extremists suggested that Lincoln be impeached and removed from office. Samuel Medary of *The Crisis*, caught in his own web of hate, advocated impeachment. So did George B. Smith, prominent Democratic politician of Wisconsin.[44] Such critics reviewed the events of 1862 with sadness and regret. "The history of the past year," wrote a Dubuque Democrat, "must be read in its disasters, rather than its conquests. It has been Fanaticism's Saturnalia...[when] the crude theories of zealots—starking mad on one idea and sane on no other—have entered into and possessed the thoughts of practical men."[45]

No other Lincoln-penned document elicited such paeans of praise and such damning denunciation as the Emancipation Proclamation of January 1, 1863. Radical Republicans, except a few who thought that the proclamation did not go far enough, emitted a chorus of huzzas and labelled January 1 an "Epochal day." "All honor to the man, who, in the face of obloquy and reproach, of detraction and misrepresentation, invoking 'the considerate judgment of mankind and the gracious favor of Almighty God,' dares to do right," wrote one Republican editor.[46] One of Lincoln's secretaries, daydreaming as he made copies of the original document, could hear the sound of clanking chains and the shouts of joy and laughter of the "newly freed." He also heard "the anger of the fierce opposition, wrath, fury, [and] dismay."[47]

Midwestern Democrats provided most of "the fierce opposition," expressing "wrath, fury, [and] dismay." "We scarcely know how to express our indignation," wrote the editor of the *Louisville Democrat*, "at this flagrant outrage of all Constitutional law, all human justice, all Christian feeling." The angry editor called Lincoln "an imbecile President," "an encourager of insurrection, lust, arson, and murder." He concluded that Lincoln had usurped authority and slandered Kentuckians.[48]

Vallandigham, willing to be a martyr for his views, called the Emancipation Proclamation unconstitutional, unnecessary, and divisive. He believed it would discourage enlistments, breed discontent in the border states, unite the South to a man, and prompt the Democrats to plump for peace.[49] Those views were shared by hundreds of Democratic newspaper editors. One termed the proclamation "a ukase" and called its author a "tyrant and usurper."[50] Another labeled it "the most foolish joke ever got off by the six-foot four Commander-in-chief."[51] One pronounced it "a youthful indiscretion,"[52] while another called it "one of a series of imbecile and disastrous steps."[53] A clever editor termed the proclamation "political medicine" which would "kill both the patient and the doctor."[54] The anger of Samuel Medary of *The Crisis*, Mahony of the *Dubuque Herald*, and John T. Logan of the *Dayton Empire* knew no bounds. Medary coined new terms of approbation, supposed that a despotism had enveloped the country, and demanded the cessation of hostilities.[55] Mahony suggested that Lincoln's proclamation excused Democrats from further support of the war. "Abolition created the Administration, has shaped its policy, has dictated its appointments," wrote the embittered Irishman, "and must be left to furnish the material requisites of men and money." He shamelessly suggested that open defiance was desirable: "The people who submit to the insolent fanaticism which dictated this last act, *are and deserve to be enslaved* to the class which Abraham Lincoln self-sufficiently declares free. If they possessed a tithe of the spirit which animated Rome when Cataline was expelled from its walls...they would hurl him into the Potomac...Cabinet, Congress, and all."[56] Logan of the *Daily Empire* spoke a like language. He recognized that emancipation negated compromise hopes—dealt a death blow to the Democratic demands for "The Constitution as it is, the Union as it was." "The old flag of the Union," he editorialized, "is hauled down, and the black flag—the true color of the Abolition party—is run up. Treason is to be made loyalty, and perjury is to be sanctified."[57]

The editors of such papers as the *Cincinnati Enquirer*, the *Hamilton True Telegraph*, the *Belleville Democrat*, the *(St. Louis) Missouri Republican* (a Democratic newspaper despite its name), the *Detroit Free Press*, and the *Chicago Times* appealed anew to the spirit of Negrophobia—a spirit which produced riots in Detroit, Chicago, and New York in 1863.

Some Democrats continued to make the Emancipation Proclamation an issue in every election during the remainder of the war. They opposed Owen Lovejoy's bill to abolish slavery by constitutional amendment and they opposed the Freedmen's Bureau Act. They later cast their votes or expressed their opinions against the civil rights acts and against the 13th, 14th, and 15th amendments. They spoke of the need of white supremacy, pretending that miscegenation and "amalgamation" were the true aims of many abolitionists. They continued to label their political opponents "Black Republicans" and spoke of turning the calendar back to the days when slavery and states rights were respected institutions. "In my heart I believe our policy [opposing emancipation] is the best for the white race, the black race, the country, and humanity," write a young Dayton lawyer who admired Clement L. Vallandigham, "and I can die on the scaffold if need be, but I cannot change my faith."[58]

The refusal of many Americans to change an erroneous "faith" explains the slow headway civil rights made in the post-Civil War years.

CHAPTER VIII

Ohio Politics in 1863*

On a mild sunny day, shortly after two o'clock on the afternoon of January 1, 1863, President Abraham Lincoln signed the Emancipation Proclamation at his cluttered desk in the White House. About the same time, while wintry winds pushed the temperature way below zero, a baby boy was born to German-American parents in a bleak farmhouse not far from Hamilton, Ohio. The proud parents, who despised President Lincoln, named their new son Clement Laird Vallandigham Horn.[1]

Clement Laird Vallandigham, the baby's namesake, was a well-known and controversial forty-two-year-old congressman from Ohio's Third District. A gadfly during the third session of the Thirty-seventh Congress, the Dayton resident was destined to become the central figure in the political battles waged in Ohio throughout 1863.[2]

While President Lincoln spent New Year's Day hosting a White House reception and then signing his proclamation on emancipation, Congressman Vallandigham was in his room in Washington writing an antiwar speech that he planned to give in the House of Representatives after the holiday recess.

As the new year began, Vallandigham could look back upon a checkered career as a lawyer, newspaperman, and politician. Ohio-born and indoctrinated with Calvinist values (his father was a Presbyterian preacher), young Vallandigham set out to earn a living and find his niche in life. After a

---

* Miami University, for permission to use material originally published as "Ohio Politics in 1863: Looking Back 125 Years," in *The Old Northwest*, 14.1 (Spring 1988): 39–66.

118

two-year stint as a grade school teacher in Maryland, he returned to New Lisbon (now Lisbon) to study law and seek honors in politics. Claiming to be an apostle of Jacksonian Democracy, he gained election to the lower house of the state legislature. There he berated the Whigs, developed an addiction to states rights, and gained the respect of his fellow Democrats. He had a ready smile, a pleasing personality, and a reputation as an excellent speaker. When Whigs opposed a resolution endorsing the Mexican War, Vallandigham taunted them and implied that they were traitors, a favor returned in full measure in 1863.[3]

In August 1847, young Vallandigham and his new wife moved to southwestern Ohio, where he went on to guide the *Dayton Western Empire* back to respectability, revive the disorganized Democratic party of Montgomery County, and become a brigadier general in the state militia. After considerable success as both editor and lawyer, he sought election to Congress. He failed twice before succeeding the third time. Re-elected in 1858 and 1860, Vallandigham was one of the most ardent supporters of compromise measures designed to prevent a military conflict between the North and the South.[4]

After the Fort Sumter affair, Vallandigham still advocated peace and compromise, too stubborn to change his views and accept reality. As a western sectionalist, he feared that a civil war would bring the ascendancy of New England and that the West would lose its political clout. He thought that President Lincoln's war measures, taken before Congress convened on July 4, 1861, merited his impeachment.[5] In the days that followed he railed against what he called "executive usurpation," opposed various "abolition measures," claimed that peace and compromise was still a realistic goal, and rebuked those who called him a "traitor" and "Southern sympathizer."[6]

Ohio Republicans, in control of the state legislature, changed the boundaries of the Third District, substituting a strong Republican county for a fifty-fifty one. This political stratagem paid dividends and Vallandigham lost his seat to a Republican contender (Robert C. Schenck) in November 1862, making him a lame duck during the last session of the Thirty-seventh Congress.[7] The lame duck congressman, busy writing a state-of-the-Union speech, stood at the crossroads of his career. He was a formidable foe—introspective, possessed of a moral righteousness, fluent, bright and well-read, tenacious, and self-serving.

On January 14, 1863, Vallandigham presented his pro-peace speech on the floor of the House of Representatives. If the war continued, he said, civil rights would be washed away. The arbitrary arrests of the previous fall, the purging of polls in the border states, the suspension of the writ of *habeas corpus*, and the mobbing of Democratic newspapers were all steps toward an eventual despotism. "The experiment of war," he insisted, "has been tried long enough." He asked for an armistice—time for passions to cool "and reason to resume sway." He hoped for "eventual reunion" and "the ultimate achievement of the nation's destiny."[8] The hour-long speech earned the lame duck congressman national notoriety, the designation "apostle of peace," and the rancor of Republicans.[9]

Four discernible cross-currents bestirred the political waters in Ohio during the first four months of 1863. One was the question of peace and compromise, for the pro-peace movement received an impetus as a result of Vallandigham's congressional speech. Some Democratic newspapers in Ohio printed the speech in its entirety and endorsed its sentiments.[10] "Peace in on a million lips," wrote John W. McElwee of the Hamilton *True Telegraph* in an editorial, "and it will like thunder, ere long, in the ears of our rulers like an Alpine storm."[11] Earlier, William T. Logan of the *Dayton Empire* had said that the country was tired of war and bloodshed:

> The earth is crimson with the blood of brave men. Desolation, ruin, and suffering follows the march of contending armies....In almost every household there is a mourner, and, in almost every heart a vacant place. The ferryman on the river Styx has done a heavy freighting business during the past twelve-month.[12]

Some Democratic members of the Ohio state legislature sought to promote a national peace convention—perhaps in Louisville; Democratic-controlled legislatures in Indiana and Illinois had taken the initiative to promote such convention. After all, defeatism and dismay were widespread throughout the upper Midwest in the early months of 1863—more so after the Union defeat and debacle at Chancellorsville on May1–5. Democratic leaders like Vallandigham hoped that a peace crusade would lead to eventual reunion and political rewards as well.[13]

Federal conscription, being debated in Congress and the public press, was the second political issue that aroused strong feelings among Ohio voters in early 1863. Vallandigham was one of the most vociferous congressional critics of the Conscription Bill; he declared it undemocratic, unnecessary, and unconstitutional.[14] Samuel S. Cox of the Columbus district also protested, saying, "Repeal the confiscation act, the emancipation proclamation, and other unconstitutional measures—withdraw the negro entirely, and a conscription bill will not be necessary to reinvigorate the country."[15]

The $300 commutation clause, which allowed a man to buy his way out of the service, galled Ohio Democrats. The intrepid editor of the *Hamilton True Telegraph* stated the case for the country's poor. "As a general thing," he editorialized, "the Abolitionists are in office or in a condition to buy themselves free. Not so with the Democracy. They are the yeomanry of the country. They live by labor and are the tillers of the earth; and [they are] not in a condition to buy their freedom of the Administration."[16] The commutation clause gave Democrats the opportunity to say that it was "a rich man's war and a poor man's fight."

The third issue, raised by Democrats during the early months of 1863, centered around civil rights. President Lincoln's suspension of the writ of habeas corpus, the trial of civilians by military commissions, arbitrary arrests, and military edicts that forbid criticism of the Lincoln administration were a threat to traditional rights of citizens. Federal marshals had arrested five Ohioans on the eve of the '62 elections the previous fall; the five were: Archibald McGregor, editor of the *(Canton) Stark County Democrat*; Peter N. Reitzell, a friend of McGregor; Lawrence W. Hall, an ex-congressman from Bucyrus; John W. Kees of the *Circleville Watchman*; and Dr. Edson B. Olds of the *(Lancaster) Ohio Eagle*.[17] Kees had called Lincoln a fool, fanatic, and fathead rolled into one while Olds was an outspoken editor as well as a three-term ex-congressman.

Olds' arrest evolved into a classic. While he was confined in the Ohio State Penitentiary, he was elected to the state senate to fill a vacancy and after he was released he was given a "royal welcome" by a crowd of ten thousand at the Lancaster railroad depot—this in December 1862.

The mobbing of Democratic newspapers also violated freedom of the press. The *(Canton) Stark County Democrat* felt the wrath of one mob. The *Marietta Democrat* felt the wrath of another. And on March 5, 1863, about one hundred soldiers, stationed at Camp Chase (on the outskirts of Columbus) raided and "thoroughly wrecked" the quarters of Medary's *The Crisis*.[18]

Democrats regarded Maj. Gen. Ambrose E. Burnside's military edict ("General Orders, No. 38") of April 13, 1863, as the last straw. Burnside, commander of the Department of the Ohio, and headquartered in Cincinnati, stated that "declaring sympathy for the enemy" would not be tolerated within his jurisdiction and that persons "committing such offenses" would be arrested and tried by military commissions.[19] Since Burnside believed that criticizing President Lincoln or administration policy constituted aiding the enemy, the brash general's decree threatened civil rights guaranteed in the first amendment. Some Democrats sincerely believed that the erosion of traditional rights would bring an end to democratic government unless the movement for peace and compromise ended the bloody war.

None of the three issues, however, engendered the emotion resulting from Lincoln's emancipation measures. They awakened the latent racism and Negrophobia so widespread in Ohio. Democrats reacted angrily to Lincoln's proclamation, terming it ridiculous, unreasonable, and unconstitutional. They also viewed it as a sop to the abolition or radical wing of the Republican party. Vallandigham called the proclamation unnecessary, divisive, and unconstitutional, adding that it would discourage enlistments, breed discontent in the border states, and unite the South to a man.[20] The indignant editor of the *Ashland Union* termed it "a ukase" and its author "a tyrant and usurper."[21] Medary of *The Crisis* advocated the impeachment of the president, supposed that a despotism was enveloping the country, and demanded the cessation of hostilities.[22] One of Vallandigham's disciples, a young Dayton lawyer named Thomas O. Lowe (his father and brother were Union officers) wrote like a racist: "In my heart I believe that our policy [opposing emancipation] is the best for the white race, the black race, the country, and humanity, and I can die on the scaffold if need be, but I cannot change my faith."[23]

Emancipation and conscription, as political issues, were of especial interest to three elements of the Democratic party: Irish-Americans, German-Americans, and Appalachian whites. The Irish-Americans, who generally lived in the cities, believed that emancipation would release a flood of cheap labor ("contrabands") and that they might lose their jobs. Cincinnati stevedores and boatmen learned that lesson in 1862 and reacted with a riot in July, burning sections of the black ghetto. Irish-American ladies and lasses learned the same lesson when forty of them were replaced by blacks at the prestigious Burnet House in Cincinnati. Irish-American workers of Toledo also learned a lesson when employers hired "contrabands" as strike-breakers, leading to another riot. It was easy for such editors as Medary of *The Crisis* and James J. Faran of the *Cincinnati Enquirer* to convince Irish-Americans that free blacks formed a threat to their jobs and their future.

Conscription also seemed to pose a threat to the Irish-Americans. The volunteer system, as it evolved, offered generous bonuses and it tempted many of the poor Irish. But conscription seemed to eliminate the bonus system. Furthermore, the poor could not raise the $300 which brought exemption from the draft. In addition, the typical Irish-American had no desire to work beside a black laborer or fight beside a black soldier. The Republican party seemed to stand for nearly everything the Irish-American detested: abolitionism, prohibition, and Know-Nothingism.

Many German-Americans, especially those of the Catholic faith, felt much the same way as the Irish-Americans. "The jealousy of the low Germans and Irish against the negro," a touring foreign correspondent wrote, "was sufficient to set them against the war which would have brought four million of their black rivals into competition for that hard and dirty work which American freedom bestowed on them."[24]

Germans, who enjoyed their schnapps the way the Irish relished their whiskey, also thought that the Republican party was tainted with temperance. Nor was the military conscription any more palpable to the German-Americans than to the Irish-Americans. When the War Department ruled that those who had voted, even though they were not yet U.S. citizens, were subject to the draft, German-Americans protested.

"Butternuts," white from Appalachia who had crossed the Ohio River to preempt the poorer soils in the Buckeye State, formed the third element in the Democratic party identified with Negrophobia. They brought their antiblack prejudices, their Democratic proclivities, and their stills with them when they settled in Ohio. "Butternut" country was characterized by poorer soils, smaller homesteads, and more widespread illiteracy.[25] These so-called "Butternuts" were the "Barefeet Democracy" of Andrew Jackson's day and sometimes were referred to as "the great unwashed, unterrified Democracy." They relished antiabolition speeches given at their backwoods gatherings. Some, like Dr. Olds, proudly wore butternut emblems and refused to change their cultural patterns and their common man beliefs.[26]

Since few "Butternuts" could afford to buy their way out of military service via the $300 commutation, they also viewed conscription as an anathema. Nor did they intend to destroy their stills and climb aboard the prohibition wagon. Kees, erratic editor of the *Circleville Watchman*, appealed to the prejudices of the "Butternuts" when he railed against abolition and the war. He referred to the abolitionists as "damned disunionists" and he wanted them hung "till the flesh rot off their bones and the winds of Heaven whistle yanky doodle through their loathsum skelitonz [*sic*]."[27]

While Ohio Democrats debated the issues of the day, Vallandigham's last two-year term as a congressman began to come to a close. In the final weeks of his last session he decided to seek the gubernatorial nomination at his party's state convention, scheduled for June 11. Assessing the political climate of the hour, Democrats were hopeful of repeating their successes of the previous fall.

Worried Republicans launched a crusade to stymie Democratic hopes and checkmate the peace movement. Party leaders, hiding behind the Union party label, represented a viable and well-led organization. Ohioans were prominent in Washington. Two sat in Lincoln's cabinet, Edwin M. Stanton as Secretary of War and Salmon P. Chase as Secretary of the Treasury. Both of the state's two U.S. Senators, Benjamin F. Wade of Jefferson and John Sherman of Mansfield, were influential and able men. So were several Republican members of the House of Representatives, especially James M. Ashley and John A. Bingham—both regarded themselves as patriots and Democrats as traitors. Ohio Republicans, in the October elections of 1861, had put David Tod in the Governor's chair, and they had control of the state legislature.

Shocked by the results in the fall elections of 1862, Republicans organized a crusade to discredit the Democrats—they saw Vallandigham and his friends as most vulnerable. Republican editors like Whitelaw Reid of the *Cincinnati Gazette* sought to fasten the term "Copperheads" to Democratic party members as a means of discrediting them. In one of the most vicious smear campaigns in the country's history, Republican editors and orators succeeded in making the "Copperhead" label stick, equating Democrats with the poisonous snake with the brown-blotched body and the copper-colored head.[28] They convinced the public that Democratic critics of the Lincoln administration were pro-Southern in their proclivities and semi-traitorous in their activities. The smear campaign paid dividends, for in patriotic circles the Democracy was discredited.[29]

Republicans tried a second political stratagem. They fashioned a strawman and tied it to the Democratic party. This strawman assumed the form of the Knights of the Golden Circle, and Republican party political propaganda made this fantasy seem real. There actually was a historical character named George Bickley and, as a Cincinnati citizen during the pre-war years, he tried to organize the Knights of the Golden Circle as an agency to colonize and "annex northern Mexico to the Dominion of the United States as in the case of Texas."[30] But Bickley's dream never reached reality, and he left Cincinnati for Washington, D.C., and then the South, leaving behind countless creditors and a shabby reputation. Ohio Republicans were the leaders in transforming Bickley's filibustering fancy into a subversive society, supposedly nurtured in Democratic councils and Copperhead conclaves. Rumors and supposition about the Knights of the Golden Circle were so numerous and so widespread that name became a household term. Many Ohio Democrats, including Vallandigham and Medary were tarnished by the Golden Circle brush. It was effective political propaganda, so effective that stories of Golden Circle perfidy in Ohio were passed off as fact into the twentieth century.[31]

Republicans tried still another tack—organizing a secret patriotic society of their own, one in which they pulled the strings. They justified the creation of this secret political society, called the Union Leagues, as an antidote to the Knights of the Golden Circle. The bigger they built the Golden Circle bogeyman, the greater the need for their secret political society to nullify its evil deeds. The Republican-directed Union Leagues, generating patriotism by circulating pamphlets and propaganda, waged war against "Copperheads" most effectively. At Cleveland, on May 20–21 , the various state and regional Union Leagues merged into a national organization, the Union League of America. It was a nationwide secret patriotic society in the hands of Lincoln's political friends and supporters. The U.L.A. sponsored mass meetings, distributed Republican campaign literature,[32] converted the unwary, won support for the war effort, and helped Lincoln's party win local, state, and national elections.[33]

The Republican stratagems paid dividends. They drove the fringe element out of the Democratic party, discredited Lincoln's opponents, slowed down the peace crusade, and boosted sagging morale in the upper Midwest. They regenerated patriotism as it bred an intolerance of Copperheads. They prompted Edwin Cowles of the *Cleveland Leader* to write: "Treat Copperheads as assassins; as men who, if they would not aim the knife at your breast, would not at least move a finger to arrest to the blow. They are assassins; they are traitors; and that last word is the sum of everything vile."[34]

Vallandigham, on his way home to Dayton after Congress adjourned, stopped over in Columbus to visit friends and seek support for his gubernatorial campaign. He was greeted by a long-time friend, William W. Armstrong, who had been elected Secretary of State the previous fall during a Democratic resurgence. Rather dogmatically, Vallandigham told Armstrong that he wanted the Democratic gubernatorial nomination, and that he expected Armstrong's support. Armstrong was shocked. "But Colonel," he said nervously, "this is not your time to run for Governor. I think that Hugh J. Jewett ought to be nominated."[35]

Taken aback by Armstrong's retort, Vallandigham restated his intention. Armstrong, in turn, argued that propriety and party practices dictated that Jewett should get the nomination if he wanted it, that having been the nominee two years earlier and having run a good campaign, Jewett was entitled to a second chance—party leaders had already cast their lot with Jewett. Vallandigham, however, put his own ego and ambition ahead of party protocol and the party's welfare. He said that the people wanted him if the party hierarchy did not, and that he must have the honor and the nomination.[36]

Vallandigham soon realized that, as an outsider, the odds were against him. But defying General Burnside and "General Orders, No. 38" might bring him the means of gaining headlines, publicity, and arrest. He had Dr. Olds' experience as a precedent: arrest had brought Olds the status of a martyr and the people rallied to his support, electing him to office. Vallandigham, therefore, baited Burnside, condemning him and "General Orders, No. 38," first in Columbus and then in Mount Vernon. Burnside countered by ordering Vallandigham's arrest. He sent a company of troops and a special train to seize the defiant Daytonian and bring him back to Cincinnati as a prisoner.[37]

General Burnside set the wheels of a military trial in motion. He selected eight army officers as members of a military commission to act out the role of a jury, named Brig. Gen. Robert B. Potter as the presiding officer, and appointed Capt. James M. Cutts as judge advocate. It was a hand-picked team.

When Vallandigham was brought before the commission he insisted that he was a citizen and that military courts had no jurisdiction over him. After all, the civil courts in Ohio were open and functioning. Brigadier General Potter, as presiding officer, ignored Vallandigham's contentions and the military commission, after a proceeding of several days, found Vallandigham guilty of violating "General Orders, No. 38." Burnside interpreted the decision to mean that his prisoner was guilty of treason and giving aid to the enemy.[38]

Through letters to editors and an address entitled "To the Democracy of Ohio," Vallandigham played the role of a martyr.[39] Democratic editors rallied to his support and a wave of indignation swept the country.

After approving the findings of his military commission, General Burnside selected Fort Warren in Boston harbor as Vallandigham's quarters for the duration of the war. President Lincoln, relying upon newspaper accounts for information about Vallandigham's arrest and trial, took up the matter at a cabinet meeting. Most cabinet members deplored Burnside's rash act, but since it was a *fait accompli*, they favored accepting what had been done in the name of practicality. One cabinet member suggested that Vallandigham be exiled to the Confederacy rather than held as a prisoner in Fort Warren. President Lincoln liked the suggestion and instructed his Secretary of War to send Vallandigham "behind the lines" supposedly to be with his friends.[40]

General Burnside, in obeying Secretary of War Edwin M. Stanton's orders, sent Vallandigham to the headquarters of Maj. Gen. William S. Rosecrans, then in Murfreesboro and commanding the Army of the Cumberland. Rosecrans, in turn, instructed two officers on his staff to conduct the prisoner "beyond the Union lines." William S. Furay, a reporter for the *Cincinnati Daily Gazette*, tagged along and wrote a detailed account of the transfer of Vallandigham into the Confederate lines.[41]

Vallandigham told the Confederate picket who "received" him that he was "a prisoner of war."[42] Eventually, Vallandigham, still insisting that he was a prisoner of war, reached the army headquarters of Lt. Gen. Braxton Bragg. The Confederate commander promptly contacted Richmond authorities for instructions. Meanwhile, Vallandigham asked for a "pass" and decided to go to Texas and cross the Rio Grande to Matamoros, Mexico, or travel to Wilmington, North Carolina, to run the blockade as the first leg of his proposed trip to Canada.[43]

The Union exile was an unwelcome guest in Dixie. Confederate authorities did not want to give substance to President Lincoln's assertion that Vallandigham was sent south to be among "friends." The Confederate press argued that Vallandigham was as much an enemy of the South as Lincoln—both wanted reunion, one through compromise and the other through military coercion. After all, the Confederacy was fighting for its independence. "So odious to us has the idea of reunion with the North become," stated the editor of the *Richmond Sentinel*, "that we denounce the party of which Vallandigham is chief as bitterly as Lincoln's supporters."[44] Vallandigham zigzagged his way to Wilmington to await an opportunity to run the blockade, get to Bermuda, and catch a ship bound for Canada.[45]

The arrest, trial, and exile of Clement L. Vallandigham became the central issue of Ohio politics in the months that followed. It overflowed the borders of the state, and editors from Iowa to New York blistered both General Burnside and President Lincoln.[46] Editor Henry N. Walker of the *Detroit Free Press* summed up the Democratic case: "When Vallandigham's rights go down, so do yours, and mine, and everyman's."[47] Democrats organized indignation meetings and tried to capitalize upon the popular reaction to the summary treatment accorded Vallandigham. Those meetings ratified resolutions that glorified civil rights, denounced General Burnside, and criticized President Lincoln. The best-known resolutions, framed in

Albany, N.Y., and sent to President Lincoln, elicited a reply—really a state paper—that contained the oft-quoted sentence: "Must I shoot a simple-minded soldier boy who deserts, while I must not touch a hair on the wiley [*sic*] agitator who induces him to desert?"[48]

Meanwhile, the political pot boiled briskly in Ohio. The popular reaction to Vallandigham's arrest, trial, and exile put his name on every lip. Some Democrats wanted him to be their gubernatorial nominee as a means to rebuke the Lincoln administration. Others had decided that Hugh J. Jewett deserved the nomination; he had been their candidate in 1861 but had lost the election to David Tod. Jewett was regarded as a moderate; he was a respected lawyer and businessman, and a party regular and an honorable man. Party tradition dictated that he be given a second chance. Party stalwarts like Samuel S. Cox (a three-term congressman) and George W. Mannypenny of the *(Columbus) Ohio Statesman* believed that nominating Vallandigham would be a mistake—it could "ruin" the party, give the Republicans a chance to discredit the Democracy, wave the flag, and appeal to patriotic emotions.[49]

There was a groundswell for Vallandigham among the masses; many viewed him as "a martyr." All members of the Democratic State Central Committee favored Jewett's nomination, but they could not check the rising tide of pro-Vallandigham sentiment. Even Jewett recognized Vallandigham's popularity and offered to withdraw his name from contention, letting the nomination go to the exile by default. Some Democrats like Cox and Mannypenny sought to sidetrack the Vallandigham boom by drafting Maj. Gen. George B. McClellan, then on the sidelines, as their party's nominee. But McClellan refused to let his name be put forth; he still believed that President Lincoln might call him to lead the Army of the Potomac one more time.

The zeal of Vallandigham's supporters and the widespread sentiment for peace and compromise insured the exile's nomination even before the Democratic State Convention met in Columbus on June 11. The excitement of the hour and the tone of defiance of Vallandigham's supporters, especially among members of "the great unterrified, unwashed Democracy," bore evil tidings to Jewett and the party hierarchy. Spectators, mostly Vallandigham's "friends," outnumbered the delegates ten to one. When those in charge of arrangements changed the meeting site from a hall to "the east front of the State-House," they inadvertently transformed the convention into "a Vallandigham rally."[50]

The election of William Medill (two-term congressman and one-time governor) over George E. Pugh (longtime political leader and a former U.S. senator) as chairman was an empty victory for members of the party hierarchy, for soon after calling the convention to order, Medill said that public sentiment decreed that Vallandigham be the gubernatorial nominee. Chaos reigned as Vallandigham supporters shouted and cheered and created a din. After order was restored, both candidates' names were put in nomination. It was a raucous roll call and a one-sided victory for the Vallandighamers; Jewett received only eleven votes.[51]

Vallandigham had guessed correctly. In seeking arrest he became a martyr in the eyes of most Democrats, and the public reaction brought him a nomination that he believed rightfully his. Once again, he placed his personal ambition ahead of party welfare.

After the tally was announced, bedlam again reigned. Then it was time to make the nomination unanimous, give George E. Pugh second place on the ticket, and adopt twenty-three resolutions. Several criticized "abolition," "radicalism," arbitrary arrests, Governor Tod, and President Lincoln. Others advocated peace and compromise: one asked for "a convention of the States" to bring about reunion and the end of the war. The twenty-third asked for the naming of members to a "Committee of Nineteen" (one for each of the state's congressional districts). That committee was instructed to meet with President Lincoln, lay the resolutions before him, and ask him to nullify the proceedings of the military commission that had tried Vallandigham, and repudiate the sentence given the exile.[52]

In time, the "Committee of Nineteen" met with the president, presented their plea in writing, and awaited his answer. Lincoln's written answer served as another state paper, intended for publication. In it, Lincoln reviewed ground that he had covered earlier in his answer to the "Albany Resolves." His central theme was that the public welfare should not be put in jeopardy by irresponsible acts of individuals.[53]

A week after the Democratic State Convention nominated Vallandigham and Pugh as the standard-bearers, Republican delegates assembled in Columbus to choose their gubernatorial candidate. Republican strategists tried to win the support of the uncommitted voters by advertising their assemblage as "the Union Party Convention." It was a clever tactic, also practiced in other states.

The name of David Tod, the incumbent governor, was on every tongue. Some delegates favored his renomination and re-election; others were critical of his administration. Many Radical Republicans thought that he might be a political liability and they were ready to discard him like an old shoe. He was useful in 1861 but apt to lose to Vallandigham in 1863.

Defeatism, popular after Union defeats at Fredericksburg and Chancellorsville, seemed to be spreading like a prairie fire as Copperheadism reached high tide in mid-June 1863. A rumbling unrest, fueled by fear of conscription, permeated the backcountry. Republicans were worried about the upcoming election while the Democrats were sanguine of success. Tod's reputation was badly tarnished. He was blamed for the arbitrary arrests made the previous year and bowing to military power in 1863. He even was blamed for the economic depression that visited Ohio early in the war.

David Tod, who believed that he merited a second term as Ohio's governor, could look back at a varied and venturesome career. Born and reared on his father's farm, "Brier Hill," he attended neighborhood schools before enrolling at Burton Academy, in Geauga County. Then he turned to law as a career, setting up a practice in Warren. He espoused Jacksonian Democracy, and added a postmaster's duties to others. He served one term in the state senate and won friends in every corner of Ohio. His party nominated him for governor in 1844 and again in 1846; he lost each time to the Whig nominee. After a five-year stint as American minister to Brazil (1847–1851), he returned home to amass a fortune through investments in coal mines, canals, and railroad lines. He served as the second president of the Cleveland Mahoning Valley Railroad Company. Although still nominally a Democrat, his views became Whiggish. As a Stephen A. Douglas supporter, he attended the Democratic National Convention in Charleston and saw his party split into two wings. He attended Douglas's convention in Baltimore in June, and, after Caleb Cushing resigned as presiding officer, he took up the gavel. He spoke in Douglas's behalf here and there in Ohio and despaired over his defeat at the hands of Lincoln.

Believing that Southern secessionists were traitors, and opposed to slavery, Tod gave the war effort rigorous support after the firing on Fort Sumter. Sloughing partisanship, he donned the mantle of a patriot and gained the favor of some Republicans. Fearful that Democrats (with Jewett heading the ticket) might win the state-house in October of 1861, Republicans drafted Tod, a late convert to their party, as their gubernatorial nominee. He won handily and served his state well: raising troops, supporting the war, governing judiciously, and cooperating with the Republican-dominated state legislature. He was, all in all, an able and impressive fellow; once a newspaperman characterized him as "aldermanic."[54] He really deserved a second term.

The situation was quite different in 1863, with Republican wire-pullers convinced that Tod could not defeat Vallandigham. Members of the party hierarchy, therefore, decided to push Tod to the side and put in a fresh face—"Honest John" Brough, also an eleventh hour convert to Republicanism. While Vallandigham's nomination was based upon the solid support of the masses, Brough's was engineered in back-room conferences, becoming a carefully planned and promoted affair.[55]

Brough was a good choice. He was a fluent and emotional speaker. He cultivated respect because of his nickname, "Honest John." He had a record of achievement to his credit: successful newspaper proprietor and editor; state legislator; two-term state auditor; respected lawyer in Cincinnati; railroad entrepreneur (president of two railroad companies); and a full-fledged supporter of the war and the Lincoln administration. He could pose as a symbol of patriotism.

It did not take long for the Vallandigham versus Brough campaign to take an ugly turn. From the first, some Republicans had viewed Vallandigham as a traitor and "worse than a Judas."[56] Another patriot wrote: "Shame! Shame! upon the professed Union men who permitted such a convention in their midst, desecrating by its unhallowed breath the fair escutcheon of a noble state...."[57]

Democrats repaid scorn with scorn and applied a series of epithets to Brough: "renegade," "fool," "turncoat," "nigger-lover," and "flailing Falstaff." They ridiculed his physical appearance with a ditty:

If flesh is grass as people say,
Then Johnny Brough's a load of hay.[58]

Three important military events occupied the public's fancy early in July. On July 1–3, the Army of the Potomac turned back General Lee's army in a dramatic three-day battle near Gettysburg and chased the Confederate invaders back into Virginia. On July 4, Lt. Gen. John C. Pemberton surrendered Vicksburg and a demoralized army of 30,000 Confederate soldiers to Maj. Gen. U.S. Grant's army. The two tremendous victories had many side effects. Republicanism and the Lincoln administration regained respectability. They boosted Northern morale, and pushed Copperheadism down a slippery slope. Brough's campaign for the governorship received a shot in the arm; Vallandigham's push for peace and compromise began to disintegrate.

A short time later, Gen. John H. Morgan and 2,500 Confederate raiders crossed the Ohio River and invaded Indiana. On July 13 they crossed into Ohio near Harrison and zigzagged their way eastward, pursued by Union troops. Ohio militia took part in the chase and helped corner the remnant of a once proud brigade in Columbiana County. This daring raid also helped Brough's case, for it stirred the fires of patriotism in Ohio and developed a greater hatred for "the damned rebels." "If there was before any doubt about the Ohio election," an astute Republican wrote, "Morgan's raid settled it. No campaign before ever damaged a political friend as much as Morgan's has damaged Vallandigham's."[59]

On July 15, while U.S. troops and Ohio volunteers were still pursuing Morgan's raiders, exile Vallandigham arrived at the Clifton House, on the Canadian side of Niagara Falls. He was met by a good-sized "welcoming party." It consisted of his wife, Ohio friends, and several newspapermen. He handed the reporters a copy of a document entitled "Address to the Democracy of Ohio." Dated July 15, 1863, the address gave several sentences to two basic issues: (1) civil rights violations, and (2) peace and reunion through compromise. Vallandigham, of course, depicted himself as a martyr and claimed that time would vindicate him and fault his enemies.[60]

After a month's stay at the Clifton House in Niagara, Vallandigham moved to the Hirons House in Windsor, across the river from Detroit and closer to Ohio. There he spent time in his second floor suite receiving visitors (including George E. Pugh), writing letters to be read at Democratic rallies, urging acquaintances to solicit voters, and rationalizing his role as martyr.[61]

As the weeks went by, the gubernatorial of 1863 lost dignity, becoming vicious and vindictive. Democrats called Brough "a fat Knight of the Corps d'Afrique" and stirred the latent racism so widespread in Ohio. They labeled the opposition party "Black Republicans." The Democratic editor of the *Dayton Empire* put his prejudices into print: "Let every vote count in favor of the WHITE man, and against the Abolition hordes, who would place negro children in your schools, negro jurors in your jury boxes, and negro votes in your ballot boxes!...Down with the flag of Abolition; mount the flag of WHITE MEN upon the citadel."[62] Democrats circulated a pamphlet entitled *The Results of Emancipation* and posters with the legend "Protect Us from Negro Equality" were popular at party rallies. Some Democrats who called Brough a "renegade" also portrayed him as an Othello in the hands of a cunning Iago, and they popularized a clever ditty:

> May every Buckeye smooth or rough,
> Denounce the renegade Jack Brough;
> May every woman, child, and man,
> Pray Heaven to bless Vallandigham.[63]

Republicans responded in kind. Their favorite ditty was:

> Hurrah for Brough and Abraham
> And a rope to hang Vallandigham.

They tried to convince voters that the Democratic gubernatorial candidate was a traitor. One self-styled patriot, inept as a speller, wrote that Vallandigham was "a Treble tongued, Hidra headed, Cloven footed, Heaven forsaken, Hell begotten, Pucilanimous curse."[64]

Some Republicans repeated old lies and invented new ones. They accused Vallandigham of belonging to the Knights of the Golden Circle, of conspiring with Gen. John H. Morgan to invade Ohio, and with being closeted with the president of the Confederacy while an exile in Dixie. A forger brought forth a letter supposedly written by Vallandigham to a rebel colonel; in it was the sentence "my heart bleeds for Dixie."[65]

Election day, October 13, brought warm sunshine and a cloudless sky. Ohioans went to the polls in record numbers. President Lincoln, worried about the possible election of Vallandigham, paced to and fro. "The President says he feels nervous," Lincoln's Secretary of the Navy wrote in his diary.[66]

Lincoln need not have worried. Vallandigham went down to defeat by 100,000 votes. Brough received a 61,752 majority on the home front and a 40,000 majority on the soldier vote (most collected in the field). Republicans celebrated. Edwin M. Stanton, Ohioan and Secretary of War, sent

Brough congratulations: "Your election is a glorious victory, worthy of the rejoicing which will greet it." Secretary of the Treasury Salmon P. Chase, another Ohioan, also sent Tod a telegram: "Count every ballot a bullet fairly aimed at the heart of the rebellion."[67]

President Lincoln, who had told one of his cabinet members that he was more worried about the Brough-Vallandigham election than his own in 1860, stayed up late to get reports on the Ohio vote. After midnight he received an encouraging message from Tod: "God be praised. Our majority on the home vote cannot be less than 30,000. Advise Sec'y Stanton." Lincoln supposedly wired back: "Glory to God in the highest; Ohio has saved the Union."[68]

While Brough and Republicans celebrated, Vallandigham took his defeat in good grace. He wrote a post-election letter to "Democrats of Ohio," thanking all for their support. "Our defeat will soon be forgotten," he stated in a key sentence, "but the glory of having rescued free discussion and free ballot will be remembered for ages even though we should lose them at last."[69]

Vallandigham whistled in the dark, reluctant to accept the fact that the Ohio electorate had rejected him and his views on peace and compromise by a decisive margin. Thomas O. Lowe, one of the exile's loyal disciples, stated the facts of the case more realistically: "The people have voted in favor of the war and the way it is at present conducted, and it has to go on of course. The case went to the jury and they have rendered their verdict, and I am not disposed to move for a new trial."[70] The editor of the Democratic newspaper in Vallandigham's home town stated a like view, but less graciously: "The people of Ohio, by their votes, have decided for war, taxation, conscription, and despotism."[71]

Having lost his case before one jury, Vallandigham sought vindication before another—the U.S. Supreme Court. He received a report that George E. Pugh had applied for a writ of certiorari on the exile's behalf and that the court might hear arguments that the military commission had no right to try a civilian when the civil courts were open. So he put faith in another lost hope.[72] Meanwhile, the martyr's halo that he had fashioned for himself lost most of its glow.

Although Brough won the governorship on October 13, he would not take office until early January 1864. Tod was still in charge and the political pot continued to boil.

Earlier, through David Wills of Gettysburg, Governor Tod had received an invitation from Gov. Andrew G. Curtin of Pennsylvania to cooperate in the establishment of a soldiers' cemetery on a portion of the three-day battlefield.[73] Governor Tod stated his "hearty approval" of the cemetery project and reported that he would "commend the same to the coming General Assembly."[74] Meanwhile, as Governor Curtin's agent, Wills made progress on the cemetery project. On September 15, Wills wrote to Tod saying that he had selected October 23 as the day for the dedication of the 17½ acre plot as "a national soldiers' cemetery" and that he had invited the venerable Edward Everett to give the day's oration. Wills asked Tod, as well as the other Northern governors, to attend in person and help to dedicate the sacred soil. Later, Wills changed the date to November 19.[75]

Taking the invitation seriously, Tod decided to arrange for a special Columbus-to-Gettysburg train to take a large entourage to the dedication ceremonies. He composed a circular letter and sent "an invitation" to many, Democrats as well as Republicans: "the officers of the State," members as well as members-elect of the state legislature, some army officers, and many newspapermen. The closing sentence of the circular letter promised "transportation at the expense of the State."[76]

Some Democratic politicians, still smarting from Vallandigham's defeat at the polls, decided to capitalize on Tod's promise of free passage to Gettysburg.[77] George L. Converse, a Democratic leader in the lower house of the state legislature, tried to organize a party boycott of Tod's proposed excursion. He viewed it as a "political junket" and "a raid upon the treasury for the benefit of the Rail Roads." Could not the money that the trip would cost be better spent by "purchasing clothing, fuel, and food for the suffering poor who had been made such by the great battle?" In his long critique, circulated among fellow state legislators and newspaper editors, Converse added a personal pique. He would not accept a personal favor from a political opponent who had been guilty of spreading lies and "misrepresentations of me personally" during the past election.[78] It was, all in all, a scurrilous and partisan letter.

Samuel Medary of *The Crisis* was the first to print Converse's lengthy letter in its entirety and endorse its contents. The contrarylike editor added a personal note, saying that it was indeed "gratifying to know that here is one man left to cry out against a system of the wildest extravagance which ever cursed any people."[79]

Others joined the fray. "We would like to know," the editor of the *Hillsboro Weekly Gazette* asked, "where Tod the thief got his authority to issues 'transportation' to the amount of $15,000 to transport 'officials' to Gettysburg!"[80] James J. Faran of the *Cincinnati Enquirer* called attention to a provision of the state constitution that read "No money shall be drawn from the treasury, except in pursuance of a specific appropriation made by law."[81]

Tod, more or less, ignored Converse's insulting letter and made arrangements for the special train to take "the Ohio party" to Gettysburg. Tod also helped to organize a special "Ohio program" to be held in a Gettysburg church at five o'clock on the afternoon of November 19 after the soldiers' cemetery had been dedicated. He asked Col. Charles Anderson (a brother of Maj. Robert Anderson of Fort Sumter fame), the lieutenant governor-elect, to give the oration at the "Ohio program."

Tod and Brough, as well as ex-governor William Dennison and Colonel Anderson, had seats on the 12'x20' platform when Edward Everett gave his two-hour oration and President Lincoln a most memorable address. The "Ohio program," held in the Presbyterian church later that afternoon was an outstanding success. Even President Lincoln and Secretary of State William H. Seward attended and offered compliments to Tod and Anderson before they boarded a special train for Washington.[82]

Tod received some accolades from his friends for sponsoring the Gettysburg excursion and the special "Ohio program." "It was good to be there," the editor of one Columbus newspaper wrote, "and to be rebaptized in the spirit of patriotism and devotion to human liberty."[83] Some Democrats continued to play the role of carping critics. Medary of *The Crisis* said nothing about the dedication ceremony but still criticized Lincoln's phrase "of the people, by the people, for the people"—it made no mention of states rights. Medary chose to publish a lengthy speech that Vallandigham, still in exile in Windsor, gave to a group of visiting University of Michigan students.[84] William H. Munnell of the *Hillsboro Gazette* was more irrational. He viewed the Gettysburg gathering as a partisan conclave, called "to make Abolition nominations for the next Presidency" and "to harmonize if possible certain unruly elements that threaten the dissolution of the [Republican] party." He had more to say: "It is thus the memories of the dead are mocked by these Jacobin Infernals. What care they about the dead? They have made too many dead to honor them. Their business is to butcher men, not mourn over dead men."[85]

Later in the month, Ohioans had a chance to celebrate General Grant's (he was a native son) victory in the battle of Murfreesboro, November 24–25. Maj. Gen. William T. Sherman, Grant's right hand man in that campaign, was also born an Ohioan. Tod sent his congratulations to both. The victory added another nail to the Copperhead coffin.

The stars in the Union galaxy shone brighter as November gave way to December. Defeatism and despair, so evident earlier in the year, were in retreat. Tod could look forward to returning to his law practice and his business interests. But he never forgave those Republicans who had denied him a second term as governor. For some strange reason, he also blamed the Lincoln administration for failing to support his bid for renomination and re-election.

CHAPTER IX

"Brick" Pomeroy: Copperhead and Curmudgeon*

Emotional oratory, mixed with vicious charges and countercharges, provided fuel for the presidential campaign of 1864. As the political pot boiled more vigorously, Marcus M. Pomeroy, editor of the *LaCrosse Democrat*, fed the flames with searing attacks upon the Lincoln administration. The arrogant editor amazed his friends and aroused his foes by placing the caption "The Widow-Maker of the 19th Century" over a front-page picture of President Lincoln.[1] Then, several weeks later, Pomeroy employed his pointed pen to administer the editorial *coup de grace*:

> The man who votes for Lincoln now is a traitor and murderer. He who pretending to war for, wars against the constitution of our country is a traitor, and Lincoln is one of these men....And if he is elected to misgovern for another four years, we trust some bold hand will pierce his heart with dagger point for the public good.[2]

Even an epigrammatic epitaph was suggested in that issue:

Beneath this turf the Widow Maker lies,
Little in everything, except in size.[3]

Pomeroy's thirst for Lincoln's blood made the assiduous editor a marked man. It won for him the notoriety he sought.[4] Attention was focused on LaCrosse, and men queried, "What manner of man is this?"[5]

❄ ❄ ❄

---

* Reprinted (with permission) from the *Wisconsin Magazine of History*, 35 (Winter 1951): 106-13, 156-57.

A score of Wisconsin citizens would have ventured an answer to that question. Many had more than a passing acquaintance with Pomeroy. In Horicon they spoke highly of the young entrepreneur who had come to town in 1857 with a few dollars in his pocket, a newspaperman's know-how,[6] and the will to succeed. He built the *Horicon Argus* into one of the better small town papers in the State, acquired the sobriquet "Brick,"[7] and served as deputy United States marshal. He shifted his base of operations to Milwaukee, where he served as city editor of the *Milwaukee Daily News* and watched the circulation of that enterprising journal double. Pomeroy's support of Stephen A. Douglas rather than President James Buchanan cost the Milwaukeean his slice of the patronage pie, and the marshalship passed into other hands. An out-of-state newspaper venture dissipated his small stake, so he returned to Wisconsin in 1860 and selected LaCrosse as a city with a future. On credit, he purchased a one-third interest in the office and equipment of the *LaCrosse Union and Democrat*.[8] Pomeroy promoted Douglas' doctrine aggressively, both in the editorial offices and in the hotel lobbies. He took a recess from his newspaper duties to attend the Baltimore Convention which named Douglas of Illinois as the standard-bearer of the Northern wing of the Democratic Party.[9]

While Pomeroy directed his editorial efforts in behalf of Douglas, another firm partner preached Buchanan's views. A six-month civil war within the editorial sanctum of the *LaCrosse Union and Democrat* endangered the life of that party paper. Sheriff's suspensions and sales, coupled with stock transfers, ended the legal existence of the *Union and Democrat*, and in November of 1860 the ambitious Pomeroy emerged with his own *LaCrosse Democrat*, debt-encumbered and circulation dwindling.

The redoubtable "Brick" took a firm stand in opposition to secession of the Southern states and to President Buchanan's "weak-kneed" policy. "We contend," wrote Pomeroy, as his paper took a new lease on life, "that no State has the right to secede—has no right to declare herself free from the laws which govern the Union; and every sane man must insist upon this principle."[10] Irritated by the president's vacillating tactics, the editor wrote: "What a weak and imbecile old fool Jim Buchanan is." Wrathful words came from Pomeroy's pen: "Buchanan is a traitor to his Country—a traitor to his party—a traitor to his word." He asked his readers to add an extra line to their prayers: "Save our Country, but damn our President."[11]

These strong words mellowed as the weeks went by. South Carolina, Pomeroy reasoned, was forced out "for her own protection." Coercion seemed to be "a pretty thing to talk," but dangerous, impractical, and impossible. His revised views on secession agreed with Greeley's—they would let the erring sisters "go in peace."[12]

South Carolina's assault upon Fort Sumter, however, produced a polemic "The Star Spangled Banner Forever." It was a fervent plea to avenge through military might the insult to Sumter's flag; it was a demand that the rebellion be speedily suppressed.[13]

Pomeroy's spirit of patriotism remained keyed to a high pitch during the early months of the war. He tried to organize his own company, to be named "The Wisconsin Tigers" and to do business in "Marion's style,"[14] but that dream faded into nothingness. When the opponents of war raised their voices after the Union debacle at Bull Run Creek, Pomeroy promised vigilante action to quash treason.[15] Truly, he appeared to be an ardent patriot!

But when time combined with realism to cool the ardor of the North, Pomeroy's patriotism also cooled. The cloud of Abolition cast its shadows over the issues preached by the party in power, so the Democratic editor issued a warning:

> There is not today half the enthusiasm in the country there was two months since....A chill has already set in....We are willing to fight till death for the common good of a common people, but will not be forced into a fight to free the slaves. The real traitors in the north are the Abolitionists, and they are the ones who will do more to put off the day of peace than all the soldiers of the South.[16]

Pomeroy endorsed a nonpartisan ticket in the county elections, although he espoused the Democratic slate in the state elections. Slowly it dawned upon the energetic editor that the Union Party ticket represented Republican Party strategy, and he denounced it as a political swindle—a political feast wherein Lincoln's party took the turkey and gave the Democrats the buzzard.[17] He condemned the abolitionists in general and Sherman M. Booth in particular. "He is to respectable people," Pomeroy wrote of this Milwaukee editor and abolition agitator, "what a blooming pole cat would be in a ballroom."[18] When Gen. John C. Fremont proclaimed the freedom of the slaves of rebels within his jurisdiction, the LaCrosse editor showered him with epithets.[19] Pomeroy did not endorse slavery as a desirable institution, but its existence was a *fait accompli*, and the United States government lacked authority to intervene when states accepted and protected it. Furthermore, the freed Negroes, moving northward, threatened the position of free white labor in the North.

The abolition crusade dampened his enthusiasm for the war. Lincoln's preliminary Emancipation Proclamation of September 23, 1862, irritated him. It seemed to be proof that the administration was perverting a war to save the Union into one to free the slaves. Lincoln had surrendered to the "abolition hounds"! Republican agitators seemed to be fiddling while Rome burned—for "nigger is a never ending theme."[20]

Yet Pomeroy was patriot enough to oppose the "Ryan Address." This statement of Democratic beliefs and policy—based upon states rights, conciliation, reason, and humanitarianism—disturbed the editor of the *LaCrosse Democrat*. "This is no time for drawing party lines....," pleaded Pomeroy. "Partisan agitation will not subdue the rebellion."[21] He refused to publish the Ryan address in his paper, and he justified his opposition in many columns of type.[22]

Pomeroy's endorsement of the war obviously was not the blind or blanket type. Administration policy often received the stamp of disapprobation on the editorial pages. The suspension of the writ of habeas corpus and the wholesale arbitrary arrests drew criticism. He expressed disgust with Lincoln's "bungling" and "experimenting." McClellan's removal seemed to be based upon political motives and the pressure of the Radical Republicans. Soldier voting-in-the-field drew a barrage from the editor, for it was a political stratagem which stifled the Democratic revival.[23] And abolition as national policy horrified him.

A three-week tour of the St. Louis sector of war and a two-month term in Arkansas at the headquarters of the Army of the Southwest undermined Pomeroy's devotion to war and wrecked his respect for Lincoln's administration. It ended, eventually, his qualified support of the effort to subdue the South by military might. It changed Pomeroy from a protestor into a full-fledged Copperhead.[24]

At St. Louis the touring editor had become acquainted with army contractors and army quartermasters who had cooperated to build private fortunes—"making money by the cord."[25] Discontented officers and friends explained army politics and practices to the eager editor and unloaded upon willing ears their tales of political patronage, rank favoritism and widespread frauds. He noted the demoralizing aspects of army life—hordes of "unlawful wives and prostitutes accompanying the army," gambling condoned on every hand, liquor shipments and sales at army bases, and stealing sanctioned as confiscation. "The horrors of war will not end on the battlefield," wrote the editor in a letter to his readers, "nor will habits so easily formed by a large mass of officers and men ever be shaken off."[26] His visits to the field hospitals seared his soul. He saw dying men, pained and disillusioned—shell-shattered bodies writhing in the shadow of death. War was a creator of cripples and beggars. "How a hospital strips the damnable crimson glory from a soldier,"[27] he wrote. Watching a lot of 500 pine coffins being unloaded at the St. Louis wharves brought forth the humanitarian's reaction: "These rough, brown, cheap, worm-eaten coffins, piled up there like oyster cans, silently waiting to fold their wooden arms about our sons, brothers and fathers, rather took the poetry out of the shoulder straps and gold-covered cord to be seen strutting around, giving orders to the glory-hunters in plain blue."[28]

His experiences at the Helena headquarters of the Army of the Southwest added to his misgivings. Pomeroy's friend, Gen. Willis A. Gorman, was assigned elsewhere, and Gen. Benjamin M. Prentiss, whose gold stars were tarnished by his surrender at Shiloh, came to Helena to replace him. Many hours were passed in chasing Confederate guerrillas and playing poker, yet Pomeroy found abundant time to write long letters to his *LaCrosse Democrat*, to Storey's *Chicago Times*, and to the *Milwaukee Evening News* revealing his conversion to Copperheadism.[29]

The Arkansas army in action saddened his heart and wounded his spirit. His hatred of war became a passion. He cursed the "devilish vandalism" of the soldiery, and he pilloried its policy of scouring the countryside for provisions and supplies.[30] "When God has forgotten us, and men rule but to plunder," he wrote, "the people may well begin to pause and tremble."[31] Dealing in confiscated cotton seemed to be the prime army activity: "If the enemy is to be conquered, why in God's great name do we not march troops to battle, instead of cotton fields?" Insolently he added: "Give us war or give us peace. This army has, for nine months, been stealing cotton, mules and niggers....The army cannot fight and steal at the same time."[32] Contractors and cotton agents, who descended upon the Arkansas bases like vultures at a carrion feast, also drew Pomeroy's wrath. To a friend he wrote:

> The army is rotten: not in its body, but its heads. The war is dishonest. It was begun by people on one side to save *themselves*, on the other to save the Union; but it has become, through the corruption of Lincoln's court and official missions, but a murderous crusade for plunder and party power. Its aim is to create a moneyed aristocracy—compel the people to support it—and the time *shall come*, if God will spare my life, when the people who are being murdered shall know the crime committed against them. I will gain an audience first, *and then*—woe betide the party in power. I will be no party to this robbery. They may denounce me but their children will not, for they shall know the truth.[33]

Watching the soldiers plod through the mud and contract the ague stirred the inevitable reaction. He wrote of a hospital ship as "a boat load of pain and agony," of mutilated men as "a deathly feast of blood." Amputated arms and disfigured faces, rather than captured battle flags and surrendered swords, seemed to be the true trophies of war.[34] "The more we see of this war," he wrote for publication, "the more do we feel like swearing at the fanatical fire-eaters and abolitionists who brought it on."[35]

> This war is not being carried on to preserve the Union. Such talk is all bosh. Once in the country simplicity of our heart, we thought so; but the truth has dawned upon our vision, full and clear. Were there no Presidents to make—did there not exist parties in the North and South which appeal to the passions and prejudices rather than reason—were there no cotton in the South—no chance to *steal* in one day more than a man can *earn* in a lifetime—were there no rich spectators and moneyed men, as selfish and unprincipled as the devil himself, now controlling this crusade, there would be peace today over the land.[36]

The LaCrosse malcontent became convinced that the South could not be whipped, that the officers were more concerned with promotions than with warfare, that the administration had ceased to command the respect so necessary to success, and that the war had degenerated into a "murderous crusade for cotton and niggers."[37]

His obsession drove Pomeroy to the brink of treason. He recognized that Patrick Henry's pronouncement "If this be treason, make the most of it"—a statement made a hundred years earlier—paralleled his own:

> The people do not want this war. Taxpayers do not wish it. Widows, orphans and overtaxed working men do not ask or need this waste of men, blood, and treasure. There is no glory to be won in a civil war, no more than in a family quarrel. If politicians would let this matter come before the people there would be an honorable peace within sixty days. But so long as blind leaders govern and fanaticism rules the day, so long will there be war, tears, and desolation. It might be treason to write this. But we cannot help it. If the truth be treason, this is the heighth [*sic*] of it, but such treason will find a cordial "Amen" in thousands of hearts both in and out of the army.[38]

The intemperate epistles of the LaCrosse letter-writer and the constant criticism of army policy prompted Prentiss to banish him from that general's jurisdiction. Prentiss' "General Order No. 19" not only dismissed Pomeroy but warned him that his return to that sector would bring about his arrest as a spy.[39]

He returned to LaCrosse to splatter poisonous passages over the editorial pages. The Conscription Act of March 3, 1863, won the editor's disapproval. He claimed that it crushed "the sovereign power of the states," that it contradicted American tradition, and that it made Lincoln a despot—a "permanent ruler of the nation." He stated his beliefs boldly: "The late Conscription act...is one that elevates Abraham Lincoln to the position of MILITARY DICTATOR..."[40] Pomeroy hoped to capitalize upon popular opposition to a measure which excused from service those who could afford to pay the $300 exemption fee.[41]

Editorials, too, denounced General Burnside's suppression of the *Chicago Times*.[42] That arbitrary act threatened the freedom of the press and was an attempt to stifle the rising tide of public opinion. The arrest of Clement L. Vallandigham[43] indicated the extension of tyranny, and his military trial represented the army's invasion of judicial fields. Storey of the *Chicago Times* and Vallandigham, Pomeroy insisted, were martyrs who sought to defend the dying liberties of a half-enslaved people. Lincoln seemed to be "intoxicated and entranced by the whirl of the mighty events around him" as he donned the garb of the "tyrant"—Burnside and Hascall were his "western satraps."[44] "Blustering Ben" Butler, too, drew Pomeroy's wrath down upon his head—Butler and Fremont seemed to be the darlings of the Radical Republicans, ultras who wanted the wheel of revolution to turn faster.[45]

By reprinting articles from Copperhead sheets like the *Chicago Times*, the *New York World*, the *Cleveland Plain Dealer*, the *Cincinnati Enquirer*, and the *Milwaukee News*, Pomeroy advocated his views through indirection. The "Ryan Address," which he had rejected a year earlier, he now endorsed.[46] When President Lincoln set aside August 5, 1863, as a day for fasting and prayer, Pomeroy printed a plea he presumed appropriate: "Remove by death the present Administration from power and give us in their place Statesmen instead of jokers and clowns—honest men instead of speculators—military ability instead of conceit and arrogant assumption."[47]

LaCrosse Unionists tried to combat Pomeroy's influence. They tied the tail of treason to Pomeroy's kite. They used "Copperhead" as a smear term. Unsigned letters threatened Pomeroy's life and property. Republicans urged that "loyal men" cancel their subscriptions to the *LaCrosse Democrat* and that businessmen cease use of that paper as a medium of advertising. Social boycotts, too, could be effective. A.P. Blakeslee launched the *LaCrosse Democratic Journal* to lure Democratic Party patrons from Pomeroy's quarters and to direct editorial blasts at the "treasonable doctrines of those who sympathize with the rebellion." "Wisconsin Democracy," Blakeslee warned, "has a few dangerous men, seeking to be leaders, whose counsels should be spurned."[48]

Tactics of intimidation and the state election fever of 1863 spurred "Brick" Pomeroy to double his accusations and intensify his charges. He dedicated a poem to Lincoln and army plundering:

There's blood upon your garments,
    There's guilt upon your soul,
For the lust of ruthless soldiers
    You let loose beyond control:
Your dark and wicked doings
    A God of mercy sees
And the wail of homeless children
    Is heard on every breeze.[49]

"Abraham Lincoln is the traitor," charged Pomeroy. "It is he who has warred upon the Constitution. We have not...He has broken his oath—lent himself to corruptionists and fanatics...."[50] When the patriots shouted, "Copperhead!" Pomeroy retorted, "Blow-snakes!"[51]

Democratic defeats in the November 1863 elections perplexed Pomeroy. He made the "Ryan Address" the scapegoat, forgetting that his diatribes were even more intemperate.[52] His failure to sell his bill of goods irritated and angered him. His sincerity and his courage drove him further to the left, and in the months that followed he reloaded his cannons with more explosive shells. He labeled the draft a "cruel failure" characterized by "inefficiency, expense, and worthlessness."[53] He searched the dictionary for denunciatory derivatives. "Lincoln," stated the abusive editor, "is but the fungus from the corrupt womb of bigotry and fanaticism."[54] In that same issue of April 23, 1864, Pomeroy fastened the phrase "widow-maker" to President Lincoln. In the months that followed it became the editor's favorite phrase of denunciation. When Lincoln sought renomination, Pomeroy's protests were filled with rancor: "May Almighty God forbid that we are to have two terms of the rottenist, most stinking, ruin-working small-pox ever conceived by fiends or mortals, in the shape of two terms of Abe

Lincoln's administration."[55] In successive issues he expanded that same theme. "The energy of the administration," he critically averred, "is devoted to secure Lincoln's re-election—to rear the widow-maker to the top of his monument of skulls—to the apex of his heap of national ruin." Dejectedly he added: "God only knows where we are drifting....A once proud nation is in tears, trouble and mourning....Patriotism is played out....All are tired of this damnable tragedy....Each hour is but sinking us deeper into bankruptcy and desolation...."[56]

When Pomeroy injected sectionalism into his array of arguments, he passed over ground which scores of midwesterners had trod—arguments that the tariff policy of the government discriminated against the agrarian West, that the eastern-owned railroads literally "skinned the West alive," and that the war was making the trans-Allegheny West both "slave and servant of New England."[57]

Appeals to sectional pride and deflated pocketbooks were supplemented by appeals to the human heart and to personal prejudices. The "widows in black" and the "orphans in tears" were paraded on the editorial pages—Lincoln was "orphan-maker" as well as "widow-maker."[58] It was at this stage of the war of words that he posted Lincoln's picture on the front page of his paper and used the caption "The Widow-Maker of the 19th Century." Popular antipathy to Negro emancipation encouraged editorials based upon that prejudice. Negro suffrage as a policy received numerous editorial blasts. Butler and Wendell Phillips shared Pomeroy's editorial abuse.[59] And Lincoln was to blame for it all! He was "hell's viceagent on earth" as well as a "flat-boat tyrant." "How much longer," Pomeroy asked, "will ye stand this insult, oh! ye willing people?"[60]

Pomeroy's fantastic yet serious censure won him national notoriety. He gloried in that publicity—it was food for his vanity.[61] It was then that he became more abusive and asked for the assassination of the President—trusting that "some bold hand will pierce his heart with dagger point for the public good."[62] That was the peak of Pomeroy's denunciation.

Pomeroy received, in full measure, abuse of the same variety that he so savagely distributed. The circulation of his weekly *LaCrosse Democrat* dropped to 360 copies[63]—proof of the unpopularity of Copperhead sentiments in western Wisconsin. The social boycott was extended. Intimidation, as the Union Leagues widened their influence, became a more popular policy. Soldiers, writing from camp sites and by campfires, threatened to shoot Pomeroy when they returned.[64] Indignant LaCrosse Unionists threatened bodily injury and mob action. The Third Minnesota Regiment, passing through LaCrosse, attempted to "clean out the *Democrat* office." Only the prompt action and the cool head of Mayor Pettibone restrained the rioters.

These constant threats infuriated Pomeroy. He feared no one—he would fight fire with fire, so he answered in kind: "When this office is destroyed, a hundred buildings in this city will keep it company. Matches are cheap and retaliation sweet. If anyone wants a little riot, they shall have a big one—one to last them forever."[65] Pomeroy advised his followers, "When they ignite the match, let us apply the torch."[66]

Pomeroy often expressed his feelings in poetry. A satirical stanza, in the closing minutes of the 1864 presidential campaign, pleaded for antiadministration votes:

And Father Abraham, it's no joke if you again split rails;
The Constitution you tried to split—in this we think you'll fail—
We'll swap you off, though in the stream—we're sure to make a raid,
McClellan is our motto now—free speech, free press, free trade![67]

The election results repudiated Pomeroy's poetry, McClellan's candidacy, and the Copperhead-sponsored peace policy. The disconsolate editor regretted Lincoln's election "more than words can tell," predicting that the union of the states was "gone forever," that the South "would never be subjugated," and that thieving army generals would work with renewed effort. He warned the administration that the North was ripe for revolution and that a Northwestern Confederacy would be formed to join an alliance with the South.[68] He claimed that the will of the masses had been overwhelmed by executive patronage.[69] "The election being over," the obtrusive editor scribbled, "we look to those who voted for Lincoln and the continuance of this war to go to the front."[70] His churlishness proved him a true curmudgeon: "...if Old Abe ever comes into our office to tell one of his stories, or crosses our path, we'll go for him with a culvereen [sic] of corn cider. Dare not assassinate Lincoln! We'd shoot him as quick as any man!"[71]

But, increasingly, national news and issues received less space in the editorial columns—local news absorbing the editor's attention. Lincoln's belated removal of General Butler, whom Pomeroy had abused unmercifully, drew a word of approval and a column of applause. A four-month circuitous tour of the East—to New York and points northeast—dulled the Copperhead's sharp criticisms. He found the country not nearly as ruined nor so war-weary as he had earlier imagined. He was convinced that General Grant was dealing the rebellion its death blow and that powder and blood had cleansed the army of the corruptionists and plunderers.[72]

Lincoln's dramatic death—at the hand of an assassin as Pomeroy had earlier suggested—shocked the country. Even the irascible editor of the *LaCrosse Democrat* showed regret. He decked his newspaper in mourning garb by turning the column rules and clamored for the assassin's blood.[73] The culprit ought to be "hung in chains to starve to death" in true pirate fashion, suggested Pomeroy. Perhaps, added the editor, Ben Butler's hand lay behind the diabolical plot—the LaCrosse curmudgeon knew no one more wicked and less principled.[74] But Pomeroy, too, was under suspicion as the threads of the conspiracy were slowly unraveled;

his enemies recalled that he had hoped that "a daggerpoint pierce Lincoln's heart."[75] Weakly the editor defended his editorial excesses of the war years. He reminded his readers that others, too, had been critical and that many comments were the product of "the heat of a fierce political campaign."[76]

The capitulation of the Confederate forces to General Grant and Sherman cancelled, as well, the commissions of the Copperhead captains. The war discredited them as prophets, so Pomeroy and his compatriots stood disgraced. Theirs, too, was a period of readjustment and the struggle to leave behind their wartime reputations and build new ones. In this rebuilding, Pomeroy enjoyed a sweeping success. By 1868 he inflated his subscription list to nearly 100,000[77]—"even his enemies could not resist buying his paper."[78] Then he sought new fields to conquer. At "Boss" Tweed's invitation, Pomeroy set up headquarters in New York and edited the *New York Democrat* until the scrupulous scribbler laid the charges which exploded the notorious "Tweed Ring." He returned, then, to the Midwest, editing *Pomeroy's Democrat* in Chicago while rising to become one of the top chieftains in the Greenback wigwam. Next, Pomeroy heeded Greeley's advice and moved to Denver, where he edited the *Great West*, invested in mines, and re-established himself financially through organizing and promoting the Atlantic-Pacific Railway Tunnel Company. He spent his last years in the state of his birth, enjoying plush offices in New York City; there he promoted his tunnel company, edited *Advance Thought*, and talked of LaCrosse in which he first won notoriety and national recognition.

❊ ❊ ❊

Pomeroy's participation in the Copperhead movement can be attributed to his personality and to his predilections. His audacity and unconventionality were fathered by his vanity and his search for notoriety.[79] He was not adverse to complimenting himself in his own newspaper. "If they [the people] wish to read the opinion of a man who fears nothing but his God," he wrote, "...the *Democrat* will suit them."[80] A friendly critic insisted that exhibitionism and impulsiveness underwrote Pomeroy's pronouncements, adding: "He neither means nor believes half what he says, politically, in the *Democrat*."[81]

His political and social philosophy, too, drove him into the Copperhead camp. He was essentially a Jeffersonian Democrat at heart, readily lending his sympathy to the underdog.[82] His individualism prompted him to stress personal rights and freedom of action. Human rights he regarded superior to property rights. Like a sage he passed on advice on values: "We are rich, my boy, in our hearts—not in our breeches pockets. Coffins have no money drawers, and if they had, it is too dark to make change down there."[83] He claimed that employers were morally obligated to pay a living wage, that the sweatshops of New York were a national disgrace, and that God did not sanction the suppression of truth and justice by the money powers.[84] "The hand of an honest laborer, calloused though it may be," read a Pomeroy epigram, "is softer than many a palm kid touched today."[85] Like Jefferson, the editor of the *Democrat* had great faith in man, a respect for constitutional government, and a reverence for individual rights; sovereignty, Pomeroy insisted, rested in the people.[86]

His opposition to war as a means to an end was rooted in his humanitarianism. Visits to hospitals embittered Pomeroy, buzzards over battlefields horrified him, crosses in cemeteries turned his thoughts to distress in far-away homes. Succinctly he stated his thesis: "Truly war is frightful. Its glories are those of death and grief—its pomp and vanities, those of crazed ambition; of sorrow and ruin."[87]

Sectionalism, too, forced his hand. He regarded the Morrill tariff as a monstrous tax upon the agrarian West.[88] He claimed that "rivers of blood" would be shed, "mainly to extend and expand New England Puritanism by force upon an unwilling people."[89] It was his loyalty to the debtor West which dictated acceptance of the treasury notes in 1862, and which directed him into the Greenback movement after the war.[90]

"Brick" Pomeroy had predicted that history would vindicate his views and sanction his course of action. Little did he understand the force of nationalism and the unfolding of events! In the popular mind—even today—he lives as a Copperhead and curmudgeon. A rival's evaluation dominates: "He out-jeffed Jeff Davis in treasonable utterances and out-deviled the Devil in deviltry."[91]

PART FOUR

Rewriting Copperhead History

The historiography of midwestern Copperheadism seeps into the first two chapters of Part Four and eventually becomes an integral part of each. The first essay, presented here as Chapter X, was a presidential address at a convention of Phi Alpha Theta (international honorary history society) in Atlanta on December 29, 1975. It was later published in *The Historian*, the respected quarterly of Phi Alpha Theta.

The second essay, "Nationalism and the Writing of Civil War History," presented here as Chapter XI, makes its first appearance in this book. It is a topic that has haunted me for fifteen years or more. Written as a rough draft years ago, it has been reworked, revised, and rewritten time and again. But something always seemed lacking and I was never fully satisfied with it. Somewhat reluctantly, it finds a place in this book.

Chapter XII deals with several different topics and closes out this book. Each topic is related, in one way or another, with Civil War dissent in the Upper Midwest. First there is a summary treatment of dissent in each of the country's earlier wars: the Revolutionary War, the War of 1812, and the Mexican War. Interestingly, Clement L. Vallandigham and Abraham Lincoln, central figures in this book, were on opposite sides in both the Mexican War and the Civil War, reversing roles in the second—in the Mexican War Vallandigham was "the patriot" and Lincoln was the dissenter; in the Civil War, Lincoln was the president and Vallandigham the dissenter.

Another section of Chapter VII deals with the three court cases concerned with military authority and civil rights. These three cases, in order, were *Ex Parte Merryman* (1861), *Ex Parte Vallandigham* (1863), and *Ex Parte Milligan* (1866). Copperheads and the courts were in agreement in the Merryman and Milligan cases. Since the Copperheads expressed views about civil rights that were ratified by the courts, the Copperheads gain some legitimacy—essential in revisionism.

The third section of Chapter XII states the case for Copperheads as dissenters rather than rascals or traitors. Wood Gray, in *The Hidden Civil War*, and George Fort Milton, in *Abraham Lincoln and the Fifth Column*, helped to fasten four assumptions or contentions upon Civil War historiography of the 1840s, 1850s, and 1860s. Revisionists, slowly and surely have challenged these assumptions and considerable headway has been made in purging Republican political propaganda from Civil War history.

It is hoped that this book, a collection of previously published articles and several new essays, will provide a convenient source for students interested in Civil War dissent and civil rights. Middle western Copperheadism is an interesting, evasive, and important subject, deserving more attention than it has received.

| CHAPTER X |

Civil War Politics, Nationalism, and Postwar Myths*

"History," Napoleon Bonaparte once stated somewhat cynically, "is a myth men agree to believe," i.e., "lies agreed upon."[1] Thomas Carlyle, dipping his pen in acid ink, offered a similar supposition by defining history as "the distillation of rumor."[2] Although American historians, preaching probity and extolling objectivity, have eliminated many legends and erroneous interpretations from the stream of Civil War history, some myths and incorrect assumptions remain as pollutants, darkening the waters and affecting its purity.

Civil War myths and legends gained respectability and acceptance as fact in the years following the conflict partly because nationalism helped to transform partisan and majority views into the "correct" ideas and interpretations. Nationalism, as a political force and a subtle operative, affects the minds of men and affects the writing of a country's history. Defined as "a psychological phenomenon" and "a state of mind," nationalism dictates that everyone owes his loyalty to the nation-state and provides a framework for consensus history.[3] It tends to promote majority contentions of an age, or an era, as the true views and proper interpretations. It tends to transform historical figures into national heroes, lauding their virtues, effacing their errors, and tarring their critics. It even tends to present partisan suppositions and incorrect assumptions of the Civil War years, the majority views of the time, as historical truths and galvanized generalizations. "Historical myths and legends," historian Thomas A. Bailey stated in an address, "are needful in establishing national identity and stimulating patriotic pride."[4]

*Reprinted (with permission) from *The Historian*, 38 (May 1976): 419–38.

Some of the Civil War myths and legends arose out of the political contentions and the political stratagems practiced by the majority party which controlled both Congress and the White House during the early 1860s. The Republican party held most of the governorships as well, and party leaders, therefore, had an opportunity to claim that they were the government, present their contentions as the true views, and practice tactics to stifle and suppress the opposition, i.e., Democratic dissenters who wanted their own views and suppositions to prevail.

The Civil War years witnessed some despicable political practices or "dirty tricks," for the greater the intensity of partisanship, the more likely immoral means will be used to serve partisan ends. Although Democrats of the war years did not have clean hands at all times, Republican practices and political claims had the far greater effect in determining what facts and generalizations weavers put into the fabric of history. Republican contentions provided much of the woof, their practices much of the warp.

Joseph Medill, an influential Republican and editor of the *Chicago Tribune*, typified party spokesmen whose misrepresentations and practices gave shape and color to the fabric of history. His opinions and assertions, made in the columns of his newspaper, provided documentation for latter-day historians writing consensus history. Patron of a young aspiring politician named Abraham Lincoln, Medill gave his protege some confidential advice in 1859: "Go in boldly, strike straight from the shoulder—his *below* the belt as well as above, and kick like thunder."[5] Nobody, not even Horace Greeley of the *New York Tribune* nor Governor Oliver P. Morton of Indiana, hit below the belt as consistently and effectively as Medill.

Civil War politics contain countless examples of artful lying, outright forgery, and smear tactics, as well as the use of such devious stratagems as fashioning bogeymen, devising conspiracies and exposés, and using the arms of the government to present falsehoods as fact—falsehoods which posterity accepted as correct events, ideas, and interpretations.

The manufacture of lies as political propaganda was a most common practice during the war years, giving substance to the principle that all was fair in love, war, and politics. "...when I get home [from Washington, D.C.]," one Republican wrote to a friend running for state office in Ohio, "I will get up some stories and tell about your opponent, whoever he is. I don't know him, and it is not necessary that I should in order to tell a few big lies about him."[6]

The presidential sweepstakes of 1864 and the Ohio gubernatorial election of 1863 provided a setting for a variety of "dirty tricks," especially "big lies" and brazen forgeries. Both elections were heated contests, and partisan feelings generated passions, hatreds, and vituperation. Both sides distorted opposition views and dispensed venom. The gubernatorial contest, especially, saw partisan bitterness at its worst, and the Democratic candidate, Clement L. Vallandigham, could not deny the lies, correct the misrepresentations,[7] and expose the forgeries as fast as they appeared. Vallandigham, regarded by Republicans as the most notorious of the critics of war policy, gained the Democratic nomination for governor, in part, because of the public reaction to the summary treatment accorded him. After Vallandigham had made public attacks upon arbitrary practices and Lincoln's war policy, federal officials arrested him, tried him before a military commission in an area where the civil courts were open—no civil jury would have found him guilty of more than intemperate remarks—and exiled him to the Confederacy, presumably "to be among friends."[8] Public reaction quashed the wishes of the party hierarchy and handed the exile the gubernatorial nomination on a badly chipped party platter. Soon thereafter, Vallandigham ran the blockade, made his way to Canada, and campaigned from his base in Windsor. Republicans, recognizing the emotional appeal made by the exile's friends, countered by naming an ex-Democrat, John Brough, as their party's candidate, stoking the fires of patriotism and nationalism and loosening a campaign of abuse and vilification against the well-known exile and gubernatorial nominee.

Four spurious documents, each discrediting Vallandigham, received an extensive circulation in the Republican press:

(1) Vallandigham's arrival in Canada coincided with the New York antidraft riots of July 13–16, 1863. Republican editors supposed that Vallandigham had been responsible, in one way or another for the violence, perhaps conniving with Confederate agents to start the rioting. The suppositions were eventually nurtured by a forged letter, reputedly written by a man who was aboard the *Lady Davis*, which Vallandigham took from Bermuda to Halifax. This forgery implicated the exile, maintaining that he planned the bloody disturbance and that his agents set it in motion.[9]

(2) Some Republicans suggested that Lee's invasion of Pennsylvania, culminating in the battle of Gettysburg, had been suggested or encouraged by Vallandigham while an exile in Dixie. A forged letter, supposedly written by an agent who had spent several weeks in Richmond, made the rounds of the Republican press. The anonymous author of the forged letter claimed that he had witnessed a conference between Vallandigham, General Robert E. Lee, and Jefferson Davis and that he had overheard the exile urging an invasion of Pennsylvania to coincide with an uprising in the upper Midwest.[10] Vallandigham's denials, including his assertion that he had never set foot in Richmond, failed to stop the widespread circulation of this forgery.

(3) Republicans circulated a similar story, one linking Vallandigham to Confederate general John H. Morgan's abortive raid into Indiana and Ohio. Vallandigham, the mythmakers contended, had helped to plan the daring Confederate excursion across the Ohio River, and it was to be timed with an uprising staged by the exile's friends in the hope of establishing a separate

"Northwest Confederacy." One tangent of the lie was that Morgan's men cheered for Vallandigham and instructed those whom they captured and paroled to vote for the exile and against the Republican-sponsored candidate.[11]

(4) The Vallandigham-to-Inshall letter, another forgery, also made the rounds of the Republican press. The letter, reports said, had been written by Vallandigham, when an exile in the South, to a rebel friend, Daniel D. Inshall, a colonel in the 8th Alabama Regiment. The letter, supposedly, was discovered when Colonel Inshall's body was searched after his death on a battlefield, and it was plucked from a pocket to become public property. In the letter, Vallandigham called himself "a friend of the South," expressed sympathy for the Confederate cause, denounced the U.S. government as "hated and tyrannical," and closed with the statement "my heart bleeds or Dixie." The forged letter, published a day or two before the fall election, received a nationwide circulation and gave Democrats and Vallandigham, waiting fitfully in Canada, little chance to denounce or repudiate it.[12]

Forged letters, perhaps, had less effect upon election returns than another tactic—devising a bogeyman to scare voters and discredit the opposition. The most popular Republican-devised bogeyman took the form of the Knights of the Golden Circle, portrayed as a subversive secret society composed of Democrats steeped in subversion. Two pamphlets, both claiming to be exposés of the Golden Circle, prepared the way for the use of a bogeyman as an election-eve stratagem.[13]

The bizarre story had its setting in Marion County, Ohio, where Thomas H. Hodder edited a Democratic newspaper noted for its vicious anti-Lincoln editorials and its opposition to the war. Known and unknown persons threatened Hodder's life and vowed to destroy his printing plant. In turn, Hodder and some of his Democratic friends organized a mutual protection society to defend each other and their property from the hands of the self-styled patriots who talked of using a halter and a torch to suppress dissent. Hodder's friends agreed upon a specific signal to be used if one of them needed help or if the office of the Democratic newspaper was threatened.

On the eve of the October 1861 election, several Republican rascals produced a set of forged documents which portrayed Hodder's ill-organized mutual protection society as a castle or council of the Knights of the Golden Circle and turned their questionable evidence over to the newspapers. Several Republican editors published election-eve extras featuring "the revelations," and a federal marshal, in on the hoax from the very beginning, arrested Hodder and other Democratic leaders in an attempt to convince the wary public that the Knights of the Golden Circle really existed in Marion County and Ohio. The very wording of the bogus oath should have made it suspect, but war psychosis served as a breeding ground for rumors and made the ridiculous seem commonplace. The bogus oath read:

And I will further promise or swear in the presence of Almighty God, and the members of the Golden Circle that I will not rest or sleep until Abraham Lincoln, now president, shall be removed out of the President's chair, and I will wade in blood up to my knees as soon as Jefferson Davis sees proper to march with his army to take the city of Washington and the White House, to do the same.[14]

Golden Circle suppositions spread to other Ohio counties, as well as neighboring states, and proved to be effective political propaganda. Democrats, of course, rushed their denials and demurs into print. "We believe that this secret organization has no existence in reality," wrote one prominent editor, "and it is our conviction that the whole affair was concocted by a few dishonest politicians to influence well-meaning men to vote against the Democratic party."[15]

Time and a postelection trial discredited Republicans responsible for devising the Golden Circle bogeyman and revealed that the evidence consisted of fraud and forgeries.[16] Having found an effective political stratagem, however, Republicans used the Golden Circle bogeyman time and again. Michigan Republicans parlayed Franklin Pierce's visit into a K.G.C. scare, even branding the ex-president "a prowling traitor spy."[17] A *Chicago Tribune* correspondent, who doubled as an aide to the Republican governor of Illinois, devised an expose of the Golden Circle in August of 1862,[18] partly to justify a series of arbitrary arrests and partly to influence the fall election returns.[19] A politically minded colonel, who played the role of man Friday to the governor of Indiana, repeatedly raised the Golden Circle bugaboo to discredit Democrats, cover his errors of judgment, influence elections, and justify the arming of the Union Leagues.[20]

When the Golden Circle bogeyman became rather tattered and torn, Republicans sewed on a new coat and brought on new names. A politician holding a colonel's rank and stationed in St. Louis devised a lengthy revelation about the Order of American Knights in 1864, entitling his exposé "Conspiracy to establish a Northwestern Confederacy."[21] Even the *New York Tribune* published the "startling revelations" in full[22] and gloried in the political effectiveness of the revived bogeyman. Indiana Governor Oliver P. Morton's man Friday, Carrington, also put a set of new clothes on the old bogeyman, and the Sons of Liberty made the headlines as the result of a lengthy expose published in the *Indianapolis Journal*.[23]

Even the Secretary of War, Edwin M. Stanton, got into the act, instructing his judge advocate general to investigate the secret society suppositions. Judge Advocate General Joseph Holt produced a fourteen thousand-word report in which he presented the suppositions as facts. Holt claimed that the Knights of the Golden Circle had evolved into the Order of American Knights and eventually into the Sons of Liberty, all hampering the war effort and plotting treason. Holt discussed eleven "specific purposes and operations" of the "serpentine" societies and estimated that half a million members practice perfidy in the upper Midwest.[24]

Republicans rushed Judge Advocate General Holt's report on secret societies into press as a campaign document[25] intended to help maintain their party in power and win a second term for Lincoln. Republican-sponsored Union Leagues disseminated one hundred thousand copies as an effective means to convert the unwary,[26] inadvertently passing on a myth to posterity. Democrats, of course, denounced Holt's report as "a conglomeration of falsehoods"[27] and denied the propriety of the Republican party using an arm of the government to manufacture "ante-election falsehoods" for its own purposes.[28]

Republicans not only made a deliberate effort to discredit the Democracy by developing the legend that thousands of dissenters belonged to subversive political societies but used a tar brush to discredit the opposition. Republicans, led by Governor Oliver P. Morton of Indiana, blatantly called all who opposed any of President Lincoln's politics a variety of smear terms: "traitors," "allies of Jeff Davis," "secessionists," "friends of the rebels," and "Copperheads." The term "Copperhead" became the favorite word of derision by the time the war reached the halfway mark, and Republicans claimed that most Democrats deserved to be named after the poisonous snake with the brown-blotched body and the copper-colored head. Radical Republicans agreed with a diarist who wrote, "A defender of slavery, a Copperhead, and a traitor differ so little from each other that a microscope magnifying ten thousand times would not disclose the difference. A pro-slaveryist, a Copperhead, and a traitor are the most perfect *tres in unum*."[29] Scores of poems appeared, some advising President Lincoln to stomp upon those whom they stigmatized as Copperheads. One such verse read:

There's a foe behind your back, Ole Abe,
    That crouches for a spring,
Besides the one [i.e., the rebels] in front of you
    whose shouts defiant ring;
It is life or death with us, Old Abe,
    Strike! ere it is too late,
And crush the traitorous, crazy crew
    that clamors at your gate.[30]

The smear campaign of the war years discredited Democratic dissenters, even the loyal opposition, most effectively and passed on to posterity a new proper noun with a degrading meaning: "Copperhead—a northern sympathizer with the South during the U.S. Civil War."[31]

The smear campaign developed an interesting tangent. Republicans developed still another type of "dirty trick" as a political device—they drew up formulas for conspiracies, used an array of detectives (some outright rascals) to transform suppositions into treasonous plots, exposed the so-called conspiracies in the public press, and used military commissions to gain convictions and produce political propaganda.

Governor Oliver P. Morton, claiming that his party monopolized patriotism, set the stage for such a political program in Indiana, for he needed reelection and a Republican victory to vindicate his dictatorial and extralegal practices and to indemnify himself. When the determined governor failed to convince two military commanders that enough evidence existed to make arrests and conduct treason trials, he succeeded in replacing the two recalcitrants with servile military men. "The Governor," one of the deposed commanders later wrote, "urged the arrest of the Indiana members [of the Sons of Liberty and the conspiracy] as essential to the success of the National cause in the autumn elections."[32] Gen. Samuel P. Heintzelman, removed as commander of the Northern Department because he would not play Governor Morton's game, learned later that he lost his post because he "did not make enough arrests" and because he did not believe that the evidence at hand supported the conspiracy theory. The deposed commander recorded his humiliation in his journal: "I have not been radical enough—won't arrest people without orders [from Washington]—would not take the responsibility of doing what Mr. Stanton would not do without Mr. Lincoln's orders. They can't make me a radical. I will do what I think best for the country & not the party. I have served my country too long to now commence to serve a party."[33]

Gen. Alvin P. Hovey, who had assured an assemblage of Republicans that the Democrats would not carry the 1864 elections if he could help it,[34] served as Governor Morton's lackey and chief executioner. He arrested some prominent Democrats as well as some second-rate ones, brought in a partisan judge advocate to serve as both prosecutor and judge over a hand-picked military commission, and wrote a wretched chapter in the history of American jurisprudence. Although the evidence consisted largely of hearsay and supposition, the military commission found four Democrats, including Lambdin P. Milligan, guilty of involvement in a conspiracy, largely because of the tactics used rather than because of the evidence presented.[35]

Republicans staged the same comic opera in Illinois, with different scriptwriters but a similar script. An editor of the *Chicago Tribune* provided the basic outline for the conspiracy plot,[36] and Col. Benjamin J. Sweet, commandant at nearby Camp Douglas, fleshed out the format. Colonel Sweet, seeking a promotion and anxious for the glory which had escaped him on the battlefield, hired six detectives to find evidence to support a nonexistent conspiracy, and he made the arrests on the eve of the November 1864 elections as proof that the plot existed. Sweet claimed that Chicago Copperheads, cooperating with rebels in Canada, had devised a plot to free the eight thousand Confederates being held in Camp Douglas, burn Chicago, sponsor an insurrection, and establish a separate confederacy sympathetic to the South.[37]

After Colonel Sweet arrested those whom he tried to involve in the nonexistent plot, the *Chicago Tribune* published an exposé with bold headlines as

election-eve propaganda. Sweet's fantasy and the grand exposé even implicated Clement L. Vallandigham, back in Ohio after a year in exile, and
Gen. George B. McClellan, Democratic presidential nominee.[38]

After the elections were over, Maj. Henry L. Burnett, who had directed
the Indianapolis treason trials so expeditiously, supervised the trial of "the
Chicago eight" before a military commission convened in Cincinnati. Colonel Sweet's chief witness, John T. Shanks, had the record of a renegade:
perjurer, forger, deserter, bigamist, liar, horse thief, and ex-rebel. Sweet's
six detectives, the principal witnesses in the trial held in Cincinnati, transformed a local Democratic club into a castle of the Sons of Liberty and
wove a web of treason around a handful of little-known Chicagoans. They
also entrapped George St. Leger Grenfell, an English soldier of fortune,
who had stopped over in Chicago when returning from a hunting safari in
south central Illinois.[39] Although the farce ended tragically for the English
adventurer Grenfell, it had a happy ending as far as the Republicans were
concerned; Republicans won the 1864 presidential contest and a "dirty
trick" of great magnitude gained respectability in history—political propaganda won widespread acceptance as a historical happening.

Republican political propaganda and Republican political ploys, practiced by the majority party during the crucial years of the Civil War, led to
the development of six myths still recited and repeated by historians 110
years later. The six myths are:

(1) *That Democratic critics of the Lincoln administration, i.e., Northern Democratic dissenters during the Civil War, were pro-Southern in their sympathies, treason-minded in their proclivities, and deserving of the smear term,
"Copperhead."* These Democratic critics of Lincoln's policies have been
presented—especially by nationalist historians—as men whose hearts were
black, whose blood was yellow, and whose minds were blank—"friends of
Jeff Davis," defeatists, "fifth columnists," and irrational critics who discouraged enlistments, sponsored antidraft riots, hampered the war effort, joined
subversive secret societies, engaged in conspiracies, and earned an appellation which equated them with the poisonous, copper-colored snake
which struck without warning. Actually, the Copperheads and (or) Democratic dissenters were conservatives who opposed the changes which the
war imposed upon the country. Their wartime slogan, "The Constitution as
it is, the Union as it was," indicated that they hung tenaciously, if ineptly, to
their conservative political, social, and economic heritage. They opposed
the transformation of the federal union into a centralized national government, the triumph of industrialism, the extension of the social revolution
(including the freeing of the slaves), and the upsetting of the three-section
balance of power. The so-called "Copperheads" of the upper Midwest drew
most of their membership from three socioeconomic elements of the population: Irish-Americans, German-American Catholics, and the "Butternuts,"
i.e., ex-Southerners who had left the upland South to preempt the poorer

sections and soils of Illinois, Indiana, and Ohio. Some were outright racists and political bigots; others were concerned constitutionalists who realized that the undercurrents of the war were affecting the country's ideas and ideals. The so-called "Copperheads" should be judged by what they said and did in their socioeconomic and political setting, rather than by Gen. Ambrose E. Burnside's suppositions about loyalty and treason or Governor Oliver P. Morton's dogmatically partisan contentions or Horace Greeley's definitions of partisanship and propriety.

(2) *That the Knights of the Golden Circle existed as a viable, extensive, pro-Southern subversive society, drawing multitudes of Democrats into its thousands of castles or councils and promoting treasonable activities.* Actually, the Golden Circle was little more than a paper-based organization and a figment of Republican imagination. It was little more than a bogeyman created by partisan propagandists to discredit the Democracy, justify the creation and arming of Union Leagues, and affect the elections returns.

(3) *That the Order of American Knights was a widespread subversive organization, lineal descendant of the Knights of the Golden Circle when exposés and expediency caused the latter to disintegrate.* Actually, the Order of American Knights was little more than another political mirage and bogeyman devised for political effect. The effort to develop the American Knights as an agency to serve Democrats fearful that their rights might be quashed collapsed completely before a politically minded colonel, stationed in St. Louis, concocted an exposé out of lies, misrepresentations, and suppositions.

(4) *That the Sons of Liberty became the lineal successor of the Knights of the Golden Circle and the Order of American Knights, that the new secret Democratic society had half a million members, and that the organization had treasonable objectives.*[40] Actually, the Sons of Liberty was little more than another paper-based proposition, charted by a second-rate Indianapolis politician and devised to serve as a mutual protection society, a fraternity to elect Democrats to office, an association to maintain free and open elections and preserve civil rights, and a means to nominate a peace man as the party's presidential candidate.

(5) *That Lambdin P. Milligan, whose name was later associated with a notable U.S. Supreme Court case (Ex Parte Milligan), was involved in a conspiracy to seize a federal arsenal, free rebels held as prisoners in Camp Morton, and revolutionize the Midwest in 1864 and that justice was dispensed by the Indianapolis treason trials.* Actually, several of Milligan's political allies, notably Harrison H. Dodd, were guilty of seditious talk and taking money dispensed by Confederate agents in Canada, but Governor Morton transformed a molehill into a mountain through the Indianapolis-based exercise in military justice. The Indianapolis treason trials were little more than a political stratagem promoted by Governor Morton to discredit the Democracy, create political propaganda, and effect his reelection and vindication.[41]

(6) *That the Camp Douglas conspiracy—supposedly a plot to free rebel pris-*
oners being held in a prison compound outside of Chicago, burn the city,
and sponsor an uprising which would lead to the establishment of a North-
west Confederacy—was real and that the subsequent treason trial in Cin-
cinnati revealed that a treasonable plot was nipped in the bud. Actually, the
formula for the so-called Camp Douglas conspiracy was devised by a partisan Republican editor of the *Chicago Tribune*, and a politically minded
colonel fleshed out the format and hired an array of detectives to frame
some Democrats and develop a plot. The subsequent exposé and the treason trial held in Cincinnati provided the substance for still another Civil War
myth.

These six Civil War myths, evolving out of Republican political propaganda and majority views, gradually gained acceptance and respectability.
The nationalistic upsurge, nurtured by the Grand Army of the Republic,
helped to transform Civil War suppositions into historical facts. So did the
gradual transformation of Lincoln from a historical figure into a folk hero.
The apotheosis of Lincoln received an assist from the manner and timeli-
ness of his death. "This murder, this oozing blood," Count Adam Gurowski
wrote in his diary while manning an observation post in Washington, "...
opens him to immortality."[42] The perceptive editor of *Leslie's Illustrated*
Weekly recognized that the Civil War president was a martyr to a cause
and an ideal, writing, "Abraham Lincoln has joined the noble army of
Freedom's Martyrs. Christ died to make men holy; he [Lincoln] died to make
men free."[43] A Connecticut clergyman also predicted the deification of the
assassinated president. In a memorial sermon he stated, "We shall hear
the name of Lincoln mentioned hereafter as the martyr of Liberty."[44]

Some prominent Republicans of the war years also had a hand in
fastening majority views upon history as the true views during the decades
following Appomattox. Having helped to devise Republican propaganda
during the war, they wrote their contentions as history after the war. Horace
Greeley, for example, repeated many of his wartime allegations about Democratic perfidy, subversive secret societies, and treason plots in a two-volume work which he entitled *The American Conflict*.[45] Whitelaw Reid, a
newspaperman whose *Cincinnati Gazette* broadcast suppositions about
the Golden Circle and subversion, wrote his views into a widely read work
entitled *Ohio in the War*.[46] Dozens of others followed suit, whether writing
formal history or personalizing their reminiscences.[47]

The 1890s proved to be the second era which helped to fasten the six
Civil War myths upon history. A nationalistic upsurge characterized the
decade—it underwrote the big navy policy, the search for world power, the
imperialist craze, and the jingoism and breast-beating of the self-styled
patriots. Nationalists applied the Horatio Alger format to Lincoln and put
him on a pedestal. Scores of regimental histories appeared, most appealing to pride and passion. Union veterans preached patriotism as they

lobbied for pensions, reviewed their wartime experiences at encampments and reunions, and developed a myopic view of "the late war." The popularity of U.S. Grant's memoirs, published during the late 1880s, stirred anew the fires of patriotism as the majority views of the Civil War years became consensus history. William D. Foulke, a newspaperman turned historian, wrote a two-volume biography—it could properly be characterized as a eulogy—in which he presented Oliver P. Morton, Indiana's Civil War governor, as patriotism personified, while he depicted the Democratic critics as evil men. Foulke incorporated Republican suppositions about Democratic disloyalty, subversive societies, and treasonable plots as historical truths. He gave respectability to the six Civil War myths which Governor Morton had helped to develop and perpetrate.

Even James Ford Rhodes, writing his *magnum opus* and unable to distinguish between wartime Republican propaganda and historical fact, presented Democratic critics of war policy in a bad light, assigned untold numbers of Democratic dissenters to subversive societies, and put his stamp of approval upon the treason trials held in Indianapolis and Cincinnati.[48]

The World War I era seemed to revive an interest in Civil War subversion and the treason trials. Mayo Fesler, an Indianapolis newspaperman who had been weaned on Civil War myths and suppositions, responded to the war psychosis of his day and decided to seek more information about the Knights of the Golden Circle and secret wartime activities. He wanted to tap the memories of the "old timers," men active in Civil War affairs, before Father Time gathered the full harvest. He formulated a questionnaire seeking information about the Golden Circle and secret society activities and sent it to five hundred "old timers," including many Indiana Democrats accused of belonging to some secret societies. In addition, Fesler personally interviewed two hundred more aged citizens, putting his questions orally.

Not a single Democratic respondent to the written questions or the oral interrogations, even those whom Republicans had publically accused of Golden Circle activities during the war, admitted membership in any secret subversive society. Nor did any know of a single council or lodge existing in their neighborhood. Republican respondents, on the other hand, repeated the suppositions about the Golden Circle and Democratic secret societies which they had read in their party's press or heard at political rallies.

Instead of accepting Democratic denials at face value, Fesler developed an interesting rationale to support his own suppositions; Democratic respondents who had once belonged to the Golden Circle lied, denying any knowledge about subversion because they regarded their secret society vows binding for life and superior to any civil oath. In other words, Fesler, inquisitor extraordinary, used the lack of tangible evidence as further proof that the subversive societies existed, spewing treason on the home front during the war.

Unable to distinguish between the Knights of the Golden Circle, the Order of American Knights, and the Sons of Liberty, Fesler lumped them all together, asserting that they were really one and the same thing—an assertion that should have made his work suspect. "These secret associations," the single-minded newspaperman concluded, "bore different names in different sections and at different periods of the war." He also repeated the old saw that hundreds of thousands of Democrats joined the "subversive orders" and that the prime purpose of the serpentine societies was to overthrow the government, thus "lending assistance to the southern rebels."[49]

The editor of the respected *Indiana Magazine of History* published Fesler's long composition, entitled "Secret Political Societies in the North during the Civil War," for it bore the trappings of scholarship. Although Fesler's pseudo-scholarly work incorporated his own suppositions and much historical hogwash, it won acceptance in the best academic circles. Fesler's contentions entered the college textbooks, and his notable article became the gospel during the 1920s and the 1930s.[50]

A generation later, when World War II stoked the fires of nationalism and patriotism again, renewing an interest in dissent and subversion associated with previous wars, George Fort Milton composed a poorly researched and hurriedly written potboiler entitled *Abraham Lincoln and the Fifth Column*. Accepting propaganda of Civil War days as historical fact, Milton blamed the Knights of the Golden Circle, the Order of American Knights, and the Sons of Liberty for draft disturbances, widespread discontent, and wartime conspiracies. Adept at drawing word portraits and dramatizing historical events, Milton wrote a book that read like a detective thriller. In the end, according to Milton, truth triumphed over evil and Lincoln over the purveyors of treason. Not only had Lincoln been elected for a second term in the November elections of 1864, Milton concluded with a literary flourish, "but he also won a complete victory over the secessionists' fifth column in the Loyal States."[51]

Important people endorsed Milton's book, inadvertently sanctioning his retelling of Civil War rumors and myths in readable fashion. President Franklin D. Roosevelt, as a favor to a friend, arranged to be photographed holding the book preparatory to boarding a plane for one of his conferences with Joseph Stalin and Winston Churchill. Roosevelt also gave the book a plug by equating dissenters of his own day with those of the Civil War era, applying the term "Copperhead" to both. Homer S. Cummings, FDR's attorney general, also endorsed Milton's book, pointing out that it dealt with "the appeasers, the seditionists, and the faint-hearted of another day when the nation was in peril."[52] Even Henry Steele Commager, one of the country's most respected historians, wrote warmly in Milton's behalf. The timely tale, Commager averred, was "a stirring and on the whole, heartening story of how Lincoln out-maneuvered and confounded the appeasers, the defeatists, the malcontents, and the fifth columnists of the Civil War era."[53]

The same year which saw the publication of Milton's popular potboiler also witnessed the appearance of Wood Gray's scholarly and stilted book, *The Hidden Civil War: The Story of the Copperheads*. The book had evolved out of Gray's doctoral dissertation,[54] which had gathered dust for ten years before World War II reawakened an interest in Civil War subversion and defeatism. More scholarly than Milton's book about Democratic dissenters in Lincoln's day, Gray's book, nevertheless, followed the nationalistic and anti-Copperhead course. Gray collected hundreds of quotations from Copperheads and their critics and hung them on the line of treason. Expressing the nationalism of the hour, he saw the Copperhead leaders as "a type that is dangerous in a democracy"—dissenters who "must be guarded against in time of crisis among a free people."[55]

Writers of college textbooks borrowed from such historians as Wood Gray, George Fort Milton, and Mayo Fesler, presenting Democratic dissenters of Civil War days as subversives active in secret societies and involved in treasonable plots. John D. Hicks's widely used one-volume textbook, *A Short History of American Democracy*, followed the patriotic line. The book, which reputedly sold a million copies, depicted Democratic critics of Lincoln's war policy in a bad light, implying that they deserved to be equated with the poisonous snake with the copper-colored head. Hicks depicted Copperheads as peace-at-any-price men who joined subversive societies like the Knights of the Golden Circle and gave aid and comfort to the Confederacy.[56]

John D. Hicks's recitation of Civil War propaganda seemed to encourage others to do likewise. Mark M. Boatner III incorporated myths about Copperheads into his oft-used reference work, *The Civil War Dictionary*. Boatner's reference work, regarded as a bible by some Civil War cultists, devoted three and one-half sentences to the best known of the secret societies of the war years:

> *Knights of the Golden Circle*. A secret order in the North of Southern sympathizers. Originally starting in the South, its purpose was the extension of slavery in the 1850's, and as the movement spread into other parts of the country, it became the organization of the Peace Democrats, who disproved of the War. In the latter part of 1863, the name was changed to the Order of American Knights, and in 1864 to the Sons of Liberty. Vallandigham was the supreme commander of this last-named order, having been active in the original organization as well.[57]

The three and one-half sentences contain eight errors of fact—more than two errors per sentence—and helped to popularize some of the myths which evolved out of Republican political propaganda of the 1860s.

Writers of historical novels borrowed from academe, transforming Civil War myths and suppositions into folklore. William Blake mixed sex and intrigue in a ratio which made his book, *The Copperheads*, a best seller. Blake began his historical novel by assuming that all Copperheads, i.e., Democratic critics of Lincoln's war policy, were traitors and that many joined the Knights of the Golden Circle. The story features a pretty New York miss (Maria Meinhardt) and three suitors. The first was a wealthy and corrupted scion of an old New York family, also a Copperhead and a member of the Knights of the Golden Circle. He sought the heroine's hand while engaging in illegal trade with the Confederacy and partaking in subversive activities. The second suitor, a fervent Unionist, possessed the finesse of Falstaff in the art of wooing a fair maiden. The third suitor wore the hero's mantle, being a staunch patriot, a brave soldier, a gentleman's gentleman, and an ardent lover wrapped up in one. After winning the fair maiden's heart and serving a stint in the Union army, the War Department sent him on a spying mission into the upper Midwest to ferret out a plot of the Knights of the Golden Circle to subsidize a rebellion and establish a Northwest Confederacy. When the hero foiled the plot and returned to New York to marry his beloved, he found her already married to suitor number two. Like a gallant gentleman, and in the manner of Tennyson's Enoch Arden, the disappointed and sad suitor tiptoed off into the night.[58]

Constance Robertson's historical novel, entitled *The Golden Circle*, also made the best seller lists. It featured less sex and more drama, with true historical characters playing minor roles in the tale of intrigue and counterintrigue. The story had its setting in Dayton, the hometown of Clement L. Vallandigham, famous Ohio Copperhead. It centered around a conspiracy scheme devised by the Knights of the Golden Circle. Zachary Granger, the hero, arrived in Dayton to investigate subversion, and he soon met Asa Ormerod, the villain who headed the Golden Circle and devised a scheme to revolutionize the upper Midwest and bring a Northwest Confederacy into being. The two not only worked backstage at cross purposes, but both sought the hand of a vivacious, astute, and wealthy widow. In the end, Granger foiled the treasonable scheme, exposed the villain (he was arrested and carried off to prison), and ended up in the widow's arms. Patriotism, truth, honor, and virtue triumphed over villainy, treason, Copperheadism, and the Golden Circle.[59]

Three other historical novels helped to popularize Civil War myths about Democratic dissenters, subversive societies, and supposed conspiracies. Ernest Haycox, being rediscovered as a worthy western writer, entitled a story *The Long Storm*; it dealt with the Knights of the Golden Circle and a treason plot centered in the far Northwest.[60] Phyllis A. Whitney wrote a romantic story, *The Quicksilver Pool*. It also dealt with the Golden Circle and a conspiracy.[61] Mary Tracy Earle told a young people's tale about an orphaned teen-ager with prorebel sympathies, his Union-minded uncle, and a Golden Circle plot. The uncle, a medical doctor kidnapped by Golden Circle members, showed such pluck that he converted the nephew to Unionism and caused the subversive society to disintegrate in south central Tennessee.[62]

Democratic dissenters of Civil War days were neither saints nor sinners; most were concerned and conservative citizens responding to the issues of their own day. They should not be viewed through the opaque spectacles of their political opponents.

Republican political propaganda, abetted by nationalism as a force and factor, evolved into some myths which were written into consensus history. Historical truth should never be adulterated with political propaganda nor colored by adding generous dosages of an intangible ingredient called nationalism.

A mythical cat has nine lives. Some Civil War myths have had ten.[63]

CHAPTER XI

Nationalism and the Writing of Civil War History:
An Essay in Historiography

Nationalism is a strange phenomenon. It is the unseen cement that holds a national state together, transforming a given geographical area into a political entity. It is a pervasive force that defies a simple definition, for it is evasive, intangible, and mystical. Anyone who would try to analyze *nationalism* and assess its role in history should be a disciple of Merlin rather than a follower of Lancelot. As an enchanting and vibrant force, nationalism affects our lives, our nation's existence, and the writing of history. Its influence is shown in transforming a piece of cloth into an emotional symbol, even reading virtues into the colors of the U.S. flag: red for courage, blue for valor, and white for purity.

Hans Kohn, the notable historian of nationalism, characterized it as "a psychological phenomenon."[1] Whether defined as "collective patriotism," "amassed loyalty," "a spiritual force," "a country's ego" (Edna Ferber's definition), "a trait peculiar to a nation," "the unseen bond which ties citizens to their countries," or "the inseparable ideological counterpart of modern civilization,"[2] it is essential to a nation's life. In the United States, nationalism draws people of different races and creeds and cultures together to form a nation.

Nationalism grows in intensity in times of war, for then the national interest seems to supersede personal wants and needs. It usually ebbs in periods of peace as individuals and groups pursue their own interests. It underwrites a country's hopes and fears, and directs its ideals and dreams of destiny. "Nationalist historiography," Kohn once wrote, "desires not only to describe a people's life but to help form it and to make its history appear as the fulfillment of a supposed national destiny."[3] The presence and prevalence of nationalism in the United States prompted a well-known New York writer to say, "America is not just a country, but a philosophy as well—a civic religion like the Roman."[4]

Nationalism seems to affect the writing of history in four ways: (1) linking the nation to God and claiming the benefit of His blessings—U.S. citizens sing "America the Beautiful" and the words "God sheds His grace on thee." (2) transforming a country's leading historical figures (especially those connected with wars) into national heroes—a social historian recently complained, "American scholars and readers have shown great interest in the nation's military heroes and exploits, but very little attention has been paid to the terrible costs of the conflicts...."[5] (3) justifying that which happened (especially the wars) and presenting the majority views of each era as the correct views—illustrated by an American historian who wrote, "...all four of the wars ["of this century"] entered into by the U.S. were 'right'... the decision for war on the balance was justified...and the world would have been a far worse place had the U.S. not fought them."[6] (4) discrediting minority movements, except those (like Jeffersonian Democracy, abolition, women's rights, Populism, and anti-Vietnam) which eventually evolved into majority movements. Each of these four, more or less, was integrated into the writing of Civil War history.

Efforts to link God and country existed long before the Civil War visited America. There was a widespread effort, especially on the popular level, to depict the United States as a country in tune with God's wishes. Coins bore the inscription "In God We Trust" and antebellum citizens expected reciprocity. George Bancroft, a prominent historian of earlier days, saw the Constitution of the United States as God's gift to the American people. He, like others of his day, believed that his country received Divine favor and blessings. In 1851 Herman Melville seemed to say the same thing when he wrote, "The Americans are the peculiar chosen people—the Israel of our time; we bear the ark of the liberties of the world."[7] Some Protestant clergymen expressed the same theme, stating that God had entered into a special covenant with the American people and had conferred great blessings upon them.[8] Some writers, after the war, saw Abraham Lincoln as "God's man," sent by Heaven to rescue a nation in crisis. John Coleman Adams, writing for *Century Magazine*, portrayed the Civil War president as "a man of God's own making, called forth to be the helmsman for the stormy hour, the pilot of mighty destinies, dowered by heaven for this task."[9]

After the Fort Sumter affair of April 12–14, 1861, inflamed passions both North and South, nationalism prompted the spokesmen of each side to align themselves with God. Northerners, led by some Protestant preachers, claimed that the Almighty was on their side and that the Confederates were allied with Satan. The Rev. George Peck, a Methodist minister, wrote that God used the North to inflict "a judicial punishment" upon the South because of the region's "iniquitous slave system." The war, the Reverend Peck added, seemed to be a part of God's plan to end "an evil institution" in the United States.[10] Julia Ward Howe's "Battle Hymn of the Republic" aptly expressed the wartime conviction that religious fulfillment appeared as a secular phenomenon. Even Lincoln came to believe that he was an instrument in God's hands and, at Gettysburg, he stated that the new nation, "under God," would have "a new birth of freedom."

Confederates, under the subtle influence of Southern nationalism, were as adept at rationalizing their alliance with God as their Northern brethren. Theirs was a simplistic creed, aptly and succinctly stated by one historian: "The creation of the Confederacy was acknowledged to be the working of the hand of God in history in a manner not unlike his creation of the kingdom of Israel under David. The prosperity, atheism, and materialism of the North had prompted the Almighty to move against the nation, to divide it, and to set apart a righteous remnant in the South to preserve His truth, justice, and honor."[11]

While Southerners were rationalizing their status and fighting a war of independence, the Lincoln administration added a second objective to the war—freeing the slaves and transforming the war into a moral crusade, *i.e.*, extending God's law into the secular conflict. The Union army became an army of liberation and John Brown's soul went marching on. At a Boston rally staged to celebrate President Lincoln's Emancipation Proclamation of January 1, 1863, emotional participants sang:

> Sound the loud timbrel o'er Egypt's dark sea;
> Jehovah hath triumphed, His people are free.[12]

Joseph Medill, the editor of the *Chicago Tribune*, also saw emancipation as God's wish and God's handiwork. President Lincoln, Medill stated in an editorial, was but obeying the Lord's admonition to "Let my people go." The nation, now involved in a moral crusade, was finally attuned to God's wishes, and victory would surely follow.[13]

Emancipation, as morality in action, casts its light upon Civil War historiography, and no historian dare question Lincoln's actions on this score. And, since the civil rights movement of the 1960s and 1970s, no historian dare write, as George Fort Milton did in the 1930s, that the four-years war was a "needless war."[14]

"Heroes," a sage once remarked, "are made, not born." The Civil War presented an array of historical figures whom nationalism helped to transform into national heroes. In part, it is accomplished through the selection and the omission of known facts and the addition of an author's interpretation and choice of adjectives.

Lincoln, of course, stands at the head of the list. But there were others like Edwin M. Stanton (the aggressive and enigmatic Secretary of War), U.S. Grant (Lincoln's favorite general), and the redoubtable Col. Elmer E. Ellsworth (the first Union officer killed in the Civil War).

The process of transforming Lincoln from a historical character into a national hero began with his tragic death. The timing and manner of his death, at the hands of an assassin, made him a martyr to the cause of reunion and emancipation.[15] Count Adam Gurowski, a Polish emigré who manned an observation post in Washington, predicted that the manner of Lincoln's death would make him immortal: "This murder, this oozing blood, almost sanctifies Lincoln. His end atones for all the shortcomings for which he was blamed and condemned....Grand and noble will Lincoln stand in the world's history. The murder's bullet opens to him immortality."[16]

Lincoln's development as a national hero received an assist by those writers who saw him as "God's man." John Coleman Adams, in that article in *Century Magazine*, commented upon Lincoln's famous reply to Horace Greeley's "Prayer of Twenty Millions," writing, "There spake God's man, instinctively grasping for the truth for which he was brought into the world."[17] The idea that Lincoln was "God's man" was also expressed by a speaker who was a member of the Lincoln Fellowship of Wisconsin; the clergyman, passing himself off as a historian, entitled his talk "The Man from Sangamon and the Man from Galilee"—even giving Lincoln first billing in the title.

Lincoln's two war-time secretaries, John G. Nicolay and John Hay, contributed considerably to the transformation of the Civil War president from a historical figure into a national hero. Their massive and monumental ten-volume work, *Abraham Lincoln: A History* (1890) was the bible for two generations; it glorified the Civil War president and discredited his critics—his warts disappeared as all critical comments were omitted. The co-authors regarded themselves as "Lincoln men through and through." In a letter to Lincoln's son, possessor of his father's letters and documents that the co-authors had borrowed, John Hay wrote, "I need not tell you that every line has been written with a spirit of reverence and regard."[18] Of course, Lincoln's son reserved the right to use a red pencil. But there was little need, for the co-authors' respect for Lincoln had evolved into reverence and their work was close to an exercise in adulation.

Carl Sandburg's six-volume portrayal of Lincoln (two volumes devoted to "the prairie years" and four to "the war years") added romance and reverence as well as detail, helping to popularize the Civil War president and solidify his place as a national hero.[19] It prompted a reviewer to write: "It has done us good to read this able, rugged book. We do not doubt that it has done Carl Sandburg much good to write it. Such is the strange blessing which Lincoln bestows on his biographers.... And the result is the living virtue that streams out of Lincoln forever."[20]

In the years that followed—and as World War I engendered nationalism—a number of historians enhanced Lincoln's reputation with books that
were widely read. George Fort Milton's *Abraham Lincoln and the Fifth Column* (1942) possessed a catchy title and it appealed to a people at war. Its
sales zoomed when President Franklin D. Roosevelt added his subtle endorsement to those previously made by such respected historians as Henry
Steele Commager, Solon J. Buck, and Allan Nevins.[21] Milton gloried that
Lincoln had triumphed over "the dissenters and appeasers of his day," slandering the president's wartime critics in the process.[22]

T. Harry Williams, one of the country's most respected historians in
his day, brought forth two books that added to Lincoln's reputation. In the
first, *Lincoln and the Radicals* (1941), Williams detailed how the Civil War
president outfoxed the left wing critics (the so-called Radical Republicans)
of his own party—treating them unfairly in the process. In the second book,
Lincoln and His Generals (1952), Williams absolved the Civil War president of some errors of judgment and presented him as a super-strategist
and a great commander in chief.[23] Williams' portrayal of Lincoln as a super-
strategist received a solid endorsement in Colin R. Ballard's book entitled
The Military Genius of Abraham Lincoln (Cleveland, 1952).

Bruce Catton, filling a shelf with his Civil War books, always treated
Lincoln sympathetically—in the best tradition of a nationalist historian. Even
Allan Nevins, in his extraordinary four-volume work, *The War for the Union*,
rules in Lincoln's favor on every score. By the time the country had finished
commemorating its Civil War centennial, Lincoln's place as the U.S.'s greatest president was secure. He not only stood on the highest pedestal, but
his rugged face was carved out of granite on the side of Mount Rushmore.

About the time that Gutzon Borglum began work on his famous four-
figure monument, a well-known historian, Thomas Beer, made "the mistake" of portraying Lincoln rather realistically—as a historical figure rather
than a national hero in an article in the *Saturday Evening Post*. A dozen
critics rebuked him. One, a nationalist historian of the first order, wrote:
"You are like all these other Bolsheviki who are trying to degrade the character of Abraham Lincoln and make him appear an ordinary man. Lincoln
was the greatest man born in the world since our Savior, *if it is fair to call
him a man at all*...."[24] Historians who treat Lincoln realistically or write studies of Lincoln's critics, be they wartime Democrats or Radical Republicans,
have a hard time getting a fair hearing if the reviewers are historians who
view Lincoln as a national hero rather than as a historical figure.

Lincoln, of course, was not the only historical figure of Civil War days
whom popular writers and historians have helped evolve into national heroes—the selection or omission of known facts are part of the process.
Nationalist historians like Bruce Catton and T. Harry Williams endorsed
General U.S. Grant's military actions as they did President Lincoln's political ones. They like to quote Lincoln's assessment of Grant: "He fights."

They recite Grant's telegraphic report to Washington in 1864: "I propose to fight it out on this line if it takes all summer." They like Grant's metaphorical comment, "Our cat has the longest tail." They fail to say that Grant never learned that it was foolhardy to attack entrenched Confederate troops as he did at Vicksburg, in the Wilderness, at Spotsylvania and Cold Harbor— that the Minie ball and the Springfield riles called for a change in tactics and that Grant was guilty of suffering staggering losses and an unnecessary loss of soldiers' lives. Catton received an assist from an array of historians, one even developing the theme that Grant was really a man of compassion, concerned for the welfare of his troops.[25]

Nationalist historians are want to portray General Grant as courageous rather than callous, tenacious rather than stubborn. They endorse Grant's war of attrition in 1864, saying that the encounters north and east of Richmond decimated Lee's army and shortened the war. Grant, they rationalized, could afford his losses of 70,000 men while Lee could not afford his far lesser losses. This, they add, made Lee's surrender inevitable. "Grant deserves the glory," T. Harry Williams once said; "he won and you can't argue with that."[26]

Stanton also receives more accolades than critical appraisal from nationalist historians—after all, he held "the right views" *re* emancipation and civil rights for the newly freed. They stress his indispensable roles in the war, his dedication and dynamism, his organizational skills, and his combative powers. They down-play his arrogance and heartlessness, his anti-Catholic bigotry, his brutal fits of temper, and his duplicity and double-dealing—Gideon Welles saw Stanton as a two-faced dissembler.

The true story of the desecration of civil rights in the Civil War, with Stanton playing the role of the principal character, has not yet been written—it simply is not the patriotic thing to do. Most of the thousands of civilian arrests (estimates vary from 10,000 to 38,000)[27] rest at Stanton's doorstep. Stanton endorsed the trial of civilians (like Clement L. Vallandigham and Lambdin P. Milligan) by military commissions where the civil courts were open—a practice repudiated by the U.S. Supreme Court in *Ex Parte Milligan* (1866) after the war.[28] Nor should the principal characters in "the Indianapolis conspiracy," the so-called "Camp Douglas Conspiracy" and the Lincoln assassination conspiracy, have been tried by military commissions rather than in the civil courts. Stanton never repudiated soldiers (whether in camp or on furlough) who mobbed and destroyed Democratic newspapers nor reprimanded generals who prohibited their circulation in the field. No Stanton biographer nor nationalist historian makes mention of the Albert J. Edgerly affair: Lieutenant Edgerly of the 4th New Hampshire Volunteer Regiment, while home on leave, campaigned for the Democratic state ticket in 1863. By order of Secretary of War Stanton, Edgerly was dismissed from the service "for circulating Copperhead tickets and doing all in his power to promote the success of the rebel cause in his

State."[29] Stanton's political bigotry caused him to equate voting for the Democratic ticket in New Hampshire with "the rebel cause."

Stanton's role regarding the so-called "Holt Report on Secret Societies"[30] was as disgraceful as his treatment of Lieutenant Edgerly. Not only was "the report" composed at the Secretary of War's instructions, but then it was circulated as propaganda during the presidential election of 1864. The report, regarded as reliable evidence by four generations of historians after the war, linked Democrats to subversion—on the whole, it was composed of lies and "*suppositions* and *understandings* and *guesses* and *loose* generalities."[31]

Nationalist historians also tend to ignore or excuse Stanton's part in the trial of the so-called "Lincoln assassination principals"—or shift the blame to Judge Advocate General Joseph Holt. Professor Ludwell Johnson III indicts Stanton in a rather savage fashion:

> The trial of the conspirators was an utter disgrace. Some witnesses were bullied into perjury by threats of hanging; others sold their false testimony for cash. Stanton and Holt first tried to hold the trial in secrecy, but word of their plan reached the press and Stanton backed down. Some members of the military commission conducted themselves so as to dishonor the uniform they wore. The commission itself, of course, lacked any jurisdiction known to either civil or military law. The blatant partisanship of Assistant Judge Advocate John Bingham, Stanton's old friend from Ohio, was shameful in a man whose official position required him to present evidence of innocence as well as guilt and to protect the rights of the defendants. Witnesses were heard and testimony admitted that would have made Sir George Jeffrey blush. As for the prisoners, they were (except for Mary Surratt) not only heavily ironed in court and out, but at Stanton's direction, were tormented to the point of madness by having to spend weeks in the cells blinded and deafened by heavy, padded canvas bags that were tied over their heads.[32]

Obviously, Stanton's star shines much brighter if he is presented as a national hero rather than as a historical figure.

In addition to linking God and nation and transforming historical characters into national heroes, nationalist historians "justify that which happened" and present the majority views of each era as the correct views. Conyers Read, in his presidential address at the American Historical Association convention in 1949—during the "Cold War" years—suggested that history be mobilized in defense of American standards and ideals. "Total war," he said, "...enlists everyone."[33] Samuel Eliot Morison, in his A.H.A. presidential address in 1950 scolded "the revisionists" for belittling wars and supposing that "no war did any good, even to the victor." Morison advocated "a friendly, almost affectionate attitude" toward our past.[34] A noted

Civil War historian, Phillip S. Paludan, seems to have taken Morison's advice to heart. In two scholarly articles he defended and justified the Civil War as "a Good Thing." The North, Paludan wrote, went to war out of a conviction that the South had broken the law and out of fear that a successful secession would encourage further division. Paludan believes that the North was right on both counts, as the war was "the necessary instrument of order, strength, wealth, and liberty." The Civil War was "worthwhile," for "we cannot pay cheap prices for things that are precious." "As a result of the war," Paludan added, "a 'new birth of freedom' did occur. Like most births it was painful."[35]

Not only do nationalist historians justify the Civil War as a critical event in American history, but they seem to endorse every act of the Lincoln administration. They justify Lincoln's use of "war powers" to issue his Emancipation Proclamations—Democrats believed them patently unconstitutional and even the president knew that he was on shaky ground.[36] They passively accept the many arbitrary arrests of civilians in the North during the war and even ignore "the fall roundup of 1862."[37] They accept as practical or necessary the trial of civilians like Edmund J. Ellis, Clement L. Vallandigham, and Lambdin P. Milligan by military commissions in areas where the civil courts were open. They justify President Lincoln's suspension of the writ of habeas corpus when even many Republicans believed that suspension was a congressional, not a presidential prerogative. And they justify the dismemberment of Virginia (the creation of the Republican-controlled state of West Virginia), refusing to accept the process as "constitutional flimflam." During the Civil War the Republican party controlled both houses of Congress as well as the presidency. Republican party views— the majority views of the Civil War era—were passed on to posterity as the true views. Pundits say that, in each war, the victors write the definitions for justice, honor, and treason. Under the subtle influence of nationalism, much Civil War-time political propaganda has been written into history as historical fact.

Nationalism, as the prompter in discrediting minority movements, worked overtime as far as Civil War Democrats were concerned. Much Republican political propaganda concerning Lincoln's Democratic critics found its way into high school and college textbooks—beginning with the smear term "Copperheads."

During the war years, especially the first half of 1863, Republican editors and orators fastened the term "Copperheads" upon Lincoln's Democratic critics in the most vicious smear campaign in American history. Editor Edgar Conkling of the *Cincinnati Gazette* led the way in labeling Democrats after the poisonous snake with the brown-blotched body and the copper-colored head. The Republican propaganda campaign was so effective that, 125 years later, dictionaries still define the word "Copperhead" as "a Northern sympathizer with the South during the Civil War."[38]

Radical Republican contentions that Lincoln's Democratic critics were "pro-Southern" found their way into books written by Lincoln's Republican contemporaries after the war. Horace Greeley's *The American Conflict* (1867), Whitelaw Reid's *Ohio in the War* (1868), and Berry R. Sulgrove's *History of Indianapolis and Marion County* (1886) exemplify books written by Republican partisans who were also newspaper editors who had been involved in the smear campaign. Lincoln's Democratic critics, naturally, were treated most unfairly and the term "Copperhead" experienced a rebirth.

The practice of portraying Lincoln's Democratic critics as "Copperheads" rather than as conservatives who opposed the changes that the war imposed upon the country continued as the nineteenth century gave way to the twentieth. This is illustrated by such books as William D. Foulke's *Life of Oliver P. Morton, Including His Important Speeches* (1899), and James Ford Rhodes' *History of the United States from the Compromise of 1850...* (1893–1906) and *History of the Civil War, 1861–1865* (1917).

The "Copperhead view" of Civil War Democrats was popular again as World War II engendered nationalism. Wood Gray's *The Hidden Civil War: The Story of the Copperheads* (1942) and George Fort Milton's *Abraham Lincoln and the Fifth Column* (1942) continued the tradition of presenting Republican-concocted Civil War propaganda as historical fact. Wood Gray collected stacks of quotations (many from Democratic as well as Republican newspapers) and hung them on the line of treason. He even characterized the so-called "Copperheads" as "a type that is dangerous in a democracy"—dissenters who "must be guarded against in time of crisis among a free people."[39] George Fort Milton, in depicting Lincoln's Democratic critics as a "Fifth Column," used a tar brush when dealing with Horatio Seymour, spokesman for many Eastern Democrats, and Clement L. Vallandigham, the controversial leader of "Peace Democrats" in the upper Midwest.[40] All in all, Milton carried the pro-Southern theme to an extreme. Yet the suppositions of Gray and Milton were endorsed by Commager, one of the most respected historians of his day; Commager characterized Milton's potboiler as "a stirring and on the whole, heartening story of how Lincoln outmaneuvered and confounded the appeasers, the defeatists, and the fifth columnists of the Civil War era."[41] Perhaps Gray and Milton, as well as Commager, were caught up in the swirling nationalism that enveloped the country during World War II.

The practice of bashing the so-called "Copperheads" and presenting them as pro-Southern in their sympathies continued into the 1980s. Richard H. Sewell, in a recent book entitled *A House Divided: Sectionalism and Civil War, 1848–1865* (1988), says that some "so-called Copperhead Democrats—men like Clement L. Vallandigham, Thomas Seymour [of Connecticut], and Fernando Wood [of New York City]...sought to discourage enlistments."[42] Although the words and actions of these three dissenters undoubtedly did discourage enlistments, the word "sought" does them an injustice and is contradicted by historical evidence.[43]

In two notable books, James M. McPherson continues the nationalist tradition of portraying the so-called "Copperheads," and especially Vallandigham, as pro-Southern in their sympathies. In the Pulitzer Prize-winning *Battle Cry of Freedom: The Civil War Era* (1988), McPherson says that Vallandigham "...added sympathy for the South produced by descent from a Virginia family and marriage to the daughter of a Maryland planter."[44] McPherson could have written that both Vallandigham's grandfather and great-grandfather were Pennsylvanians and that the grandfather served in the Revolutionary War as a colonel, mixed farming and law, and condemned "the Whiskey rebels" for using "foolish and illegal tactics" to achieve their ends.[45] But such a statement would not fit the pro-Southern scheme for Vallandigham and the so-called "Copperheads." Furthermore, William McMahon, whose daughter Vallandigham married, hardly fit the "planter" category; he was "the leading merchant" of Cumberland, Maryland, but was also active as "a progressive farmer"[46]—and he died in 1838, eight years before young Clem Vallandigham married his daughter Louisa. Finally, the Census of 1860 did not list any McMahon in Allegany County, Maryland, as a slaveholder.[47] Interestingly, both of Abraham Lincoln's grandparents were Virginians, and he married the daughter of a prominent Kentucky slaveholder.

In McPherson's notable work, *Ordeal by Fire: The Civil War and Reconstruction* (1982), the theme that Peace Democrats deserved to be called "Copperheads" and labeled "pro-Southern" also persists. The respected author even goes so far as to imply that Vallandigham's arrest, trial, and exile provided the historical basis for Edward Everett Hale's great story "The Man Without a Country"[48]—another myth that indirectly discredits Vallandigham.

The wartime Republican propaganda campaign against the so-called "Copperheads" possessed an interesting tangent—that thousands and thousands of Democrats belonged to subversive secret societies and were involved in two conspiracies, one based in Indianapolis and the other in Chicago. During the war such terms as Knights of the Golden Circle, Order of American Knights, and Sons of Liberty became household terms because of exposés concocted by Republicans for political gain.[49] These Republican-sponsored exposés, composed to discredit the Democracy and affect the election returns, found their way into Joseph Holt's infamous report, published as a campaign document under the title *Report of the Judge Advocate General on the "Order of American Knights," alias "Sons of Liberty": A Western Conspiracy in Aid of the Southern Rebellion.*[50]

These tales of subversion had nine lives, being repeated in the decades after the war by Republicans who became authors. Historian James Ford Rhodes, bestirred by the nationalism that engulfed the 1890s, repeated the subversion tales about the three secret societies and the two midwestern conspiracies when fashioning his seven-volume history of the last half of the nineteenth century.[51] Mayo Fesler, influenced by the nationalistic surge associated with World War I, wrote an article that bore the trappings of scholarship; it expressed the conviction that the Golden Circle, American Knights, and Sons of Liberty had extensive membership lists and had plotted treason in Indianapolis and Chicago in 1864.[52] Both Gray's *The Hidden Civil War* and Milton's *Abraham Lincoln and the Fifth Column* gave considerable space to the so-called "Copperhead secret societies" and to the supposed conspiracies. Fesler's article and Gray's and Milton's books were the wells from which writers of college textbooks drew polluted water, with John D. Hicks' *A Short History of American Democracy* (1943) being a classic example.[53] Then, in 1970, Professor Oscar A. Kinchen raised the tales of subversive societies and treason in Chicago to a higher level with a book entitled *Confederate Operations in Canada and the North*.[54]

In *Ordeal by Fire*, historian McPherson restates his contention that the so-called "Copperhead secret societies" hatched treason in their councils. "There were several plots to free Confederate prisoners," he contends, "including one to stage an uprising in Chicago during the Democratic national convention to cover the liberation of war prisoners from nearby Camp Douglas."[55] He claims that some historians who have debunked the Golden Circle tales and the "Camp Douglas conspiracy" have carried "revisionism a bit too far." He even believes that Clement L. Vallandigham "lied under oath when he denied all knowledge of conspiracies at the treason trials of the Chicago conspirators in early 1865."[56]

Copperheadism, as a minority movement, fared badly at the hands of Radical Republicans who were anxious to discredit the political opposition and win elections. It continued to fare badly at the hands of nationalist historians for a hundred years, as much Republican wartime propaganda was accepted as historical fact. During the past thirty years some revisionist historians have discredited and discarded some of that political propaganda.[57] But much separating wheat from chaff remains to be done, for nationalism—subtle and evasive—still affects the writing about the so-called "Copperheads," Democratic critics of the Lincoln administration who opposed the changes that the Civil War foisted upon their country.

T.S. Eliot, with insight, cautioned practitioners of Clio's craft to be wary when writing history:

> Think now
> History has many cunning passages,
>   contrived corridors and issues,
> Deceives with whispering ambitions,
> Guides us by our vanities.[58]

CHAPTER XII

In Retrospect and More

Civil War dissent in the form of Democratic criticism of the Lincoln administration had its peaks and valleys and seemed to be driven by the winds of chance. It was not a new phenomenon, for dissent was prevalent in every previous American War. During the Revolutionary War the majority (the so-called "Patriots"), holding the reins of power, penalized the dissenters (the so-called "Loyalists"); they used threats and violence, confiscated their property, and drove many into exile—"to hell, Hull, or Halifax." Patriots characterized Loyalists as "traitors" and "a thing whose head is in England, whose body is in America, and [whose] neck ought to be stretched."[1] Thousands of the Loyalists ended up in Canada and their descendants still comprise an element of the population bearing a grudge for past events. After the war the Patriots wrote their own definition for such terms as "justice," "honor," and "treason." Revolutionary War dissenters, in recent years, have regained some respectability and have been put in their historical setting.

The War of 1812 also had many who qualified as dissenters, and partyism as well as sectionalism and economics, provided the ingredients. The Northeast furnished most of the critics of the war, including a young man named Daniel Webster. As a congressman from New Hampshire, Webster defended the Federalist point of view and honed his speaking skills. President James Madison and "War Hawks" like Henry Clay contended that those who attended the Hartford Convention of 1814 flirted with treason. "The Federalist party, from its apparent sympathy with the Hartford Convention," a nationalist historian wrote more than a hundred years later, "received a death blow from which it did not recover."[2] National-ist historians transformed "a questionable conflict" into "a fight for a free sea" and "a crusade in defense of national honor." They viewed the Hart-ford Convention as "an ugly incident" and wrote that the war itself gave "strength and splendor to the chain of the Union."[3] So again, the dissenters wore the black hats.

As in the Civil War, blatant partyism formed the chief factor in dissent during the Mexican War. The Whigs were the "outs" and Democrats the "ins" during that three-year war. Henry Clay, a "War Hawk" during the War of 1812, was "the Dove of Peace" during the Mexican War—his bitter op-position to the War was intensified when his favorite son and namesake was killed in one of the battles. Abraham Lincoln, as a freshman con-gressman, let party loyalty shape his opposition to the Mexican War. Lin-coln, jousting with President Polk, introduced a series of resolutions intended to embarrass the man who sat in the White House. Lincoln con-tended that "the spot" where American blood had been first shed was not American soil but a Mexican corn field. Later Lincoln voted for a partisan resolution declaring that the Mexican War "was unconstitutionally and unnecessarily begun by the President [Polk]."[4] Later, flag-waving histori-ans wrote that Lincoln and other dissenters played "an ignoble role" during the 1846–1848 war, argued that the conflict "had strengthened the fibers of the country," and that wars, sometimes, are "the only means of advanc-ing civilization."[5]

While Lincoln was opposing the Mexican War, Clement L. Vallandigham endorsed it—ironically, those roles would be reversed in the Civil War. As a young state legislator, Vallandigham chided the Whigs for their opposition to the Mexican War. "Sirs," he said as he shook his finger at the Whig dissenters, "if ye will howl over its calamities in the name of the living, by the blood of its slain ye shall have no part in its glories."[6] Vallandigham's taunts, implying that the Whigs were traitors, were repaid a hundredfold during the Civil War.

Vallandigham and Indiana's Daniel W. Voorhees carried the torch for civil liberties during the first half of the Civil War. Some of the infractions, represented by Burnside's "General Orders, No. 38" and Hascall's "Gen-eral Order No. 9," deserved to be rebuked, and most historians today con-demn them. Three Civil War court cases dealt with the issue of civil rights, and two of them ended with decisions in favor of the Democratic dissenters.

The first case, *Ex Parte Merryman* (1861), had a Maryland seces-sionist of pro-Southern sympathies as the central figure. The story dated back to the day when Massachusetts troops, going on their way to Wash-ington, were attacked by a mob in Baltimore. So on April 27, 1861, Presi-dent Lincoln authorized his general in chief, Winfield Scott, to suspend the writ of habeas corpus along the railroad lines from Philadelphia to Wash-ington.[7] On May 21, 1861, Gen. George Cadwalader, commanding in the area, ordered Merryman arrested for "drilling secessionist volunteers near Cockeysville, Maryland." Brig. Gen. William Kein, a subordinate officer, made Merryman a prisoner and hustled him off to Fort McHenry. No grounds having been stated for Merryman's arrest, Chief Justice Roger B. Taney of the U.S. Supreme Court, sitting as a judge in the Maryland district, issued a writ of habeas corpus in behalf of the prisoner; Taney ordered General Cadwalader to bring Merryman into his court for a hearing—after all, the Sixth Amendment promised "a speedy and public trial by an impartial jury in the district where the [supposed] crime had been committed." General Cadwalader refused to respect Taney's writ, contending that he was acting under authority of the president. Justice Taney, in turn, sent a marshal to serve the uncooperative general with a contempt of court citation. When the marshal arrived at Cadwalader's quarters, he was confronted by soldiers with bayonets and they prevented the delivery of the citation.

Rebuked by the military, Chief Justice Taney prepared a written statement—known as *Ex Parte* Merryman—that claimed that the president *did not* have the right to suspend the writ of habeas, contended that the right rested with Congress, and that Lincoln had overstepped the boundary of constitutional rights. Taney added that since the courts were "open and functioning," any "suspected treason" should be reported to a district attorney and should be dealt with by a judicial process. Taney did not stop there, for he scolded the president for violating the very Constitution that he had sworn to uphold, and the president's responsibility was to maintain constitutional guarantees. He even called Lincoln's action regarding habeas corpus "an act of usurpation."[8]

Taney's decision shocked President Lincoln as well as members of his cabinet. Attorney General Edward Bates, in a confidential letter to Secretary of War Edwin M. Stanton, expressed the fear that a decision declaring arbitrary arrests illegal, would "do more to paralyze the Executive... than the worst defeat our armies have yet sustained."[9] President Lincoln, it seems, shared the same view when he stated that he would be faithless to his oath of office "if the government should be overthrown, when it was believed that disobeying the single law would tend to preserve it." Lincoln, more or less, ignored Taney's decision as well as his admonition, and, time and again, would authorize generals to suspend the writ of habeas corpus in special cases or areas.

Democrats like Dennis A. Mahony of the *Dubuque Herald*, Samuel Medary of *The (Columbus) Crisis*, and Clement L. Vallandigham endorsed Chief Justice Taney's decision and line of reasoning. Like Taney, they were convinced that only congress had the right to suspend the writ of habeas corpus, and they criticized Lincoln in the months and years that followed. They brought out their best siege guns after Secretary of War Stanton, concerned with the enforcement of the Militia Act of July 17, 1862 ("the limping draft law"), issued a suspension order on August 8, 1862.[10] Even a

state supreme court entered the fray. Wisconsin's three-member state supreme court, in a case known as *In Re Kemp*, stated that martial law must
be restricted only to "those places which are the actual theatre of war" and
that "only Congress had the power to suspend the writ of habeas corpus—
this on January 13, 1863.

In Re Kemp had its origins in the Port Washington antidraft riot of
November 10, 1862, and the arrests made after its suppression. It centered around three of the more than 150 arrests made following the riot,
with a Luxembourger-American named Nicholas Kemp capturing the spotlight. On December 4, 1862, and through his attorney, Kemp petitioned the
Wisconsin State Supreme Court for a writ of habeas corpus. The petition
stated that Kemp's imprisonment was illegal, for it was not based upon a
court decision and that all citizens "were entitled to a fair trial under the
Constitution of the United States." The court granted the writ, but the commanding general of the Department of the Northwest declined to release
Kemp from military custody; he cited "General Order No. 141" of the War
Department and Lincoln's suspension of the writ of habeas corpus as justification for his refusal.

Edward G. Ryan, a Copperhead and self-styled Constitutionalist, vol-
unteered his services in behalf of the prisoner and made a stirring plea for
legality and fair play. He argued, as so many others had, that Lincoln's
suspension of the writ of habeas corpus was unconstitutional *because only
Congress had that power*. But, even if he had the power, it should not be
used illegally. He closed his plea in a fervent manner: "I want to see this
Court have the courage to set this brute law of the sword at defiance."[11]

Each of the three judges, in separate decisions, agreed with Ryan
and challenged the president's right to suspend the writ of habeas corpus.[12] The decision aroused some apprehension in Washington—"severely
jolted the national authorities." Secretary of War Stanton met with Lincoln
and considered appealing the case to the U.S. Supreme Court. They decided to send U.S. Senator Timothy Howe back to his home state to obtain
a transcript of the case record. But Attorney General Bates advised against
any appeal, for Chief Justice Taney might use his influence to rebuke
Lincoln's again, as he had done in *Ex Parte Merryman*. Lincoln and Stanton
must have heeded Bates' advice, for the case was never brought to the
U.S. Supreme Court. Stanton, in time, ordered the prisoners (about fifty
were still being held) released.[13]

The Wisconsin court's decision prompted Lincoln's friends in Congress to introduce a bill that authorized the president to suspend the bill of
habeas corpus—it would cut the ground from under Copperhead contention that Lincoln was guilty of violating the Constitution in this area. The
Habeas Corpus Act of March 3, 1863, gave Lincoln the legal authority that
he had lacked earlier and the issue in the Kemp case became moot.

The right of military authorities to defy writs of habeas corpus or try civilians via military commissions in areas where the civil courts were open arose again in *Ex Parte Vallandigham* (1863). The case dated back to Gen. Ambrose E. Burnside's instructions to arrest Clement L. Vallandigham, a Dayton resident and a well-known critic of the Lincoln administration and the war.

Vallandigham, once a three-term congressman, had played the part of a gadfly during the 37th Congress, denouncing abolition measures, conscription, and the numerous violations of civil rights. Vallandigham was defeated for re-election in November of 1862 because the state legislature, as a political stratagem, had changed the boundaries of his district. When he came home from Washington in mid-May of 1863, he decided that he wanted his party's gubernatorial nomination. He found the cards stacked against him. The party hierarchy had already decided to hand the nomination to Hugh J. Jewett, a respected middle-of-the-roader. Jewett had been the Democratic gubernatorial nominee two years earlier, losing the governorship to David Tod in a close race. But tradition dictated that he be given a second chance. Many Democrats thought that Vallandigham, with a reputation as an antiwar man, was less likely to defeat the Republican nominee than Jewett.

After appraising the situation, Vallandigham, clever and calculating, decided to seek arrest, become "a martyr to civil rights," and use the public reaction to gain the gubernatorial nomination at the state convention scheduled for June 11, 1863.

General Burnside, commander of the Department of the Ohio and headquartered in Cincinnati, provided a golden opportunity for Vallandigham to set up his dominoes when the arrogant military man issued a decree known as "General Orders, No. 38." There was also General Milo S. Hascall's "General Order No. 9," issued in a subdivision of Burnside's department; Hascall, based in Indianapolis and commanding the Military District of Indiana, restated Burnside's edict in his own words and added some threats and trimmings of his own. Then Hascall proceeded to suppress several Democratic newspapers and arrest some editors, including one who had done little more than call Hascall "a donkey."[14]

Vallandigham had every reason to believe that getting arrested and posing as a martyr to freedom of speech would pay dividends. That, in effect, is what had happened to Dr. Edson B. Olds of Lancaster. Editor of the *Ohio Eagle* and a "Butternut" and critic of the Lincoln administration, Olds was arrested by an order of the War Department and shipped off to a prison in Columbus. The arrest made him a kind of popular hero in his area, and when a vacancy developed in the upper house of the state legislature, public indignation swept him into that office. And, after his release (no charges were filed against him), he returned home to Lancaster, he received "a royal reception"—supposedly a crowd of ten thousand celebrated. Vallandigham, bright and perceptive, anticipated similar results.

Friends arranged two speeches for Vallandigham so he could bait General Burnside, one in Columbus and the second in Mount Vernon. When it was his turn to speak at Mount Vernon, Vallandigham knew that two of Burnside's agents were near the platform, instructed to take notes, and he decided to give the general both barrels. After condemning Burnside, Hascall, and President Lincoln, Vallandigham centered his invective upon "General Orders, No. 38." Holding a copy of it aloft, he denounced it as the edict of a despot. He could spit upon it, he said, or trample it underfoot—he stood on "General Orders No. 1," the Constitution of the United States.[15]

The dominoes fell exactly as Vallandigham had anticipated. Burnside saw to it that the Dayton dissenter was arrested, found guilty by a military commission, and exiled to the Confederacy (at Lincoln's suggestion). While Vallandigham was in Wilmington, N.C., awaiting a blockade runner to take him to Bermuda and then a mail steamer to Canada, the Democratic state convention met in Columbus on June 11, 1863, and named the self-styled martyr its gubernatorial candidate for the October 13 election. The entire scenario proved that Vallandigham was perceptive enough to appraise the situation correctly, calculating enough to plan it, and bold enough to carry it off.[16]

While Vallandigham was being held as a military prisoner and before he was shipped southward, the Hon. George E. Pugh moved for a writ of habeas corpus in behalf of the self-styled martyr before Judge Humphrey H. Leavitt of the U.S. Court for the Southern District of Ohio. Judge Leavitt asked that Pugh's plea be presented to General Burnside so that he could state his side of the case to the court. Burnside, in turn, claimed that he had a legal and constitutional right, as commander of the Department of the Ohio, to arrest and try Vallandigham.

Pugh presented emotional arguments in Vallandigham's behalf, citing English and American precedents and contending that civil and constitutional rights were not at the whim of military commanders. "We cannot move a single step," Pugh asserted, "but we do not see with what jealous care our fathers handcuffed military power." Vallandigham was a civilian in a non-combative area, entitled, according to the Constitution, to be tried only in civil courts and by a jury of his peers. The "doctrine of necessity," Pugh added, is an invalid excuse that opens the door to abuses.[17]

In a decision known as *Ex Parte Vallandigham*, Judge Leavitt refused to grant the writ, siding with Burnside and ignoring court decisions like *United States vs. Burr* (1806) and *Ex Parte Merryman* (1861). Finding little support for his decision in the Constitution and in precedent, Leavitt fashioned his arguments around "moral guilt." There was a type of treason, the waffling judge argued, that was not covered by the U.S. Constitution and the laws of the land. Those who live under the protection and enjoy the benefits of a benign government "must learn that they cannot stab its vitals with impunity." Those who criticize a government during "a time of crisis," when necessity is the law of self-preservation, should expect to be treated arbitrarily. Judge Leavitt ended with an interesting statement: "The sole question is whether the arrest was legal.. [and] its legality depends on the necessity which existed for making it, and of that necessity...this Court cannot judiciously determine."[18]

After Leavitt's decision the score was *one* and *one*: Leavitt's decision in *Ex Parte Vallandigham* pleased the Lincoln administration; Taney's decision in *Ex Parte Merryman* had earlier been endorsed by those who would become Lincoln's critics. Taney's decision, more or less, was ignored by the Lincoln administration; Leavitt's decision, after the war, would be repudiated by the U.S. Supreme Court.

Democrats, generally, criticized Leavitt and his decision, depicting him as a spineless tool of the Lincoln administration, afraid to challenge a blustering general. After the war, Vallandigham expressed his scorn: "Such ignorance and disregard of law, and of the administration of justice, are a disgrace to the profession, and a libel upon American jurisprudence. The position assumed in this opinion is equal in ignorance and audacity...an insult to the intelligence of the American people...."[19]

Lincoln, on the other hand, was pleased that Leavitt had not challenged military authority and wrote two long "briefs" in defense of Vallandigham's arrest. In one Lincoln wrote that the Dayton Democrat was arrested "because he was damaging the army...warring upon the military." Then Lincoln added, "...he who dissuades one man from volunteering, or induces one soldier to desert, weakens the Union cause as much as he who kills a Union soldier in battle."[20] This was well said, but Democrats could counter with an assertion that Lincoln's Emancipation Proclamations brought on more desertions than all the editorials of Democratic editors and all the speeches of Democratic spokesmen.

Lincoln's second defense of Vallandigham was occasionally on weak ground. It was not done as *punishment*, Lincoln said, but was an act of *prevention* "for what probably would be done."[21] Democratic dissenters could have had a lot of fun with this strange assertion.

The third case concerned with military power and habeas corpus was entitled *Ex Parte Milligan* (1866) and it far outshadowed the other two. This case dated back to the last half of 1864 when Gov. Oliver P. Morton of Indiana was seeking stratagems to win reelection and tilt public opinion in favor of the Lincoln administration. With the help of sympathetic generals, Governor Morton orchestrated the arrest of a dozen Indiana citizens and two military trials. In the first of the two "treason trials," set in motion before the state's gubernatorial elections, Harrison H. Dodd was tried by a seven-member military commission. Dodd was guilty of more than indiscretions: in a meeting of a dozen Democrats he openly espoused a rebellion, to be launched when the state Democratic convention met in Indianapolis; then he received a shipment of two dozen revolvers from New York City.

Supposedly, Dodd's Sons of Liberty was involved in the conspiracy. During the trial, Dodd escaped from his second-story room and fled to Canada, leaving behind a supposition of guilt. The commission, to no one's surprise, found Dodd guilty.[22]

The second military trial, little more than a farce, provided the basis for *Ex Parte Milligan* (1866). The military commission reconvened in late November, and in the end, found four second-rate Indiana Democrats guilty of "disloyal practices"—three, including Lambdin P. Milligan, were sentenced "to be hanged by the neck." Joseph E. McDonald, the lawyer for Milligan, filed a petition for a writ of habeas corpus in his client's behalf in a federal court in Indiana. The two sitting judges disagreed as to the verdict so the case could move up to the U.S. Supreme Court. Both sides added counsel, with Jeremiah S. Black presenting the case for Milligan. Black, citing cases and precedent, argued that the trial of Milligan and others by a military commission in areas where the civil courts were open and functioning, was unhistorical, unconstitutional, and contrary to democratic concepts.

On April 3, 1866, the U.S. Supreme Court handed down its opinion in that landmark case known as *Ex Parte Milligan*. Associate Justice David Davis, a Lincoln appointer, wrote the majority decision for the court, tossing Leavitt's decision in *Ex Parte Vallandigham* into a wastepaper basket and rebuking both Governor Morton and President Lincoln for using military courts to achieve political ends. "A citizen, not connected with the military service, and a resident in a State where the courts are all open, and in the proper exercise of their jurisdiction," Judge Davis stated, "cannot, even when the privilege of habeas corpus is suspended, be tried, convicted or sentenced otherwise than by the ordinary court of law." Then came the two sentences that reprimanded the governor and the president: "The Constitution of the United States is a law for rulers and people, equally in war and peace and covers with its shield of protection all classes of men, at all times and under all circumstances. No doctrine involving more pernicious circumstances was ever invented by the wit of man than that any of its great provisions could be suspended during any of the great exigences of Government."[23] Since Judge David Davis' decision had negated and repudiated Judge Leavitt's decision in *Ex Parte Vallandigham*, the revised score then stood at *two* to *zero*—dissenting Democrats concerned with civil rights had *Ex Parte Merryman* (1861) and *Ex Parte Milligan* (1866) in their favor; those who had sided with Leavitt and Lincoln and Stanton held an empty bag.

Henry Adams, in his famous book *The Education of Henry Adams*, stated that the "duty of an opposition is to compel government to prove the propriety of its measures." Democrats who were dissenters, especially in the Upper Midwest, tried to do just that —though sometimes with too much rancor and partyism, both of which made their protests less effective. Nevertheless, editors like James J. Faran of the *Cincinnati Enquirer*, and Peter V. Deuster of the *(Milwaukee) See-Bote*, congressmen like Daniel W. Voorhees of Indiana and Samuel S. Cox of Ohio, and lawyers like Charles Mason of Iowa and Edward G. Ryan of Wisconsin articulated the concerns of their constituents—*and these were real and legitimate concerns.* Their constituents, it has been stated time and again, belonged to four socioeconomic elements of the population of the Upper Midwest: (1) Irish-Americans, (2) German-American Catholics, (3) the "Butternuts," and (4) middle class Americans who regarded themselves as disciples of Jeffersonian Democracy and apostles of Jacksonian Democracy. These groups, legitimately, resented the intrusion of New England Puritanism into politics and governmental policies.

After the war, Clement L. Vallandigham often said that Democratic protests during the war checked further violations of civil liberties and helped to preserve civil rights. This also seems to be the contention of historian Mark E. Neely in his Pulitzer Prize-winning book:

> Their [Democratic opposition] opportunistic protests played a role crucial to a democratic country involved in war. They helped prevent the U.S. Army from an increasing reliance on military justice for the sake of convenience (for example in the Indiana court decision on selling liquor to soldiers). Their protests about political abuse of the internal security system forced Abraham Lincoln, in his last habeas-corpus proclamation (the one for Kentucky issued in 1864) to disclaim any attempt to interfere with the electoral process. The Democratic party was a loyal opposition. If their rhetoric was calculated to goad Republicans, it also played a legitimate role in preserving civil liberties in wartime America.[24]

Neely helps to counter some of the contentions of Wood Gray's *The Hidden Civil War* and George Fort Milton's *Abraham Lincoln and the Fifth Column*—he helps to discredit their suppositions that the "Copperheads" were pro-Southern in their sympathies and proclivities and that the Lincoln administration was not with sin.

Despite the work of the revisionists there is still much work to be done. There is the need for a scholarly book that centers on the military trial of civilians by military commissions. There is a need to discredit Joseph K.C. Forrest of Illinois and Henry B. Carrington of Indiana, both disciples of Baron Munchhausen, as fabricators of Golden Circle tales. There is the need for a scholarly book that puts the historical microscope upon the Camp Douglas conspiracy and rebukes those who fastened a fantasy upon history. There is need for a book entitled "Republican Political Propaganda of Civil War Days, Analyzed and Evaluated." There is a need to delve more deeply in Governor Oliver P. Morton's role in staging the Indianapolis-based "treason trials" and in myth-making. There is need to discredit the myth, that the arrest, trial, and exile of Vallandigham was the historical base for Edward Everett Hale's *The Man Without a Country* (1863). Civil War history needs to be purged of Republican political propaganda, Lincoln needs to be presented as a historical figure rather than as a national hero, and the role of Civil War Copperheads needs to be placed in reality.

NOTES

INTRODUCTION

1. *The Lincoln Ledger,* 2.4 (Nov. 1994): 10.
2. Mark E. Neely, Jr., *The Fate of Liberty: Abraham Lincoln and Civil Liberties* (New York: Oxford UP, 1991), xii.
3. *The Lincoln Ledger,* 2.4 (Nov. 1994): 8.
4. Eugene C. Murdock, *The Civil War in the North: A Selective Annotated Bibliography* (New York: Garland Publishing, Inc., 1987), 724, 726, 733. The book lists fifty-three items for Bearss, thirty for Catton, and twenty-seven for Klement.
5. Frank L. Klement, "Catholics as Copperheads During the Civil War," *Catholic Historical Review,* 80.1 (Jan. 1994): 36–57.
6. Andrea Bletzinger, "Lifetime Research on Lincoln Continues," Neenah/Menasha (Wisconsin) *Daily Northwestern,* Mar. 7, 1979, 9. The author wishes to thank John Joseph Klement of Marinette, Wisconsin, and Irene Klement of Wisconsin Rapids, Wisconsin, Frank's brother and sister-in-law, who supplied a copy of his paternal grandparents' passports and disclosed additional pertinent family information, and to Paul F. Klement, Frank's eldest son, who provided facts about his family. Vital statistics on the Klement family are as follows:

    Jakob Klement (grandfather), b. 1840, d. 1920
    Maria Klement (grandmother), b. 1842, d. 1921
    Jacob Klement (father), b. 1876, d. 1956
    Barbara (Kutil) Klement (mother), b. 1882, d. 1962
    Mary (Klement) Bahr (sister), b. 1902, d. 1966
    George Joseph Klement (brother), b. 1906
    Frank Ludwig Klement, b. 1908, d. 1994
    Vencil Louis Klement (a.k.a. "W. James"; brother), b. 1910
    Helen Jennie (Klement) Ebert (sister), b. 1914
    John Joseph Klement (brother), b. 1916
    Donald Anthony Klement (brother), b. 1919, d. 1993
    Marcella Evelyn (Klement) Nelson (sister) b. 1927
7. Academic Transcript, 2 pp., Shawano High School, Shawano, Wisconsin.

184

8. *Shawnee*, 1927, 19, Marquette University Archives, Milwaukee, Wisconsin.

9. Academic Transcript, 2 pp., Shawano High School, Shawano, Wisconsin.

10. *The Shawano High School Annual*, 1926, 30, 31, 32, 33, Marquette University Archives; *Shawnee*, 1927, 19, 26, Marquette University Archives.

11. *The Shawano High School Annual*, 1926, 11, 16, 17, 25, 29, 32; *Shawnee*, 1927, 19, 25.

12. Steven K. Rogstad interviews Frank L. Klement, audio cassette, Milwaukee, Wisconsin, May 15, 1988, ninety minutes. Cassette in possession of author. Cited hereafter as Frank L. Klement interview.

13. "Our War and its Historians," *Marquette University Magazine*, 5.4 (Summer 1964): 2.

14. *The Shawano High School Annual*, 1926, 10, Marquette University Archives; *Shawnee*, 1927, 18, Marquette University Archives.

15. *The Shawano High School Annual*, 1926, 12, 29, 35, 92; *Shawnee*, 1927, 18.

16. *Shawnee*, 1927, 52–3, Marquette University Archives.

17. Academic Transcript, 2 pp., Shawano High School, Shawano, Wisconsin; Frank L. Klement interview, May 15, 1988; Academic Transcript, 2 pp., Central State Teachers College, University of Wisconsin-Stevens Point, Stevens Point, Wisconsin. The university was previously known as Stevens Point Normal School (1894–1926), Central State Teachers College (1926–1951), Wisconsin State College-Stevens Point (1951–1964), and Wisconsin State University-Stevens Point (1964–1971).

18. *The Iris*, 1932, 21, Central State Teachers College. Additional information about Herbert R. Steiner during Frank's years at Stevens Point is found in ibid., 30; *The Iris*, 1933, 23, 29, 105, Central State Teachers College; *The Iris*, 1934, 21, 30, Central State Teachers College; *The Iris*, 1935, 10, 19, Central State Teachers College.

19. *The Iris*, 1933, 23, Central State Teachers College.

20. Frank L. Klement interview, May 15, 1988. The forty-four page scrapbook contains mementos from his high school and college years, and is in the Marquette University Archives.

21. *The Iris*, 1934, 78, Central State Teachers College; *The Iris*, 1935, 97, Central State Teachers College.

22. *The Iris*, 1935, 97, Central State Teachers College. Frank graduated from Central State Teachers College on June 12, 1935; see Academic Transcript, 2 pp., Central State Teachers College, University of Wisconsin–Stevens Point.

23. Ibid.

24. Frank L. Klement interview, May 15, 1988.

25. Ibid.

26. Ibid. Dr. Laura Gellott, professor of history at the University of Wisconsin-Parkside, had Klement as an instructor at Marquette. She told the author: "I remember him telling us this story in class—saying that he was the 'greenest' grad. student who ever enrolled in grad. school."

27. Richard N. Current, "William Best Hesseltine 1902–1963," *Lincoln Herald*, 66.1 (Spring, 1964): 14.

28. Richard N. Current, ed., *Sections and Politics: Selected Essays By William B. Hesseltine* (Madison: State Historical Society of Wisconsin, 1963), v; Richard N. Current, "Recollections of the Man and the Teacher," *Wisconsin Magazine of History*, 66.2 (Winter 1982–1983): 121. Hesseltine's papers were deposited in the State Historical Society of Wisconsin after his death in 1963, which are housed in seventy-five archive boxes. His thirty-two Ph.D.s are listed in the abstract for the collection, as well as in Current, *Sections and Politics*, 149–50.

29. Frank L. Klement interview, May 15, 1988; Academic Transcript, 2 pp., University of Wisconsin-Madison.

30. Current, *Sections and Politics*, v–vi; Robert G. Gunderson, "William Best Hesseltine and the Profession of History: A Retrospective," *Wisconsin Magazine of History*, 66.2 (Winter 1982–1983): 106; Current, "Recollections of the Man and the Teacher," 121.

31. Frank L. Byrne, "The Trainer of Historians," *Wisconsin Magazine of History*, 66.2 (Winter 1982–1983): 115.

32. Ibid.

33. Current, *Sections and Politics*, vi–vii; Current, "Recollections of the Man and the Teacher," 120; Byrne, "The Trainer of Historians," 116.

34. Byrne, "The Trainer of Historians," 116.

35. Current, *Sections and Politics*, vii; Byrne, "The Trainer of Historians," 116.

36. Byrne, "The Trainer of Historians," 116; Gunderson, "William B. Hesseltine and the Profession of History: A Retrospective," 109; Current, *Sections and Politics*, vii; "Our War and its Historians," 5. The following version of Hesseltine's stylistic rules for writing is owned by Horace Samuel Merrill, who earned his Ph.D. under him in 1942. Robert G. Gunderson says that this is "Merrill's version of what WBS said. Hesseltine's version in fact sounded more convincing, though only WBH would have had the temerity to add five to the Biblical ten. As WBH delivered them, they sounded more awesome, less wordy, and more Biblical." Robert G. Gunderson, letter to Steven K. Rogstad, [Bloomington], Oct. 28, 1995, in possession of author.

"PROFESSOR WILLIAM B. HESSELTINE'S 'COMMANDMENTS' ON HISTORICAL WRITING"

1. Thou shalt not use the present tense, nor the passive voice.

2. Thou shalt not split thy infinitives nor dangle thy participles, *nor* end thy sentences with prepositions.

3. Thou shalt not use slang, except as it be contemporary with thy subject and clearly explained, and then only when it adds seasoning to thy work. Above all thou shalt avoid and abhor all modern jargon, even though it be the words of thy instructors. Trite statements and dead metaphors are an abomination to the true believer.

4. Thou shalt not use the personal pronoun either implicitly or explicitly.

5. Thou shalt not use *this* for *the* nor *the* for *a*.

6. Thou shalt place thy time clauses first.

7. Thou shalt not use the rhetorical question to avoid an intelligent beginning—thou shalt strike thy reader hard with thy first sentence.

8. Thou shalt set down things as they happen—thou shalt have no reference later in time than the subject thou'rt treating.

9. Thou shalt be aware of quotations. A secondary source or the author thereof speaketh not from his own knowledge, he is no better than thou—use him but quote him not, nor mention his name in thy text. Neither shalt thou quote anything thou canst say better thyself, nor shalt thou quote to carry thy story, nor to establish a fact, except when the word itself is the fact. In short, thou shalt quote only to "season" thy story, and then no "blocks,"—never more than three lines.

10. Thy footnotes shall be the field of all thy battles, and thou shalt combine footnotes wherever possible. In thy footnotes thou shall cite material to the standard source, for verily the greatest scholar is not he who can cite the most obscure document but he who alloweth his reader to check for himself, in the most convenient source available.

11. Thy methodology is not the theme of thy story, therefore shalt thou discuss thy subject, and not the documents concerning thy subject, nor thy methods in finding and arranging them.

12. Thou shalt clearly identify in relation to thy subject, any personality or incident mentioned in the text, be it Abraham Lincoln, the Battle of Gettysburg, or Jesus of Nazareth. Only after thou hast performed this ceremony or purification mayest thou use familiar terms such as Lee, Sheridan, Shiloh, Mud March or Monitor.

13. Thou shalt not write the history of a wheat field regardless of how "naturally" it develops, for history is the story of people, and everyday natural processes do not have to do with history.

14. Thou shalt not pass judgements on mankind in general, yet thou shalt not pardon any man for anything. If a man is in error thou shalt seek the reasons for his error, but not the excuses.

15. Thou shalt avoid negations, as these revelations, alas, have failed to do. Thou shalt be neither a "no-er" nor a "not-er."

37. Byrne, "The Trainer of Historians," 117.

38. Frank L. Klement, "Vallandigham and the Civil War," address before the Civil War Round Table of Chicago, Dec. 8, 1966, audio cassette tape, Civil War Round Table of Chicago. His paraphrasing was taken from Act III, Scene II of Shakespeare's play, "Julius Caesar." Klement used the following list of literary rules during his years of teaching at Marquette, which are on file in the Marquette University Archives.

"DEVELOP A GOOD LITERARY STYLE!"

1. Use active rather than passive voice.
2. Use past tense—do not change tense like a chameleon changes colors.
3. Avoid use of personal pronouns in the body of a thesis or term paper.
4. Give full name of an individual the first time he is introduced to the reader.
5. Use figurative speech—metaphors, similies, and alliteration add color to good composition.
    a. He pushed back the curtain of racial prejudice. (metaphor)
    b. Words gushed forth like water from a spring. (similie)
    c. He possessed the industry and intelligence to succeed. (alliteration).
6. Weave quotations into the text with smoothness and skill. A term paper is not a compilation—many long quotations cemented together with a few original sentences.
7. Use transitional sentences to link paragraphs, so that abruptness does not characterize your writing. Occasionally use terms like "on the other hand," "nevertheless," "in spite of," etc.
8. Your opening and closing paragraphs are the most important ones, even in a one thousand page composition.
9. Avoid misplaced parenthetical expressions or misplaced phrases.
    a. Webb advertised for a lady to wrap sandwiches twenty-one years old.
    b. He went to Denver, hoping to find gold.
    c. Washington crossed the Delaware, father of his country.
10. Use words, phrases, or clauses in clusters of three.
11. Only a lazy person refuses to write and rewrite and rewrite and rewrite.
12. Your thesaurus should be at your elbow, helping you to find appropriate words and to prevent repetitive use of a particular word.
13. Good writing has a form of rhythm—it should read like poetry.

39. No comprehensive bibliography for Hesseltine is available. "William Best Hesseltine Bibliography," 11 pp., William Best Hesseltine Papers, State Historical Society of Wisconsin, Madison, Wisconsin, does not include any reviews. A similar list, including

some reviews, is contained in Current, *Sections and Politics*, 135–48. Also see Gunderson, "William Best Hesseltine and the Profession of History: A Retrospective," 107–8, 109, 110; Current, *Sections and Politics*, xix. Frank L. Klement interview, May 15, 1988.

40. Frank retained three notebooks from his college days. One labeled "Summer Session, 1940" contains course outlines and notes for History 115 ("The American Revolution and the Constitution, 1760–1789"), History 118 ("Reconstruction and the New Nation"), and History 261 ("Seminary, American History"). A thesis entitled "Rebels in the Ranks" is mentioned on the cover, although the paper itself is missing. The second is titled "Summer Session, 1941" and contains course outlines and notes for History 114 ("Sectionalism and the Civil War"), History 142a ("England Under the Tudors, 1485–1603"), and History 261. A paper included in this notebook is titled "The Democratic Party in Wisconsin During the Civil War," although he listed it on the cover as "Wisconsin's Opposition to the Civil War." The third notebook contains a course outline and notes for History 111 ("History of the West, 1837–1893"). These three notebooks, as well as all of Dr. Klement's library, yearbooks, manuscripts, research notes and materials, correspondence, and some personal effects were given to the author by his children after their father's death. Most of this material has been subsequently deposited with the Marquette University Archives in Milwaukee, Wisconsin.

41. Remarks of Richard N. Current and Herman Viola found in *The Lincoln Ledger*, 2.4 (Nov. 1994): 7, 10–11. Klement told this author several times about Hesseltine's anti-Catholic statements.

42. Frank L. Klement, "John Buchanan ('Scapegoat') Floyd: A Study of Virginia Politics Through a Biography." M.S. dissertation, University of Wisconsin, 1938, 205 leaves; Frank L. Klement interview, May 15, 1988; *The Beloiter*, 1941, 17, 25, 77, 82, Beloit Senior High School; *The Beloiter*, 1942, 15, 22, 25, 104, 108, Beloit Senior High School.

43. Laurel Marie Fosnot, "Gestalt Psychology Applied to the Graphic and Plastic Arts." M.S. dissertation, University of Wisconsin, 1938, 78 leaves; *The Badger*, 1935, 71, 257, 281, University of Wisconsin-Madison. Vital statistics for the Frank L. Klement family are as follows:

> Frank L. Klement (father), b. Aug. 19, 1908, d. July 29, 1994
> Laural M. Fosnot (mother), b. June 21, 1913, d. Sept. 29, 1991
> Paul F. Klement (son), b. Oct. 8, 1941
> Richard E. Klement (son), b. Mar. 25, 1944
> Kenneth R. Klement (son), b. Apr. 23, 1951

44. Frank L. Klement, college notebook labeled "Summer Session 1940," Marquette University Archives; Frank L. Klement, "The Democratic Party in Wisconsin During the Civil War," 37 leaves, History 261, contained in college notebook labeled "Summer Session 1941," Marquette University Archives. An outline for this paper indicates that Frank originally intended the scope of the work to be for the entire duration of the war, but the paper itself concludes with the year 1862. He renamed the paper on the notebook's cover, "Wisconsin's Opposition to the Civil War." He also wrote a thirty-page paper during that same session entitled "Colonization During the Tudor Era," for History 142a (see note 39).

45. Byrne, "The Trainer of Historians," 116–17; Current, "William Best Hesseltine 1902–1963," 14; Freidel, "The Teacher and His Students," 112, 113, 114; Current, *Sections and Politics*, viii, ix, xi; Gunderson, "William Best Hesseltine and the Profession of History: A Retrospective," 106.

46. Frank L. Klement interview, May 15, 1988. Besides obtaining the Charles Kendall Adams Fellowship for 1942–43, Klement was the recipient of several other special grants, including a Ford Foundation Fellowship (1951); Fund for the Advancement of Education (1952–53); Social Science Research Council Grant-In-Aid (1952); Marquette University Research Grant (1960, 1962, 1968); Midwest Research Committee Award (1964); American Philosophical Society Research Grant (1964); Huntington Library Fellowship from Sacramento State University (1967); Marquette University Summer

Faculty Fellowship (1972); Leverhulme Research Fellowship from the University of Sussex, England (1975–76).

47. Frank L. Klement interview, May 15, 1988.

48. Ibid.

49. Ibid. Frank L. Klement, "Wisconsin and the Civil War," *Wisconsin Blue Book*, 1962 (Madison: Wisconsin Legislative Reference Library, 1962), 72–180. Hesseltine's comments are found on page 71. Frank L. Klement, *Wisconsin and the Civil War* (Madison: State Historical Society of Wisconsin, 1963). The book was limited to 3,000 copies; see Frank L. Klement, letter to Steven K. Rogstad, [Milwaukee], Aug. 19, 1992, in possession of author. Klement finished a revision and expansion of the work in 1994 which was published as *Wisconsin in the Civil War: The Home Front and the Battle Front, 1861–1865* (Madison: State Historical Society of Wisconsin, 1997). Quotations taken from the 1997 edition, v.

50. Frank L. Klement interview, May 15, 1988. See note 28 for information about Hesseltine's graduate students.

51. Frank L. Klement, "Senior Chapel Address," (Lake Forest College) *Stentor*, May 26, 1945: 4. Frank is pictured on page 32 of the 1945 (Lake Forest) *Forester*, but no information about his duties is provided.

52. Ibid.; *Periscope*, 1946, 23, Eau Claire State Teachers College; *Periscope*, 1948, 9, Eau Claire State Teachers College; *Wisconsin Academy Review*, 13.3 (Summer 1966): 44. The university's chronology is as follows: Eau Claire State Normal School (1916-1926); Eau Claire State Teachers College (1926–1951); Wisconsin State College-Eau Claire (1951–1964); Wisconsin State University-Eau Claire (1964–1971); University of Wisconsin-Eau Claire (1971–present).

53. Remarks of John E. Walsh and Mercedes Maloney contained in *The Lincoln Ledger*, 2.4 (Nov. 1994): 8, 11–12.

54. John E. Walsh, *To Print the News and Raise Hell: A Biography of William F. Storey* (Chapel Hill: University of North Carolina Press, 1968).

55. *The Lincoln Ledger*, 2.4 (Nov. 1994): 11–12. Viola's remarks appear on pages 10–11.

56. Ibid.; Frank L. Klement, "Seven Who Witnessed Lincoln's Gettysburg Address," Lincoln Fellowship of Wisconsin *Historical Bulletin*, No. 40 (1985), 1; (Marquette University) *News & Views*, 21.1 (Aug. 23, 1994): 2. Four annual Klement lectures have been delivered so far: "Confederate Bastille: Jefferson Davis and Civil Liberties" by Mark E. Neely, Jr. (1992); "What is an American? Abraham Lincoln and Multiculturalism" by Richard N. Current (1993); "The 'Wicked Rebellion' and the Republic: Henry Tuckerman's Civil War" by Robert W. Johannsen (1994); "Jubal A. Early; The Lost Cause, and Civil War History: A Persistent Legacy" by Gary W. Gallagher (1995); "Grant and Halleck: Contrasts in Command" by John Y. Simon (1996); "Momentous Events in Small Places: The Coming of the Civil War in Two American Communities" by Edward L. Ayres (1997). Marquette established an endowment fund to support the lecture series. Inquiries about contributions should be made to the College of Arts and Sciences at (414) 288–5968.

57. Frank L. Klement, "History and the Humanities," *Transactions of the Wisconsin Academy of Sciences, Arts and Letters*, 63 (1975): 72–80.

58. "A Different View of Lincoln," *The Milwaukee Journal*, Feb. 5, 1976, 6; "Honest Abe Was Far From Being a Saint, Wisconsin Prof Says," *The Miami Herald*, Feb. 4, 1976, 8–B; "Say it ain't so, Abe," *The Providence Journal*, Feb. 3, 1976; "Lincoln's image tarnished?" *Kenosha News*, Feb. 3, 1976, 1; "Researcher says Lincoln not above a few dirty tricks," *Oshkosh Daily Northwestern*, Feb. 3, 1976, 2; "Lincoln no saint, professor says," *Wisconsin State Journal*, Feb. 3, 1976, 4–4; "Abe's halo is slipping," Feb. 3, 1976, 1; Baraboo *News Republic*, Feb. 3, 1976, 1; "Prof says Abe used dirty tricks," *Racine Journal Times*, Feb. 3, 1976, 9A; "Abe Lincoln myth shred by historian," *Portage Daily Register*, Feb. 3, 1976, 1; "Professor attacks Lincoln's legend," unidentified; "Historian Says Myths Immortalized Lincoln," unidentified. For Klement's account of

the controversy see Frank L. Klement, letter to Steven K. Rogstad, [Milwaukee], Nov. 16, 1992, in possession of author.

59. Lance J. Herdegen, letter to Frank L. Klement, Feb. 4, 1976, Marquette University Archives; "We don't have to have perfect heroes," *(Wisconsin Rapids) Daily Tribune*, Feb. 11, 1976, 4.

60. Wood Gray, *The Hidden Civil War: The Story of the Copperheads* (New York: Viking Press, 1942); George Fort Milton, *Abraham Lincoln and the Fifth Column* (New York: Vanguard Press, 1942).

61. Arthur C. Cole, rev. of *The Hidden Civil War: The Story of the Copperheads*, by Wood Gray, and *Abraham Lincoln and the Fifth Column*, by George Fort Milton, *The American Historical Review*, (Oct. 1943), 122–24; Howard C. Perkins, rev. of *The Hidden Civil War: The Story of the Copperheads*, by Wood Gray, *The Journal of Southern History*, (May 1943), 270–72.

62. Elbert J. Benton, *The Movement for Peace Without Victory During the Civil War* (Cleveland: Collections of the Western Reserve Historical Society, Publication No. 99, 1918); Edward Chase Kirkland, *Peacemakers of 1864* (New York: Macmillan, 1927). A shorter study is Mayo Fesler, "Secret Political Societies in the North During the Civil War," *Indiana Magazine of History*, 14 (Sept. 1918): 183–286. Howard C. Perkins, rev. of *The Hidden Civil War: The Story of the Copperheads*, by Wood Gray, *The Journal of Southern History* (May 1943), 272.

63. Frank L. Klement, "Middle Western Copperheadism: Jeffersonian Democracy in Revolt." Ph.D. dissertation, University of Wisconsin, 1946, 342 leaves.

64. Ibid.; Frank L. Klement, "Economic Aspects of Middle Western Copperheadism," *The Historian*, 14.1 (Autumn 1951): 27–45. The article was reprinted as "The Democrats as Sectionalists" in James A. Rawley, ed., *Lincoln and Civil War Politics* (Huntington: Robert E. Krieger, 1969), 95–103. Many of Klement's conclusions concerning Northern dissenters focused on how regional economies determined different Copperhead ideologies which escaped definitive analysis because each was uniquely complex. There is no doubt that his adherence to a basically economic interpretation was greatly influenced by several lectures which he heard in graduate school at Madison, notes for which appear in his college notebooks (see note 40).

65. Frank L. Klement, "Lincoln's Critics in Wisconsin," Lincoln Fellowship of Wisconsin *Historical Bulletin*, No. 14 (1956): 5.

66. Frank L. Klement, "Middle Western Copperheadism and the Genesis of the Granger Movement," *Mississippi Valley Historical Review*, 38.4 (Mar. 1952): 679.

67. Frank L. Klement, "Economic Aspects of Middle Western Copperheadism," 27.

68. Klement, "Middle Western Copperheadism and the Genesis of the Granger Movement," 679–80.

69. Frank L. Klement, *The Copperheads in the Middle West* (Chicago: University of Chicago Press, 1960), viii.

70. Wayne C. Temple, rev. of *The Copperheads in the Middle West*, by Frank L. Klement, *Lincoln Herald* (Winter 1960), 190; Richard N. Current, rev. of *The Copperheads in the Middle West*, by Frank L. Klement, New York *Herald-Tribune Book Review*, Sept. 25, 1960; Emma Lou Thornbrough, rev. of *Copperheads in the Middle West*, by Frank L. Klement, *The Historian* (Nov. 1960), 128–29.

71. Frank L. Klement, "Vallandigham and the Civil War," Dec. 8, 1966. Charles Hubert Coleman (Feb. 21, 1900–Jan. 11, 1972) is most remembered for his books *The Election of 1868: The Deliberate Effort to Regain Control* (New York: Columbia University Press, 1933) and *Abraham Lincoln and Coles County, Illinois* (New Brunswick: Scarecrow Press, 1955). Two of his earliest Copperhead essays were "The Use of the Term 'Copperhead' During the Civil War," *Mississippi Valley Historical Review*, 25.2 (Sept. 1938): 263–64, and "The Middle Western Peace Democracy, 1861–1865," *Mississippi Valley Historical Review*, 28.2 (Sept. 1941): 209–10. Interestingly, although Klement credited

Coleman for performing some of the earliest research on Vallandigham, he never referred to anything which Coleman wrote about the subject in his books or articles.

72. Frank L. Klement, *The Limits of Dissent: Clement L. Vallandigham and the Civil War* (Lexington: University Press of Kentucky, 1970), 2.

73. Frank L. Klement, "Vallandigham and the Civil War," Dec. 8, 1966.

74. Michael Les Benedict, rev. of *The Limits of Dissent: Clement L. Vallandigham and the Civil War*, by Frank L. Klement, *American Historical Review* (Spring 1972), 211; Wayne C. Temple, rev. of *The Limits of Dissent: Clement L. Vallandigham and the Civil War*, by Frank L. Klement, *Lincoln Herald* (Spring 1972), 70.

75. Mark E. Neely, Jr., "The Embarrassing Case of Dr. Blanchard: A Newly Discovered Lincoln Document," *Lincoln Lore*, No. 1741 (Mar. 1983).

76. "Professor Klement Replies," *Lincoln Lore*, No. 1748 (Oct. 1983): 3; Frank L. Klement, letter to Steven K. Rogstad, [Milwaukee], Mar. 2, 1993, in possession of author.

77. Frank L. Klement, *Dark Lanterns: Secret Political Societies, Conspiracies, and Treason Trials in the Civil War* (Baton Rouge: Louisiana State University Press, 1984), 6; Frank L. Klement, "Civil War Politics, Nationalism, and Postwar Myths," *Historian*, 38.3 (May 1976): 438.

78. Frank L. Klement, "The Most Critical Year: Events of 1863," unpublished, 1986, 835 leaves.

79. Frank L. Klement, "Ohio and the Dedication of the Soldiers' Cemetery at Gettysburg," *Ohio History*, 79.2 (Spring 1970): 76–100; Frank L. Klement Interview, May 15, 1988.

80. Leonne M. Hudson, rev. of *The Gettysburg Soldiers' Cemetery and Lincoln's Address: Aspects and Angles*, by Frank L. Klement, *Ohio History* (Winter-Spring 1995), 112.

81. Frank L. Klement, letter to Richard Sloan, [Milwaukee], May 3, 1994, copy in possession of author.

82. Frank L. Klement, letter to Steven K. Rogstad, [Milwaukee], Apr. 18, 1989, in possession of the author.

83. Richard O. Curry, "The Union as it Was: A Critique of Recent Interpretations of the 'Copperheads,'" *Civil War History*, 13.1 (Mar. 1967): 29–30.

84. *The Lincoln Ledger*, 2.4 (Nov. 1994): 12–13.

85. James McPherson, *Battle Cry of Freedom: The Civil War Era* (New York: Oxford UP, 1988), 878.

86. David E. Long, "Frank Klement Revisited: Disloyalty and Treason in the American Civil War," *Lincoln Herald*, 97.3 (Fall 1995): 99. Long makes similar arguments in his book, *The Jewel of Liberty: Abraham Lincoln's Re-Election and the End of Slavery* (Mechanicsburg, Pa.: Stackpole Books, 1994).

87. *The Lincoln Ledger*, 2.4 (Nov. 1994): 13.

88. "Our War and Its Historians," 2.

89. Klement, *Dark Lanterns*, 6.

90. *The Lincoln Ledger*, 2.4 (Nov. 1994): 8; see Robert H. Abzug, "The Copperheads: Historical Approaches to Civil War Dissent in the Midwest," *Indiana Magazine of History*, 66.1 (Mar. 1970): 40–55.

91. Frank L. Klement interview, May 15, 1988.

92. Mark E. Neely, Jr., *The Fate of Liberty: Abraham Lincoln and Civil Liberties* (New York: Oxford UP, 1991), 229.

CHAPTER I

1. Allan Nevins, "Not Capulets, Not Montagus," *American Historical Review*, 65 (Jan. 1960): 259–60.

2. *The American Heritage Dictionary* (Boston, 1992), 415.

3. Wood Gray, *The Hidden Civil War: The Story of the Copperheads* (New York, 1942), 164–75. He also called Vallandigham (page 158) "a near fanatic."

4. Ibid., 224.

5. Ibid., 134.

6. Ibid., 168–69, 181.

7. Ibid., 224.

8. George Fort Milton, *Abraham Lincoln and the Fifth Column* (New York, 1942), 133, 136, 206, 334. For example, page 36, Milton wrote, "With the early summer [1861], a secret society [the Knights of the Golden Circle] spread over the whole region [the Upper Midwest], with a full panoply of oaths, grips, recognition signs—and determined to aid the Confederate cause."

   Milton's *The Age of Hate: Andrew Johnson and the Radicals* (New York, 1930) was anti-Radical and pro-Johnson—in the best William A. Dunning tradition. Milton's *Eve of Conflict: Stephen A. Douglas and the Needless War* (Boston, 1934) won accolades, but it was strongly pro-Douglas and anti-Radical. Milton's *Conflict: The American Civil War* (New York, 1941) stressed the military aspects in a most readable fashion. One historian called it the "best" one-volume history of the war.

9. Ibid., 187, 248.

10. Ibid., 18–19, 334.

11. Ibid., 117, 158, 209, 252.

12. Ibid., 334.

13. Commager, quoted on the dust jacket of *Abraham Lincoln and the Fifth Column*.

14. Several books that present the traditional suppositions about the so-called "Copper-heads" include: (1) Edward C. Smith, *The Borderland in the Civil War* (New York, 1927), (2) James I. Horan, *Confederate Agent: A Discovery in History* (New York, 1954), and (3) Stephen Z. Starr, *Colonel Greenville: The Life of A Soldier of Fortune* (Baton Rouge, 1971). In his much-praised book, *Abraham Lincoln: A Biography* (New York, 1952), Benjamin P. Thomas called the so-called "Copperheads" "seditionists" and wrote: "Throughout the North—but especially in those counties of the Midwest where the majority of the people were of Southern antecedents—secret societies, known variously as Knights of the Golden Circle, the Order of American Knights, and the Sons of Liberty, enrolling thousands of members, spoke openly in favor of the Southern cause, and committed acts of violence against the government" (pages 376–77).

   Three articles exemplify the many that preach the same suppositions as Wood Gray and George Fort Milton: (1) Bethania M. Smith, "Civil War Subversives," in *Journal of the Illinois State Historical Society*, 45 (Autumn 1952): 220–40; (2) Frederic S. Klein, "The Great Northwest Conspiracy," in *Civil War Times Illustrated*, 4 [3] (June 1965): 21–26; and (3) Stephen Z. Starr, "Was There a Northwest Conspiracy?" in *Filson Club Historical Quarterly*, 38 (Apr. 1964): 328–41.

   Mark M. Boatner, *Civil War Dictionary* (New York, 1953) is replete with historical errors; his three and a-half sentence sketch on the Knights of the Golden Circle contains eight factual errors—more than two per sentence.

   Historical novels that give writers a literary license overplay the conspiracies and discredit to Lincoln's Democratic critics number close to ten. Two of the more popular were: (1) Constance Robertson, *The Golden Circle* (1951), and (2) Dee Brown, *Conspiracy of Knaves* (1986).

15. Lawrence J. McCaffrey, *The Irish Diaspora in America* (Washington, D.C., 1984), 92. The role of Irish-Americans in the Copperhead movement in the North is treated in Frank L. Klement, "Catholics As Copperheads During the American Civil War," *Catholic Historical Review*, 80 (Jan. 1994).

16. *Freeport Journal* (n.d.), quoted in the *Dayton Daily Empire*, Feb. 14, 1860.

17. *Chicago Tribune* (n.d.), quoted in the *(Springfield) Illinois State Register*, July 25, 1863.

18. *Cincinnati Daily Commercial*, Jan. 15, 1862.

19. *Detroit Advertiser and Tribune* (n.d.), quoted in the *Detroit Free Press*, Sept. 13, 1863.

20. *(Chicago) Western Railroad Gazette*, Apr. 25, 1863. The entire critique reads as follows: "It was right enough to sicken a decent man to behold the kind of voting cattle (each with a Democratic ticket in hand) brought in interminable rows at the ward voting places. Such beastly faces, bloated carcasses, filthy, stinking, God-forsaken wretches; jail birds turned loose; dirty offal vomited forth from the sinks, and gutters, and sloughs of Kilgubbin; men whose vile countenances, fiery with rum, suggested proficiency in every crime from perjury to murder as a fine art; men swearing, cursing, blaspheming; men who couldn't read a single letter of a single word of the ticket they voted; men who signed their name with a cross; the upturned substrata of city corruption; human swine all blotched and reeking with congenial mire; loathsome, ignorant, brutal, disgusting, debased in body and mind to a level with the beasts of the field; excrescences and running sores upon the unhealthy body politic—*such* votes elected the Copperhead municipal ticket."

21. *Times* (London), July 15, 1863. This noted journalist was William H. Russell whose diary (printed in two volumes in London in 1863 and entitled *My Diary North and South*) is an invaluable historical source. Russell could be called "the first war reporter" for earlier he had toured the area of the Crimean War. He was, without question, the best-known reporter of his day.

22. This is the thesis of John L. Stipp, "Economic and Political Aspects of Western Copperheadism" (Ph.D. dissertation, Ohio State University, 1940). The title is really a misnomer, for Stipp centered his study, almost in entirety, upon Ohio.

23. Samuel P. Heintzelman, "Journal," entry of Oct. 20, 1864, Samuel P. Heintzelman Papers, Library of Congress. At the time that General Heintzelman wrote that journal entry, he was commander of the Department of the Ohio, with headquarters in Cincinnati. Heintzelman replaced Gen. Ambrose E. Burnside soon after the president revoked Burnside's suspension of the *Chicago Times* in 1863.

24. Letter, John W. Kees to Samuel S. Cox, Apr. 12, 1862, Samuel S. Cox Papers, Brown University Library, Providence, Rhode Island. The author used microfilm copies of the Cox Papers loaned (via an inter-library program) by the Hayes Memorial Library, Fremont, Ohio.

25. The author has one of the Olds' butternut emblems, given to him by Dr. Olds' great granddaughter when she was a student at Marquette University.

26. Eugene Roseboom, "Southern Ohio and the Union in 1863," *Mississippi Valley Historical Review*, 39 (June 1952): 29–44. Roseboom discredited the supposition that southern Ohio was the stronghold of Copperheadism. The Democratic counties in Ohio were scattered here and there with a tier across the center—in the less desirable farming areas.

27. Charles R. Wilson, "Cincinnati as a Southern Outpost in 1860–1861," *Mississippi Valley Historical Review*, 24 (Mar. 1938): 473–82; Charles R. Wilson, "Cincinnati's Reputation during the Civil War," *Journal of Southern History*, 2 (Nov. 1936): 468–79; Henry C. Hubbart, "Pro-Southern Influences in the Free West, 1840–1865," *Mississippi Valley Historical Review*, 20 (June 1933): 45–62; Earle D. Ross, "Northern Sectionalism in the Civil War Era," *Iowa Journal of History and Politics*, 30 (Oct. 1932): 455–512; Frank L. Klement, "Economic Aspects of Middle Western Copperheadism," *The Historian*, 14 (Autumn 1951): 27–44.

28. Letter, Matt Martin to Samuel S. Cox, Dec. 3, 1861, Cox Papers.

29. Report of Gen. John A. McClernand, published in *Official Records of the Union and Confederate Armies* (128 vols.; Washington, D.C., 1880–1901), series 1, vol. 17, part 2, 332–33.

30. Harry E. Pratt, "The Repudiation of Lincoln's War Policy in 1862—Stuart-Swett Congressional Campaign," *Journal of the Illinois State Historical Society*, 24 (Apr. 1931): 129–40.

31. *The (Columbus) Crisis*, June 27, Oct. 24, Nov. 28, 1861, Jan. 23, 1862; *(Springfield) Illinois State Journal*, June 22, 1862; *Congressional Globe*, 37th Congress, 2nd session, 170.

32. Stanley L. Jones, "Agrarian Radicalism in the Illinois Constitutional Convention of 1862," *Journal of the Illinois State Historical Society*, 48 (Autumn 1955): 271–82; Frank L. Klement, "Middle Western Copperheadism and the Genesis of the Granger Movement," *Mississippi Valley Historical Review*, 38 (Mar. 1952): 679–94.

33. Clement L. Vallandigham, *Speeches, Arguments, Addresses and Letters of Clement L. Vallandigham* (New York), 326.

34. Quoted in John H. Holliday, *Indianapolis and the Civil War* (Indianapolis, 1911), 572–73.

35. Letter, Frederic W. Horn to Gov. Alexander Randall, Apr. 18, 1861, Wisconsin Civil War Governors' Letters, Wisconsin State Historical Society, Madison.

36. Samuel S. Cox, *Puritanism and Politics. Speech of Hon. S.S. Cox of Ohio, before the Democratic Union Association*, Jan. 13, 1863 (New York, 1863); Vallandigham's famous "There Is a West" speech is in *Cong. Globe*, 36th Cong., 1st session, Appendix, 43–44.

37. Letters, James A. Craven to William H. English, Apr. 9, July 28, 1861, William H. English Papers, Indiana State Historical Society, Indianapolis.

38. See Frank L. Klement, "Midwestern Opposition to Lincoln's Emancipation Policy," *Journal of Negro History*, 40 (July 1964): 169–83.

39. *Oshkosh Courier*, Feb. 21, 1862.

40. *Macomb (Ill.) Eagle* (n.d.), quoted in *Indianapolis Daily State Sentinel*, Dec. 23, 1861.

41. *Cincinnati Daily Commercial*, July 11, 16–17, 1862; William H. Lofton, "Northern Labor and the Negro during the Civil War," *Journal of Negro History*, 39 (July 1949): 251–73; Frank L. Klement, "Sound and Fury: Civil War Dissent in the Cincinnati Area," *Cincinnati Historical Bulletin*, 35 (Summer 1977): 99–114.

42. *Dubuque Democratic Herald*, Jan. 3, 8, 10, 1863.

43. Letter, Thomas O. Lowe to "Dear Will" (brother-soldier), Jan. 23, 1863, Thomas O. Lowe Papers, Dayton and Montgomery County Public Library, Dayton, Ohio.

44. Emma Lou Thornbrough, *Indiana in the Civil War Era, 1850–1860* (Indianapolis, 1865), 205.

45. *The Crisis*, Mar. 11, 18, 1863; *(Columbus) Ohio State Journal*, Mar. 7, 1863; Eugene H. Roseboom, "The Mobbing of *The Crisis*," *Ohio State Archaeological and Historical Quarterly*, 59 (Apr. 1950): 150–53.

46. Mark E. Neely, *The Fate of Liberty: Abraham Lincoln and Civil Liberties* (New York, 1991), 54–55.

47. Chapter XI, in Frank L. Klement, *The Limits of Dissent: Clement L. Vallandigham and the Civil War* (Lexington, Ky., 1970), 156–73, is entitled "Arrest and Trial."

48. See Chapter X, "The Northwest Confederacy Scheme and the Indianapolis Treason Trials," and Chapter XI, "The Camp Douglas Conspiracy and the Cincinnati Treason Trial," in Frank L. Klement, *Dark Lanterns: Secret Political Societies, Conspiracies, and Treason Trials in the Civil War* (Baton Rouge, 1984), 151–86, 187–217.

49. Hamilton *True Telegraph*, Feb. 23, 1863.

50. *(Milwaukee) See-Bote*, Oct. 25, 1862, Feb. 11, Mar. 25, Apr. 30, 1863.

51. Hamilton *True Telegraph*, Feb. 29, 1863.

52. Chapter XI, pages 156–72, in Frank L. Klement, *The Limits of Dissent* deals with Vallandigham's arrest and trial. Chapter III, in Klement, *The Copperheads in the Middle West* (Chicago, 1960), pages 73–133, is entitled "The High Tide of Midwestern Copperheadism," while Chapter IV (pages 107–33) is entitled "Formation of the Peace Movement."

53. William K. Beaudot and Lance J. Herdegen, *An Irishman in the Iron Brigade: The Civil War Memoirs of James P. Sullivan, Sergt., Company K, 6th Wisconsin Volunteers* (New York, 1993), 83. This is a remarkable book for it expresses a line soldier's feelings time and again. It is a book that belongs on all Civil War bookshelves.

54. Letter (virtually a state paper), Lincoln to "Hon. Erastus Corning and others," June 12, 1863, published in the *New York Tribune*, June 15, 1863. The autographed copy in the Robert Todd Lincoln Papers, Library of Congress, was somewhat revised before being released to the press.

55. Letter, Lincoln to Greeley, Aug. 22, 1862, *The Collected Works of Abraham Lincoln*, edited by Roy P. Basler (9 vols.; New Brunswick, NJ, 1953), 5:388–89.

56. *Cincinnati Daily Gazette*, Nov. 9, 1863.

57. *Times* (London), Mar. 17, Oct. 7, 20, 1863.

58. *Proceedings of the State Grand Council of the U.L.A. of Michigan at Its Special Meeting Held in Detroit...March 2, 1864* (n.p., n.d.), 13.

59. Letter, James M. Edmunds to Lincoln, Dec. 12, 1864, Robert Todd Lincoln Papers. A brief history of the Union League is in Klement, *Dark Lanterns*, Chapter II, pp. 34–63.

60. *American Heritage Dictionary* (Boston, 1992), 415.

61. See Klement, *Dark Lanterns*, 7–33, 64–90, 91–135, 136–50. The closing sentence (page 33) of the chapter entitled "George Bickley and the Knights of the Golden Circle" reads: "The Golden Circle was a bogeyman devised for political gain." The closing sentence of Chapter III ("Phineas G. Wright, the Order of American Knights, and the Sanderson Expose") says that Republican propaganda maligned Vallandigham and "created a subversive-society legend with nine lives" (page 90). Chapter IV is entitled "H.H. Dodd, the Sons of Liberty, and the Carrington Exposé."

62. This contention is developed in Frank L. Klement, "The Soldier Vote in Wisconsin during the Civil War," in *Wisconsin Magazine of History*, 28 (Sept. 1944): 39–47. Also see T. Harry Williams, "Voters in Blue: The Citizen Soldiers of the Civil War," *Mississippi Valley Historical Review*, 31 (Sept., 1944): 187–204.

63. A Democratic soldier wrote: "...a soldier is under too much influence to cast a free and independent vote....Our Colonel made a speech to the regiment on the eve of election, in favor of Amasa Cobb [Republican congressional incumbent]," soldier's letter published in *Madison (Wis.) Patriot*, Nov. 21, 1862.

64. Ibid., Nov. 25, 1862.

65. Report of the Secretary of State, *Wisconsin Executive Documents, 1863–1864* (Madison, 1865), 73.

66. Madison *Patriot*, Sept. 19, 1862.

67. Equally as important as Woodward's defeat, as far as President Lincoln was concerned, was the defeat of Walter W. Lowie in the same election. Lowie, as Chief Justice of the Pennsylvania State Supreme Court, was one of the judges (in a 2 to 1 decision) that had written the court opinion that the Conscription Act of Mar. 3, 1863, was unconstitutional and null and void within Pennsylvania's borders. President Lincoln considered arresting Lowie. After the election the court, by a 2 to 1 vote, reversed the decision. The vote of furloughed soldiers defeated Lowie.

68. One encyclopedia has the "new definition." See *World Book Encyclopedia* (Chicago, 1991), vol. 4, page 1046; the definition reads: "a name given to a group of Democrats who criticized Abraham Lincoln's Administration during the Civil War."

69. James M. McPherson, *Abraham Lincoln and the Second American Revolution* (New York, 1990) argues persuasively that the war possessed a "truly revolutionary character." Interestingly, McPherson, a nationalist historian still mired in the Wood Gray-George Fort Milton interpretation of Lincoln's Democratic critics, sees eye to eye with the Copperhead interpretation that the war was revolutionary in nature.

70. Frank L. Klement, *The Copperheads in the Middle West* (Chicago, 1960), 1.

71. Appraiser's report (re. Clement L. Vallandigham), Probate Records (Packet No. 9875), Montgomery County Court House, Dayton, Ohio. In addition to the more than 1,200 books in his personal library, he had another 263 books in his law library.

72. I have discredited the Republican contentions about the Knights of the Golden Circle in a series of articles. See Frank L. Klement, "Carrington and the Golden Circle Legend in Indiana during the Civil War," *Indiana Magazine of History*, 61 (Mar. 1965): 31–52. Others include: "The Hopkins Hoax and Golden Circle Rumors in Michigan, 1861–1862," *Michigan History*, 47 (Mar. 1863): 1–14; "Rumors of Golden Circle Activity in Iowa during the Civil War years," *Annals of Iowa*, 27 (Spring 1965): 523–36; "Copperhead Secret Societies in Illinois during the Civil War," *Journal of the Illinois State Historical Society*, 48 (Summer 1955): 152–80; "Ohio and the Knights of the Golden Circle: The Evolution of a Civil War Myth," *Cincinnati Historical Society Bulletin*, 32 (Spring-Summer 1974): 7–27.

73. The four booklets are described in a chapter entitled "H.H. Dodd, the Sons of Liberty, and the Carrington Exposé," pp. 91–135, in Frank L. Klement, *Dark Lanterns*, 105–6. The Order of American Knights is debunked in Frank L. Klement, "Phineas C. Wright, the Order of American Knights, and the Sanderson Expose," *Civil War History*, 18 (Mar. 1972): 5–23.

74. See Frank L. Klement, Chapter V entitled "The Indianapolis Treason Trials and *Ex Parte Milligan* (1866)," in Michael R. Belknap, editor, *American Political Trials* (Westport, Conn. 1981), 101–27.

75. Testimony of Edward Thomas Courtney, Samuel Remington, and Richard Patten at the Cincinnati treason trial, Feb. 8–10, Apr. 7, Mar. 22, 1865, in *House Executive Documents*, 30th Cong., 2nd sess., 196–230, 359–60, 472–76.

76. See Chapter VII, "The Camp Douglas Conspiracy and the Cincinnati Treason Trial," in Klement, *Dark Lanterns*, 187–217.

77. The socioeconomic aspects of Ohio Copperheadism are explored in John Stipp, "Economic and Political Aspects of Western Copperheadism," (Ph.D. dissertation, Ohio State University, 1942). The religious, social, and political relationships of Republicans and Democrats in the Upper Midwest were studied in Harvey L. Carter, "The Origins of Political Patterns in the Older Middle West, 1856–1864" (manuscript in possession of the author, Harvey L. Carter). Also see Gilbert R. Tredway, *Democratic Opposition to the Lincoln Administration in Indiana* (Indianapolis, 1973) and the two articles by Frank L. Klement, "Economic Aspects of Middle Western Copperheadism," *The Historian*, 14 (Autumn 1951): 27–44, and "Middle Western Copperheadism and the Genesis of the Granger Movement," *Mississippi Valley Historical Review*, 38 (Mar. 1952): 679–94.

78. *Address to the People by the Democracy of Wisconsin, Adopted in State Convention at Milwaukee, Sept. 3, 1862* (Milwaukee, 1862), 3–5. This Democratic platform was drafted by Edward G. Ryan and came to be known as the "Ryan Address." Ryan argued a case (*In Re Kemp*) before the Wisconsin State Supreme Court and the judges agreed with Ryan that Lincoln's suspension of the writ of habeas corpus was unconstitutional and that suspending habeas corpus was a congressional right. Also see Alfonso J. Beitzinger, "The Father of Copperheadism in Wisconsin," *Wisconsin Magazine of History*, 39 (Autumn 1955): 17–25.

79. Neely, *The Fate of Liberty*, 209.

80. Gray, *The Hidden Civil War*, 224; Milton, *Abraham Lincoln and the Fifth Column*, 334.

81. Philadelphia *Press* (n.d.), quoted in William Dusinberre, *Civil War Issues in Philadelphia, 1856–1865* (Philadelphia, 1965), 158.

82. Entry of Aug. 12, 1861, Daniel L. Medlar, "Journal, Sept. 1, 1859–Apr. 30, 1862," Dayton and Montgomery County Public Library, Dayton, Ohio.

83. Section 3 of Article III reads: "Treason against the United States, shall consist only in levying war against them, or in adhering to Her Enemies, or giving them Aid and Comfort. No person shall be convicted of Treason unless on the Testimony of Two Witnesses to the same overt Act, or on Confession in an open court."

84. Chief Justice Marshall, in *United States v. Burr* (1807), argued that, under the Constitution, "treason" included only *overt acts*, not verbal plans, and that a conviction would require "the testimony of two witnesses to the same overt act."

85. Judge Davis' two sentences are in *Ex Parte Milligan* (1866), 71, U.S. (4 Wallace), 431–32.

86. John A. Marshall, *American Bastile: A History of the Illegal Arrests, and Imprisonment of American Citizens during the Late War* (Philadelphia, 1878), 375–84.

87. *Indianapolis Daily Journal*, Sept. 5, 1864; letters, William A. Bowles to "Dear Brother," May 31, 1863 and Bowles to Gen. Gideon J. Pillow, Aug. 18, 1861, both in Union Provost Marshal's File of One-Name Papers *re* Citizens, National Archives, Washington, D.C. Bowles and Pillow fought together in the Mexican War.

88. Neely, *The Fate of Liberty*, 209; Joel H. Sibley, *A Respectable Minority: The Democratic Party in the Civil War Era, 1860–1868* (New York, 1977) treats Lincoln's Democratic critics as "a loyal opposition." So does Jean A. Baker, *Affairs of Party: The Political Culture of Northern Democrats in the Mid-Nineteenth Century* (Ithaca, NY, 1983).

89. *American Heritage Dictionary*, 381.

90. *Dubuque Democratic Herald*, Jan. 10, 18, 1863.

91. *LaCrosse Weekly Democrat*, Aug. 24, 1864.

92. Neely, *The Fate of Liberty*, 209.

CHAPTER II

1. Gabor S. Boritt, *Lincoln and the Economics of the American Dream* (Memphis, 1978), 130.

2. Mark E. Neely, *Lincoln and the Constitution* (Historical Bulletin No. 38, Lincoln Fellowship of Wisconsin, Madison, 1983), 5.

3. Ibid., 5; Mark E. Neely, *The Fate of Liberty: Abraham Lincoln and Civil Liberties* (New York, 1991), 7.

4. Lincoln to Greeley, Aug. 22, 1862, in *Collected Works of Abraham Lincoln*, edited by Roy P. Basler (9 vols.; New Brunswick, N.J., 1953), 5:388–89.

5. Lincoln to Albert G. Hodges, Apr. 4, 1864, ibid., 281.

6. Lincoln, "To Erastus Corning and Others," June 12, 1863, ibid., 6: 266. Lincoln added an interesting note: "I think the time not unlike to come when I shall be blamed for having made too few arrests rather than too many."

7. Neely, *Fate of Liberty*, xii, 137.

8. Quoted to Arnold M. Shankman, "Conflict in the Old Keystone: Antiwar Sentiment in Pennsylvania, 1860–1865" (Ph.D. dissertation, Emory University, 1972), 216.

9. Ibid., 126.

10. Ibid., 127.

11. Accounts of the Duff and Blanchard arrest are detailed in John A. Marshall, *American Bastile: A History of the Illegal Arrests and Imprisonment of American Citizens During the Late War* (Philadelphia, 1878), 174–79, 293–302.

12. Ibid., 586–603. Dr. Olds' speech of July 26, 1862, is included.

13. *The (Columbus) Crisis*, Oct. 22, 1863, said, "The abolitionists have only this satisfaction. They beat him by *legislation*, not by voting."

14. William W. Armstrong, "Personal Recollections," published in the *Cincinnati Daily Enquirer*, Mar 20, 1886; Frank L. Klement, *The Limits of Dissent: Clement L. Vallandigham and the Civil War* (Lexington, Ky., 1970), 87–155. James L. Vallandigham, *A Life of Clement L. Vallandigham* (Baltimore, 1872) is as much a eulogy as it is a biography.

15. *War of the Rebellion: A Compilation of the Official Records of the Union and Confederate Armies* (4 series, 128 vols.; Washington, D.C., 1800–1901), ser. 1, 23: part 2, 168. Hereafter cited as *Official Records*.

16. *The Crisis*, May 6,1863; Armstrong, "Personal Recollections"; Klement, *Limits of Dissent*, 152–53.

17. *Mount Vernon Democratic Banner*, May 9, 1863; *The Crisis*, May 13, 1863.

18. Larned "Journal," entry of May 5, 1863, Daniel Read Larned Papers, Library of Congress (the diarist was a member of the military expedition); Klement, *Limits of Dissent*, 153–54.

19. *Huntington Democrat*, July 30, 1862, and *Huntington Democrat*, Oct. 2, 1862, both quoted in Darwin Kelley, *Milligan's Fight Against Lincoln* (New York, 1973), 48.

20. John C. Walker to "Editor," June 23, 1863, published in *Indianapolis Daily State Sentinel*, June 25, 1863.

21. Marshall, *American Bastile*, 73–74.

22. Shankman, "Conflicts in the Old Keystone," 161.

23. *Indianapolis Daily Journal*, May 21, 22, 1863; *Indianapolis Daily State Sentinel*, May 21, 22, 1863.

24. The trains bound for Cincinnati and Peru were stopped along Pogue's Run, a mid-sized creek. When the car-by-car search began, some of the passengers tossed their revolvers and pistols through the open windows into the nearby creek rather than surrender them. Mockingly, this incident became "the Battle of Pogue's Run" and Republicans tried to build a treason tale of out it. See Gen. Milo S. Hascall, manuscript (an autobiographical report), in Archives Division, Indiana State Library, Indianapolis, and William D. Foulke, Life of Oliver P. Morton, *Including His Important Speeches* (2 vols.; Indianapolis, 1899), 2:274–77.

25. *Indianapolis Daily Journal*, May 22, 23, 1863.

26. Dodd's various ordeals are reported in Frank L. Klement, *Dark Lanterns: Secret Political Societies, Conspiracies, and Treason Trials in the Civil War* (Baton Rouge, 1984), 95–101.

27. Dodd founded the Sons of Liberty in 1864—to protect rights of Democrats and to promote "conservative doctrine." See Klement, *Dark Lanterns*, 91–135.

28. Shankman, "Conflict in the Old Keystone," 156.

29. Dennis A. Mahony, *The Prisoner of State* (New York, 1863), 117–19.

30. Robert S. Harper, *Lincoln and the Press* (New York, 1951), 127–28.

31. Ibid., 128–29.

32. Emma Lou Thornbrough, *Indiana in the Civil War Era, 1850–1800* (Indianapolis, 1965), 205.

33. Harper, *Lincoln and the Press*, recites many of the arrest incidents, but he also misses quite a few.

34. Ibid., 109.

35. Ibid., 112, 113.

36. Quoted in Thornbrough, *Indiana in the Civil War Era, 1850–1880*, 205.

37. Quoted in Harper, *Lincoln and the Press*, 122.

38. *Official Records*, ser. 1, 23; part 2, 147, 237. The event was discussed in scholarly fashion in Mrs. L.E. Ellis, "The Chicago Times during the Civil War," in *Illinois Historical Society Transactions* (1932), 135–82.

39. Lincoln to Secretary of War Edwin M. Stanton, June 4, 1863, in *Collected Works of Abraham Lincoln*, 6:248.

40. Harper, *Lincoln and the Press*, 109.

41. Ibid., 149.

42. Ibid., 189.

43. *The Crisis*, Mar. 11, 18, 1863; *(Columbus) Ohio State Journal*, Mar 7, 1863; Eugene H. Roseboom, "The Mobbing of *The Crisis*," *Ohio State Archaeological and Historical Quarterly*, 59 (Apr. 1950): 150–53.

44. Harper, *Lincoln and the Press*, 232.

45. *Official Records*, ser. 2, 5:741.

46. Marcus Mills Pomeroy, *Journey of Life: Reminiscences and Recollections of "Brick" Pomeroy* (New York, 1890), 182–94. General Prentiss's "General Order No. 19," expelling Pomeroy from the Department of the Southwest, was published in the *Milwaukee Sentinel*, Apr. 1, 1863.

47. Letter (in cipher), Lincoln to Burnside, May 29, 1863, *Collected Works of Abraham Lincoln*, 6:237. Lincoln's use of the word "necessity" is interesting.

48. Morton to Lincoln, May 30, 1863, Robert Todd Lincoln Papers, Library of Congress.

49. Lincoln to Schofield, July 13, 1863, *Collected Works of Abraham Lincoln*, 6:326.

50. Lincoln to Schofield, Oct. 1, 1863, ibid., 6:492.

51. Neely, *Fate of Liberty*, 28.

52. *Philadelphia Press* (n.d.), quoted in William Dusinberre, *Civil War Issues in Philadelphia, 1856–1865* (Philadelphia, 1965), 158.

53. *Congressional Globe*, 37th Congress, 1st session, 23, 100, 348.

54. This issue is discussed in scholarly fashion in Bertram W. Korn, "Congressman Clement L. Vallandigham's Championship of the Jewish Chaplaincy in the Civil War," *American Jewish Historical Review*, 53 (Dec. 1963): 188–91.

55. *Papers of U.S. Grant*, edited by John Y. Simon (vols. 1–; Carbondale, Ill., 1967–): 7:51n–56n.

56. Henry Clay Dean wrote his reasons for opposing the war into the preface of his strange book. *Crimes of the Civil War, and Curse of the Funding System* (Baltimore, 1868), 1–24.

57. *(Springfield) Illinois State Register*, Oct. 13, 1863. The two clergymen were Rev. W.R. Howard and Rev. W. P. Paxson. Rather than surrender their political convictions, both laid aside their clerical garb.

58. The clergyman was Rev. James L. Vallandigham, an older brother of Clement L. Vallandigham. In the eyes of some Radical Republicans, that was reason enough for the arrest. The entire beatitude reads: "Blessed are the peacemakers, for they shall be called children of God."

59. Rev. P.S. Bennett, *History of Methodism in Wisconsin* (Cincinnati, 1890), 207.

60. 17 Federal cases 144 (1861).

61. Shankman, "Conflict in the Old Keystone," 84.

62. Eugene C. Murdock, *One Million Men: the Civil War Draft in the North* (Madison, Wis., 1971), 59.

63. Ibid., 48.

64. Ibid., 58.

65. Marshall, *American Bastile*, 451–62.

66. Ibid., 139–52.

67. *Cleveland Leader*, Oct. 10, 16, 18, 1861; *The Crisis*, Nov. 7, 1861, *(Columbus) Ohio Statesman*, Oct. 8, 12, 15, 16, 19, 1861; *History of Marion County, Ohio* (Chicago, 1883), 448–49.

68. Henry B. Carrington, "The Constable Case" (typewritten mss.), in Henry B. Carrington Papers, Archives Division, Indiana State Library, Indianapolis.

69. The best narrative account, devoid of interpretation is in the *History of Washington and Ozaukee Counties* (Chicago, 1881), 493–96. Peter Leo Johnson, "Port Washington Draft Riot of 1862," *Mid-America*, 1 (Jan. 1930): 212–20, blames the failure to appoint Catholic chaplains for nearly all-Catholic regiments in earlier days as the root of antidraft discontent among Luxembourgers and German-Americans of the area.

70. Adrian Cook, *Armies of the Street: New York City Draft Riots of 1863* (Lexington, Ky., 1974), and Iver Bernstein, *The New York Draft Riots: Their Significance for American Society and Politics in the Age of the Civil War* (New York, 1990) are contrasting accounts; the first is basically a narrative while the second practices class analysis as the approach to the riots.

71. Shankman, "Conflict in the Old Keystone," 224–27.

72. William A. Bross, *Biographical Sketch of the Late General B.J. Sweet* [and] *History of Camp Douglas: A Paper Read Before the Chicago Historical Society, June 18, 1878* (Chicago, 1878), 44, or see, Chapter VII "The Camp Douglas Conspiracy and the Cincinnati Treason Trial" in Frank L. Klement, *Dark Lanterns: Secret Political Societies, Conspiracies, and Treason Trials in the Civil War* (Baton Rouge, 1984), 187–217.

73. Neely, *Lincoln and the Constitution*, 6, estimates the number as "at least 14,000." Alexander Johnson, in *Encyclopedia of Political Science* (edited by John I. Lalor), 2:432–34, gives a 38,000 figure—evidently borrowed from [Appleton's] *Annual Cyclopedia and Register of Important Events of the Year, 1865* (New York, 1866), 414.

74. *Official Records*, ser. 2, 1:453–57.

75. "Proceedings of a Military Commission, Convened in Cincinnati, May 6, 1863," in Citizens' File, 1861–1865. War Department Collection of Confederate Records, National Archives.

76. *Diary of Gideon Welles*, edited by Howard H. Beale (3 vols.; New York, 1960), 1:306; telegram (in cipher), Lincoln to Burnside, May 29, 1863, Special Collections Division, Brown University Library, Providence.

77. "Proceedings of a Military Commission Convened in Indianapolis on Oct. 21, 1864," General Courts-Martial Records, Records of the Office of the Judge Advocate General, National Archives; Chapter VI. "The Northwestern Confederacy Scheme and the Indianapolis Treason Trials," in Klement, *Dark Lanterns*, 151–86.

78. "Proceedings of a Military Commission Convened in Cincinnati on January 11, 1865," General Courts-Martial Records, Record of the Office of the Judge Advocate General, National Archives.

   George St. Leger Grenfell's death sentence was changed to life imprisonment at Fort Jefferson, in the Dry Tortugas off the coast of Florida, where he died in the shark-filled waters in an escape attempt and while wearing a ball and chain.

79. Ludwell H. Johnson III (Professor of History, William and Mary College), book review of Floyd Risvold, *A True History of the Assassination of Abraham Lincoln and the Conspiracy of 1865* (New York, 1975), in *Civil War History* 22 (Mar. 1976): 77–81.

80. Neely, *Fate of Liberty*, 28.

81. Ibid.

82. Shankman, "Conflict in the Old Keystone," 247.

83. Ibid., 288.

84. John W. Kees to Samuel S. Cox, Apr. 12, 1862, Samuel S. Cox Papers, Brown University Library, Providence (microfilm copy in Hayes Memorial Library, Fremont, Ohio).

85. *Dubuque Democratic Herald*, Jan. 3, 6, 10, 18, 1863.

86. *LaCrosse Weekly Democrat*, Oct. 3, 1864.

87. Ibid., Aug. 29, 1864.

88. Ibid.

89. Ibid., June 19, July 3, 1865.

90. In practice, Pomeroy was abused by various LaCrosse residents and soldiers on furlough. There were threats to mob his printing plant. Subscribers quit taking his newspaper and some businesses ceased to advertise in the *LaCrosse Democrat*. The rival Republican editor wrote this evaluation: "He out-Jeffed Jeff Davis in treasonable utterances and out-deviled the devil in deviltry."

91. Marshall, *American Bastile*, xiii.

92. *Cincinnati Daily Enquirer*, Jan. 21, 1863.

93. Lincoln, "Memorandum," dated Aug. 23, 1864, in *Collected Works of Abraham Lincoln*, 7:514–15.

94. *Ex Parte Milligan* (1866), 71 I.S. (4 Wallace), 431–32; Frank L. Klement, "The Indianapolis Treason Trials and *Ex Parte Milligan*," in *American Political Trials*, edited by Michal R. Belknap (Westport, Conn., 1981), 101–28.

95. Neely, *Fate of Liberty*, 209.

CHAPTER III

1. Traditional views of Copperheadism are presented in Wood Gray, *The Hidden Civil War: The Story of the Copperheads* (New York, 1942) and George Fort Milton, *Abraham Lincoln and the Fifth Column* (New York, 1942). Milton treats the entire Northern scene, while Gray's book is concerned with those states formed out of the Old Northwest. Professor Gray's impressive bibliography is mute testimony to intensive research. He has collected hundreds of Copperhead incidents and quotations, hung them on the line of treason, and arranged them chronologically by chapters.

2. *Congressional Globe*, 36th Cong., 2nd sess., Dec. 10, 1860, 38 ff.; Clement L. Vallandigham, *The Record of the Hon. C. L. Vallandigham on Abolition, the Union, and the Civil War* (Columbus, 1863), 43.

3. *Chicago Times*, Dec. 10, 1860.

4. An excellent evaluation of the editorial views of the *Enquirer* is available in Charles R. Wilson, *The Cincinnati Daily Enquirer and Civil War Politics: A Study of Copperhead Opinion* (unpublished Ph.D. dissertation, University of Chicago, 1934). Wilson recognized that the *Enquirer*'s Copperheadism was pro-western and held that "regardless of who won the war, the West was certain to lose it."

5. *(Columbus) The Crisis*, Jan. 31, 1861; Feb. 7, 14, 21, 1861.

6. Cyrus H. McCormick to Joseph Smith, Staunton, Virginia, May 9, 1861; William S. McCormick to James Henry, May 9, 1861, Cyrus H. McCormick Letters and Records, MSS., McCormick Historical Association Library, Chicago. After the start of hostilities, and on June 8, 1861, McCormick sold the *Chicago Times* to Wilbur Fisk Storey, who had achieved success in editing and publishing the *Detroit Free Press*.

7. The Ohioan proposed "to establish four [Northeast, Northwest, South, and Southwest]...grand sections of the Union," giving each section the right to veto Congressional measures in the Senate and assuring each section a voice in the selection of the president. *Congressional Globe*, 36th Cong., 2nd sess., Feb. 20, 1861, Appendix, 23–42; James L. Vallandigham, *A Life of Clement L. Vallandigham* (New York, 1872), 19.

8. Appleton's *Annual Cyclopedia and Register of Important Events, 1861* (New York, 1862), 312, reported 582 business failures in Ohio, 441 in Illinois, 253 in Indiana, and more than 500 in other midwestern states. The number of failures would have been much higher but two circumstances modified the impact. "One was that the panic of 1857 had weeded out, so to speak, the weakest of the houses, while in Nov., 1860, when affairs became threatening, the fall trade was passed, stocks of goods on hand were light, and there was little effort to prepare for a large spring business. Hence the payments due in the spring were, to a considerable extent, realized before non-intercourse took place." Ibid., 311–13.

9. W. F. Switzler, *Report of the Internal Commerce of the United States, House Executive Documents*, 49th Cong., 2nd sess., part 2, 21. Albert L. Kohlmeier, *The Old Northwest as the Arch of the Federal Union: A Study in Commerce and Politics* (Bloomington, 1938) reassesses the importance of the growing West-East trade.

10. *Eighth Census: Agriculture*, "Introduction" (Washington, 1870), clviii; *Hunt's Merchants' Magazine*, 44 (Jan. 1861): 102. *De Bow's Review*, New Series, 1 (Jan. 1861): 253–54, claimed that the states of Arkansas and Mississippi produced very little more than one-fourth of their necessary provisions; they were dependent upon the river trade for the other three-fourths. Studies important in revealing the significance of the Ohio-Mississippi river trade include Louis B. Schmidt, *The Internal Grain Trade of the United States, 1850–1860* (Iowa City, 1920); Thomas S. Berry, *Western Prices before 1861: A Study of the Cincinnati Market* (Cambridge, 1943); Henry C. Hurlburt, *The Older Middle West, 1840–1880* (New York, 1836); R. B. Way, "The Commerce of the Lower Mississippi in the Period 1830–1860," in *Proceedings of the Mississippi Valley Historical Association*, 10 (July 1920): 57–68; E. Merton Coulter, "Effects of Secession upon the Commerce of the Mississippi Valley," *Mississippi Valley Historical Review*, 3 (Dec. 1916): 264–85; Gerald L. Barnett, *Trade Relations between Southern Illinois and the South, 1855–1870* (unpublished M.S. thesis, University of Alabama, 1935), and Daniel W. Snepp, *Evansville's Channels of Trade and the Secession Movement* (Indianapolis, 1928).

11. *The Crisis*, May 16, 1861.

12. Charles R. Wilson, "Cincinnati, a Southern Outpost in 1860–61?" *Mississippi Valley Historical Review*, 24 (Mar. 1938): 481.

13. Logan Esarey, *A History of Indiana* (Indianapolis, 1918), 2:777.

14. *Chicago Daily Tribune*, Mar. 15, 1861; Barnett, *Trade Relations between Southern Illinois and the South, 1855–1870*, 14.

15. Charles H. Lanphier, "Recollections," in *Chicago Times*, Oct. 31, 1876.

16. Robert M. Sutton, *The Illinois Central Railroad in Peace and War, 1858–1868* (unpublished Ph.D. dissertation, University of Illinois, 1948), 120, 159.

17. Letter, John M. Dennison Letterbooks, Sept. 4, 1861, Burlington & Missouri River Railroad MSS., the Newberry Library, Chicago.

18. *Chicago Times*, Jan. 28, 1861.

19. "Report of the Commission of Statistics," in *Ohio Executive Documents*, 1860, II, 453–59; *Eighth Census: Manufacturing*, "Introduction," xxi; Wilson, "Cincinnati, a Southern Outpost in 1860–61?", 476 ff.

20. *Cincinnati Daily Enquirer*, Mar. 30, 1862.

21. William S. McCormick to James Henry, May 9, 1861; C.H. McCormick to Joseph Smith, May 7, 1861, McCormick MSS., McCormick Historical Association Library.

22. *Chicago Daily Tribune*, Feb. 12, 1861.

23. The five states which made up the Old Northwest contained 233 distilleries in 1860. Production for that year totalled 29,447,395 gallons. Peoria distilleries alone had a daily capacity of 11,650 bushels of grain.

24. *House Executive Documents*, 37th Cong., 3rd sess., Document No. 25, 200; *Report, United States Comptroller of the Currency, 1876* (Washington, 1877), 116; *Chicago Weekly Journal*, Apr. 17, May 15, 1861; Rollin G. Thomas, *The Development of State Banks in Chicago* (unpublished Ph.D. dissertation, University of Chicago, 1930), 30 ff.; George W. Dowrie, *The Development of Banking in Illinois, 1817–1863* (Urbana, 1913), 2:168–69.

25. Appleton *Annual Cyclopedia...1861*, 66–67; *Madison Wisconsin Patriot*, June 28, 29, 1862; *Milwaukee Daily Wisconsin*, July 12, 1861; Frederick Merk, *Economic History of Wisconsin During the Civil War Decade* (Madison, 1918), 193 ff.

26. Russell H. Anderson, *Agriculture in Illinois During the Civil War* (abstract of Ph.D. dissertation, University of Illinois, 1929), 4; George L. Anderson, "Western Attitude Toward National Banks, 1873–1874," *Mississippi Valley Historical Review*, 23 (Sept. 1936): 206–8.

27. Paul M. Angle, "An Illinois Farmer During the Civil War: Extracts from the Journal of John Edward Young, 1859–66," *Journal of the Illinois State Historical Society*, 26 (Apr.–July 1933): 92.

28. General Superintendent Arthur to William H. Osborn, Apr. 24, 1861, "President's Letter Book, W.H. Osborn, Nov. 19, 1861–July 1, 1862, Illinois Central Railroad Company MSS., the Newberry Library, Chicago; *History of Washington and Ozaukee Counties* (Chicago, 1881), 194–5.

29. Sylvannus (pseud.) to Paul, June 29, 1861, George H. Paul MSS., Wisconsin State Historical Society Library, Madison; *Milwaukee Daily Wisconsin*, July 12, 1861.

30. John M. Dennison Letterbooks, Aug. 17, 1861, Burlington & Missouri River Railroad MSS., the Newberry Library; C.L. Vallandigham, *Speeches, Arguments, Addresses and Letters of Clement L. Vallandigham* (New York, 1864), 326; *The Crisis*, July 25, 1861; Letter of Henry Hamlin Turner, published in *Boston Herald*, Jan. 26, 1929, cited in Paul W. Gates, *The Illinois Central Railroad and Its Colonization Work* (Cambridge, 1934), 274.

31. *Congressional Globe*, 37th Cong., 2nd sess., Dec. 23, 1861, 169; *The Crisis*, July 25, 1861; *Milwaukee Daily Wisconsin*, July 9, 1861; Chicago Board of Trade, *Annual Report*, 1862, 32.

32. *The Crisis*, June 27, Oct. 24, Nov. 28, 1861; Ibid., Jan. 23, 1862; Vallandigham, *Speeches*, 328.

33. "Proceedings of the Illinois State Constitutional Convention, 1862," in *(Springfield) Illinois State Journal*, Jan. 22, 1862; Appleton *Annual Cyclopedia...1861*, 107; Wesley C. Mitchell, *A History of the Greenbacks* (Chicago, 1903), 492.

34. *Wisconsin Farmer*, Feb. 1, 1862.

35. *Official Records of the Union and Confederate Armies* (128 vols., 1880–1901), Series 1, 17, Part 2, 332–33.

36. Osborn to H.V. Poor, Feb. 18, 1863, "President's Letter Book, W.H. Osborn, Nov. 19, 1861–July 1, 1862," Illinois Central Railroad Company MSS., the Newberry Library.

37. *Congressional Globe*, 37th Cong., 2nd sess., Dec. 23, 1861, 170.

38. *Journal of the Constitutional Convention of the State of Illinois Convened at Springfield on January 7, 1862* (Springfield, 1862), 27 ff.; "Proceedings of the Illinois State Constitutional Convention...January 21, 1862," in *Illinois State Journal*, Jan. 22, 1862.

39. *Congressional Globe*, 35th Cong., 2nd sess., Feb. 24, 1859, Appendix, 234 ff.; Vallandigham, *Speeches*, 326–28.

40. *Cincinnati Daily Enquirer*, Feb. 12, 1862.

41. *Madison Wisconsin Patriot*, Feb. 20, 1861.

42. F.W. Horn to Gov. Alexander Randall, Apr. 18, 1861, Wisconsin Civil War Governors' Letters, MSS., Wisconsin State Historical Society Library.

43. *Milwaukee See-Bote*, Apr. 30, 1862.

44. *The Crisis*, Feb. 28, Apr. 4, Aug. 15, 1861; Ibid., Jan. 21, 1863.

45. *Congressional Globe*, 36th Cong., 2nd sess., Feb. 25, 1861, 1192.

46. *Cincinnati Enquirer*, Nov. 21, 1863.

47. Cited in John H. Holliday, *Indianapolis and the Civil War* (Indianapolis, 1911), 572–73.

48. The act of July 1, 1862, levied a tax of 20 cents per gallon upon distilled spirits. The act of Mar. 7, 1864, increased the tax to 60 cents per gallon, and later war revenue measures raised the rate to $1.50 per gallon.

49. *The Crisis*, Mar. 4, 18, 1863.

50. *Cincinnati Enquirer*, Feb. 24, 1863.

51. *Congressional Globe*, 37th Cong., 3rd sess., Jan. 14, 1863, Appendix, 52–58; James G. Blaine, *Twenty Years in Congress* (New York, 1884), 1:480.

52. Ibid.

53. F. W. Horn to Governor Randall, Apr. 18, 1861, Wisconsin Civil War Governors' Letters, MSS., Wisconsin State Historical Society Library.

54. *LaCrosse Weekly Democrat*, Feb. 7, 1862; Ibid., July 7, 1863; Ibid., Oct. 17, 1864; Marcus Mills Pomeroy, *Condensed History of the War: Its Causes and Results* (n.p., 1868), 4–7.

55. *Milwaukee See-Bote*, Oct. 1, 1862. The translations from the *See-Bote* were made by Ekkehard Eickhoff, a graduate assistant at Marquette University, who aided the author in examining the views expressed in editorials of German-language newspapers.

56. "Proceedings of the Illinois State Constitutional Convention...1862," in *Illinois State Journal*, Feb. 13, 1862.

57. *TImes* (London), Dec. 1, 1863.

58. John R. Commons, et al., *Documentary History of American Industrial Society* (Cleveland, 1909), 2:5.

59. *Times* (London), Sept. 26, 1863. See also *Harper's Weekly*, Aug. 1, 1863 and *New York Tribune*, Aug. 8, 28, 1863.

60. *Milwaukee See-Bote*, Apr. 9, 23, 30, Oct. 15, Nov. 3, 1862; Ibid., Apr. 30, 1863; Ibid., Aug. 31, 1864.

61. *The Crisis*, Jan. 16, July 2, 16, 1862; Feb. 7, 1863; Aug. 24, 1864; *Cincinnati Weekly Gazette*, Sept. 2, 1862; *Cincinnati Enquirer*, Apr. 18, 1862; *Chicago Times*, Sept. 26; Oct. 5, 19, 1862.

62. Appleton's *Annual Cyclopedia...1862*, 754.

63. *Cincinnati Daily Enquirer*, July 11, 15–18, 1863.

64. Williston H. Lofton, "Northern Labor and the Negro during the Civil War," *Journal of Negro History,* 34 (July 1949), treats the economic issue realistically. A section of his article is entitled "Labor and the Conscription Law."

65. *Milwaukee See-Bote*, Nov. 18, 1863.

66. *Official Records*, Series 1, 17, Part 2, 332–34.

67. Osborn to James Caird, Esq. (London) Feb. 18, 1863, "President's Letter Book. W.H. Osborn, Nov. 19, 1861–July 1, 1862, Illinois Central Railroad Company MSS., the Newberry Library, "Proceedings of the Legislature...1863," in *Illinois State Journal*, Feb. 20, 1863.

68. *Cincinnati Daily Gazette*, Nov. 9, 1863.

69. *TImes* (London), Mar. 17, 1863; Ibid., Oct. 7, 20, 1863.

CHAPTER IV

1. Presented in part as a paper at the joint session of the Mississippi Valley Historical Association and the Economic History Association at Oklahoma City, Apr. 21, 1950.

2. In handing down the decision in Mann v. Illinois, 94 U.S. 113 (1876), Chief Justice Morrison R. Waite followed the argument of Edward G. Ryan in Pike v. The Chicago, Milwaukee & St. Paul Railway Company, 40 Wis. 583 (1876).

3. *Milwaukee See-Bote,* Oct. 31, 1860. This German-language newspaper, the unofficial organ of German Catholics of Milwaukee and vicinity, continuously reminded its readers that many Republicans had been Know-Nothings. Ekkehard Eickhoff of Braunschweig, Germany, a graduate student and research assistant at Marquette University in 1949–1950, aided the author in examining the editorial columns of the *See-Bote* and other Milwaukee German-language newspapers. The author hereby

expresses his appreciation to Mr. Eickhoff and the University for the aid both have given—one by helping in research and the other by furnishing the helper.

4. Peter L. Johnson, "Port Washington Draft Riot of 1862," *Mid-America* (Chicago), I (Jan. 1930): 212–20.

5. Frederic W. Horn to Governor Alexander Randall, Apr. 18, 1861, Wisconsin Governor's Letters, Civil War Period, Manuscripts (Wisconsin State Historical Society Library, Madison).

6. John L. Stipp, "Economic and Political Aspects of Western Copperheadism" (Ph.D. dissertation, Ohio State University, 1944), confines his study almost wholly to the Copperhead country of Ohio. It is a work which deserves more recognition and circulation.

7. Marcus M. Pomeroy, *Journey of Life: Reminiscences and Recollections of "Brick" Pomeroy* (New York, 1890), 182–94; *LaCrosse (Wis.) Weekly Democrat*, Feb. 10, Mar. 3, 17, 1863.

8. The sectional aspects are emphasized in James D. McCabe (Edward Winslow Martin, pseud.), *History of the Grange Movement: or, The Farmer's War Against Monopolies* (Chicago, 1873), and the easterner's answer is convincingly presented in Charles Francis Adams, Jr., "The Granger Movement," *North American Review* (Boston, New York), 120 (Apr. 1875): 394–424.

9. Clement L. Vallandigham, *Speeches, Addresses, and Letters of Clement L. Vallandigham* (New York, 1864), 211.

10. *Cong. Globe*, 36 Cong., 1 Sess., Appendix, 43.

11. *Chicago Times*, Dec. 10, 1860.

12. Samuel S. Cox, *Puritanism in Politics. Speech of Hon. S.S. Cox, of Ohio, before the Democratic Union Association, Jan. 13, 1863* (New York, 1863).

13. *Cong. Globe*, 36 Cong., 1 Sess., Appendix, 43–44; Vallandigham, *Speeches, Arguments, Addresses, and Letters*, 7.

14. Horn to Governor Randall, Apr. 18, 1861, Wisconsin Governor's Letters, Civil War Period, Manuscripts.

15. *Milwaukee See-Bote*, Apr. 23, 30, Oct. 1, Dec. 15, 1862.

16. Washington McLean, co-owner of the *Cincinnati Enquirer*, was the Democratic boss of Hamilton County, the political ally of Samuel Medary, and political patron of Vallandigham. McLean, always expressing pro-western sentiments, owned several boiler-plate factories and resented the competition of the Pennsylvania interests. Editorial opinions have been adequately examined in Charles R. Wilson, "The Cincinnati Enquirer and Civil War Politics: A Study in Copperhead Opinion" (Ph.D. dissertation, University of Chicago, 1934).

17. O.B. Ficklin, quoted in the *Springfield Illinois State Journal*, Jan. 9, 1863.

18. Illinois *Journal of the House of Representatives, 1863* (Springfield, 1863), 279.

19. *Chicago Daily Tribune*, Jan. 9, 1863.

20. *Indianapolis Indiana Daily State Sentinel*, Jan. 9, 1863.

21. Typical are the claims of the editorial writer of the *Milwaukee See-Bote*, Oct. 1, 1862: "It is the tender yoke of the factory barons, the blessed working of the Puritan oligarchy which now dispose of us. New England is really now our ruler and master; nay it is more—it is the creditor, we are its debtors. To her we are tributary. New England has the bonds in her hands which the other states have to pay....The money monopoly of New England is absolutely controlling and the labor of the others, especially the Western states, is tributary to it."

22. General Superintendent William R. Arthur to William H. Osborn, Apr. 24, 1861, "President's Letter Book, W.H. Osborn," Illinois Central Railroad Company Manuscripts (Newberry Library, Chicago).

23. *Eighth Census of the United States, 1860* (Washington, 1864), *Agriculture*, xxix, xxxi, cxxix, 6–9, 84–87.

24. *Prairie Farmer* (Chicago), 22 (Dec. 27, 1860): 406.

25. Henry C. Hubbart, *The Older Middle West, 1840–1880* (New York, 1936), 82. Those interested in the commercial ties of the West should not bypass such works as Albert L. Kohlmeier, *The Old Northwest as the Keystone of the Arch of the American Federal Union: A Study in Commerce and Politics* (Bloomington, 1938); E. Merton Coulter, "Effects of Secession upon the Commerce of the Mississippi Valley," *Mississippi Valley Historical Review* (Cedar Rapids), III (Dec. 1916): 264–85; Charles R. Wilson, "Cincinnati a Southern Outpost in 1860–1861?" Ibid., 24 (Mar. 1938): 473–82; R.B. Way, "The Commerce of the Lower Mississippi in the Period 1830–1860," *Proceedings of the Mississippi Valley Historical Association* (Cedar Rapids), 10, Pt. I (1920): 57–68; and Thomas S. Berry, *Western Prices before 1861; A Study of the Cincinnati Market* (Cambridge, 1943).

26. *Eighth Census of the United States, 1860, Agriculture*, clviii. Russell H. Anderson, "Agriculture in Illinois During the Civil War Period, 1850–1870" (Ph.D. dissertation, University of Illinois, 1929), contends that probably one fourth of the surplus agricultural produce of the Northwest went southward in the late fifties.

27. *The (Columbia) Crisis*, Nov. 28, 1861; *Cong. Globe*, 37 Cong., 2 Sess., 170.

28. *Carlyle (Ill.) Constitution and Union*, Oct. 3, 1863.

29. *Sheboygan (Wis.) Journal*, Feb. 18, 1862.

30. Illinois *Journal of the House of Representatives, 1863*, p. 279.

31. *The (Columbia) Crisis*, Aug. 15, 1861.

32. *Cong. Globe*, 37 Cong., 2 Sess., 169; Vallandigham, *Speeches, Arguments, Addresses, and Letters*, 326.

33. *The (Columbus) Crisis*, Nov. 28, 1861.

34. Ibid., Oct. 24, 1861; Jan. 23, 1862.

35. *Eighth Census of the United States, 1860, Agriculture*, xli.

36. "Proceedings of the Illinois State Constitutional Convention...January 21, 1862," Springfield *Illinois State Journal*, Jan. 22, 1862.

37. *Cong. Globe*, 37 Cong., 2 Sess., 170.

38. *The (Columbus) Crisis*, Jan. 28, 1863.

39. *Official Records*, Ser. 1, Vol. 17, Pt. 2, 333.

40. Illinois Central Railroad Company, *Annual Report, 1861* (Chicago, 1862).

41. Quoted in *Chicago Times*, June 3, 1863.

42. Vallandigham, *Speeches, Arguments, Addresses, and Letters*, 278.

43. *Chicago Times*, Oct. 31, 1863.

44. Richard Yates, "Message to the Legislature, January 5, 1863," *Chicago Daily Tribune*, Jan. 7, 1863.

45. Osborn to "My dear Sir," Feb. 18, 1863, "President's Letter-Book, W.H. Osborn," Illinois Central Railroad Company Manuscripts.

46. Osborn to David Dowst Company, New York, Feb. 18, 1863, ibid.

47. Osborn to H.V. Poor, New York, Feb. 18, 1863, ibid. The italics are the author's.

48. *Chicago Tribune*, June 5, 1862. Criticism of the *Tribune's* charges was voiced from the floor of the convention. See *Journal of the Constitutional Convention of the State of Illinois convened at Springfield on Jan. 7, 1862* (Springfield, 1862), 941–44.

49. William Butler to Lyman Trumbull, Feb. 4, 1862, Lyman Trumbull Manuscripts (microfilm in Illinois State Historical Society, Springfield).

50. "Proceedings of the Illinois State Constitutional Convention, January 21, 1862," Springfield *Illinois State Journal*, Jan. 22, 1862.

51. Springfield *Illinois State Journal*, Feb. 11, 12, 18, 1862.

52. Ibid., Feb. 6, 1862.

53. Ibid., Jan. 22, 1862. See also D.C. Wilbur, in *Transactions of the Illinois State Agricultural Society, 1861–64* (Springfield, 1865), 631.

54. Ibid.

55. *Journal of the Constitutional Convention of the State of Illinois...1862*, p. 55.

56. Ibid., 593.

57. Osborn's correspondence, [Nov. 19, 1861–July 1, 1862], "President's Letter-Book, W.H. Osborn," Illinois Central Railroad Company Manuscripts, reveals the fears of the road's chief executive and shows the company's interest in the convention's daily deliberations. Osborn's letter of Mar. 12, 1862, to John D. Caton expresses the president's disgust: "To add to our troubles the Constitutional Convention stirs up something every week—and I sometimes wish I could go away as fast as a telegraph message." Another letter of Mar. 12, 1862, to Thomas E. Walker proves that the lobbying activities concerning the Illinois Central constitutional clause were not wholly futile: "The resolution as at first adopted would have been almost fatal to us. D. [Douglas, chief lobbyist for the road] succeeded in getting out the fatal word—and as at last determined we are in the same position we have always been in. I think we may yet improve the resolution, but...[it is] hazardous to touch it." Much earlier Osborn had written the treasurer: "We have muzzled the only mischievous fellow who had appeared thus far." Osborn to Walker, Feb. 7, 1862, ibid. Douglas' lobbying activities on behalf of the road are revealed in "Letter-Book, J.M. Douglas, Attorney, March 6, 1860–January 25, 1864," J.M. Douglas, Out-Letters file, Illinois Central Railroad Company Manuscripts. See especially Douglas to John Barnard, Feb. 19, 1862, ibid.

58. *Journal of the Constitutional Convention of the State of Illinois...1862*, 27; Oliver M. Dickerson, *The Illinois Constitutional Convention of 1862* (Urbana, 1905), 27; *Chicago Times*, June 3, 1862.

59. "Proceedings of the Illinois State Constitutional Convention...January 21, 1862," Springfield *Illinois State Journal*, Jan. 22, 1862.

60. Joseph Medill's paper continued to preach against the "Springfield abomination" which the editor contended was "conceived in sin and brought forth in iniquity." *Chicago Daily Tribune*, June 2, 5, 6, 7, 9, 14, 16, 1862.

61. Osborn to Walker, Mar 19, 1862, "President's Letter-Book, W.H. Osborn," Illinois Central Railroad Company Manuscripts.

62. *Chicago Daily Tribune*, June 17, 1862.

63. *Chicago Times*, June 20, 1862.

64. John F. Tucker to Osborn, June 20, 1862, "President's Letter-Book, W.H. Osborn," Illinois Central Railroad Company Manuscripts.

65. *Chicago Daily Tribune*, June 21, 1862.

66. *Chicago Weekly Journal*, Jan. 16, June 19, 1863; Springfield *Illinois State Journal*, June 16, 1863; *Western Railroad Gazette* (Chicago), 7 (May 30, 1863); *Chicago Tribune*, Feb. 12, 1863.

67. Illinois *Journal of the Senate, 1863* (Springfield, 1863), 70–71.

68. "Proceedings of the Legislature, 1863," summarized in *Springfield Daily Illinois State Journal*, Jan. 14, 1863; *Chicago Weekly Journal*, Feb. 13, 1863; *Illinois Journal of the Senate, 1863*, pp. 89, 193–94, 210–11.

69. *Chicago Weekly Journal*, Feb. 13, 1863; *Chicago Tri-Weekly Tribune*, Feb. 5, 6, 1863.

70. Charles Butler, president of the St. Louis, Alton & Terre Haute, to W.D. Griswold, Jan. 9, 1863, "St. Louis, Alton & Terre Haute Out-Letters," Illinois Central Railroad Company Manuscripts.

71. Edward L. Baker to Amos T. Hall, treasurer, Jan. 17, 1863, "E.L. Baker Out-Letters," Chicago, Burlington & Quincy Railroad Manuscripts (Newberry Library).

72. *Western Railroad Gazette*, 7 (May 30, June 13, 1863).

73. Yates, "Message to the Legislature, January 5, 1863," *Chicago Daily Tribune*, Jan. 7, 1863.

74. *Chicago Daily Tribune*, Jan. 7, Feb. 12, 16, 1863.

75. *Chicago Tri-Weekly Tribune*, Feb. 6, 1863.

76. Illinois *Journal of the House of Representatives, 1863*, pp. 117, 502–3, 681.

77. *Western Railroad Gazette*, 7 (June 13, 1863).

78. *Journal of the Constitutional Convention of the State of Illinois...1862*, p. 438.

79. "Proceedings of the Illinois State Constitutional Convention...January 21, 1862," Springfield *Illinois State Journal*, Jan. 22, 1862.

CHAPTER V, SECTION ONE

1. See Arthur Schlesinger, Jr., *The Age of Jackson*, Boston, 1945; Bray Hammond, *Banks and Politics in America From the Revolution to the Civil War*, Princeton, 1957; Marvin Meyers, *The Jacksonian Persuasion*, Stanford, 1957; Lee Benson, *The Concept of Jacksonian Democracy: New York A Test Case*, Princeton, 1961; Edward Pessen, *Most Uncommon Jacksonians: The Radical Leaders of the Early Labor Movement*, Albany, New York, 1967.

2. Frederick Merk, "Eastern Antecedents of the Grangers," *Agricultural History*, 23 (Jan. 1949): 1–8; Mildred Thorne, "The Grange in Iowa, 1868–1875," *Iowa Journal of History*, 47 (Oct. 1949): 289–324; George Miller, "The Granger Laws," unpublished Ph.D. dissertation, University of Michigan, 1951 and "Origins of the Iowa Granger Law," *Mississippi Valley Historical Review*, 40 (Mar. 1954): 657–80; Earl S. Beard, "The Background of State Regulation in Iowa," *Iowa Journal of History*, 51 (Jan. 1953): 1–36; Lee Benson, *Merchants, Farmers and Railroads*, Cambridge, Mass., 1955; Gabriel Kolko, *Railroads and Regulations, 1877–1916*, Princeton, 1965.

3. Joseph Dorfman, *The Economic Mind in American Civilization, 1606–1865*, New York, 1946, 2 vols.; Bray Hammond, "Banking in the Early West, Monopoly, Prohibition, and Laissez Faire," *Journal of Economic History*, 8 (May 1948): 1–25, and *Banks and Politics in America*; James Roger Sharp, "Banking and Politics in the States: The Democratic Party After the Panic of 1837," unpublished Ph.D. dissertation, University of California, Berkeley, 1966.

4. See Robert Sharkey, *Money, Class, and Party: An Economic Study of Civil War and Reconstruction*, Baltimore, 1959; Irwin Unger, *The Greenback Era: A Social and Political History of American Finance 1865–1879*, Princeton, 1964; Walter T.K. Nugent, *Money and American Society, 1865–1880*, New York, 1968.

5. Thomas P. Govan, "Agrarian and Agrarianism: A Study in the Use and Abuse of Words," *Journal of Southern History*, 30 (Feb. 1964): 35–47.

6. For two studies asserting the "conservative" nature of Copperheadism see: R. Roseboom, "Southern Ohio and the Union in 1863," *Mississippi Valley Historical Review*, 39 (June 1952): 29–44; and the excellent article by Richard O. Curry, "The Union as It Was: A Critique of Recent Interpretation of the Copperheads," *Civil War History*, 13 (Mar. 1967): 25–39. While agreeing with these two articles our intention is to examine the implicit empirical claims of the concept of agrarian radicalism rather than dispute the subjective matter of what is and what is not "radical."

7. *Mississippi Valley Historical Review*, 38 (Mar. 1952): 680. This thesis can be traced to Charles Beard, *The Rise of American Civilization*, New York, 1930, 1:677–78, and Wilfred E. Brinkley, *American Political Parties: Their Natural History*, New York, 1943, 263–68, but it is also found in the revisionist works of Unger and Sharp noted above, both of which refer for support to the thesis of Klement's article.

8. *The Copperheads in the Middle West*, Chicago, 1960, 266.

9. *Journal of the Illinois State Historical Society*, 48 (Autumn 1955): 271–82. (This journal will appear hereafter as *JISHS*.)

10. Klement, "Middle Western Copperheadism and the Genesis of the Granger Movement," 688.

11. Ibid., 275.

12. Jones, "Agrarian Radicalism in Illinois' Constitutional Convention of 1862," 273.

13. Ibid., 275.

14. Miller, "The Granger Laws," 24.

15. Jones, "Agrarian Radicalism in Illinois Constitutional Convention of 1862," 278.

16. Arthur C. Cole, *The Era of the Civil War: The Centennial History of Illinois*, Springfield, 1919, vol. 3:267; O.M. Dickerson, "The Illinois Constitutional Convention of 1862," *University of Illinois Studies*, vol. 1, No. 9 Urbana, Mar. 1905, 391. The figures are from Cole. Different figures appear elsewhere, confusion probably owing to the fusion candidates. At any rate, the Democrats had a commanding majority.

17. *Chicago Tribune* (Nov. 1861).

18. Dickerson, "The Illinois Constitutional Convention of 1862," 392; John Moses, *Illinois, Historical and Statistical*, Chicago, 1892, 655.

19. F. Cyril James, *The Growth of Chicago Banks*, New York, 1938, 1:246–90; Klement, *The Copperheads of the Middle West*, 1–39.

20. Cole, *The Era of the Civil War*, 3:272–82; *Journal of the Constitutional Convention, State of Illinois Convened at Springfield*, Jan. 7, 1862, Springfield, 1862, passim. Hereafter cited as *Journal*.

21. Wood Gray, *The Hidden Civil War: The Story of the Copperheads*, New York, 1942, 80–81.

22. For more of Forrest's mischief see Klement, *Copperheads in the Middle West*, 142–44, 150–52. A report from the committee on Mar 19 cleared all delegates of the charges. *Journal*, 943.

23. Cole, *The Era of the Civil War*, 3:271.

24. Ibid., 270.

25. Ibid., 268; Dickerson, "The Illinois Constitutional Convention of 1862," 3–6.

26. "The inverted triangle which is 'Egypt' rests with its peak at Cairo and its base running from Chester to Carmi. Included in this area in 1860 were sixteen counties, predominantly rural, populated by Southerners by birth or extraction and overwhelmingly Democratic in their political sentiments." Jasper W. Cross, "The Civil War Comes to 'Egypt,'" *JISHS*, 44 (June 1951): 160. This is a somewhat more restricted area than Klement refers to as Egypt.

27. *Chicago Tribune*, Feb. 13, 1862.

28. Klement, *Copperheads in the Middle West*, 267.

29. *History of Gallatin, Salina...and Williamson Counties Illinois*, Chicago, 1887, 845–46; Cross, "The Civil War Comes to 'Egypt,'" 162; Oliver A. Harker, "Fifty Years with Bench and Bar of Southern Illinois," *Transactions of the Illinois State Historical Society for the Year 1920*, 50; Cole, *Era of the Civil War*, 227–28, 400–401, 411; Ernest Ludlow Bogart and Charles Manfred Thompson, *The Industrial State, 1870–1893; Centennial History of Illinois*, Springfield, 1920, 104–54. In these biographical sketches, mention of individuals will usually be cited by the journal, volume, and page number. Author and title of the article in which they appeared will only be cited when of interest.

30. *JISHS*, 6, 243–45; Cole, *Era of the Civil War*, 196; J.M. Hofer, "Development of the Peace Movement in Illinois During the Civil War," *JISHS*, 24 (Apr. 1931): 117.

31. *Biographical Encyclopedia of Illinois*, 331–32; *Chicago Tribune*, Feb. 2, Mar. 7, 1862; "Middle Western Copperheadism," 682; *JISHS*, 8:498.

32. William H. Collins and Cicero F. Perry, *Past and Present of the City Quincy and Adams County*, Illinois, Chicago, 1905, 186; Usher F. Linder, *Reminiscences of the Early Bench and Bar of Illinois*, Chicago, 1879, 244–46; Cole, *Era of the Civil War*, 127, 144, 149, 256, 321; *JISHS*, 5:476, 18:400, 406; Chester McArthur Destler, *American Radicalism, 1865–1901: Essays and Documents*, New York, 1963, 41; *History of Adams County, Illinois*, Chicago, 1879; *Historical Encyclopedia of Illinois*, Chicago, 1920, 1:414. (Hereafter cited as *Hist. Ency.*)

33. *Chicago Tribune*, Jan. 8, 1862.

34. Cole, *Era of the Civil War*, 129. There are numerous mentions of Wentworth in this volume.

35. Don Fehrenbacher, *Chicago Giant*, Madison, 1957, is an excellent biography of Wentworth.

36. *Chicago Post*, Feb. 20, 1861, in Fehrenbacher, *Chicago Giant*, 193.

37. Freemont O. Bennet, *Politics and Politicians of Chicago, Cook County, and Illinois*, Chicago, 1886, 169.

38. *Chicago Tribune*, Jan. 11, 1862.

39. *History of Lee County*, Chicago, 1888, 143, 148; Frank E. Stevens, *History of Lee County*, Chicago, 1914, 1:342; Frank E. Stevens, "Life of Stephen Arnold Douglas," *JISHS*, 16:288–90; *JISHS*, 6:218–19, n. 8, 20:287, 295.

40. Arthur Charles Cole, ed., *The Constitutional Debates of 1847*, Springfield, 1919, 101–3, 808; Sidney Breese to Augustus C. French, Jan. 5 and 17, 1852, the French Papers, Illinois Historical Library; *Journal*, 449.

41. Homer H. Cooper, "The Lincoln-Thornton Debate of 1866 at Shelbyville, Illinois," *JISHS*, 10:101–22; John P. Senning, "The Know Nothing Movement in Illinois," *JISHS*, 7: 21, n. 1; Dickerson, "The Illinois Constitutional Convention of 1862," 405; *Hist. Ency.*, 392.

42. *Hist. Ency.*, 152–53; *Portrait and Bibliographical Album of Sangamon County*, Chicago, 1891, 920; *JISHS*, 2:33–35, 14:235–36.

43. *Biographical Encyclopedia of Illinois of the Nineteenth Century* (Philadelphia, 1875), 344; Josephine Craven Chandler, "The Spoon River Country," *JISHS*, 14:306–15.

44. *Hist. Ency.*, 436–37; *JISHS*, 8:26.

45. Alexander Davidson and Bernard Stuve, *A Complete History of Illinois from 1673 to 1873...*Springfield, 1874, 553–54; Cole, *Era of the Civil War*, 34–35, 55–57, 88–89, 94–98.

46. *Hist. Ency.*, 503; *History of Pike County*, Chicago, 1880, 104–905; *Pike and Calhoun Counties, Illinois*, Chicago, 1881, 188–89.

47. Alfred H. Kelly and Winfred A. Harbison, *The American Constitution: Its Origins and Developments*, New York, 1936, 514.

48. Willard L. King, *Melville Weston Fuller, Chief Justice of the United States, 1888–1910*, Chicago, 1950, 77. King's book is the main source on Fuller although it can be supplemented by *Hist. Ency.*, 179, and Horace Samuel Merrill, *Bourbon Democracy of the Middle West, 1865–1896*, Baton Rouge, 1953, 74–75, 142, 181.

49. *Hist. Ency.*, 68, 202, 351, 371, 409, 496, 543; *History of Greene and Jersey Counties*, Springfield, 1885, 601–2; *History of Alexander, Union and Pulaski Counties*, Chicago, 1883, 489.

50. Cole, *Era of the Civil War*, 103.

51. See Merrill's characterization of the "Bourbons" in *Bourbon Democracy of the Middle West*, 1–4, passim.

52. See Stanley Llewellyn Jones, "Anti–Bank and Anti-Monopoly Movements in Illinois, 1845–1862," unpublished Ph.D. dissertation University of Illinois, 1947, and William

G. Shade, "The Politics of Free Banking in the Old Northwest, 1837–1863," unpublished Ph.D. dissertation, Wayne State University, 1966, passim.

53. Jones, "Anti-Bank and Anti-Monopoly Movements in Illinois, 1845–1862," 177.

54. *Illinois State Register*, July 20, 27, Aug. 13, 16, Oct. 17, 31, and Nov. 17, 1861.

55. *Journal*, 10.

56. Ibid., 51, 130–31, 143, 144–46, 268, 335, 494, 663, 938. Edwards' speeches are in the *Illinois State Register*, Feb. 6 and Mar. 8, 1862.

57. *Journal*, 51, 181–87.

58. Sharkey, *Money, Class and Party*, 101–5; Destler, *American Radicalism*, 8–9, 60, 61, 76; Unger, *The Greenback Era*, 97–101; Alexander Campbell to Salmon P. Chase, June 22, 1861, Chase Papers, Library of Congress; *Journal*, 449. See also Alexander Campbell to Elihu Washburne, Feb. 18, 1863, Washburne Papers, Library of Congress. There is some question concerning Kellogg's influence since their plans while similar had crucial differences. Campbell praised Kellogg in *The True American System of Finance*, 7, but he may not have read this work until sometime after 1861 since he refers to *A New Monetary System* which was the title used on the 1861 reissue of Kellogg's older book, *Labor and other Capital*.

59. *Journal*, 449; *Illinois State Register*, Feb. 15, 1862. The *State Register* was campaigning against both state banks and a federally issued currency at the time.

60. Max Cortis Kelley, "The Greenback Party in Illinois, 1876–1884," unpublished M.A. thesis, University of Illinois, 1926, passim; Unger, *The Greenback Era,* passim; Fred E. Haynes, *Third Party Movements since the Civil War with Special Reference to Iowa: A Study in Social Politics*, New York, 1966 ed., 105–52; A[lexander] Campbell, *The True American System of Finance; The Rights of Labor and Capital and the Common Sense Way of Doing Justice to the Soldiers and Their Families. No Banks: Greenbacks the Exclusive Currency*. Chicago, 1864. Campbell states his plan "contemplates no agrarian or other distribution of property," 3.

61. Thomas Weber, *The Northern Railroads and the Civil War, 1861–65*, New York, 1952, 87–88; Jones, "Agrarian Radicalism," 278; *Tribune*, Jan. 22, 1862.

62. *Journal*, 32, 33, 53, 55, 132–33.

63. *Illinois State Register*, Jan. 17, 28, Feb. 1, 1863.

64. *Journal*, 418–22; Richard Yates to Lyman Trumbull, Feb. 14, 1862, Trumbull Papers, Library of Congress. See also *Illinois State Journal*, Jan. 7 and 14, 1862; J.M. Palmer to Lyman Trumbull, Mar. 26, 1862.

65. Jones, "Agrarian Radicalism," 278.

66. Paul Wallace Gates, *The Illinois Central Railroad and Its Colonization Work*, Cambridge, Mass., 1934, 276–77, 283, 303, 386–89.

67. Klement, "Middle Western Copperheadism," 688–89. The spelling here is from the *Journal*.

68. *Journal*, 88.

69. *Journal*, 131; *Chicago Tribune*, Jan. 23, 1862.

70. *Journal*, 265. His resolution to make bank or railroad presidents ineligible for the state legislature and other public offices was humorously dismissed. Ibid., 879; *Tribune*, Mar. 18, 1862.

71. Cole, *Era of the Civil War*, 270–71.

72. *Journal*, 55.

73. *Biographical Encyclopedia of Illinois*, 96.

74. Jones, "Agrarian Radicalism," 279.

75. *Journal*, 148; Robert E. Cushman, *The Independent Regulatory Commissions*, New York, 1941, 25–26.

76. *Hist. Ency.*, 23–24. One of his brothers became a Granger; another a railroad promoter.

77. *JISHS*, 9, 186, 18, 41; *Quincy Herald* in the *Illinois State Register*, July 20, 1861.

78. *Journal*, 409. Brooks' "warlike and impetuous" newspaper attacks on his political opponents often involved him in "physical combats." In 1860 as a state senator, Brooks resigned his post in an outburst over some minor matter. In the late sixties he was converted to Methodism during a revival, after which a friend noted that he "lost his grip as Democratic editor." *Transactions of the Illinois State Historical Society*, No. 9, 210–11; ibid., no. 13, 158–59.

79. *Quincy Herald* in the *Illinois State Register*, Mar. 27, 1862.

80. *Journal*, 118; *Hist. Ency.*, 202; Cole, *Era of the Civil War*, 270–71.

81. *History of Mercer County*, Chicago, 1882, 887, 909–10. *Journal*, 95, 122, 131–32. Simpson also introduced a resolution dealing with investigation of the Illinois Central's accounts.

82. *Journal*, 112, 795, 1115.

83. Jones, "Agrarian Radicalism," 279; Earl S. Beard, "Local Aid to Railroads in Iowa," *Iowa Journal of History*, Jan. 1952, 1–34; Carter Goodrich, *Government Promotion of American Canals and Railroads, 1800–1890*, New York, 1960, 230–62; Miller, "The Granger Laws," 73–115.

84. Uri Manly to Augustus C. French, Mar. 2, 1851, Elam Rust to French, Apr. 10, 1851, E.B. Ames to French, Mar. 2, 1851, M.E. Lasher to French, Apr. 14, 1851, Elam Rust to French, Nov. 21, 1851, French Papers; *Illinois Legislature. House Journal*, 1849, 2 Sess., 7–16; Cole, *Era of the Civil War*, 35–44.

85. Ibid., 36–41; Gates, *The Illinois Central Railroad*, 21–65; Charles LeRoy Brown, "Abraham Lincoln and the Illinois Central Railroad," *JISHS*, 36 (June 1943): 147–418.

86. Miller, "The Granger Laws," 116–92; Harold D. Woodman, "Chicago Businessmen and the Granger Laws," *Agricultural History*, 36 (Jan. 1962): 16–24.

87. *Journal*, 1092–93.

88. This is basically the structure of Klement's argument. In *Copperheads in the Middle West*, 102, 251, 253, 266, he refers to five Copperheads—William Allen, Henry C. Dean, Dennis Mahoney, Marcus M. Pomeroy, and George H. Pendleton—who were later Greenbackers or "prophets" of Greenbackism. Here he confuses support for the "Ohio Idea" and opposition to the national banks with advocacy of currency expansion. Henry Clay Dean was a strong "hard money" man before the war and there is nothing in *Crimes of the Civil War and the Curse of the Funding System*, Baltimore, 1869, to indicate that he went any further than supporting the payment of the bonds in Greenbacks. He openly attacks the inflation scheme of John Law (412–19) and the paper Assignats (424–29). See also Unger, *The Greenback Era*, 73–85.

89. Gates, *The Illinois Central Railroad*, 249; Gray, *Hidden Civil War*, 57–59, 71, 91. Cole, *Era of the Civil War*, Chapter 12, passim. Klement, *Copperheads in the Middle West*, passim.

90. Gates, *The Illinois Central Railroad*, 9, 12, 13.

91. Ibid., 3–20; Cole, *Era of the Civil War*, 1–12; Richard Lyle Power, *Planting Corn Belt Culture*, Indianapolis, 1853, passim.

92. Cole, *Era of the Civil War*, 270–71.

93. Klement, "Middle Western Copperheadism," 680.

94. Kelley, "The Greenback Party in Illinois, 1876–1884," 52–55.

95. Ibid., 53–55.

96. Alfred W. Newcombe, "Alson J. Streeter—An Agrarian Liberal," *JISHS*, 38 (Dec. 1945): 414–45, 39 (Mar. 1946): 68–95.

97. Kelley, "The Greenback Party in Illinois, 1876–1884," 56–60.

98. Woodman, "Chicago Businessmen and the 'Grange Laws,'" passim.

99. Miller, "The Granger Laws," 146.

100. Ibid., 161. The vote on the 1870 law was 6–1 in favor. Ten counties in the northwest voted 18,309 for and 554 against. In the eleven southernmost counties the total vote was 3,065 for and 2,230 against; Ibid., n. 107, 161. See also 116–20, 128, 136, 140.

101. Paul W. Gates, "Large Scale Farming in Illinois, 1850–1870," *Agricultural History*, 16 (Jan. 1932): 14–25; Harvey L. Carter, "The Origins of Political Patterns in the Older Middle West," an unpublished paper which Professor Carter allowed the authors to read.

102. Solon J. Buck, "Agricultural Organization in Illinois, 1870–1880," *JISHS*, 3:10–23; Roy V. Scott, "Grangerism in Champaign County, Illinois, 1873–1877," *Mid-America*, 43 (July 1961): 141.

103. Paine, "Granger Movement in Illinois," 343. The Patrons of Husbandry had been preceded in Illinois by a State Agricultural Society formed in 1853 and grew "first in the northern and central counties and later in southern Illinois." Cole, *Era of the Civil War*, 78.

104. Solon J. Buck, *The Agrarian Crusade*, New Haven, 1921, 73; Scott, "Grangerism in Champaign County, Illinois, 1873–1877," 149–51.

105. *Alton Tri-Weekly Telegraph*, Nov. 20, 1851, quoted in Jones, "Anti-Bank and Anti-Monopoly Movements in Illinois, 1845–1862," 105.

106. Klement has, for example, effectively criticized the partisan Republican view of Copperheads which emphasizes their treasonable or defeatist attitudes which is often echoed in our textbooks. Gray, *Hidden Civil War*, is a sophisticated example which has recently been re-issued in paperback.

107. David Potter, "Explicit Data and Implicit Assumption," in Louis Gottschalk, ed., *Generalization in the Writing of History*, Chicago, 1963, 191.

CHAPTER V, SECTION TWO

1. Ronald P. Formisano and William G. Shade, "The Concept of Agrarian Radicalism," *Mid-America*, 62 (Jan. 1970): 5.

2. Ibid.

3. Since I do not wish to get into an argument whether Messrs. Formisano and Shade interpreted Stanley L. Jones' article correctly or incorrectly, I am confining my rebuttal to what I have written about midwestern Copperheads and where I believe I have been misrepresented and misinterpreted.

4. Charles H. Coleman, "Copperheads," in *Dictionary of American History*, edited by James T. Adams (5 vols., New York, 1940), 2:57–58.

5. Whitelaw Reid, *Ohio in the War* (2 vols., Columbus, Ohio., 1869) and Horace Greeley, *The American Conflict* (2 vols., Hartford, Conn., 1867) typify the "history" written by patriotic participants.

6. William Dudley Foulke, *Life of Oliver P. Morgan: Including His Important Speeches* (2 vols., Indianapolis, 1897) contributed mightily to the subversive society myth. Morton's role in creating a political bogeyman is exposed in Frank L. Klement, "Carrington and the Golden Circle Legend in Indiana during the Civil War," *Indiana Magazine of History*, 61 (Mar. 1965): 31–52.

7. Constance Robertson, *The Golden Circle* (New York: Random House, 1951) had a midwestern historical setting revolving around the supposed "Northwest Conspiracy" of the Knights of the Golden Circle. William Blake (pseudonym of William J. Blech), *The Copperheads* (New York: Dial Press, 1941) dealt with a New York girl and three suitors, one of whom was a Copperhead (and a member of the Knights of the Golden Circle), while another suitor (the hero) ended up as a special government agent responsible for nullifying the Copperhead and Golden Circle plots to establish a "Northwest Confederacy."

8. James Ford Rhodes, *History of the United States from the Compromise of 1850 to the McKinley-Bryan Campaign of 1896* (7 vols., New York, 1893–1906), 4:227–29, 245–46.

9. Edward Channing, *A History of the United States* (6 vols., New York, 1905–1925), 1:v–vi. The sixth volume, entitled *The War for Southern Independence*, won the Pulitzer Prize in 1925. Channing's *A Student's History of the United States* (New York, 1897), shows to what extent this noted historian was influenced by the nationalistic surge which helped to make the nation a naval and imperialistic power.

10. Randall's views are best expressed in "The Blundering Generation," *Mississippi Valley Historical Review*, 27 (June 1940): 3–28. Craven's contentions are revealed in "The Coming of the War between the States," *Journal of Southern History*, 2 (Aug. 1936): 303–22 and in his classic work, *The Coming of the Civil War* (New York, 1942).

11. Benjamin P. Thomas, *Abraham Lincoln: A Biography* (New York, 1952), 527. Thomas' scholarly and readable book is far and away the best one-volume work. T. Harry Williams tarnished the halos of those who dominated the Joint Committee on the Conduct of War in a book entitled *Lincoln and the Radicals* (Madison, Wis., 1941)—this book evolved out of a doctoral dissertation entitled "The Committee on the Conduct of the War: A Study of Civil War Politics" (University of Wisconsin, 1937). Richard N. Current handled one of the best known of the Radicals rather roughly in a book entitled *"Old Thad" Stevens* (Madison, 1942).

12. Mary Scrugham, *The Peaceable Americans of 1860–61: A Study in Public Opinion* (New York, 1921), ll ff., 25 ff., 64–66, 99, 104, 124–25.

13. Edward Kirkland, *The Peacemakers of 1864* (New York, 1927) received favorable reviews and merits a "revisionist" label.

14. Stuart Mitchell, *Horatio Seymour of New York* (Cambridge, Mass., 1938) was based upon extensive research but reviewers generally were critical of the author's defense of his subject.

15. Earle D. Ross, "Northern Sectionalism in the Civil War Era," *Iowa Journal of History and Politics*, 30 (Oct. 1932): 455–512.

16. Charles H. Coleman and Paul H. Spence, "The Charleston Riot, Mar 28, 1864," *Journal of the Illinois State Historical Society*, 33 (Mar. 1940): 7–56.

17. Arthur M. Schlesinger, Jr., "The Causes of the Civil War: A Note on Historical Sentimentalism," *Partisan Review*, 16 (Oct. 1949): 969–81, is an interesting assault upon revisionism. Schlesinger, who saw U.S. participation in World War II as a moral crusade against Nazism and Fascism, envisioned the Civil War as a moral crusade against slavery—historians need not apologize for moral crusades or wars in behalf of freedom.

18. Wood Gray, *The Hidden Civil War: The Story of the Copperheads* (New York, 1942), 24. Singing "Remember Pearl Harbor" and waving the flag vigorously, Wood Gray added: "The assessment of these men is not simply an effort to pass moral judgment on individuals long dead and almost forgotten. They were a type that has appeared repeatedly in our history and which we may encounter in times to come. Narrow, clinging to prejudice as though it were principle, capable of plausible but twisted logic, they necessitate a constant vigilance in any period that they may be identified and combated. It is a mark by which they may be known that they appeal always to the basest and most selfish instincts, and call pandering to such motives wisdom."

19. George Fort Milton, *Abraham Lincoln and the Fifth Column* (New York, 1942). Despite the publisher's claims that Milton "made an exhaustive study of the pertinent material in the National Archives" the book was based upon cursory research and belongs in the same pseudo-historical limbo as James Horan, *Confederate Agent: A Discovery in History* (New York, 1954).

20. Commager, quoted on the dust-jacket of Milton, *Abraham Lincoln and the Fifth Column*.

21. Homer S. Cummings, quoted on the dust jacket of Milton's *Abraham Lincoln and the Fifth Column.*

22. Stampp's book, *Indiana Politics during the Civil War* (Indianapolis, 1949), evolved out of a doctoral dissertation begun before World War II in Professor William B. Hesseltine's seminar. In an article entitled "The Milligan Case and the Election of 1864 in Indiana," *Mississippi Valley Historical Review*, 31 (June 1944): 41–58, Stampp ripped off the cloak Governor Morton wore when posing as patriotism personified.

23. Gilbert R. Tredway, "Indiana against the Administration, 1861–1865" (Ph.D. dissertation, Indiana University, 1962), 397.

24. Frank L. Klement, *The Copperheads in the Middle West* (Chicago, 1960), 1.

25. The socio-economic aspect of Copperheadism in Ohio was earlier expounded by John L. Stipp in his doctoral dissertation, "Economic and Political Aspects of Western Copperheadism" (Ohio State University, 1944).

26. Clement L. Vallandigham, in *Congressional Globe*, 37th Congress, 3rd session, "Appendix," 58.

27. "I became and am a *Western sectionalist*," Vallandigham once said, "and so shall continue to the day of my death." Milligan's devotion to the West and the principle of states rights is best revealed in his famous speech of Aug. 13, 1864. See Darwin Kelley, ed., "Lambdin P. Milligan's Appeal for States Rights and Constitutional Liberty during the War," *Indiana Magazine of History*, 66 (Sept. 1970): 263–83.

28. Klement, *The Copperheads in the Middle West*, 6.

29. Emancipation, Professor Curry emphasized, was not the political issue in West Virginia which it had been in the upper Midwest.

30. Curry, *Blueprint for Modern America...*, 33–34.

31. Solon J. Buck, *Granger Movement: A Study of Agricultural Organization and Its Political, Economic, and Social Manifestations, 1870–1880* (Cambridge: Harvard University Press, 1913) emphasized the antirailroad activities of the Grange. Edward W. Martin has the latest book on the Grangers. Martin thinks the antirailroad activities of the Grangers have been overemphasized.

32. Clarence L. Barnhart, ed., *The American College Dictionary* (text edition, New York, 1948), 998.

33. Klement, "Middle Western Copperheadism and the Genesis of the Granger Movement," *M.V.H.R.*, 38 (Mar. 1952): 690.

34. Professor John D. Hicks defined "the Granger idea" as "that the state should regulate the railroads, if necessary to the point of fixing minimum rates"—Hicks, *A Short History of American Democracy* (Boston, 1943), 457.

35. In their article, "The Concept of Agrarian Radicalism," Messrs. Formisano and Shade not only misspelled Reilly's name but misrepresented my characterization of the voluble fellow. In my article "Middle Western Copperheadism and the Genesis of the Granger Movement," I characterized Reilly as "the miller who spoke for the farmers of Randolph County" (pages 688–89). Messrs. Formisano and Shade (page 20 of their article) wrote: "Reily was a miller, who Klement believes spoke for the farmers of southern Illinois."

To point out all errors of misrepresentation would tend to transform a historiographical debate into an exercise in quibbling. Two more examples of misrepresentation, therefore, will suffice:

(1) On page 11 of their article Messrs. Formisano and Shade stated: "Categorizing [James Washington] Singleton as an 'agrarian radical' divests the term of any meaning." I agree, for I never categorized Singleton as an "agrarian radical" neither in my Copperhead book nor in the article "Middle Western Copperheadism and the Genesis of the Granger Movement." And as stated earlier, I never used the term in either work. Yet their implication is there, black on white.

(2) On page 9 (footnote no. 26), Messrs. Formisano and Shade misrepresent my interpretation of the term "Egypt." They took their definition of "Egypt" from Jasper V. Cross,

"The Civil War Comes to 'Egypt,'" *Journal of the Illinois State Historical Society,* 44 (June 1951): 160 and it read: "The inverted triangle which is 'Egypt' rests with its peak at Cairo and its base running from Chester to Carmi. Included in this area in 1860 were sixteen counties, predominantly rural, populated by Southerners by birth or extraction and overwhelmingly Democratic in their political sentiments." This is exactly my definition/characterization of Egypt. It is incorrect, therefore, for Messrs. Formisano and Shade to add: "This is a somewhat more restricted area than Klement refers to as Egypt." Since I did not use the term "Egypt" in the text of my article "Middle Western Copperheadism and the Genesis of the Granger Movement" (although the term appeared twice in one of Reilly's quotations which I used), Messrs. Formisano and Shade misread my mind. I used the terms "downstate Democrats" or "downstate delegates" repeatedly, but I do not regard these terms as synonymous with "Egypt."

36. "Proceedings of the Illinois State Constitutional Convention, January 21, 1862," published in the *(Springfield) Illinois State Journal,* Jan. 22, 1862.

37. Ibid., Feb. 11, 12, 18, 1862.

38. Ibid., Feb. 6, 1862.

39. Ibid., Jan. 22, 1862. Also see D.C. Wilbur, in *Transactions of the Illinois State Agricultural Society, 1861–64* (Springfield, 1865), 631.

40. *Journal of the Constitutional Convention of the State of Illinois Convened at Springfield on Jan. 7, 1862* (Springfield, 1862), 148.

41. "Proceedings of the Illinois State Constitutional Convention...January 21, 1862," *(Springfield) Illinois State Journal,* Jan. 22, 1862.

42. *Journal of the Constitutional Convention of the State of Illinois...1862,* 27.

43. *Chicago Times,* June 20, 1862.

44. Letter, John F. Tucker to William H. Osborn (president of the Illinois Central RR Company), June 20, 1862, in "President's Letter-Book," W.H. Osborn, Illinois Central Rail Road Company MSS., Newberry Library.

45. State of Illinois, *Journal of the Senate, 1863* (Springfield, 1863), 70–71.

46. "Proceedings of the Legislature, 1863," summarized in the *(Springfield) Illinois State Journal,* Jan. 14, 1863; *Chicago Weekly Journal,* Feb. 13, 1863; State of Illinois, *Journal of the Senate, 1863,* 89, 193–94, 210–11.

47. State of Illinois, *Journal of the House of Representatives, 1863* (Springfield, 1863), 117, 502–3, 681.

48. *(Chicago) Western Railroad Gazette,* June 13, 1863.

49. See Frederick Merk, "Eastern Antecedents of the Grangers," *Agricultural History,* 23 (Jan. 1949): 1–8.

50. *Journal of the Constitutional Convention of the State of Illinois...1862,* 438.

51. Klement, "Middle Western Copperheadism and the Genesis of the Granger Movement," *M.V.H.R.,* 38 (Mar. 1952): 694.

CHAPTER VI

1. Lawrence J. McCaffrey, *The Irish Diaspora in America* (Washington, D.C., 1984), 92.

2. *The Poetical Works of Charles G. Halpine [Miles O'Reilly],* edited by Robert B. Roosevelt (New York, 1869), 289.

3. Letter, Horn to Governor Alexander Randall, Apr. 18, 1861, in Civil War Governors' Letters, 1861–1865, Wisconsin State Historical Society, Madison.

4. Dennis A. Mahony, *The Prisoner of State* (New York, 1863), 30.

5. *Dubuque Herald,* May 18, 1861.

6. Darwin Kelley, *Milligan's Fight Against Lincoln* (New York, 1973) emphasized the Indiana Copperheads' straight-laced constitutionalism.

7. Letter, Matt Martin to Samuel Cox, Dec. 3, 1861, in Samuel Sullivan Cox Papers (microfilm), Hayes Memorial Library, Fremont, Ohio.

8. *Dubuque Herald*, Nov. 23, 1861.

9. Cincinnati employers had paid Irish boathands forty dollars a month; the "contrabands" received thirty. See Wilson H. Lofton, "Northern Labor and the Negro during the Civil War," *Journal of Negro History*, 34 (July 1949): 251-73.

10. *Times* (London), July 15, 1863. The reporter, William H. Russell, was a world-renowned newsman, due to his stories about the Crimean War. He was the author of *My Diary North and South* (2 vols.; London, 1863), an invaluable Civil War source.

11. *Cincinnati Daily Enquirer*, July 15, 1862.

12. *Cincinnati Gazette*, July 16, 1862; *Cincinnati Daily Enquirer*, July 16, 17, 1862.

13. *Catholic Telegraph* (n.d.), quoted in Bucyrus *Weekly Journal*, Aug. 14, Sept. 18, 1863. Archbishop Purcell's support of the war is treated in scholarly fashion in Anthony Deye, "Archbishop John Baptiste Purcell and the Civil War" (Ph.D. dissertation, University of Notre Dame, 1944).

14. The antiwar movement in southwestern Ohio is discussed and analyzed in Frank L. Klement, "Sound and Fury: Civil War Dissent in the Cincinnati Area," in *Cincinnati Historical Society*, 35 (Summer 1977): 99–114. On election day, Oct. 13, 1863, Archbishop Purcell went to the polls to cast his ballot publicly for John Brough rather than the Democratic gubernatorial candidate, Clement L. Vallandigham.

15. Two studies of Dennis A. Mahony as a dissenter deserve mention. Mercedes Maloney, "With Malice Toward One: Dennis A. Mahony During the Civil War" (M.A. essay, Marquette University, 1979) is perceptive and scholarly. Hubert H. Wubben, "Dennis Mahony and the *Dubuque Herald*, 1860–1863, "*Iowa Journal of History*, 56 (Oct. 1958), 289–320, treats its subject in a rather cursory fashion.

16. *Dubuque Herald*, May 18, June 5, 14, 1861; Mahony, *The Prisoner of State*, 46–109.

17. Mahony incorporated Stanton's order of Aug. 8, 1862, in his book, *The Prisoner of State*, 111–12.

18. The detailed story of Mahony's arrest is included in his strange book, *The Prisoner of State* as well as in John A. Marshall, American Bastile: *A History of the Illegal Arrests and Imprisonment of American Citizens during the Late Civil War* (Philadelphia, 1878), 403–16.

19. Mahony, *The Prisoner of State*, 404.

20. Letter, Annie to Charles Taylor, Oct. 22, 1862, quoted in Arnold M. Shankman, *The Pennsylvania Antiwar Movement*, 1861–1865 (Rutherford, N.J., 1980), 103–4.

21. *See-Bote*, Apr. 9, 16, 23, 30, June 4, 1862.

22. Alfons J. Beitzinger, "The Father of Copperheadism in Wisconsin," *Wisconsin Magazine of History*, 39 (Sept. 1955): 17–35, analyzes Ryan's role as a Lincoln critic.

23. *See-Bote*, Aug. 19, Sept. 16, 1863.

24. Ibid., Oct. 25, 1862.

25. Rev. Francis Fulleder, an Austrian-born priest, quoted in Peter Leo Johnson, "Port Washington Draft Riot of 1862," *Mid-America*, new series, 1 (Jan. 1930): 220.

26. Lawrence H. Larson, "Draft Riot in Wisconsin, 1862, "*Civil War History*, 7 (Dec. 1961): 421-27, is short on analysis. John W. Oliver, "Draft Riots in Wisconsin during the Civil War," *Wisconsin Magazine of History*, 2 (Mar. 1919): 334–37 is both brief and superficial. So is Lynn I. Schoonover, "A History of the Civil War Draft in Wisconsin" (M.A. thesis, University of Wisconsin, 1915). The best narrative, devoid of interpretation, is the account in *History of Washington and Ozaukee Counties* (Chicago, 1881), 306–66, 493–96.

27. Both Lincoln's proclamation of Sept. 24, 1862, and Secretary of War Stanton's of Aug. 8, 1862, are given in full in Mahony, *The Prisoner of State*, 111–14. Lincoln's proclamation suspending the writ of habeas corpus is in *The Collected Works of Abraham Lincoln*, edited by Roy Basler (9 vols.; New Brunswick, N.J., 1953), 6:436-37.

28. (Madison) *Wisconsin Patriot*, Dec. 23, 1862. The case bore the name of Nicholas Kemp, one of the rioters, for whom Ryan had sought a writ of habeas corpus.

29. *In Re Kemp*, 16 Wisconsin 396 (1863); [Appleton's] *Annual Cyclopedia and Register of Important Events...1863* (New York, 1864), 469–70.

30. Letter, Edward Bates to Edwin M. Stanton, Jan. 31, 1863, in Edwin M. Stanton Papers, Library of Congress.

31. William V. Shannon, *The American Irish: A Political and Social Portrait* (New York, 1966), 59.

32. Lincoln, "To Whom It May Concern" (no date), in *The Collected Works of Abraham Lincoln*, 8:428. Mary Denis Maher, *To Bind the Wounds: Catholic Sister Nurses in the U.S. Civil War* (Westport, Conn., 1989) details the merciful work of the sisters who were nurses.

33. Cpl. Felix Brannigan, 74th New York Volunteer Regiment, quoted in Benjamin Quarles, *The Negro in the Civil War* (Boston, 1953), 31.

34. Letter, Thomas Dudley to John J. Crittenden, Dec. 8, 1862, John J. Crittenden Papers, Library of Congress.

35. Adam Gurowski, *Diary...From March 4, 1861 to November 2, 1865* (3 vols.; Boston, 1862–1866), 2:60. Gurowski was not a Democrat, but an ally of Radical Republicans and a critic of Lincoln.

36. *Dubuque Democratic Herald*, Jan. 3, 8, 1863. Because of legal complications the *Herald* became the *Democratic Herald*.

37. Ibid., Jan. 10, 1863.

38. *Metropolitan Record*, Jan. 3, 10, 1863, quoted in Joseph George, Jr., "A Catholic Family Newspaper' Views the Lincoln Administration: John Mullaly's Copperhead Weekly," *Civil War History*, 24 (June 1978): 20.

39. Mullaly, quoted in the *New York Herald*, May 19, 1863.

40. *See-Bote*, Jan. 6, 13, 20, 1863.

41. Ibid., Feb. 11, Mar. 25, Apr. 30, 1863.

42. *Metropolitan Record*, Mar. 14, 1863, quoted in George, "'A Catholic Family Newspaper'...," 122.

43. Robert Harper, *Lincoln and the Press* (New York, 1951), 127.

44. Mahony, *The Prisoner of State*, iii–iv.

45. *The American Heritage Dictionary* (Boston, 1992), 415.

46. Frank L. Klement, *Dark Lanterns: Secret Political Societies, Conspiracies, and Treason Trials in the Civil War* (Baton Rouge, 1984) has separate chapters dealing with the so-called Copperhead secret societies (Knights of the Golden Circle, Order of the American Knights, and Sons of Liberty) as well as one on the Union Leagues.

47. Shannon, *The American Irish*, 57.

48. *New York Herald*, July 13, 1863.

49. Report, Col. Robert Nugent to Provost Marshal Gen. James B. Fry, July 9, 1863, cited in Adrian Cook, *The Armies of the Streets: The New York City Draft Riots of 1863* (Lexington, Ky., 1974), 54.

50. *New York Herald*, July 14, 1863.

51. Ibid.; [Appleton's] *Annual Cyclopedia . . . 1863*, 811.

52. Herman Melville, "The House-Top: A Night Piece (July, 1863)" in *The Works of Herman Melville* (16 vols.; London, 1924), 16:64.

53. *New York Herald*, July 18–23, 1863; *New York Evening News*, July 13, 1863; Orestes Brownson, "Catholics and the Anti-Draft Riots," *Brownson's Review*, 3rd series, 4 (Oct. 1863): 386; Albon P. Man, Jr., "The Church and the New York City Draft Riots of 1863," *Records of the American Catholic Historical Society of Philadelphia*, 62 (Mar. 1951): 48.

54. Letter, Seymour to Archbishop Hughes, July 13, 1863, published in Cook, op. cit., 106.

55. Archbishop Hughes' letter, dated July 15, 1863, published in *New York Herald*, July 15, 1863.

56. The flyer, addressed "To the Men of New York, Who Are Now Called in Many of the Papers 'Rioters'," dated July 15, 1863, in [Appleton's] *Annual Cyclopedia . . . 1863*, 815–16.

57. *New York Herald*, July 17, 1863.

58. Cook, op. cit., is the best single account. It is excellent as to description but rather weak on interpretation. Iver Bernstein, *The New York City Draft Riots: Their Significance for American Society and Politics in the Age of the Civil War* (New York, 1989), has two chapters summarizing the events of July 13–16, while the last five chapters render a challenging socio-economic analysis. Ernest A. McKay, *The Civil War and New York City* (Syracuse, 1990), gives considerable attention to the riots.

59. *New York Herald*, Aug. 20–26, 1863; James A. Frost, "The Home Front in New York During the Civil War," *New York History*, 41 (July 1961): 289.

60. Shankman, op. cit., 148.

61. This included two state gubernatorial elections in which President Lincoln had an intense interest. "Copperhead candidates," Clement L. Vallandigham and George W. Woodward, lost in Ohio and Pennsylvania respectively.

62. *Indianapolis Daily Journal*, Aug. 22, 23, Oct. 8, 19, 1864.

63. "The Proceedings of the Military Commission Convened in Indianapolis" are in the General Courts-Martial Records, in the Records of the Office of the Judge Advocate General, National Archives. The other three sentenced to be hanged with Milligan were William A. Bowles of French Lick, Andrew Humphreys of Linton, and Stephen Horsey of Martin County.

64. The Milligan story is recounted in Frank L. Klement, "The Indianapolis Treason Trials and *Ex Parte Milligan*" (Chapter V), in Michael R. Belknap, (ed.), *American Political Trials* (Westport, Conn., 1981), 101–37.

65. Letter, Governor Richard Yates, William Butler, O.M. Hatch, and Jesse K. Dubois to President Lincoln, Mar. 1, 1863, in Robert Todd Lincoln Papers, Library of Congress.

66. Testimony of William Hull, Edward Thomas Courtney, and William Remington, Feb. 14, Mar. 1–3, 1865, before the Cincinnati Military Commission, published in *House Executive Documents*, 39th Congress, 2nd session, 263–66, 292–301, 319–21.

67. *Chicago Daily Tribune*, Nov. 7–9, 1863; William A. Bross, *Biographical Sketch of the Late General B.J. Sweet [and] History of Camp Douglas: A Paper Read Before the Chicago Historical Society, June 18, 1878* (Chicago, 1878). Also see Chapter VII, "The Camp Douglas Conspiracy and the Cincinnati Treason Trial," in Klement, *Dark Lanterns*, 187–217.

68. Stephen Z. Starr, *Colonel Grenfell's Wars: The Life of a Soldier of Fortune* (Baton Rouge, 1971), details Grenfell's role in the "conspiracy"; Starr believes that a conspiracy actually existed. Also see Starr, "Was There a Northwest Conspiracy?" *Filson Club, Historical Quarterly*, 38 (Sep. 1964): 328–41. Klement, *Dark Lanterns*, 187–217, discredits and debunks the so-called conspiracy.

CHAPTER VII

1. *Congressional Globe*, 36 Cong., 2 sess., "Appendix," 168.

2. *Hastings Democrat*, Dec. 10, 1859; *Dayton Daily Empire*, Dec. 17, 1859.

3. *The Record of Hon. C.L. Vallandigham on Abolition, the Union, and the Civil War* (Columbus, 1863), 51.

4. *Dayton Daily Empire*, Mar. 16, 1860; *Cong. Globe*, 35 Cong., 2 sess., Part III, 2320; *Political Debates between Hon. Abraham Lincoln and Hon. Stephen A. Douglas...* (Columbus, 1860), 71–72.

5. Reynolds entitled his tract *'The Balm of Gilead': An Inquiry into the Right of American Slavery* (Belleville, Ill., 1860). The Rev. Walther's treatise is well analyzed in Joel S. Torstenson, "The Attitude of the Lutheran Church toward Slavery" (M.A. thesis, University of Minnesota, 1940).

6. Democrat Thomas W. McNeeley (delegate from Cass and Menard Counties), in "Proceedings of the Illinois State Constitutional Convention...1862," published in the (Springfield) *Illinois State Register,* Feb. 13, 1862.

7. *Cong. Globe*, 36 Cong., 1 sess., "Appendix," 43; Samuel S. Cox, *Puritanism and Politics: Speech before Democratic Union Association, January 3, 1863* (New York, 1863), passim. Vallandigham publicly boasted that he was a "good Western fireeater" and an outspoken "Western sectionalist."

8. *(Chicago) Western Railroad Gazette*, Apr. 25, 1863; *Cincinnati Daily Commercial*, Jan. 15, 1862; *Indianapolis State Sentinel,* Jan. 15, 1862. Erin Township, Washington County, Wisconsin, contained a one hundred percent Irish-American population. Prior to 1859, there was not a single vote cast by any but a Democrat when it could be claimed as a party test. In 1860 the solid Democrat phalanx was broken for the first time, 182 votes being cast for Douglas, and one for Lincoln. The tally-clerks ruled the vote for Lincoln invalid--the voter obviously had made a mistake! In the election of 1864 Lincoln received two votes, and the two were counted.

9. *Times* (London), Dec. 1, 1863. "The jealousy of the Low German and Irish against the free negro," wrote the touring reporter for the *Times*, "was sufficient to set them against the war which would have brought four million of their black rivals into competition for that hard and dirty work which American freedom bestowed of them."

10. Samuel P. Heintzelman, "Journal," entry of Oct. 20, 1864, Samuel P. Heintzelman Papers, Library of Congress. Heintzelman watched a Democratic rally in the Ohio backwoods, and noted that many of the women wore riding skirts "so old, rusty, ragged, & dirty, they might have belonged to their grandmothers." A historian put the historical microscope upon the Democratic counties of Ohio and concluded that the anti-Lincoln country was characterized by smaller homesteads, poorer soils and more widespread illiteracy. See John Stipp, "Economic and Political Aspects of Western Copperheadism" (Ph.D. dissertation, Ohio State University, 1942). The conflict of Southern and Yankee culture is admirably treated in Richard L. Powers, *Planting Corn Belt Culture: The Impress of the Upland Southerner and Yankee in the Old Northwest* (Indianapolis, 1953).

11. Adam Gurowski, *Diary...from March 4, 1861, to November 2, 1862* (Boston, 1862), 23.

12. Gideon Welles, *Diary of Gideon Welles, Secretary of the Navy under Lincoln and Johnson,* ed. by John T. Morse (3 vols., Boston, 1911), 1:89-90.

13. Letter, M.S. Shuck to "Dear Cousin," July 4, 1862, M.S. Shuck Papers, Filson Club Library, Louisville.

14. *Detroit Free Press*, Aug. 6, 1861.

15. *Official Records of the Union and Confederate Armies* (128 vols., Washington, 1890–1901), Series 1, 2:466–67.

16. Letter, Joshua F. Speed to Joseph Holt, Sept. 7, 1861, Joseph Holt Papers, Library of Congress.

17. Letter, Ben Wade to Z. Chandler, Sept. 23, 1861, Zachariah Chandler Papers, Library of Congress; *Chatfield Republican*, Sept. 28, Oct. 26, 1861; *Cincinnati Gazette*, Nov. 8, 1861; *St. Louis Democrat*, Nov. 9, 1861.

18. *Indianapolis State Sentinel*, Sept. 9, Oct. 22, 1861; *Chatfield Democrat*, Sept. 21, Oct. 19, 1861; *Louisville Journal*, Sept. 14, 1861; *Detroit Free Press*, Sept. 19, Oct. 4, 25, 1861; Charles Mason, "Diary," entries of Sept. 8, Oct. 20, Nov. 7, Charles Mason Papers, State Department of History and Achives, Iowa State History Library.

19. *La Crosse Weekly Democrat*, Sept. 20, 27, Oct. 11, Nov. 15, Dec. 13, 1861. The editor was Marcus Mills "Brick" Pomeroy. Later in the war Pomeroy became the most

notorious and ill-tempered of all of Lincoln's critics. Pomeroy's role as critic of President Lincoln has been treated in two historical articles: (1) Frank L. Klement, "'Brick' Pomeroy: Copperhead and Curmudgeon," *Wisconsin Magazine of History*, 35 (Winter 1951): 106–13, 156–57. (2) Frank L. Klement, "A Small-Town Editor Criticizes Lincoln: A Study in Editorial Abuse," *Lincoln Herald*, 55 (Summer 1952): 27–32, 60.

20. Letter, John W. Kees to S.S. Cox, Apr. 12, 1861, Samuel Sullivan Cox Papers (microfilm copy), Hayes Memorial Library, Fremont, Ohio.

21. *Circleville Watchman*, Apr. 18, 1862.

22. *Oshkosh Courier*, Feb. 21, 1862.

23. *Cong. Globe*, 37 Cong., 2 sess., 903–7, 1112; ibid., "Appendix," 69; *Detroit Free Press*, March 8, 1862; *Indianapolis State Sentinel*, Mar. 15, 1862; letter, O.H. Bentrick to Joseph A. Wright, Mar. 13, 1862, Joesph A. Wright Papers, Indiana Division, Indiana State Library.

24. Clement L. Vallandigham et al., "Address of the Democratic Members of Congress to the Democracy of the United States" (Washington, D.C., Apr. 9, 1862), passim.

25. *(Milwaukee) See-Bote*, Apr. 23, 1862.

26. "Report of the Democratic State Convention, 1862" (Columbus, July 4, 1862), in Samuel Medary Papers, Ohio Historical Society.

27. *Indianapolis State Sentinel*, July 7, 14, 15, 18, 25, 1862; *The (Columbus) Crisis*, July 9, 16, 30, 1862; *Dubuque Herald*, July 18, 1862.

28. *Cincinnati Daily Commercial*, July 10, 11, 16, 17, 1862; *Cincinnati Daily Enquirer*, July 10–12, 1862; *Circleville Watchman*, July 18, Sept. 26, 1862; *Detroit Free Press*, July 25, Sept. 5, 1862. The Cincinnati riot is treated briefly in Williston H. Lofton, "Northern Labor and the Negro during the Civil War," *Journal of Negro History*, 34 (July 1949): 251–73.

29. *Official Records*, Ser. 1, 14:333–34; *(Milwaukee) See-Bote*, May 21, 1862; *Detroit Free Press*, May 17, 1862; *Dubuque Herald*, May 21, 29, 1862; *Chatfield Democrat*, May 24, 1862; *Faribalt Central Republican*, May 28, 1862; *St. Cloud Democrat*, May 29, 1862; letter, H.S. Bundy to Ben Wade, May 20, 1862, Benjamin F. Wade Papers, Library of Congress.

30. Calvin Fletcher, "Diary," entry July 14, 1862, Calvin Fletcher Papers, Indiana State Historical Society.

31. Roy P. Basler, ed., *The Collected Works of Abraham Lincoln* (9 vols., 1953), 5:327–28, 388–89; *New York Tribune*, Aug. 19, 1862.

32. *Louisville Journal*, Sept. 25, 1862; *Chatfield Democrat*, Sept. 27, 1862.

33. *Indianapolis State Sentinel*, Sept. 24, 1862; *Cincinnati Daily Enquirer*, Sept. 24, 1862.

34. Letter, W.R. Hanley to J.J. Crittenden, Oct. 3, 1862, John J. Crittenden Papers, Library of Congress.

35. *Canton (Ohio) Stark County Democrat*, Sept. 24, 1862.

36. *Dayton Daily Empire*, Oct. 18, 1862; *Indianapolis State Sentinel*, Oct. 16, 1862.

37. *Dayton Daily Empire*, Oct. 25, 1862.

38. *(Springfield) Illinois State Register*, Nov. 5, 1862.

39. Letter, Thomas Dowling to John J. Crittenden, Dec. 1, 1862, Crittenden Papers; *Milwaukee Banner & Volksfreund*, Nov. 12, 19, 1862; *Hamilton True Telegraph*, Oct. 30, Nov. 14, 1862. Two historical articles deal with the repudiation theme; see Harry E. Pratt, "The Repudiation of LIncoln's War Policy in 1862--Stuart-Swett Congressional Campaign," *Journal of the Illinois State Historical Society*, 24 (Apr. 1931): 129–40, and Winfred A. Harbison, "The Election of 1862 as a Want of Confidence in President Lincoln," *Papers of the Michigan Academy of Sciences, Arts, and Letters* (1930), 499–513. Some Republicans publicly admitted that Lincoln's preliminary proclamation of emancipation brought forth unfavorable election returns. See William T. Coggeshall "Diary," entry of Jan. 2, 1863, William T. Coggeshall Papers, Ohio Historical Society;

letter, Issac Welsh to Ben Wade, Jan. 31, 1863, Wade Papers; *CIncinnati Daily Commercial*, Oct. 3, 1862; letter, Richard Smith to Samuel P. Chase, Nov. 7, 1862, Samuel P. Chase Papers, Library of Congress.

40. Letter, John Reynolds to Lyman C. Draper, Nov. 8, 1862, Lyman C. Draper Papers, State Historical Society of Wisconsin.

41. Letter, Thomas Dudley to John J. Crittenden, Dec. 8, 1862, Crittenden Papers.

42. *Lexington Observer* (n.d.), quoted in *Indianapolis State Sentinel*, Dec. 17, 1862.

43. *Dayton Daily Empire*, Dec. 5, 1862.

44. *The Crisis*, Dec. 31, 1862; George B. Smith, final entry in "Diary, 1862," George B. Smth Papers, State Historical Society of Wisconsin.

45. *Dubuque Herald*, Jan. 1, 1863.

46. *(Springfield) Illinois State Journal*, Jan. 3, 1863; *St. Cloud Democrat*, Feb. 26, 1863; *New York Tribune*, Jan. 23, 1863.

47. William O. Stoddard, Jr., ed., *Lincoln's Third Secretary: The Memoirs of William O. Stoddard* (New York, 1955), 170.

48. *Louisville Democrat* (n.d), quoted in *Dayton Daily Empire*, Jan. 7, 1863.

49. *Cong. Globe*, 37 Cong., 3 sess., 130; C.L. Vallandigham, *Speeches, Arguments, Addresses, and Letters of Clement L. Vallandigham* (New York, 1864), 438; *The Crisis*, Jan. 28, 1863.

50. *Ashland (Ohio) Union*, Jan. 7, 1863.

51. *Chatfield Democrat*, Jan. 10, 1863.

52. *Sheboygan Journal*, May 7, 1863.

53. *Green Bay Advocate*, Mar. 3, 1863.

54. *Oshkosh Courier*, Jan. 1, Oct. 31, 1863.

55. *The Crisis*, Jan. 8, 15, 22, Feb. 5, 19, 26, 1863.

56. *Dubuque Democratic Herald*, Jan. 3, 8, 10, 1863.

57. *Dayton Daily Empire*, Jan. 3, 5, 7, 10, 16, 24, 1863.

58. Letter, Thomas O. Lowe to "Dear WIll" (brother), Jan. 23, 1863, Thomas O. Lowe Papers, Dayton and Montgomery County Public Library.

CHAPTER VIII

1. On Sept. 9, 1970, I talked about Democrats as critics of the Lincoln administration to members of the Hamilton Civil War Round Table. After the meeting an elderly gentleman came up to me and stated that his grandfather's name was Clement Laird Vallandigham Horn and that his grandfather was born on the afternoon of Jan. 1, 1863. He added that the day was "bitter cold," the coldest day of that winter.

2. The Third Session lasted from Dec. 1, 1862, to Mar. 3, 1863. Chapter VII (pages 86–110) of my book *The Limits of Dissent: Clement L. Vallandigham and the Civil War* (Lexington, Ky., 1970) is entitled "Gadfly" and it treats in detail Vallandigham's role in Congress.

3. *Journal of the House of Representatives of the State of Ohio* (Columbus, 1847), 40–42.

4. *Congressional Globe*, 36 Congress, 2nd session, 220, 237–42, 279–80.

5. Letter, Clement L. Vallandigham to Richard K. Hendrickson et al., May 13, 1861, published in *The (Columbus) Crisis*, May 23, 1861.

6. *Cong. Globe*, 36 Congress, 2 sess., 130; entry of Aug. 12, 1861, Daniel L. Medlar "Journal" (mss)., Dayton and Montgomery County Public Library; "Address of the Democratic Members of the Congress to the Democracy of the United States," published in *Washington National Intelligencer*, May 8, 1862.

7. Samuel Medary, a defender of Vallandigham, said, "They beat him by *legislation*, not by voting" in *The Crisis*, Sept. 22, 1862.

8. *Cong. Globe*, 37 Cong., 3rd sess., Appendix, 52–60.

9. *Dayton Empire*, Jan. 24, 1863. James J. Faran, editor of the *Cincinnati Daily Enquirer*, Jan. 20, 1863, wrote, "It is a speech which would add the fame of a Clay, or a Webster, or a Burke, or a Chatham."

10. The *Dayton Empire*, the *Hamilton True Telegraph*, the *Cincinnati Enquirer*, and *The Crisis* led the way in praising Vallandigham and promoting the peace crusade.

11. *Hamilton True Telegraph*, Jan. 29, 1863.

12. *Dayton Weekly Empire*, Jan. 3, 1863.

13. Wood Gray, *The Hidden Civil War: The Story of the Copperheads* (New York, 1942),118–47, deals with this six-month period in Chapter VI entitled "The Period of Despair."

14. *Cong. Globe*, 37 Cong., 3 sess., 172–77.

15. Cox, quoted in *(Springfield) Illinois State Register*, Mar. 3, 1863.

16. *Hamilton True Telegraph*, Feb. 29, 1863.

17. See John A. Marshall, *American Bastile: A History of the Illegal Arrests and Imprisonment of Americans During the Late Civil War* (Philadelphia, 1878), 117–26, 586–606. Ellen R. Young, "Arbitrary Arrests during the War" (M.A. thesis, 1924) treats the arrests of 1862 in Ohio both superficially and inadequately.

18. A brief but scholarly account of the destruction of Medary's newspaper offices and printing plant appears in Eugene H. Roseboom, "The Mobbing of the *Crisis.*" *Ohio State Archaeological and Historical Quarterly*, 59 (Apr. 1950): 150.

19. Burnside's "General Orders, No. 38," was published in *Official Records of the Union and Confederate Armies* (128 vols.; Washington, D.C., 1880–1901), series 3, 23, part 2, 237.

20. *Cong. Globe*, 37 Cong., 3 sess., 130; Clement L. Vallandigham, *Speeches, Arguments, Addresses, and Letters of Clement L. Vallandigham* (New York, 1864), 438.

21. *Ashland (Ohio) Union*, 7 Jan. 1863.

22. *The Crisis*, Dec. 31, 1862; Jan. 8, 15, 22, and Feb. 5, 19, 26, 1863.

23. Letter, Thomas O. Lowe to "Dear Will" [brother], Jan. 25, 1863, in Thomas O. Lowe Papers, Dayton and Montgomery County Public Library, Dayton, Ohio. Also see, Frank L. Klement, "Midwestern Opposition to Lincoln's Emancipation Policy," *Journal of Negro History*, 49 (July 1964): 169–83.

24. *The Times* (London), Dec. 1, 1863. The touring correspondent was William H. Russell.

25. This is the theme of John Stipp, "Economic and Political Aspects of Western Copperheadism" (Ph.D. dissertation, Ohio State University, 1942). Despite its title, Stipp's scholarly study is concerned almost exclusively with the Ohio scene.

26. The author has a butternut that Dr. Edson B. Olds wore during the Civil War. It was given to him by Dr. Olds' great-granddaughter, then a student at Marquette University.

27. Letter, John W. Kees to Samuel S. Cox, Apr. 12, 1862, Samuel S. Cox papers (microfilm), Ohio Historical Society, Columbus: *Circleville Watchman* (n.d.), quoted in *Indianapolis State Sentinel*, Apr. 28, 1862.

28. Readers interested in this topic should read Charles H. Coleman, "The Use of the Term 'Copperhead' during the Civil War," *Mississippi Valley Historical Review*, 25 (Sept. 1938): 263–64.

29. Even today, *Harper's American College Dictionary* defines a "Copperhead" as "A Northern sympathizer with the South during the Civil War" rather than as "a Democratic critic of the Lincoln administration."

30. George Bickley, "Statement of Facts," dated Aug. 8, 1863, in George Bickley Papers, Reports on the Order of American Knights, Records of the Office of the Judge Advocate General, National Archives.

31. Ohio's contributions to the building of the Golden Circle legend are discussed extensively in Frank L. Klement, "Ohio and the Knights of the Golden Circle: The Evolution of a Civil War Myth," *Cincinnati Historical Society Bulletin*, 32 (Spring–Summer 1974): 7–27.

32. The Loyal Publication Society, subsidized by the Union League of New York, published 900,000 copies of ninety different pamphlets and distributed them to 649 different Union League councils, 474 ladies' associations, 744 editors, 26,160 private individuals, and countless soldiers in the field. The New England Loyal Publication Society also published and circulated many tracts. See Frank Freidel, "The Loyal Publication Society: A Pro-Union Propaganda Agency," *Mississippi Valley Historical Review*, 26 (Dec. 1939): 359–76.

33. Chapter II, "The Union Leagues: Patriotic Secret Societies," in Frank L. Klement, *Dark Lanterns: Secret Political Societies, Conspiracies, and Treason Trials in the Civil War* (Baton Rouge, 1964), 34–63, summarizes the Union League story. The best account of the establishment and spread and influence of the Union Leagues is Guy Gibson, "Lincoln's League: The Union League Movement During the Civil War" (Ph.D. dissertation, University of Illinois, 1957).

34. *Cleveland Leader* (n.d.), quoted in *Dayton Weekly Empire*, Apr. 4, 1863.

35. Armstrong, "Personal Reminiscences," published in *Cincinnati Daily Enquirer*, Mar. 20, 1886.

36. Armstrong.

37. *Official Records*, series 2, V, 555; entry of May 6, 1863, Daniel Read Larned "Journal," in Daniel Read Larned Papers, Library of Congress; *Cincinnati Daily Gazette*, May 5, 6, 1863; *Cincinnati Daily Enquirer*, May 5, 6, 1863.

38. The lengthy proceedings of the trial were published in *Official Records*, series 2, 5: 633–46.

39. "To the Democracy of Ohio," published in *The Crisis*, May 13, 1863; letters, Vallandigham to Manton Marble (editor of the *New York World*), May 12, 15, 1863, in Manton Marble Papers, Library of Congress. The story of Vallandigham's arrest and trial is related in detail in Klement, *The Limits of Dissent*, 156–72.

40. Entry of May 19, 1863, *Diary of Gideon Welles, Secretary of the Navy under Lincoln and Johnson*, edited by Howard K. Beale and Alan W. Brownsword (3 vols.; New York, 1960), 1:306; telegrams (2), Secretary of War Stanton to General Burnside, May 19, 1863, published in *Official Records*, series 2, 5:666.

41. *Cincinnati Daily Gazette*, May 29, 1863.

42. Letter, Merritt Miller to "Bro. Clement," May 30, 1863, Merritt Miller Papers, in possession of V.L. Rockwell, Union Grove, Wis. Vallandigham's memorized words were: "I am a citizen of Ohio, and the United States. I am here within your lines by force and against my will. I therefore surrender myself to you as a prisoner of war."

43. Report (copy), Lt. Gen. Braxton Bragg to Adj. Gen. Samuel Cooper, May 27, 1863, in Clement L. Vallandigham Papers, Western Reserve Historical Society, Cleveland. A copy of the pass, dated May 26, 1863, is also in the Vallandigham Papers.

44. *Richmond Sentinel*, June 6, 1863.

45. Vallandigham's three-week stay within Confederate lines is told in detail in Frank L. Klement, "Clement L. Vallandigham's Exile in the Confederacy, 25 May–17 June 1863," *Journal of Southern History*, 31 (May 1965): 149–63.

46. *Dubuque Herald*, May 14, 1863; *New York World*, May 12, 14, 1863.

47. *Detroit Free Press*, May 8, 1863.

48. The "Albany Resolves" of May 16, 1863, were published in Edward McPherson, *The Political History of the United States...during the Great Rebellion* (Washington, D.C., 1864), 163, and in [Appleton's] *Annual Cyclopedia and Register of Important Events...1863* (New York, 1864), 799–800. Lincoln's reply of June 12, 1863, written as a letter to "Hon. Erastus Corning & others," appeared in the *New York Tribune*, June 15, 1863, and other newspapers; it now appears in *The Collected Works of Abraham Lincoln*, edited by Roy P. Basler (9 vols.; New Brunswick, N.J., 1953), 6:260–72.

49. Letter, Samuel S. Cox to Manton Marble [editor of the New York *World*], June 1, 1863, in Manton Marble Papers, Library of Congress; *Cleveland Leader*, June 8, 1863.

50. Armstrong, "Personal Recollections," in *Cincinnati Daily Enquirer*, Mar. 20, 1886; *(Columbus) Daily Ohio State Journal*, June 12, 1863; Klement, *The Limits of Dissent; Clement L. Vallandigham and the Civil War*, 183–86.

51. *Daily Ohio State Journal*, June 12, 13, 1863; *(Columbus) Daily Ohio Statesman*, June 12, 13, 1863.

52. *The Crisis*, June 13, 1863; *Daily Ohio Statesman*, June 13, 1863.

53. The twenty-three resolutions, put in abridged form by Mathias Birchard and his compatriots, are incorporated in footnote #1, *The Collected Works of Abraham Lincoln*, 6:300–301. Lincoln's long reply follows (pages 300–306). The originals of both are in the Robert Todd Lincoln Papers.

54. *Cincinnati Commercial*, Nov. 23, 1863.

55. Letters, A. Denny to John Sherman, Apr. 25, 1863, and James J. James to John Sherman, June 18, 1863, in John Sherman Papers, Library of Congress; letter, R.H. Stephenson to William Henry Smith, Aug. 17, 1863, William Henry Smith Papers, Ohio Historical Society; *Daily Ohio State Journal*, June 16, 1863; *Cleveland Leader*, June 17, 1863.

56. Entry of Aug. 12, 1861, Daniel L. Medlar, "Journal, September 1, 1859, April 30, 1862."

57. Letter, A. Pierce to his wife, June 12, 1863, published in the *McArthur (Ohio) Register*, n.d., in Sherman Papers. Letter, James A. Connolly to "Dear Wife," June 12, 1863, published in *Three Years in the Army of the Cumberland: The Letters and Diary of Major James A. Connolly*, edited by Paul Angle (Bloomington, Ind., 1959), 88–89.

58. Armstrong, "Personal Recollections," in *Cincinnati Daily Enquirer*, Mar. 30, 1886.

59. Letter, Lyman Trumbull to Zachariah Chandler, Aug. 14, 1864, Zachariah Chandler Papers, Library of Congress.

60. "Address to the Democracy of Ohio," July 15, 1863, published in *Cincinnati Daily Enquirer*, July 20, 1863; *Buffalo Morning Courier*, July 16, 1863. Vallandigham's one-month stay at Niagara, Canada West, is detailed in Frank L. Klement, "Exile Across the Border: Clement L. Vallandigham at Niagara, Canada West," *Niagara Frontier*, 11 (Autumn 1964): 69–73.

61. Letter, Vallandigham to Alexander S. Boys, Sept. 1, 1863, in Alexander S. Boys Papers, Ohio Historical Society. The exile's year-long residence in Canada is related in Frank L. Klement, "Vallandigham as an Exile in Canada, 1863–1864," *Ohio History*, 74 (Summer 1965): 151–68.

62. *Dayton Daily Empire*, Aug. 21, 24, 1863; *Cincinnati Daily Empire*, Sept. 7, 1863.

63. *Mount Vernon Democratic Banner*, July 11, 1863. The pamphlet *The Results of Emancipation* (New York, 1863), was written by Samuel F.B. Morse and published and distributed by his Society for the Diffusion of Political Knowledge.

64. Letter, Clemens L. Clendenen to his wife, June 12, 1863, published in McArthur *Register* (n.d.), clipping in John Sherman Papers.

65. The forged Vallandigham-to-Inshall letter was published in most Republican newspapers, including the *Daily Ohio State Journal*, Oct. 10, 1863.

66. Entry of Oct. 13, 1863, *Diary of Gideon Welles*, 1:469–70.

67. Stanton's telegram was published in the *Dayton Daily Journal*, Oct. 17, 1863, Chase's in the *Indianapolis Daily State Sentinel*, Oct. 16, 1863.

68. Entries of Oct. 13, 14, 1863, *Diary of Gideon Welles*, 1:470; telegram, Tod to Lincoln, Oct. 14, 1863, Robert Todd Lincoln Papers. No copy of the Lincoln-to-Tod telegram has been located to date.

69. Vallandigham's "open letter," dated Oct. 14, 1863, published in *Ohio Daily Statesman*, Oct. 20, 1863.

70. Letter, Thomas O. Lowe to "Dear William" [brother], Oct. 26, 1863, Lowe Papers.

71. *Dayton Daily Empire*, Oct. 14, 1863.

72. The decision in *Ex Parte Vallandigham*, rendered on Feb. 15, 1864, stated that the U.S. Supreme Court could not "originate a writ of certiorari to review...the proceedings

of a military commission." In other words, the judges ruled that the Constitution did not specifically provide that a military commission decision could be appealed to the federal courts. The court reversed itself two years later in *Ex Parte Milligan* (1866).

73. Telegram, David Wills [or Governor Curtin] to David Tod, Aug. 1, 1863, published in *Documents Accompanying the Governor's Message of January 1864* (Columbus, 1864), 158.

74. Letter, Tod to David Wills, Aug. 23, 1863, ibid., 160.

75. Letters, "David Wills to Governor Tod," Sept.15, Oct. 13, 1863, ibid., 160–61. Wills' role in the cemetery project is treated in Frank L. Klement, "'These Honored Dead': David Wills and the Soldiers' Cemetery at Gettysburg," *Lincoln Herald*, 74 (Fall 1972): 123–35.

76. Circular letter, dated Oct. 25, 1863, and signed by Governor Tod, ibid.

77. *The Crisis*, Nov. 4, 1863.

78. Letter, George L. Converse to Tod, Oct. 31, 1863, David Tod Papers, Ohio Historical Society.

79. *The Crisis*, Nov. 4, 1863.

80. *Hillsboro Weekly Gazette*, Nov. 26, 1863.

81. *Cincinnati Daily Enquirer*, Nov. 9, 1863.

82. Anyone interested in Colonel Anderson's oration can see Earl W. Wiley, "Colonel Charles Anderson's Gettysburg Address," *Lincoln Herald*, 54 (Fall 1952): 14–21. Those seeking more information about Ohio's role in the Gettysburg Cemetery story can see Frank L. Klement, "Ohio and the Dedication of the Soldiers' Cemetery at Gettysburg," *Ohio History*, 79 (Spring 1970): 76–100.

83. Editor W.H. Foster, in the *Columbus Express*, Nov. 23, 1863.

84. *The Crisis*, Nov. 25, 1863.

85. *Hillsboro Weekly Gazette*, Nov. 26, 1863.

CHAPTER IX

1. *LaCrosse Weekly Democrat*, Aug. 2, 1864.

2. Ibid., Aug. 24, 1864.

3. Ibid. This was a reprint from the *Appleton Crescent* (issue not given).

4. R.F. Howard, "'Brick' Pomeroy's Life and Schemes in LaCrosse," in *LaCrosse Chronicle*, Jan. 1, 1905. This author, who knew Pomeroy personally, entitled one section of his story "Pomeroy Sought Publicity."

5. No Pomeroy letters have been uncovered. For some phases of his life it is necessary to rely upon Marcus Mills Pomeroy, *Journey of Life: Reminiscences and Recollections of "Brick" Pomeroy* (New York, 1890). This autobiography, written twenty-five years after the Civil War, justifies its author's course of action.

6. He served his newspaper apprenticeship in the East, first as a journeyman printer, and then as editor of newspapers in Corning, New York and Athens, Pennsylvania.

7. While editing the *Argus*, Pomeroy carried on a friendly feud with the editor of the Beaver Dam newspaper. A satire on Beaver Dam was reprinted by the *Louisville (Ky.) Journal* and that editor labeled the satirist a "perfect brick." Pomeroy quickly accepted the sobriquet "Brick" and popularized its use.

8. C.P. Sykes and A.P. Swineford established the *LaCrosse Daily Union* in Oct. 1859 to support President James Buchanan and his Lecompton policy and to combat Douglas' bid to take over leadership of the Democratic Party. In November, the Sykes-Swineford partnership absorbed the *LaCrosse Democrat*, which had been launched by A.P. Blakeslee and F.A. Moore in 1859. On Apr. 28, 1860, "Brick" Pomeroy purchased his one-third interest in the merged newspapers, sharing ownership with Swineford and Moore. *Annotated Catalogue of Newspaper Files in the Library of the State Historical Library of Wisconsin* (Madison, 1911), 350; *LaCrosse Weekly Democrat*, Nov. 22, 1861.

9. Franklin J. Meine, "Marcus Mills Pomeroy," *Dictionary of American Biography*, 15:53–54. Meine's brief survey of Pomeroy's life is historically sound, generally. Fairy-tale features are incorporated in Mrs. Mary E. Tucker, *Life of Mark M. Pomeroy, A Representative Young Man of America: His Early History, Character, and Public Service in Defense of the Rights of States, Rights of the People, and the Interests of Working Men* (London, 1868). R.F. Howard's account, "'Brick' Pomeroy's Life and Schemes in LaCrosse" in the *LaCrosse Chronicle*, Jan. 1, 1905, is replete with inaccuracies and vagaries. The Works Progress Administration (W.P.A.) projected biographical account, consisting of twenty-two typewritten pages, in the Manuscript Section of the State Historical Society Library of Madison, needs revision. There is a brief sketch in *The National Cyclopedia of American Biography*, 2:502. Obituaries, with omissions and inaccuracies, are included in Appleton's *Annual Cyclopedia and Register of Important Events of the Year 1896* (page 579) and in the *Brooklyn Daily Eagle*, May 30, 1896. James A. Watrous' "Editors of LaCrosse as Watrous Sees 'Em," in *LaCrosse Chronicle*, Feb. 6, 1910, possesses little historical value as far as Pomeroy is concerned.

10. *LaCrosse Democrat*, Dec. 24, 1860.

11. Ibid., Dec. 26, 1860. Cited in *History of LaCrosse County, Wisconsin* (Western Historical Company, Chicago, 1881), 550. The section entitled "The Press" in this excellent volume of local history was written by Charles Seymour, Pomeroy's newspaper rival of the Civil War and post-War days.

12. *LaCrosse Democrat*, Jan. 11, 1861. In the *New York Tribune* of Nov. 9, 1860, Editor Horace Greeley had said: "If the Cotton States shall become satisfied that they can do better out of the Union than in it, we insist on letting them go in peace. The right to secede may be a revolutionary one, but it exists nevertheless...We hope never to live in a republic whereof one section is pinned to the residue by bayonets." Greeley later became a war radical, although occasionally he advocated the cause of compromise and peace.

13. *LaCrosse Weekly Democrat*, Apr. 19, 1861.

14. Ibid., Apr. 26, May 2, 1861.

15. *History of LaCrosse County*, 552.

16. *LaCrosse Democrat*, Aug. 19, 1861, cited in the W.P.A. biographical sketch, 8.

17. *LaCrosse Weekly Democrat*, Sept. 6, 20, Oct. 4, 11, 1861.

18. Ibid., Sept. 26, 1861. Booth was Wisconsin's most noted Abolitionist. He is listed in history as a principal in the famous fugitive slave case, *Ableman vs. Booth*. During the early years of the Civil War, Booth edited the *Milwaukee Daily Life* in which he espoused immediate emancipation of the slaves.

19. Ibid., Oct. 11, 1861.

20. Ibid., Apr. 18, 23, May 7, June 16, Sept. 28, 1862.

21. Ibid., Sept. 8, 1862.

22. Ibid., Aug. 19, Sept. 8, 1862.

23. Ibid., Feb. 2, Sept. 30, Nov. 25, Dec. 5, 1862. Pomeroy accepted the views of the editor of the Madison *Wisconsin Daily Patriot*, Nov. 12, 1862. "The whole thing of this army voting is a most consummate humbug...The scheme is like a jug handle—on one side."

24. Pomeroy left for St. Louis on Nov. 24, 1862, and returned to LaCrosse in mid-December suffering from a mild form of smallpox. After his recovery, and on Jan. 1, 1863, he left for Helena, Arkansas, to serve in an unofficial capacity upon the staff of his friend from Minnesota, Gen. Willis A. Gorman. Pomeroy arrived in Helena on Jan. 15, 1863, and, sometime later, his commission came. This first lieutenant's commission, signed by Gov. Edward G. Salomon, contained a note on its margin: "By request of M.M. Pomeroy no pay chargeable against the State under this commission." That pseudo-commission assigned Pomeroy to no regiment, company, detachment, or duty. It was, in fact, little more than a roving newspaperman's pass. When the governor, later,

revoked the commission, Pomeroy denied that it was a commission, insisted that he had never accepted it, and claimed that revocation of something which was nonexistent bordered on absurdity.

25. *LaCrosse Weekly Democrat*, Dec. 9, 1862.

26. Ibid., Dec. 16, 1862.

27. Ibid., Dec. 9, 1862.

28. Ibid.

29. Wilbur Fisk Storey, who had built up the *Detroit Free Press* into a well-known paper, purchased the *Chicago Times* early in 1861. He supported the war until emancipation became national policy. Then he became a caustic and candid critic of Lincoln and the war.

30. *LaCrosse Weekly Democrat*, Feb. 17, Mar. 17, 1863.

31. Ibid., Feb. 17, 1863.

32. Ibid., Apr. 7, 1863.

33. Tucker, *Life of Mark M. Pomeroy*, 91.

34. *LaCrosse Weekly Democrat*, Feb. 10, 1863.

35. Ibid., Mar. 3, 1863.

36. Ibid., Mar. 17, 1863. After the war Pomeroy always referred to the Civil conflict as a "bond-holder's war." Lincoln's supporters he termed "robbers, insulters, cotton thieves, contract swindlers, grave robbers, hospital plunderers, nigger lovers, whiteman-haters and Union separatists." See "Brick" Pomeroy, *Soliloquies of the Bondholder, the Poor Farmer, the Soldier's Widow, the Political Preacher, the Poor Mechanic, the Freed Negro, the "Radical" Congressman, the Returned Soldier, the Southerner, and Other Political Articles* (New York, 1866), 5, 30. This pamphlet reveals Pomeroy's mastery of satire and sarcasm. In another publication, *Condensed History of the War: Its Causes and Results: Plain Home-Told Facts for the Young Men and Working Men of the United States* (n.p., 1868), Pomeroy contended that the war fastened upon America "a monied power and aristocracy greater than ever known before in the world" (page 7). Pomeroy's views drove him into the Greenback movement.

37. *LaCrosse Weekly Democrat*, Mar. 17, 1863.

38. Pomeroy's letter of Feb. 26, 1863, from Helena appeared in the Mar. 17 issue of the *LaCrosse Weekly Democrat*.

39. Prentiss' order is stated in full in the *Milwaukee Sentinel*, Apr. 1, 1863. The Republican press jubilantly circulated the contents of General Prentiss' charges. See also Ibid., Mar. 16–17 and the *LaCrosse Weekly Democrat*, Mar 31, 1863. The Republican press circulated charges that Pomeroy was dismissed because he played poker with the Army paymaster and inveigled him out of government funds, and that he was dismissed because of his dealing in confiscated cotton. The complete and detailed story of Pomeroy's Arkansas adventure needs to be told and merits a separate historical article. The LaCrosse editor's vindication of his action is well told in his autobiography, *Journey of Life: Reminiscences and Recollections of 'Brick' Pomeroy*. Pages 182–94 of this interesting work contain Pomeroy's Arkansas experiences.

40. *LaCrosse Weekly Democrat*, Feb. 17, 1863.

41. Ibid., Apr. 14, 1863.

42. Gen. Ambrose E. Burnside suspended the *Chicago Times* by military order in June 1863. The charges were "disloyal and incendiary sentiments." Burnside's order was promptly revoked by the president.

43. Clement L. Vallandigham, prominent Ohio Democrat, was arrested on May 5, 1863, for criticizing the Lincoln administration and for "declaring sympathies for the enemy." A military commission found Vallandigham guilty and he was sentenced to closed confinement. Lincoln altered the sentence to banishment within the Confederate lines.

44. *LaCrosse Weekly Democrat*, June 2, 1863. Brig. Gen. Milo S. Hascall commanded in Indiana and Illinois, and he was responsible for the suppression of the *South Bend Forum* and the *Columbia* City *News.*

45. Pomeroy is responsible for the turbulent general being popularly known as "Spoon" Butler. Benjamin F. Butler, *Butler's Book: Autobiography and Personal Reminiscences of Major-General Benjamin F. Butler* (Boston, 1892), 43. Pomeroy's contempt for Butler the general repaid in kind.

46. *Milwaukee Sentinel*, Sept. 26, 1863; *LaCrosse Democratic Journal*, Sept. 13, 20, 23, 1863; *LaCrosse Weekly Democrat*, June 27, 1863.

47. Ibid., July 28, 1863.

48. *LaCrosse Democratic Journal*, June 17, 24, 1863.

49. *LaCrosse Weekly Democrat*, Aug. 25, 1863.

50. Ibid., Oct. 27, 1863.

51. Ibid., Aug. 4, 11, 1863.

52. *Milwaukee Sentinel*, Nov. 6, 9, 1863; *LaCrosse Weekly Democrat*, Nov. 10, 1863.

53. *LaCrosse Weekly Democrat*, Dec. 22, 1863.

54. Ibid., Apr. 23, 1864.

55. Ibid., July 5, 1864.

56. Ibid., July 19, 1864.

57. Ibid., Oct. 17, 1864. Earlier the Democratic editor of the *Madison Wisconsin Patriot* and the *Sheboygan Journal* had emphasized the economic grievances of the West. See also Pomeroy, *Condensed History of the War*, 4–7.

58. *LaCrosse Weekly Democrat*, Aug. 2, 1864. To the tune of "When Johnny Comes Marching Home Again," Pomeroy wrote an eight-verse song. The following verse, Ibid., Oct. 3, 1864, illustrates its manner of appeal:

    "The widow maker soon must cave! Hurrah! Hurrah!

    We'll plant him in some nigger's grave! Hurrah! Hurrah!

    Torn from your shop, your farm, your raft,

    Conscript! how do you like the draft?

    And we'll stop that, too,

    When Little Mac takes the helm!"

59. Wendell Phillips, a prominent advocate of abolition, had toured the Midwest. Butler was described as "a beast and thief," "murderer in shoulder straps," "this representative of hell on earth," and a blunderer "destitute of all moral principles—base, selfish, and unscrupulous." Ibid., July 19, 1864, Jan. 23, 1865.

60. *LaCrosse Weekly Democrat*, Aug. 24, 1864.

61. Howard, "'Brick' Pomeroy's Life and Schemes in LaCrosse," in *LaCrosse Chronicle*, Jan. 1, 1905; *Milwaukee Sentinel*, Oct. 12, 1865.

62. *LaCrosse Weekly Democrat*, Aug. 2, 1864.

63. *History of LaCrosse County*, 546.

64. *LaCrosse Weekly Democrat*, Oct. 3, 1864.

65. *LaCrosse Democrat*, Apr. 2, 1864. Earlier he had told his friends how to protect themselves: "Matches are cheap. If fanatics and fools seek mob law and anarchy, by all means let them have it. Burn down and destroy theirs as they have or may yours. By dark or by daylight—by fire or by powder—feed those who may injure you the dish they prepare. On no account inaugurate violence or excitement, but for every dime of your property destroyed by political opponents, destroy a dollar's worth in return. Stores, houses, barns, offices, and churches burn." Ibid., Feb. 19, 1864.

66. *LaCrosse Weekly Democrat*, Oct. 10, 1864.

67. Ibid., Nov. 7, 1864.

68. Ibid., Nov. 21, 1864.
69. Ibid., Nov. 7, 1864.
70. Ibid., Nov. 14, 1864.
71. Ibid., Nov. 21, 1864.
72. Ibid., Jan. 23, Apr. 3, 1865.
73. *History of LaCrosse County*, 553.
74. *LaCrosse Weekly Democrat*, Apr. 24, 1865.
75. *Milwaukee Sentinel*, May 8, 1865; *LaCrosse Weekly Democrat*, Apr. 24, 1865.
76. *Milwaukee Sentinel*, May 8, 1865, *Weekly Democrat*, May 8, 1865.
77. L.H. Pammel, *Some Reminiscences of LaCrosse and Vicinity* (LaCrosse, 1928), 67. Pammel states that the circulation of Pomeroy's paper was "some 90,000 copies per issue." Appleton's *Annual Cyclopedia and Register of Important Events of the year 1896* sets the circulation at 100,000. Pomeroy—never known for his modesty—claimed that his circulation, early in 1865 had dwindled to 27 copies of his weekly, and that in 1868 it reached 100,000. Pomeroy, *Journey of Life*, 197, 203.
78. Benjamin F. Bryant, *Memoirs of LaCrosse County* (Madison, Wis., 1907), 116.
79. Ibid. Also Howard, in *LaCrosse Chronicle*, Jan. 1, 1905; *Milwaukee Sentinel*, Jan. 10, Oct. 12, 1865.
80. *LaCrosse Weekly Democrat*, Sept. 12, 1864. Republican newspapers circulated a story that Pomeroy's unpopular criticisms aroused public indignation to the point that he was forced into hiding in the woods forty miles away, and that he sent the editorials by messenger to the offices of the *Democrat*. Although these libels varied with historical fact, they continued in circulation, e.g., Appleton's *Annual Cyclopedia and Register of Important Events of the Year 1896*, 579.
81. *Round's Printers' Cabinet*, cited in *Milwaukee Sentinel*, Oct. 12, 1865.
82. In *D.A.B.*, 15:54.
83. Marcus M. ("Brick") Pomeroy, *Sense, or Saturday-Night Musings and Thoughtful Papers* (New York, 1868), 201.
84. *LaCrosse Weekly Democrat*, Sept. 3, 27, 1863, June 23, 1865.
85. Pomeroy, *Sense*, 13.
86. *LaCrosse Weekly Democrat*, Mar 1, 1864.
87. Ibid., Apr. 18, 1862.
88. Ibid., Feb. 7, 1862.
89. Ibid., July 7, 1863.
90. Ibid., Dec. 30, 1862.
91. *History of LaCrosse County*, 545.

CHAPTER X

1. J. Christopher Herold, *The Mind of Napoleon: A Selection from his Written and Spoken Words* (New York, 1955), 50.
2. Thomas Carlyle, *The French Revolution: A History*, 3 vols. (London, 1898), I:256.
3. Hans Kohn, *The Idea of Nationalism, A Study of Its Origins and Background* (New York, 1944), 16. Boyd Shafer, president of Phi Alpha Theta during the 1972–73 biennium, is the author of two books which deal with nationalism as a world force: (1) *Nationalism, Myth and Reality* (New York, 1935), and (2) *Faces of Nationalism, New Realities and Old Myths* (New York, 1972). Also see Shafer, "Webs of Common Interests: Nationalism, Internationalism and Peace," *The Historian*, 36 (May 1974): 403–33.
4. Thomas A. Bailey (presidential address at the 1968 convention of the Organization of American Historians), "The Mythmakers of American History," *Journal of American History*, 60 (June 1968): 5.

5. Joseph Medill to Abraham Lincoln, Sept. 10, 1859, Robert Todd Lincoln Papers, Library of Congress.

6. James B. McCullough to William Henry Smith, May 31, 1864, William Henry Smith Papers, Ohio Historical Society, Columbus.

7. "The disunion [Republican] newspapers of Ohio," complained one of Vallandigham's friends, "are filling their columns with garbled and mutilated extracts from the speeches of Vallandigham in order to deceive the people." Cited in *Dayton Daily Empire*, Aug. 22, 1863.

8. The author has dealt with the subject in chapters entitled "Arrest and Trial" and "A Prisoner Becomes an Exile" in *The Limits of Dissent: Clement L. Vallandigham and the Civil War* (Lexington, Ky., 1970), 156–72, 190–201.

9. *Dayton Daily Journal*, July 15, 1863, and Nov. 22, 1867.

10. *Detroit Free Press*, Sept. 14, 1863. The *Free Press* attributed the forgery, which linked Vallandigham to Lee's invasion of Pennsylvania, to Henry Reinish.

11. *Dayton Daily Journal*, July 15 and 16, 1864; *Cleveland Leader*, July 30, 1863; *New Lisbon Buckeye State*, Aug. 13, 1863; *Bucyrus (Ohio) Weekly Journal*, Aug. 14, 1863; *Columbus Daily Ohio State Journal*, July 20, 1863; and *Buffalo Morning Express*, July 18, 1863. This myth is perpetuated in such widely read works as James D. Horan, *Confederate Agent: A Discovery in History* (New York, 1954).

12. *Cincinnati Gazette*, Oct. 12, 1863; and *Columbus Daily Ohio State Journal*, Oct. 10, 1863.

13. The first, Joseph W. Pomfrey, *A Disclosure and Exposition of the Knights of the Golden Circle, including the Secret Signs, Grips, and Charges, of the Three Degrees, as Practiced by the Order* (Cincinnati, 1861), came off the same presses as the Republican-oriented *Cincinnati Gazette*. The second, credited to "a member of the Order," was really written by a young Republican, Dr. John M. Hiatt of Indianapolis. It was entitled *An Authentic Exposition of the "K.G.C.," Knights of the Golden Circle...*and published by C.C. Perrine & Company of Indianapolis in July 1861.

14. The bogus oath and other supporting documents appeared as part of the exposé published by the *Columbus Daily Ohio State Journal*, Oct. 8, 1861.

15. *The (Columbus) Crisis*, Nov. 7, 1861.

16. *Cleveland Leader*, Oct. 10, 16, and 18, 1861; and *History of Marion County, Ohio* (Chicago, 1883), 448–49.

17. *Detroit Tribune*, n.d., quoted in the *Detroit Free Press*, Sept. 25, 1861.

18. *Chicago Tribune*, Aug. 26, 1862.

19. The use of the K.G.C. bogeyman in Illinois is treated more extensively in my "Copperhead Secret Societies in Illinois During the Civil War," *Journal of the Illinois State Historical Society*, 48 (Summer 1955): 152–80.

20. The role of Gov. Oliver P. Morton and Col. Henry B. Carrington in giving headlines to the K.G.C. is reviewed in my "Carrington and the Golden Circle Legend in Indiana during the Civil War," *Indiana Magazine of History*, 51 (Mar. 1965): 31–52. The full story of the K.G.C. is summarized, more or less, in my "Ohio and the Knights of the Golden Circle: The Evolution of a Civil War Myth," *Cincinnati Historical Society Bulletin*, 32 (Spring-Summer 1974): 7–27.

21. The undated document is in the John P. Sanderson Papers, Ohio Historical Society, Columbus. It was first published in the *St. Louis Missouri Democrat*, July 28, 1864, and then broadcast over the country.

22. *New York Tribune*, July 29, 1864.

23. *Indianapolis Journal*, June 29, 1864.

24. Report, Joseph Holt to Hon. Edwin M. Stanton, Oct. 8, 1864, published in *Official Records of the Union and Confederate Armies*, series 2, 128 vols. (Washington, D.C., 1880–1901), 7:930–53.

25. *Report of the Judge Advocate General on the Order of American Knights, alias the Sons of Liberty: A Western Conspiracy in Aid of the Southern Rebellion* (Washington, D.C., 1864).

26. William B. Lord to Joseph Holt, Nov. 13, 1864, Joseph Holt Papers, Library of Congress; and John McGaffey to William Henry Smith, Nov. 17, 1864, William Henry Smith Papers.

27. *(Springfield) Illinois State Register*, Oct. 18 and 21, 1864.

28. *Cincinnati Daily Enquirer*, Oct. 16, 1864.

29. Adam Gurowski, *Diary...from March 4, 1861 to November 10, 1864*, 3 vols. (Washington, D.C., 1862–66), 2:302.

30. *Hartford (Wisconsin) Home League*, Nov. 15, 1862.

31. *The American College Dictionary*, text edition (1948), s.v. "Copperhead."

32. Henry B. Carrington, "Indiana War Documents Cleared of Error" (thirteen-page undated typed ms.), 8, Henry B. Carrington Papers, Archives Division, Indiana State Library, Indianapolis. General Alvin P. Hovey replaced Carrington as commander of the District of Indiana.

33. Samuel P. Heintzelman, Journal, entry of Aug. 8, 1864, Samuel P. Heintzelman Papers, Library of Congress. Gen. Joseph Hooker replaced Heintzelman as commander of the Northern Department. The District of Indiana was a subdivision of the Northern Department.

34. *Indianapolis State Sentinel*, Sept. 9, 1864.

35. Gilbert R. Tredway, *Democratic Opposition to the Lincoln Administration in Indiana* (Indianapolis, 1973) is a watered-down version of his dissertation, "Indiana Against the Administration, 1861–1865" (Indiana University, 1862), and both discredit Governor Morton's tactics, the military proceedings, and the judge advocate's high-handed practices. Kenneth M. Stampp, "The Milligan Case and the Election of 1864 in Indiana," *Mississippi Valley Historical Review*, 31 (June 1944): 41–58, recognizes the political implications in the Indianapolis trials.

36. William A. "Deacon" Bross, financial and commercial editor of the *Chicago Tribune*, later gave two different and conflicting accounts of how he first heard of the Confederate-sponsored conspiracy. See Bross, *Biographical Sketch of the Late General B.J. Sweet* [and] *History of Camp Douglas: A Paper Read Before The Chicago Historical Society, June 18, 1878* (Chicago, 1878), 18; and Tracy E. Strevey, "Joseph Medill and the *Chicago Tribune* during the Civil War Period" (Ph.D. dissertation, University of Chicago, 1930), 188–89.

37. Report, Col. Benjamin J. Sweet to Brig. Gen. James Fry, Nov. 23, 1864, in *Official Records*, series 1, 45: part 1, 1077–80.

38. *Chicago Daily Tribune, Nov. 8 and 9, 1864.*

39. The traditional story, repeated in such well-known books as George Fort Milton, *Abraham Lincoln and the Fifth Column* (New York, 1942), 278–304, 323–34, is challenged in my book, *The Copperheads in the Middle West* (Chicago, 1960), 199–202.

40. Traditional interpretations of the Order of American Knights and the Sons of Liberty are summarized in Bethania Meredith Smith, "Civil War Subversives," *Journal of the Illinois State Historical Society*, 45 (Autumn 1952): 220–40; and Elbert J. Benton, *The Movement or Peace Without Victory during the Civil War* (Cleveland, 1918). The traditional story of the Order of American Knights has been debunked in my article, "Phineas C. Wright, the Order of American Knights, and the [John P.] Sanderson Exposé," *Civil War History*, 18 (Mar. 1972): 5–23.

41. Tredway, *Democratic Opposition to the Lincoln Administration in Indiana*, discredits the Indianapolis treason trials effectively. Lorna Lutes Sylvester, on the other hand, follows a more pro-Morton line in "Oliver P. Morton and Hoosier Politics during the Civil War," (Ph.D. dissertation, Indiana University, 1968).

42. Gurowski, *Diary...from March 4, 1861 to November 10, 1865*, 3:398.

43. *Leslie's Illustrated Weekly* (New York), Apr. 29, 1865.

44. *Funeral Observances at New London, Connecticut, in Honour of Abraham Lincoln...including the Public Addresses of Rev. G.B. Willcox and Rev. Thomas P. Field, D.D.* (New London, 1865), 32–33.

45. Horace Greeley, *The American Conflict: A History of the Great Rebellion in the United States, 1860–1865*, 2 vols. (Hartford, Conn., 1867), 1:350, 492–93; 2:18–19, 556–58.

46. Whitelaw Reid, *Ohio in the War*, 2 vols. (Cincinnati, 1868), passim.

47. The term "dozens of others" includes such diverse works as (a) Berry R. Sulgrove, *History of Indianapolis and Marion County* (Philadelphia, 1886); (b) William H.H. Terrell, *Report of the Adjutant General of Indiana*, 8 vols. (Indianapolis, 1869); (c) Felix G. Stidger, *Treason History of the Order of the Sons of Liberty...*(Chicago, 1903); (d) I. Winslow Ayer, *The Great Northwestern Conspiracy in All Its Startling Details...*(Chicago, 1865); (e) Edmund Kirke [James R. Gilmore], "The Chicago Conspiracy," *Atlantic Monthly* 16 (July 1865): 108–20; (f) William A. Bross, *Biographical Sketch of the Late B.J. Sweet: History of Camp Douglas* (Chicago, 1878); (g) Eugene F. Baldwin, "The Dream of the South: The Story of Illinois during the Civil War," in *Transactions of the Illinois State Historical Society, 1911* (Springfield, 1913); (h) Jubal A. Early, "The Story of the Attempted Formation of a N.W. Confederacy," *Southern Historical Society Papers*, 10 (Apr. 1882): 154–58; (i) John B. Castleman, *Active Service* (Louisville, Ky., 1917); and (j) Henry B. Carrington, "Indiana War Documents Cleared of Error" (ms.) in Carrington Papers.

48. James Ford Rhodes, *History of the United States from the Compromise of 1850 to the McKinley-Bryan Election of 1896*, 7 vols. (New York, 1893–1906), 5:317.

49. Mayo Fesler, "Secret Political Societies in the North during the Civil War," *Indiana Magazine of History* 14 (Sept. 1918): 183–85, 280–86.

50. During the 1920s, Curtis H. Morrow wrote a doctoral dissertation entitled "Politico-Military Societies in the Northwest" (Clark University, 1927). It covered much of the same ground earlier tilled by Fesler, and its conclusions also paralleled Fesler's. Portions of the dissertation were published in five installments in *Social Science* 4 (Nov. 1928–Aug. 1929): 9–31, 222–42, 348–61; and ibid. 5 (Nov. 1929): 73–84.

51. George Fort Milton, *Abraham Lincoln and the Fifth Column,* 334.

52. Homer S. Cummings, quoted on the dust jacket of Milton's *Abraham Lincoln and the Fifth Column.*

53. Henry Steele Commager, ibid.

54. Wood Gray, "The Peace Movement in the Old Northwest, 1862–1865: A Study in Defeatism" (Ph.D. dissertation, University of Chicago, 1934).

55. Wood Gray, *The Hidden Civil War: The Story of the Copperheads* (New York, 1942), 224.

56. John D. Hicks, *A Short History of American Democracy* (Boston, 1943), 403.

57. Mark M. Boatner, *The Civil War Dictionary* (New York, 1959), 175. Some of the same errors appeared in the *Encyclopedia Britannica*, 1951 edition, 13:441–42.

58. William Blake [Blech], *The Copperheads* (New York, 1941).

59. Constance Robertson, *The Golden Circle* (New York, 1951).

60. Ernest Haycox, *The Long Storm* (Roslyn, N.Y., 1946). In all, Haycox wrote twenty novels, each having a western setting. His best work might well be *Bugles in the Afternoon* (Boston, 1944), an excellent fictional presentation of the Custer massacre.

61. Phyllis A. Whitney, *The Quicksilver Pool* (Greenwich, Conn., 1955). The story is available only in paperback.

62. Mary Tracy Earle, *The Flag on the Hilltop* (Boston, 1902).

63. Respected historians still repeat the myths about subversive secret societies and their conspiracies. A recent article in *The Historian*, for example, justifies President Lincoln's use of arbitrary measures because of "seditious, if not treasonous, conduct by elements of the sizable and influential 'Copperhead' press and by such covert organizations as the Order of the Knights of the Golden Circle"—both "threatened irreparably to

undermine the war effort"—Robert Neil Mathis, "Freedom of the Press in the Confederacy: A Reality," *The Historian*, 37 (Aug. 1975): 647.

CHAPTER XI

1. Hans Kohn, *The Idea of Nationalism: A Study of Its Origins and Background* (New York, 1944), 16.

2. Gerald Newman, *The Rise of English Nationalism: A Cultural History, 1740–1830* (New York, 1987), 53.

3. Hans Kohn, *American Nationalism: An Interpretive Essay* (New York, 1957), 29.

4. Peter Fleming, *Promises to Keep* (New York, 1978), 87.

5. Maris A. Vinovskis, "Have Social Historians Lost the Civil War? Some Preliminary Demographic Speculations," *Journal of American History*, 75 (June 1989): 57–58. Professor Vinovskis added, "Most historians have neglected the social history of all wars, instead focusing mainly on military strategy and battles" (p. 35 n).

6. Letter, "To the Sentinel," n.d., signed "HISTORY PROF. Milwaukee," published in the *Milwaukee Sentinel*, Jan. 7, 1984. Interestingly, the history professor wished to remain anonymous.

7. Melville, quoted in Martin E. Marty, *Righteous Empire: The Protestant Spirit in America* (New York, 1970), 46.

8. James H. Moorhead, *American Apocalypse: Yankee Protestants and the Civil War, 1860–1869* (New Haven, Conn., 1978), 10–11.

9. John Coleman Adams, "Lincoln's Place in History," *Century Magazine*, 47 (Apr. 1894): 594–95.

10. George Peck, *Our Country: Its Trials and Triumphs* (New York, 1865), 46, 118.

11. W. Harrison Daniel, "Southern Protestantism and Secession," *The Historian*, 29 (May 1967): 406.

12. *The Liberator*, Jan. 9, 1863.

13. *Chicago Daily Tribune*, Jan. 1, 3, 1863.

14. Milton entitled his most scholarly work *The Eve of Conflict: Stephen A. Douglas and the Needless War* (Boston, 1934).

15. Hazel C. Wolf, *On Freedom's Altar: The Martyr Complex in the Abolition Movement* (Madison, Wis., 1952), devotes a chapter to Lincoln as "a martyr to the cause of abolitionism and freedom."

16. Count Adam Gurowski, *Diary...from March 4, 1861 to November 10, 1865* (3 vols., Washington, D.C., 1862–1865), 3:398. Gurowski, as a self-styled radical, was often critical of Lincoln.

17. Adams, in *Century Magazine*, 47 (Apr. 1894): 594–95. Greeley's open letter to Lincoln was printed in the *New York Tribune* of Aug. 20, 1862. Lincoln's reply of Aug. 22, 1862—really a state paper—is included in *The Collected Works of Abraham Lincoln*, edited by Roy P. Basler (9 vols.; New Brunswick, N.J., 1953), 5:388–89.

18. Letters, John Hay to John G. Nicolay, Aug. 10, 1865, and John Hay to Robert Todd Lincoln, Jan. 27, 1884, both published in *Letters of John Hay & Extracts from His Diary*, edited by Mrs. John Hay (3 vols.; New York, 1969), 2:87, 93–96.

19. Most students of the Civil War have read Sandburg's *Abraham Lincoln: The Prairie Years* (2 vols.; New York, 1926) and *Abraham Lincoln: The War Years* (4 vols.; New York, 1939). The latter won the Pulitzer Prize in 1940.

20. *Boston Daily Transcript* (n.d.), quoted in Benjamin P. Thomas, *Portrait for Posterity: Lincoln and his Biographers* (Freeport, N.Y., 1927), 292.

21. Nevins praised the book in his presidential address at the convention of the American Historical Association; Commager and Buck (archivist of the U.S.) wrote complimentary comments for the book's dust jacket. F.D.R. arranged to be photographed holding Milton's book as he was embarking for one of his conferences with Churchill and Stalin.

22. George Fort Milton, *Abraham Lincoln and the Fifth Column* (New York, 1942), 334. The author tried to obtain the number of copies printed without success.

23. Williams, *Lincoln and the Radicals* (Madison, Wis., 1941) evolved out of his doctoral dissertation, a history of the Joint Committee on the Conduct of the War, and that, in the main, explains why he slighted Radical Republican governors and others like Wendell Phillips and Horace Greeley. Both books were reprinted as paperbacks and were popular as supplementary textbooks in collegiate Civil War courses.

24. Thomas Beer, *Hanna* (New York, 1929), 34n. Beer related the incident in a lengthy footnote.

25. Brooks D. Simpson, "Butcher? Racist? An Examination of William S. McFeely's *Grant: A Biography*," in *Civil War History*, 33 (Mar. 1987): 63–83.

26. Williams made this statement orally to the author during a friendly discussion that followed his formal lecture on "Grant and the Civil War" at Marquette University during the Civil War centennial.

27. Mark E. Neely, Jr., set the number arrested during the Civil War at 14,000; see Neely, *Lincoln and the Constitution*, Historical Bulletin No. 38 of the Lincoln Fellowship of Wisconsin (Madison, 1983), 3. Alexander Johnson, in the *Encyclopedia of Political Science* (edited by John I. Lalor), 2:432–34, suggested that 38,000 were arrested.

28. *Ex Parte Milligan*, 71 U.S. (4 Wall) 2, 83 (1866). Two notable lines of the Court's decision read as follows: "The Constitution of the United States is a law for rulers and people, equally in war and peace, and covers with the shield of protection all classes of men, at all times and under all circumstances. No doctrine involving more pernicious consequences was ever invented by the wit of man than that any of its great provisions could be suspended during any of the great exigencies of Government." The decision was written by Justice David Davis, a Lincoln appointee to the court.

29. Adj. Gen. Lorenzo Thomas (at Stanton's instruction), order dated Mar. 13, 1863, quoted in [Appleton's] *Annual Cyclopedia and Register of Important Events...1863* (New York, 1864), 681.

30. The lengthy report, compiled by Judge Advocate General Joseph Holt at Stanton's insistence, and dated Oct. 8, 1864, was later incorporated into the *Official Records of the Union and Confederate Armies* (128 vols.; Washington, 1880–1901), series 2, 7:930–53. Through Stanton's conniving, Holt's report was published as an 1864 campaign document entitled *Report of the Judge Advocate General on the Order of the American Knights* (Washington, 1864). Holt's report is debunked and discredited in Frank L. Klement, *Dark Lanterns: Secret Political Societies, Conspiracies, and Treason Trials in the Civil War* (Baton Rouge, 1984), 136–50.

31. Letter, S. Corning Judd to President Lincoln, Mar. 13, 1863, in John G. Nicolay-John Hay Papers, Illinois State Historical Library, Springfield.

32. Ludwell Johnson III (Professor of History, William & Mary College), book review of Floyd E. Risvold, *A True History of the Assassination of Abraham Lincoln and the Conspiracy of 1865* (New York, 1975), in *Civil War History*, 23 (Mar. 1976): 77–81.

33. Conyers Read, "Social Responsibilities of a Historian," *American Historical Review*, 55 (Jan. 1950): 283–84.

34. Samuel Eliot Morison, "Faith of a Historian"; ibid., 56 (Jan. 1951): 266–67, 272.

35. Phillip S. Paludan, "The American Civil War: Triumph Through Tragedy," *Civil War History*, 20 (Sept. 1974): 239–50, and "The American Civil War as a Crisis in Law and Order," *American Historical Review*, 77 (Oct. 1972): 1013–34.

36. Richard N. Current, *Lincoln, the Constitution, and Presidential Leadership*, Historical Bulletin No. 44 of the Lincoln Fellowship of Wisconsin (Madison, 1989), 5–6; Lincoln, response to a serenade, Feb. 1, 1865, in *Collected Works of Abraham Lincoln*, 8:254–55.

37. The fall roundup of 1862, especially in Illinois, was an attempt to intimidate Democrats as the fall elections approached—half of whom were accused of belonging to the Knights

of the Golden Circle (a Republican-concocted myth as far as Illinois was concerned). The arrests in Illinois were chiefly the work of a partisan and dishonest federal marshal (David W. Phillips). The fifteen Illini arrested included congressman William J. Allen, Judge Andrew D. Duff, lawyers Madison Y. Johnson and David Sheean of Galena, and doctor-lawyer Israel Blanchard of Carbondale. Highly distorted accounts of the arrests (compiled by a Lincoln-hater) appear in John A. Marshall, *American Bastile: A History of the Illegal Arrests and Imprisonment of Civilians During the Late Civil War* (Philadelphia, 1878), 174–79, 293–302, 317–20, 385–99, 449–50, 451–62, 509–35, 538–39, 580–81.

38. [Harper's] *American College Dictionary*, edited by Clarence L. Barnhart (New York, 1948), 224.

39. Wood Gray, *The Hidden Civil War: The Story of the Copperheads* (New York, 1942), 224.

40. George Fort Milton, *Abraham Lincoln and the Fifth Column* (New York, 1942), 112–26, 157–90.

41. Commager, quoted on the dust jacket of Milton's *Abraham Lincoln and the Fifth Column*.

42. Sewell, *A House Divided: Sectionalism and Civil War, 1848–1865* (Baltimore, 1988), 112.

43. Although Vallandigham had opposed the Conscription Bill as a congressman, he made it clear in his homecoming speech of Mar. 13, 1863, that the Conscription Act of Mar. 3, 1863, was the law of the land and must be obeyed—he would not counsel disobedience and the people could use their votes to change the laws. See *Dayton Daily Empire*, Mar. 14, 1863; Frank L. Klement, *The Limits of Dissent: Clement L. Vallandigham and the Civil War* (Lexington, Ky., 1970), 142. In an article that depicts Thomas Seymour as a Southern sympathizer, Joanna D. Cowden offers no evidence that the Connecticut dissenter ever advised the party faithful not to obey the Conscription Act. See Cowden, "The Politics of Dissent: Civil War Democrats in Connecticut," *New England Quarterly*, 56 (Dec. 1983): 538–54. As mayor of New York City (1861–1862) and congressman (elected in 1862), Fernando Wood preferred volunteerism to conscription, but no evidence exists that he counseled disobedience as far as the Conscription Act was concerned.

44. McPherson, *Battle Cry of Freedom*, 591.

45. James L. Vallandigham, *A Life of Clement L. Vallandigham* (Baltimore, 1872), 4.

46. James W. Thomas and T.J.C. Williams, *A History of Allegany County [Maryland]* (Baltimore, 1923), 310.

47. The Slave Schedules, 1860 Census of the United States, districts 1–3, Allegany County, Maryland (microfilm copy, Wisconsin State Historical Society).

48. McPherson, *Ordeal by Fire: The Civil War and Reconstruction* (New York, 1982), 348.

49. These three so-called secret societies have been discredited in Klement, *Dark Lanterns*, 7–33, 64–90, 91–135.

50. The report was published by the Union Congressional Committee in Washington in 1864 as a campaign document and distributed through the Union Leagues. The purpose of the document, one Republican worker wrote, was to bolster Lincoln's stock and depress McClellan's. See letter, D.N. Cooley to Elihu B. Washburne, Oct. 20, 1864, in Elihu B. Washburne Papers, Library of Congress.

51. James Ford Rhodes, *History of the United States from the Compromise of 1850...*(7 vols.; New York, 1893–1906), passim.

52. Mayo Fesler, "Secret Political Societies in the North During the Civil War," *Indiana Magazine of History*, 14 (Sept. 1918): 183–286.

53. Hicks, *Short History of American Democracy* (Boston, 1943), 403.

54. Kinchen, *Confederate Operations in Canada and the North* (North Quincy, Mass., 1970).

55. McPherson, *Ordeal by Fire*, 448.

56. McPherson, *Battle Cry of Freedom*, 783. This writer believes otherwise and Chapter VII ("The Camp Douglas Conspiracy and the Chicago Treason Trial") of my book, *Dark Lanterns*, 187–317, supports my contention.

57. Frank L. Klement, "Civil War Politics, Nationalism, and Postwar Myths," *The Historian*, 38 (May 1976): 419–38, illustrates what Professor McPherson calls "revisionism."

58. T.S. Eliot, "Gerontion," in *Complete Poems and Plays, 1909–1950* (New York, 1958), 22.

CHAPTER XII

1. Quoted in Merle Curti et al., *An American History* (2 vols.; New York, 1950), 2:159.

2. John Spencer Bassett, *A Short History of the United States* (New York, 1921), 338.

3. S.E. Foreman, *Our Republic* (New York, 1924), 215; Christopher R. Greene, *An Oration Delivered in St. Michael's Church, on Tuesday, the Fourth of July, 1815* (New York, 1946), 152.

4. *The Collected Works of Abraham Lincoln*, edited by Roy P. Basler (9 vols.; New Brunswick, N.J., 1953), 1:420–22, 431–42; (Springfield) *Illinois State Register*, Feb. 25, Mar. 10, June 13, 1848, Donald Riddle, *Congressman Abraham Lincoln* (Urbana, Ill., 1957) deals with Lincoln's stand on the Mexican War at length and in scholarly fashion.

5. Nahum, Capen, *The Republic of the United States* (Boston, 1948), 37–38.

6. *Journal of the House of Representatives of the State of Ohio, 1846* (Columbus, 1847), 40–42.

7. *Collected Works of Abraham Lincoln*, 4:341.

8. *Ex Parte Merryman*, 17 Federal Cases 144 (1861). This Merryman story is borrowed, in a large measure, from Frank L. Klement, "John Merryman: Suspension of the Writ of Habeas Corpus," in *Political Trials in History: From Antiquity to the Present*, edited by Ron Christenson (New Brunswick, N.J., 1991), 291–92. The *Ex Parte Merryman* decision, it must be emphasized, *was not* a U.S. Supreme Court decision, but a statement by Taney sitting in a circuit court.

9. Letter, Bates to Stanton, Jan. 31, 1863, Edwin M. Stanton Papers, Library of Congress. Also see *Diary of Gideon Welles*, edited by John T. Morse (3 vols.; New York, 1911), 2:242, 245–46.

10. Mark E. Neely, *The Fate of Liberty: Abraham Lincoln and Civil Liberties* (New York, 1991), 52–53. Neely added: "Stanton issued the orders on August 8, 1862, thus making the secretary of war rather than President Lincoln the first official to suspend the writ of habeas corpus across the whole United States. Stanton later swore under oath that Lincoln gave him 'verbal direction' to issue the order and that the President read Stanton's draft of the order before the secretary signed it in his presence."

11. *(Madison) Wisconsin Patriot*, Dec. 23, 1863; *(Madison) Wisconsin State Journal*, Dec. 22, 23, 1863; Alfons J. Beitzinger, "The Father of Copperheadism in Wisconsin," *Wisconsin Magazine of History*, 39 (Autumn 1955): 20.

12. *In Re Kemp*, 16 Wis. 282 (1863).

13. Letter, Bates to Stanton, Jan. 31, 1863, Stanton Papers; Beitzinger, "The Father of Copperheadism in Wisconsin," 21.

14. Emma Lore Thornbrough, *Indiana in the Civil War Era, 1850–1880* (Indianapolis, 1965), 204–5; Kenneth M. Stampp, *Indiana Politics During the Civil War* (Indianapolis, 1949), 198–202.

15. Vallandigham's speech was published in the *Mount Vernon Democratic Banner*, May 9, 1863. The speech, as reported by one of the secretaries (James Irvine) of the meeting, was republished in James L. Vallandigham, *A Life of Clement L. Vallandigham* (Baltimore, 1872), 248–59.

16. William W. Armstrong, "Personal Recollections," published in the *Cincinnati Enquirer*, Mar 20, 1886; *The (Columbus) Crisis*, June 13, 1863; Frank L. Klement, *The Limits of Vincent: Clement L. Vallandigham and the Civil War* (Lexington, Ky., 1970), 156–89.

17. Quoted in *Cincinnati Daily Gazette*, May 16, 1863; Klement, *The Limits of Dissent*, 168–69.

18. *Ex Parte Vallandigham*, [28 Federal Cases 923 (1863)]; *Cincinnati Daily Enquirer*, May 16, 1863.

19. John A. Marshall, *American Bastile: A History of the Illegal Arrests and Imprisonment of American Citizens during the Late Civil War* (Philadelphia, 1878), 732. It is likely that the account about Clement L. Vallandigham in Marshall's book was written by Clement's brother, John L. Vallandigham.

20. Letter, Lincoln "To Erastus Corning and Others", June 12, 1863, published in *The Collected Works of Abraham Lincoln*, 6:264, 266.

21. Marshall, *American Bastile*, 732. The quotation is a mangled summary of a paragraph from Lincoln's letter "to Matthew Birchard and others," June 29, 1863, included in *The Collected Works of Abraham Lincoln*, 6:303.

22. See Chapter 4 "H.H. Dodd, the Sons of Liberty, and the Carrington Exposé" and Chapter 6 "The Northwestern Confederacy Scheme and the Indianapolis Treason Trials," in Frank L. Klement, *Dark Lanterns: Secret Political Societies, Conspiracies, and Treason Trials in the Civil War* (Baton Rouge, 1984), 91–135, 151–86.

23. *Ex Parte Milligan*, 4 Wallace 2 (1866), 431–32; Samuel Klaus, editor, *The Milligan Case*, American Trials Series (New York, 1929); Frank L. Klement, "The Indianapolis Treason Trials and *Ex Parte Milligan*," in Michael R. Belknap, editor, *American Political Trials* (Westport, Conn., 1981), 101–28.

24. Neely, *The Fate of Liberty*, 209.

FRANK L. KLEMENT
BIBLIOGRAPHY

Compiled by Steven K. Rogstad

BOOKS

The Copperheads in the Middle West. Chicago: University of Chicago Press, 1960: reprint. Gloucester: Peter Smith, 1972.

Wisconsin and the Civil War. Madison: State Historical Society of Wisconsin, 1963.

The Limits of Dissent: Clement L. Vallandigham and the Civil War. Lexington: University Press of Kentucky, 1970: reprint. Bronx: Fordham University Press, forthcoming.

Dark Lanterns: Secret Political Societies, Conspiracies, and Treason Trials in the Civil War. Baton Rouge: Louisiana State University Press, 1984.

The Gettysburg Soldiers' Cemetery and Lincoln's Address: Aspects and Angles. Shippensburg, Pa.: White Mane Publishing, 1993.

Wisconsin in the Civil War: The Battle Front and the Home Front, 1861–1865. Madison: State Historical Society of Wisconsin, 1997.

Lincoln's Critics: The Copperheads of the North. Shippensburg: White Mane Books, 1998.

CHAPTERS IN BOOKS

Chapter I, "Clement L. Vallandigham," in *For the Union: Ohio Leaders in the Civil War*, edited by Kenneth W. Wheeler (Columbus: Ohio State University Press, 1968), 4–76.

"The Democrats as Sectionalists," in *Lincoln and Civil War Politics*, edited by James A. Rawley (Huntington: Krieger Publishing Co., 1969): 95–103. [reprint of the article, "Economic Aspects of Middle Western Copperheadism," *The Historian* 14.1 (Autumn 1951): 27–44].

Chapter XIV, "Middle Western Copperheadism and the Genesis of the Granger Movement," in *The Old Northwest: Studies in Regional History, 1787–1910*, edited by Harry N. Scheiber (Lincoln: University of Nebraska Press, 1969): 323–40. [reprint of the article, "Middle Western Copperheadism and the Genesis of the Granger Movement," *Mississippi Valley Historical Review* 38.4 (Mar. 1952): 679–94].

"The Critics: Union," in *America's Major Wars: Crusaders, Critics, and Scholars, 1775–1972*, 2 vols., edited by Leslie E. Decker and Robert Seager II (Reading: Addison-Wesley Publishing Co., 1973): 1: 305–32. [reprint of Chapter IV, "Formation of the Peace Movement," pp. 107–33, in *Copperheads in the Middle West* (Chicago, 1960)]. [in Vol. 1, "1775–1865." in "The Civil War: The War of the Rebellion," Section 2, "The Critics: Union"].

"'Brick' Pomeroy," in *The Badger State: A Documentary History*, edited by Justus F. and Roberta Dotts Paul (Grand Rapids: William B. Eerdman's Publishing Co., 1979): 194–203. [reprint of the article, "'Brick' Pomeroy: Copperhead and Curmudgeon," *Wisconsin Magazine of History* 35.2 (Winter 1951): 106–13, 156–57.

"Wisconsin Copperheads," in *The Badger State: A Documentary History*, edited by Justus F. and Roberta Dotts Paul (Grand Rapids: William B. Eerdman's Publishing Co., 1979): 203–7. [reprint of the article, "Copperheads and Copperheadism in Wisconsin: Democratic Opposition to the Lincoln Administration," *Wisconsin Magazine of History* 42.3 (Spring 1959), 182–88].

Chapter V, "The Indianapolis Treason Trials and *Ex Parte Milligan*," in *Ten Famous American Political Trials*, edited by Michael R. Belknap (Westport: Greenwood Press, 1981): 101–27.

"John Merryman" [*Ex Parte Merryman*, 1861], (pp. 291–92); "Lambdin P. Milligan" [*Ex Parte Milligan*" 1866], (pp. 293–94); "Clement L. Vallandigham" [*Ex Parte Vallandigham*, 1863], (pp. 463–64), in *Political Trials in History: From Antiquity to the Present*, edited by Ron Christenson (New Brunswick: Transaction Publishers, 1991).

"The Indianapolis Treason Trials and *Ex Parte Milligan*, in *American Political Trials*" (revised, expanded edition), edited by Michael R. Belknap (Westport: Praeger Publishers, 1994), 97–118.

ARTICLES

"The Soldier Vote in Wisconsin During the Civil War." *Wisconsin Magazine of History* 28.1 (Sept. 1944): 37–47.

"General John B. Floyd and the West Virginia Campaigns of 1861." *West Virginia History Quarterly* 8.3 (Apr. 1947): 319–33.

"Debunking the Debunkers." *The Social Studies* 38.8 (Dec. 1947): 366–69.

"Jane Grey Swisshelm and Lincoln: A Feminist Fusses and Frets." *Abraham Lincoln Quarterly* 6.4 (Dec. 1950): 227–38.

"The Abolition Movement in Minnesota." *Minnesota History* 32.1 (Mar. 1951): 15–33.

"Economic Aspects of Middle Western Copperheadism." *The Historian* 14.1 (Autumn 1951): 27–44.

"'Brick' Pomeroy: Copperhead and Curmudgeon." *Wisconsin Magazine of History*, 35.2 (Winter 1951): 106–13, 156–57.

"Middle Western Copperheadism and the Genesis of the Granger Movement." *Mississippi Valley Historical Review* 38.4 (Mar. 1952): 679–94. Republished in the Bobbs-Merrill *Reprint Series in American History* (Indianapolis, 1967).

"A Small-Town Editor Criticizes Lincoln: A Study in Editorial Abuse." *Lincoln Herald* 54.2 (Summer 1952): 27–32, 60.

"Edwin B. Bigelow: A Michigan Sergeant in the Civil War." *Michigan History* 38.3 (Sept. 1954): 193–99.

"Copperhead Secret Societies in Illinois During the Civil War." *Journal of the Illinois State Historical Society* 48.2 (Summer 1955): 152–80.

"Lincoln's Critics in Wisconsin." Lincoln Fellowship of Wisconsin *Historical Bulletin* No. 14 (1956).

"Copperheads and Copperheadism in Wisconsin: Democratic Opposition to the Lincoln Administration." *Wisconsin Magazine of History* 42.3 (Spring 1959): 182–88.

"Columbus—A Lesson in Faith." *Columbia* 39 (Oct. 1959): 11, 39–47.

"Milwaukee Critics of Lincoln." Milwaukee County Historical Society *Historical Messenger* 16.3 (Sept. 1960): 2–7.

"Peter V. Deuster, the 'See-Bote', and the Civil War." Milwaukee County Historical Society *Historical Messenger* 16.4 (Dec. 1960): 2–6.

"Franklin Pierce and the Treason Charges of 1861–1862." *The Historian* 23.4 (Sept. 1961): 436–48.

"Wisconsin and the Civil War." *Wisconsin Blue Book, 1962* (Madison: Wisconsin Legislative Reference Library, 1962): 72–180.

"'As Others See Us:' Milwaukee in 1858." Milwaukee County Historical Society *Historical Messenger* 18.3 (Sept. 1962): 13–15.

"That Thirty-seventh Congress." *Illinois History* 16.2 (Nov. 1962): 38–9.

"The Hopkins Hoax and Golden Circle Rumors in Michigan: 1861–1862." *Michigan History* 47.1 (Mar. 1963): 1–14.

"'Brick' Pomeroy and the Democratic Processes: A Study in Civil War Politics." *Transactions of the Wisconsin Academy of Sciences, Arts and Letters* 51 (1963): 159–69.

"'I Whipped Six Texans:' A Civil War Letter of an Ohio Soldier." *Ohio History* 73.3 (Summer 1964): 180–82.

"Milwaukee Women and the Civil War." Milwaukee County Historical Society *Historical Messenger* 21.1 (Mar. 1965): 9–14.

"Rumors of Golden Circle Activity in Iowa During the Civil War Years." *Annals of Iowa* 37.7 (Winter 1965): 523–36.

"Carrington and the Golden Circle Legend in Indiana During the Civil War." *Indiana Magazine of History* 61.1 (Mar. 1965): 31–52.

"Clement L. Vallandigham's Exile in the Confederacy, May 25–June 17, 1863." *Journal of Southern History* 31.2 (May 1965): 149–63.

"Vallandigham as an Exile in Canada, 1863–1864." *Ohio History* 74.3 (Summer 1965): 151–68, 208–10.

"Wisconsin and the Re-Election of Lincoln in 1864: A Chapter of Civil War History." Milwaukee County Historical Society *Historical Messenger* 22.1 (Mar. 1966): 20–42.

"Deuster as a Democratic Dissenter During the Civil War: A Case Study of a Copperhead." *Transactions of the Wisconsin Academy of Sciences, Arts and Letters* 55 (1966): 21–38.

"Kilbourn Gives Advice to Lincoln." Milwaukee County Historical Society *Historical Messenger* 23.1 (Mar. 1967): 8–9.

"Ohio and the Dedication of the Soldiers' Cemetery at Gettysburg." *Ohio History* 79.2 (Spring 1970): 76–100.

"The Copperheads." *History of the English Speaking People* No. 102 (Sept. 1971): 3271–77 (a European publication edited by Peter Humble).

"Phineas C. Wright, The Order of American Knights, and the Sanderson Exposé." *Civil War History* 18.1 (Mar. 1972): 5–23.

"'These Honored Dead:' David Wills and the Soldiers' Cemetery at Gettysburg." *Lincoln Herald* 74.3 (Fall 1972): 123–35.

"Governor Edward Salomon, W. Yates Selleck, and the Soldiers' Cemetery at Gettysburg." *Transactions of the Wisconsin Academy of Sciences, Arts and Letters* 61 (1973): 11–28.

"Ohio and the Knights of the Golden Circle: The Evolution of a Civil War Myth." *Cincinnati Historical Society Bulletin* 32.1–2 (Spring–Summer 1974): 7–27.

"History and the Humanities." *Transactions of the Wisconsin Academy of Sciences, Arts and Letters* 63 (1975): 72–80.

"Civil War Politics, Nationalism, and Postwar Myths." *The Historian* 38.3 (May 1976): 419–38.

"Sound and Fury: Civil War Dissent in the Cincinnati Area." *Cincinnati Historical Society Bulletin* 35.2 (Summer 1977): 99–114.

"Lincoln, the Gettysburg Address, and Two Myths." *Blue & Gray* 2.2 (Oct.– Nov. 1984): 7–11.

"Ward H. Lamon and the Dedication of the Soldiers' Cemetery at Gettysburg." *Civil War History* 31.4 (Dec. 1985): 293–308.

"Seven Who Witnessed Lincoln's Gettysburg Address." Lincoln Fellowship of Wisconsin *Historical Bulletin* No. 40 (1985).

"The Ten Who Sat in the Front Row on the Platform During the Dedication of the Soldiers' Cemetery at Gettysburg." *Lincoln Herald* 88.4 (Winter 1985): 106–13.

"A Milwaukeean Witnesses Lincoln's Gettysburg Address." *Milwaukee History* 9.2 (Summer 1986): 34–49.

"Benjamin B. French, the Lincolns, and the Dedication of the Soldiers' Cemetery at Gettysburg." *Historical New Hampshire* 42.1 (Spring 1987): 36–63.

"Ohio Politics in 1863: Looking Back 125 Years." *The Old Northwest* 14.1 (Spring 1988): 39–65.

"Lincoln's First Gettysburg Address: A Little Known Impromptu Speech Perhaps Best Forgotten." *Blue & Gray* 8.2 (Dec. 1990): 36–38.

"Sergeant Edwin B. Bigelow's Exciting Adventures, with Excerpts from the Wolverine Cavalryman's Civil War Diary." *Blue & Gray* 8.6 (Aug. 1991): 36–38.

"President Lincoln, the Civil War, and the Bill of Rights." *Lincoln Herald* 94.1 (Spring 1992): 10–23.

"Thirteen and Three Tidbits Concerning Lincoln's Address and the Dedication of the Gettysburg Soldiers' Cemetery." Lincoln Fellowship of Wisconsin *Lincoln Ledger* 1.5 (Nov. 1993): 1, 3.

"Catholics as Copperheads During the Civil War." *Catholic Historical Review* 80.1 (Jan. 1994): 36–57.

ENTRIES IN ENCYCLOPEDIAS AND DICTIONARIES

Bacon, Donald C., Roger H. Davidson, and Morton Keller, eds. *The Encyclopedia of the United States Congress.* New York: Simon & Schuster, 1995.

    1. "Clement L. Vallandigham," 4:2028–29

Catholic Encyclopedia for School and Home. 12 vols. New York: McGraw-Hill, 1965.

    1. "James Hoban," 5:204–5

    2. "Abraham Lincoln," 6:400–403

    3. "Reconstruction Period," 11:241–43

Current, Richard N., ed. *Encyclopedia of the Confederacy.* 4 vols. New York: Simon & Schuster, 1993.

    1. "Copperheads," 1:411–13

    2. "Northwestern Conspiracy," 3:1158–59

Dictionary of Wisconsin Biography. Madison: State Historical Society of Wisconsin, 1960.

    1. "Marcus Mills 'Brick' Pomeroy," 289

    2. "George Baldwin Smith," 331

Garraty, John A., ed. *Encyclopedia of American Biography.* New York: Harper & Row, 1974.

    1. "Clement L. Vallandigham," 1119–20

Garraty, John A., ed. *American National Biography* 25 vols. New York: Oxford University Press, forthcoming.

    1. "Lambdin P. Milligan"

Hubbell, John, and James W. Geary, eds. *Biographical Dictionary of the Union: Northern Leaders of the Civil War.* Westport: Greenwood Press, 1995.

    1. "Samuel Medary," 348

    2. "Lambdin P. Milligan," 356–57

    3. "Clement L. Vallandigham," 551–52

Roller, David C., and Robert W. Twyman, eds. *Encyclopedia of Southern History.* Baton Rouge: Louisiana State University Press, 1979.

    1. "Knights of the Golden Circle," 691–92

    2. "Order of American Knights," 41–42

Tarter, Brent, Sandra Treadway, and John Kneebone, eds. *Dictionary of Virginia Biography.* Richmond: Virginia State Library and Archives, forthcoming.

    1. "George Washington Lafayette Bickley"

The New Catholic Encyclopedia. New York: McGraw-Hill, 1967.

    1. "James Shields," 13:175–76.

World Book Encyclopedia. 22 vols. Chicago: World Book, Inc., 1991.

    1. "Brooks Adams," 1:33

    2. "Anti-Masonic Party," 1:556

    3. "Black Codes," 2:403

    4. "Cassius Marcellus Clay," 4:658

    5. "Copperheads," 4:1046

    6. "Fort Pickens," 7:415

    7. "Proslavery Movement," 15:832

    8. "Edmund Ruffin," 16:518

    9. "Scalawags," 17:169

10. "Lyman Trumbull," 19:473

11. "Clement Laird Vallandigham," 20:281

MISCELLANEOUS

"Senior Chapel Address." [Lake Forest College] *The Stentor*, May 26, 1945: 4.

Comments about "The Education of Abraham Lincoln" by Arnold Gates, a lecture delivered at the 195th meeting of the Civil War Round Table of Milwaukee, *Newsletter*, General Order 106 (Mar. 1968): 1–2.

"About the Author" (biographical sketch of Edward Noyes). Lincoln Fellowship of Wisconsin *Historical Bulletin* No. 25 (1970): 15.

"Meet the Author" (biographical sketch of Wayne C. Temple). Lincoln Fellowship of Wisconsin *Historical Bulletin* No. 26 (1971): 19.

"About the Author" (biographical sketch of Lloyd Ostendorf). Lincoln Fellowship of Wisconsin *Historical Bulletin* No. 27 (1972): 10.

"Kathryn Whitford" (biographical sketch of Kathryn Whitford). Lincoln Fellowship of Wisconsin *Historical Bulletin* No. 28 (1973): 9.

"Professor Klement Replies." *Lincoln Lore* No. 1748 (Oct. 1983): 3.

"Philip J. Hohlweck: In Memoriam." The Civil War Round Table of Milwaukee *Newsletter*, General Order 271 (Mar. 1985): 1.

"The Last Lincoln Descendant." The Civil War Round Table of Milwaukee *Newsletter*, General Order No. 280 (Feb. 1986): 4.

"A Tribute to Mrs. Carl H. Wilhelm." Lincoln Fellowship of Wisconsin *Historical Bulletin* No. 43 (1988): inside front cover.

"Dr. Richard N. Current" (biographical sketch of Richard N. Current). Lincoln Fellowship of Wisconsin *Historical Bulletin* No. 44 (1989): 1.

"Historical Bulletin No. 45 is hereby dedicated to Edward Noyes." Lincoln Fellowship of Wisconsin *Historical Bulletin* No. 45 (1990): inside front cover.

"Arthur C. Hansen" (tribute to Arthur C. Hansen). Lincoln Fellowship of Wisconsin *Historical Bulletin* No. 47(1992): inside front cover.

REVIEWS

(*A Volunteer's Adventures: A Union Captain's Record of the Civil War* by John W. DeForrest), *Mississippi Valley Historical Review*, 33.2 (Sept. 1946): 354–55.

(*Uncollected Works of Abraham Lincoln: His Letters, Addresses and Other Papers, Volume 1, 1824–40*, edited by Rufus Rockwell Wilson), *Wisconsin Magazine of History*, 31.4 (June 1948): 469–71.

(*A Union Officer in the Reconstruction by John W. DeForrest*, edited by James H. Croushore and David M. Porter), *Wisconsin Magazine of History*, 32.2 (Dec. 1948): 225–27.

(*Lincoln's Vandalia: A Pioneer Portrait* by William E. Baringer), *Wisconsin Magazine of History*, 33.2 (Dec. 1949): 225–26.

(*And the War Came: The North and the Secession Crisis, 1860–1861* by Kenneth M. Stampp), *Minnesota History*, 31.4 (Dec. 1950): 243–44.

(*And the War Came: The North and the Secession Crisis, 1860–1861* by Kenneth M. Stampp), *Milwaukee Journal*, Aug. 5, 1951: sec. 5, p. 4.

(*The Army of the Pacific: Its Operations in California, Texas, Arizona, New Mexico, Utah, Nevada, Oregon, Washington, Plains Region, Mexico, etc., 1860–1866* by Aurora Hunt), *Catholic Historical Review*, 37.3 (Oct. 1951): 361.

(*Dred Scott's Case* by Vincent C. Hopkins), *Catholic Historical Review*, 38.2 (July 1952): 234.

(*On Freedom's Altar: The Martyr Complex in the Abolition Movement* by Hazel Catherine Wolf), *Minnesota History*, 33.5 (Spring 1953): 217–18.

(*Lincoln the President: Midstream* by James G. Randall), *Catholic Historical Review*, 39.1 (Apr. 1953): 82–83.

(*Lincoln and Greeley* by Harlan Hoyt Horner), *Wisconsin Magazine of History*, 37.4 (Summer 1954), 231–32.

(*Harvard Guide to American History* by Oscar Handlin, Arthur Meier Schlesinger, Samuel Eliot Morison, Frederick Merk, Arthur Meier Schlesinger, Jr., and Paul Herman Buck), *Catholic Historical Review*, 40.3 (Oct. 1954): 344–46.

(*Confederate Agent: A Discovery in History* by James D. Horan), *Journal of the Illinois State Historical Society*, 47.4 (Winter 1954): 432–33.

(*Americans Interpret Their Civil War* by Thomas J. Pressly), *Catholic Historical Review*, 40.4 (Jan. 1955): 474–75.

(*Lincoln's Third Secretary: The Memoirs of William O. Stoddard* edited by William O. Stoddard, Jr.), *Michigan History*, 39.4 (Dec. 1955): 507.

(*History of Nebraska* by James C. Olson), *Historical Bulletin*, 34 (Jan. 1956): 119–20.

(*Federalist Delaware, 1775–1815* by John A. Monroe), *Historical Review*, 34 (Mar. 1956): 185–86.

(*The Far Western Frontier, 1830–1860* by Ray Allen Billington), *Catholic Historical Review*, 43.1 (Apr. 1957): 87–88.

(*The Confederate Reader,* edited by Richard B. Harwell), The Civil War Round Table of Milwaukee *Newsletter*, General Order No. 3 (Jan. 1958), 2.

(*The Confederate Reader* edited by Richard B. Harwell), *Manuscripta*, 2.2 (July 1958): 121.

(*Civil War in the Making, 1815–1860* by Avery O. Craven), *Wisconsin Magazine of History*, 43.2 (Winter 1959–1960): 139.

(*Frontier America: The Story of the Westward Movement* by Thomas D. Clark), *Catholic Historical Review*, 46.1 (Apr. 1960): 90–91.

(*Crosier on the Frontier: A Life of John Martin Henni* by Peter Leo Johnson), *Wisconsin Magazine of History*, 43.3 (Spring 1960): 221.

(*In The Name of the People: Speeches and Writings of Lincoln and Douglas in the Ohio Campaign of 1859*, edited by Harry V. Jaffa and Robert W. Johannsen), *Wisconsin Magazine of History*, 44.1 (Autumn 1960): 73–74.

(*The Crusade Against Slavery, 1830–1860* by Louis Filler), *Catholic Historical Review*, 47.2 (July 1961): 252–53.

(*The Blue and the Gray on the Nile* by William B. Hesseltine and Hazel C. Wolf), *Milwaukee Journal*, Aug. 6, 1961: sec. 5, p. 4.

(*The Stakes of Power, 1845–1877* by Roy Nichols), *Civil War History*, 7.4 (Dec. 1961): 460.

(*Old Gentleman's Convention: The Washington Peace Conference of 1861* by Robert G. Gunderson), *The Historian*, 24.2 (Feb. 1962): 242–43.

(*Politics and the Crisis of 1860*, edited by Norman Graebner), *Wisconsin Magazine of History*, 45.4 (Summer 1962): 304.

(*The Holy See and the Nascent Church in the Middle Western United States, 1826–1850* by Robert F. Trisco), *Indiana Magazine of History*, 58.4 (Dec. 1962): 379–80.

(*Prelude to Greatness: Lincoln in the 1850's* by Don E. Fehrenbacher), *Wisconsin Magazine of History*, 46.2 (Winter 1962–1963): 153–54.

(*The First Volunteers: History of the First Minnesota Volunteer Regiment, 1861–1865* by John Q. Imholte), *Minnesota History*, 38.7 (Sept. 1963): 330–31.

(*Benjamin Franklin Wade: Radical Republican From Ohio* by Hans L. Trefousse), *The Historian*, 26.1 (Nov. 1963): 117.

(*Mr. Lincoln and the Negroes: The Long Road to Equality* by William O. Douglas), *Journal of the Illinois State Historical Society*, 57.1 (Spring 1964): 56–57.

(*A House Divided: Statehood Politics and the Copperhead Movement in West Virginia* by Richard O. Curry), *Journal of American History*, 51.4 (Mar. 1965): 720–21.

(*The Empty Sleeve: A Biography of Lucius Fairchild* by Sam Ross), *Catholic Historical Review*, 51.2 (July 1965): 229–30.

(*Never Call Retreat* by Bruce Catton), *Milwaukee Journal*, Aug. 22, 1965: sec. 5, p. 4.

(*Lincoln and the Gettysburg Address: Commemorative Papers*, edited by Allan Nevins), *Civil War History*, 11.3 (Sept. 1965): 297–98.

(*Lincoln's Gettysburg Declaration: "A New Birth of Freedom"* by Louis A. Warren), *Civil War History*, 11.3 (Sept. 1965): 297–98.

(*Lee* by Clifford Dowdey), *Milwaukee Journal*, Nov. 28, 1965: sec. 5, p. 8.

(*The House Divides: The Age of Jackson and Lincoln From the War of 1812 to the Civil War* by Paul I. Wellman), *Milwaukee Journal*, Feb. 6, 1966: sec. 5, p. 4.

(*The Historians' History of the United States*, 2 vols., edited by Andrew S. Berky and James P. Shenton), *Milwaukee Journal*, Nov. 27, 1966: sec. 5, p. 8.

(*Erie Water West: A History of the Erie Canal, 1792–1854* by Ronald E. Shaw), *Indiana Magazine of History*, 62.4 (Dec. 1966): 354–55.

(*George Washington Julian, Radical Republican: A Study in Nineteenth-Century Politics and Reform* by Patrick W. Riddleberger), *Civil War History*, 13.1 (Mar. 1967): 80–82.

(*Descriptive Bibliography of Civil War Manuscripts in Illinois* by William L. Burton), *Indiana Magazine of History*, 63.1 (Mar. 1967): 75–76.

(*Robert E. Lee: The Complete Man, 1861–1870* by Margaret Sanborn), *Milwaukee Journal*, Sept. 24, 1967: sec. 5, p. 4.

(*Mr. Lincoln's Washington: Selections From the Writings of Noah Brooks, Civil War Correspondent* by P.J. Staudenraus), *Journal of the Illinois State Historical Society*, 60.3 (Autumn 1967): 329–31.

(*Turning Points of the Civil War* by James A. Rawley), *The Historian*, 30.1 (Nov. 1967): 132–34.

(*A Short History of the American Civil War* by Roy P. Basler), *The Historian*, 30.1 (Nov. 1967): 133–34.

(*Lincoln's Lost Speech: The Pivot of His Career* by Elwell Crissey), *Milwaukee Journal*, Dec. 17, 1967: sec. 5, p. 6.

(*A Layman's Guide to Negro History,* compiled and edited by Erwin A. Salk), *Milwaukee Journal*, Jan. 7, 1968: sec. 5, p. 4.

(*The Negro American: A Documentary History* by Leslie J. Fishel, Jr. and Benjamin Quarles), *Milwaukee Journal*, Mar. 10, 1968: sec. 5, p. 4.

(*Twelve Again Empire: The Anti-Imperialists, 1898–1900* by Robert L. Beisner), *Milwaukee Journal*, Apr. 14, 1968: sec. 5, p. 4.

(*The Papers of Ulysses S. Grant, Volume 1*, edited by John Y. Simon), *The Historian*, 30.3 (May 1968): 506–7.

(*The Gettysburg Campaign: A Study in Command* by Edwin B. Coddington), *Milwaukee Journal*, June 30, 1968: sec. 5, p. 4.

(*The Inner Civil War: Northern Intellectuals and the Crisis of the Union* by George M. Frederickson), *Catholic Historical Review*, 54.3 (Oct. 1968): 544–45.

(*Sections and Politics: Selected Writings by William B. Hesseltine*, edited by Richard N. Current), *Milwaukee Journal*, Dec. 29, 1968: sec. 5, p. 4.

(*De Stael-Du Pont Letters: Correspondence of Madame de Stael and Pierre Samuel de Pont de Nemours and of other Members of the Necker and Du Pont Families,* edited by James F. Marshall), *Milwaukee Journal,* Jan. 26, 1969: sec. 5, p. 4.

(*Grant Takes Command* by Bruce Catton), *Milwaukee Journal,* Mar. 2, 1969: sec. 5, p. 4.

(*My Life With History* by John H. Hicks), *Milwaukee Journal,* Mar. 16, 1969: sec. 5, p. 4.

(*The War of 1812* by Reginald Horsman), *Milwaukee Journal,* Apr. 27, 1969: sec. 5, p. 4.

(*Black Abolitionists* by Benjamin Quarles), *Milwaukee Journal,* July 6, 1969: sec. 5, p. 4.

(*Blueprint For Modern America: Nonmilitary Legislation of the First Civil War Congress* by Leonard P. Curry), *Journal of the Illinois State Historical Society,* 62.3 (Autumn 1969): 324–26.

(*To Print the News and Raise Hell: A Biography of Wilbur F. Storey* by Justin E. Walsh), *Civil War History,* 15.4 (Dec. 1969): 350–52.

(*Right Hand Grove Uplifted: A Biography of Archbishop Michael Heiss* by Sister M. Melita Ludwig), *Records of the American Catholic Historical Society of Philadelphia,* 80.4 (Dec. 1969): 251–52.

(*The Papers of Ulysses S. Grant, Volume 2: April–September, 1861,* edited by John Y. Simon), *The Historian,* 32.2 (Feb. 1970): 306–7.

(*Black Freedom: The Nonviolent Abolitionists From 1830 Through the Civil War* by Carleton Mabee), *Milwaukee Journal,* June 14, 1970: sec. 5, p. 4.

(*The Territorial Papers of the United States, Volume 27,* edited by John P. Bloom), *Milwaukee Journal,* Aug. 9, 1970: sec. 5, p. 4.

(*Ordeal of Ambition: Jefferson, Hamilton, Burr* by Jonathan Daniels), *Milwaukee Journal,* Dec. 20, 1970: sec. 5, p. 4.

(*Clio's Servant: The State Historical Society of Wisconsin, 1846–1954* by Clifford L. Lord and Carl Ubbelhode), *Catholic Historical Review,* 57.1 (Apr. 1971): 177–78.

(*William Henry Seward* by Glyndon G. Van Duesen), *Catholic Historical Review,* 57.1 (Apr. 1971): 176–77.

(*Spectator of America by Edward Dicey,* edited by Herbert Mitgang), *Milwaukee Journal,* Sept. 12, 1971: sec. 5, p. 4.

(*White Terror: The Ku Klux Klan Conspiracy and Southern Reconstruction* by Allen W. Trelease), *Milwaukee Journal,* June 6, 1971: sec. 5, p. 4.

(*The Organized War, 1863–1864,* Volume 3 of *The War for the Union* by Allan Nevins), *Milwaukee Journal,* Aug. 1, 1971: sec. 5, p. 4.

(*The Siege of Charleston, 1861–1865* by E. Milby Burton), *The Historian,* 33.4 (Aug. 1971): 696.

(*Radicalism, Racism, and Party Realignment: The Border States During Reconstruction,* edited by Richard O. Curry), *The Social Studies,* 62.5 (Oct. 1971): 232.

(*Free Soil: The Election of 1848* by Joseph G. Rayback), *Journal of American History,* 58.3 (Dec. 1971): 741–42.

(*The Organized War For Victory, 1864–1865,* Volume 4 of *The War for the Union* by Allan Nevins), *Milwaukee Journal,* Dec. 5, 1971: sec. 5, p. 4.

(*Iowa on the Eve of the Civil War: A Decade of Frontier Politics* by Morton M. Rosenberg), *The Historian,* 35.1 (Nov. 1972): 136–37.

(*Frederick Jackson Turner: Historian, Scholar, Teacher* by Ray Allen Billington), *Milwaukee Journal,* Feb. 25, 1973: sec. 5, p. 4.

(*Milligan's Fight Against Lincoln* by Darwin Kelley), *Indiana Magazine of History,* 69.3 (Sept. 1973): 279–81.

(*Gideon Wells: Lincoln's Secretary of the Navy* by John Niven), *Milwaukee Journal,* Dec. 16, 1973: sec. 5, p. 4.

(*Gettysburg: The Final Fury* by Bruce Catton), *Milwaukee Journal,* Feb. 24, 1974: sec. 5, p. 4.

(*Democratic Opposition to the Lincoln Administration in Indiana* by Gilbert R. Tredway), *Journal of American History,* 61.1 (June 1974): 197–98.

(*The Fiery Trial: A Life of Lincoln* by Herbert Mitgang), *Milwaukee Journal,* July 21, 1974: sec. 5, p. 4.

(*The Civil War: A Narrative, Red River to Appomattox* by Shelby Foote), *Milwaukee Journal,* Dec. 15, 1974: sec. 5, p. 4.

(*Holy Warriors: The Abolitionists and American Slavery* by James Brewer Stewart), *Milwaukee Journal,* Dec. 26, 1976: sec. 5, p. 4.

(*With Malice Toward None: The Life of Abraham Lincoln* by Stephen B. Oates), *Milwaukee Journal,* Feb. 13, 1977: sec. 5, p. 4.

(*Union and Confidence: The 1860s* by Harold Hyman), *American Historical Review,* 82.4 (Oct. 1977): 1076.

(*Soldiering: The Civil War Diary of Rice C. Bull, 123rd New York Volunteer Infantry* edited by K. Jack Bauer), *Milwaukee Journal,* Jan. 29, 1978: sec. 5, p. 3.

(*A Respectable Minority: The Democratic Party in the Civil War Era, 1860–1868* by Joel H. Silbey), *Journal of American History,* 65.3 (Dec. 1978): 785–86.

(*Conservative Ordeal: Northern Democrats and Reconstruction, 1865–1868* by Edward L. Gambill), *Minnesota History,* 47.7 (Fall 1981): 297.

(*Essays on American Antebellum Politics, 1840–1860,* edited by Stephen E. Maizlish and John J. Kushma), *Louisiana History,* 24.4 (Fall 1983): 428–29.

UNPUBLISHED WORKS

THESES:

"John Buchanan ('Scapegoat') Floyd: A Study of Virginia Politics Through a Biography." M.S. dissertation, University of Wisconsin-Madison, 1938, 205 leaves.

"Middle Western Copperheadism: Jeffersonian Democracy in Revolt." Ph.D. dissertation, University of Wisconsin-Madison, 1946, 342 leaves.

BOOK MANUSCRIPTS:

"A Civil War Fantasy: The Story of the Knights of the Golden Circle." 1973. 242 leaves.

"The Most Critical Year: Events of 1863." 1985. 835 leaves.

ESSAYS:

"Clement L. Vallandigham and the Civil War." Undated. 98 leaves.

"Clio and the Copperheads: Looking Back at Democratic Dissent During the Civil War." Undated. 10 handwritten sheets.

"Colonization During the Tudor Era." Aug. 4, 1941. 30 leaves.

"John A. Roebuck's Motion (in the House of Commons) to Recognize the Confederacy." Paper presented before the American Historical Association on Dec. 28, 1976. 33 leaves.

"Lincoln and His Critics." Undated. 6 handwritten sheets.

"Lincoln and the Gettysburg Address." Paper presented before the Military Order of the Loyal Legion of the United States on Oct. 8, 1983. 13 leaves.

"Nationalism, Civil War, and the Historians." Undated. 11 handwritten sheets.

"Six Controversies Regarding Lincoln's Gettysburg Address." 1994. Incomplete. 23 handwritten sheets.

"The Causes and Roots of the Civil War." Undated. 6 handwritten sheets.

"The Democratic Party in Wisconsin During the Civil War." 1941. 37 leaves.

"The Democratic Party in Wisconsin During the Civil War." Undated. 95 leaves.

"Wisconsin in the Civil War Era, 1850–1865." Undated. 16 leaves.

INDEX

Compiled by Steven K. Rogstad